Lecture Notes in Computer Science 11286

Commenced Publication in 1973
Founding and Former Series Editors:
Gerhard Goos, Juris Hartmanis, and Jan van Leeuwen

More information about this series at http://www.springer.com/series/7410

Vashek Matyáš · Petr Švenda
Frank Stajano · Bruce Christianson
Jonathan Anderson (Eds.)

Security Protocols XXVI

26th International Workshop
Cambridge, UK, March 19–21, 2018
Revised Selected Papers

Editors
Vashek Matyáš
Masaryk University
Brno, Czech Republic

Petr Švenda
Masaryk University
Brno, Czech Republic

Frank Stajano
University of Cambridge
Cambridge, UK

Bruce Christianson
University of Hertfordshire
Hatfield, UK

Jonathan Anderson
Memorial University of Newfoundland
St. John's, NL, Canada

ISSN 0302-9743 ISSN 1611-3349 (electronic)
Lecture Notes in Computer Science
ISBN 978-3-030-03250-0 ISBN 978-3-030-03251-7 (eBook)
https://doi.org/10.1007/978-3-030-03251-7

Library of Congress Control Number: 2018959144

LNCS Sublibrary: SL4 – Security and Cryptology

This Springer imprint is published by the registered company Springer Nature Switzerland AG
The registered company address is: Gewerbestrasse 11, 6330 Cham, Switzerland

Preface

This volume collects the revised proceedings of the 26th International Security Protocols Workshop, held at Trinity College, Cambridge, UK during March 19–21, 2018.

The theme of this workshop was "Fail-safe and fail-deadly concepts in protocol design". The dictionary definition[1] reveals:

fail-safe:

1: incorporating some feature for automatically counteracting the effect of an anticipated possible source of failure
2: being or relating to a safeguard that prevents continuing on a bombing mission according to a preconceived plan
3: having no chance of failure : infallibly problem-free

We all know that security protocols fail. Fortunately, they do not fail all the time, although sometimes their failure is less evident than we would like. In some situations, specific partial protocol failures that are properly observed and recorded can by design lead to responses that will still drive the protocol execution to a successful end. At other times, we deliberately aim for an all-or-nothing mindset: fail-deadly is a concept from nuclear military strategy, suggesting deterrence by an immediate and forceful response to an attack. It is interesting to investigate what differentiates these two design approaches to security protocols, and what they have in common when we consider a family of protocols where both fail-safe and fail-deadly versions are considered.

As usual, this theme was not prescriptive. It was not intended to restrict the topic of the papers, but to help provide a particular perspective for the authors and focus of the discussions, for any paper in some way related to security protocols. The authors were strongly encouraged to consider the theme as a springboard, not a fence. Our intention was to stimulate discussion likely to lead to conceptual advances, or to promising new lines of investigation, rather than to consider finished work.

The first three papers formed a starting block (Warmup – failures and attacks), the following two by Becerra et al. and Nemec et al. then presented novel protocols. The core block on Tuesday, titled "Threat models and incentives," comprised eight papers. The last day of the workshop started with two papers on cryptomoney (McCorry et al. and Anderson et al.), and the workshop closed with two final papers on the interplay of cryptography and dissent.

As with previous workshops in this series, each paper was revised by the authors to incorporate ideas that emerged during the workshop. These revised papers are followed by a curated transcript of the presentation and ensuing discussion.

Our thanks go to all the authors for their kind and timely collaboration in revising these transcripts and their position paper. Particular thanks to Seb Aebischer, Kat Krol, and David Llewellyn-Jones for assisting Frank Stajano with the recordings of the

[1] Merriam-Webster Dictionary, accessed September 6, 2018.

workshop discussions. Last but not least, we thank Trinity College, Cambridge, for hosting the workshop.

We hope that reading these proceedings will encourage you to join in the debate yourselves, and perhaps even to send us a position paper for the next workshop.

September 2018

Vashek Matyáš
Petr Švenda
Frank Stajano
Bruce Christianson
Jonathan Anderson

Previous Proceedings in This Series

The proceedings of previous International Security Protocols Workshops are also published by Springer Verlag as *Lecture Notes in Computer Science,* and are occasionally referred to in the text:

25th Workshop (2017)	LNCS 10476	ISBN 978-3-319-71074-7
24th Workshop (2016)	LNCS 10368	ISBN 978-3-319-62032-9
23rd Workshop (2015)	LNCS 9379	ISBN 978-3-319-26095-2
22nd Workshop (2014)	LNCS 8809	ISBN 978-3-319-12399-8
21st Workshop (2013)	LNCS 8263	ISBN 978-3-642-41716-0
20th Workshop (2012)	LNCS 7622	ISBN 978-3-642-35693-3
19th Workshop (2011)	LNCS 7114	ISBN 978-3-642-25866-4
18th Workshop (2010)	LNCS 7061	ISBN 978-3-662-45920-1
17th Workshop (2009)	LNCS 7028	ISBN 978-3-642-36212-5
16th Workshop (2008)	LNCS 6615	ISBN 978-3-642-22136-1
15th Workshop (2007)	LNCS 5964	ISBN 978-3-642-17772-9
14th Workshop (2006)	LNCS 5087	ISBN 978-3-642-04903-3
13th Workshop (2005)	LNCS 4631	ISBN 3-540-77155-7
12th Workshop (2004)	LNCS 3957	ISBN 3-540-40925-4
11th Workshop (2003)	LNCS 3364	ISBN 3-540-28389-7
10th Workshop (2002)	LNCS 2845	ISBN 3-540-20830-5
9th Workshop (2001)	LNCS 2467	ISBN 3-540-44263-4
8th Workshop (2000)	LNCS 2133	ISBN 3-540-42566-7
7th Workshop (1999)	LNCS 1796	ISBN 3-540-67381-4
6th Workshop (1998)	LNCS 1550	ISBN 3-540-65663-4
5th Workshop (1997)	LNCS 1361	ISBN 3-540-64040-1
4th Workshop (1996)	LNCS 1189	ISBN 3-540-63494-5

No published proceedings exist for the first three workshops.

Contents

Raven Authentication Service
Attacks and Countermeasures

Graham Rymer(✉) and David Llewellyn-Jones

Computer Laboratory, University of Cambridge,
William Gates Building, 15 JJ Thomson Avenue, Cambridge CB3 0FD, UK
{Graham.Rymer,David.Llewellyn-Jones}@cl.cam.ac.uk

Abstract. Raven is the name of the University of Cambridge's central web authentication service. Many online resources within the University require Raven authentication to protect private data. Individual users are uniquely identified by their Common Registration Scheme identifier (CRSid), and protected online resources refer users to the Raven service for verification of a password. We perform a formal analysis of the proprietary Ucam Webauth protocol and identify a number of practical attacks against the Raven service that uses it. Having considered each vulnerability, we discuss the general principles and lessons that can be learnt to help avoid such vulnerabilities in the future.

Keywords: Web authentication · Single-Sign-On · Vulnerability
Network security

1 Introduction

Most large organisations use some form of Single-Sign-On or Web authentication system for their own internally authenticated services. A variety of frameworks are used for this, including CAS, WebAuth (Stanford), Shibboleth, and Ucam Webauth. All of these are based on similar principles: the user is redirected to a centralised authentication portal, where they enter their credentials (username and password). Once the user is successfully authenticated, their browser redirects back to the original site, which they may then be granted access to. The original site never sees the password, but instead receives an unforgeable token from the portal attesting to the user's identity.

Such Web authentication offers many opportunities for the introduction of vulnerabilities, since it combines a three-party authentication protocol with a "messy" HTTP-redirect-based channel. In this paper, we consider Raven's Ucam Webauth protocol. This is an example that has demonstrated how this combination can lead to vulnerabilities of both design and implementation.

At the University of Cambridge a proposal for a "central, password-based web authentication service" was initially approved in December of 2002 by a committee of the University's Computing Service (now part of University Information Services). In August 2003, a "central web authentication system" was

V. Matyáš et al. (Eds.): Security Protocols 2018, LNCS 11286, pp. 1–14, 2018.
https://doi.org/10.1007/978-3-030-03251-7_1

announced, which was launched as a supported service in September of the following year. By October 2005, both CamSIS (Cambridge's comprehensive system for handling student information, records and transactions) and CamCORS (the Cambridge Colleges' Online Reporting System for Supervisions) had adopted Raven authentication. Today the Raven service operates as an identity provider (IdP) for all current (and some former) members of the University of Cambridge. Originally supporting only the proprietary Ucam Webauth protocol, it has also supported Shibboleth since 2007. Although little known outside the University, Ucam Webauth has been silently protecting a number of important information assets for many years. Despite its singular deployment, it counts amongst its former users a number of high profile alumni, including domestic royal persons (e.g. Prince William, Duke of Cambridge), as well as other high profile figures. Raven offers an exemplar with which to demonstrate the pitfalls of a roll-your-own web authentication scheme. Raven also continues to touch the lives of globally influential individuals, and for this reason is perhaps worth a closer look, despite its niche application.

2 Ucam Webauth

2.1 Protocol

The main agents of the protocol include the Web Application Agent (WAA) and the Web Login Service (WLS). We consider a third agent, a web browser (WB), as simply the communication channel between the WAA and the WLS. In a lower-level view we might consider that the WB also stores and transmits secret credentials for verification by the WLS, but such interactions (although present in Fig. 1) are superfluous to the subsequent discussion, and so have been omitted for brevity.

Figure 1 serves to illustrate a normal login sequence, and was modelled on observations of an actual login sequence involving the University's Raven service and the C-based authentication handler for Apache marshalling access to some Raven-protected content. We will continue by presenting a high-level abstract description of the Ucam Webauth protocol, focussing only on the messages in Fig. 1 depicted as solid lines, which we will call the reduced protocol.

Raven is broadly comparable (at least in the service it provides, if not in all aspects of technical implementation) to similar services deployed at other universities, including Yale's CAS[1], and Stanford's WebAuth[2], which were both developed around the same time. However, unlike both these alternative systems, Raven is different in that it provides no back channel between the WAA and the WLS, i.e. all communication is passed through the user's browser. This is one feature which makes Raven very easy to deploy. It should be noted that Raven provides an authentication service only, not an authorisation service. Authorisation is the duty of subscribing WAAs.

1 https://apereo.github.io/cas/5.0.x/protocol/CAS-Protocol-Specification.html.
2 http://webauth.stanford.edu/protocol.html.

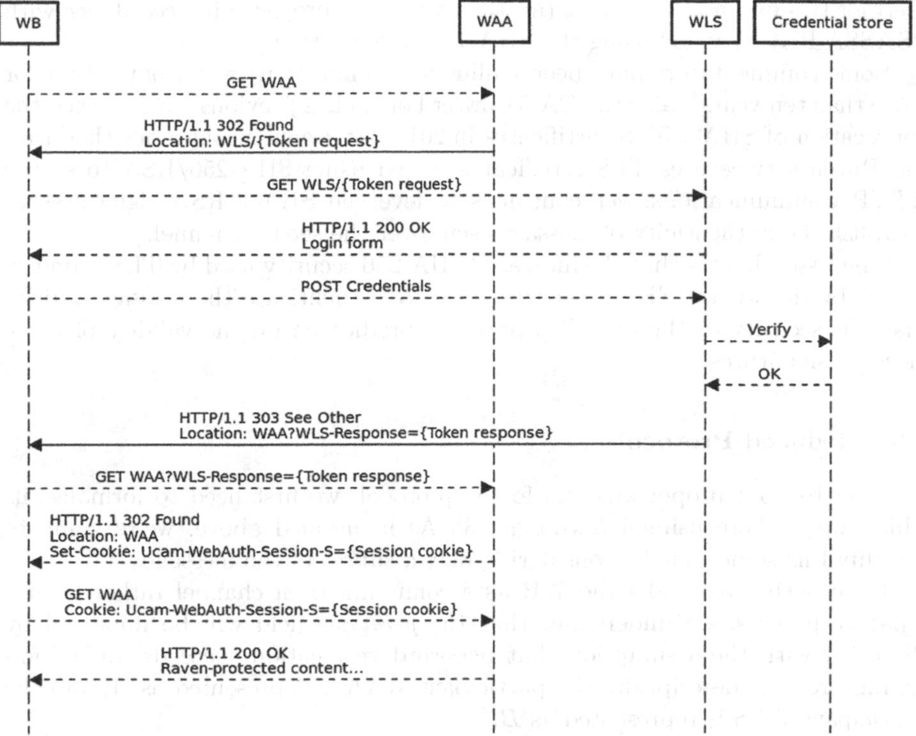

Fig. 1. Ucam Webauth login sequence, showing successful authentication by the Web Login Service (WLS) and authorisation by the Web Application Agent (WAA) via the Web Browser (WB).

2.2 Message Space

Protocol participants exchange two types of message: a token request, and a token response (illustrated with solid unbroken lines in Fig. 1). These messages are exchanged between the WLS and the WAA, relayed via the WB.

$$\text{Token request} := ver|url|desc|aauth|iact|msg|params|date|skew|fail$$

$$\text{Token response} := ver|status|msg|issue|id|url|principal|ptags|auth|sso|life|params|kid|sig$$

We will further simplify subsequent analysis by ignoring some of the more arcane fields in these message formats. Noteworthy fields include *ver* (the supported protocol version, dictating the expected message format), *url* (the return URL, i.e. the WAA), *params* (an optional nonce generated by the WAA for each request), *msg* (an optional custom message to be displayed to the user), *id* (a nonce generated by the WLS for each response), *principal* (an authenticated user's CRSid), *kid* (identifies which key pair from the deployed service set is being used for this exchange), and *sig* (an RSA signature prepared in accordance with RSASSA-PKCS1-v1_5[3] using the SHA-1 hash algorithm.

Some commentators have been calling for a migration away from SHA-1 for more than ten years[4], also the CA/Browser Forum has previously announced the deprecation of SHA-1 TLS certificates in 2014[5]. It seems incongruous then that the Raven service uses TLS certificates signed using SHA-256/RSA to secure HTTP communications, yet continues to leverage SHA-1/RSA signatures to establish the authenticity of messages sent over the secure channel.

The lesson here is that the increased SHA-256 security used by TLS is undermined by the weaker SHA-1 security used to authenticate the messages, given that the security of the overall protocol is predicated on the validity of these message signatures.

2.3 Reduced Protocol

In order to do a proper analysis fo the protocol, we first need to formalise it, which we do here using BAN-Logic [3]. As mentioned above, we're going to simplify this somewhat by considering only a subset of the messages.

By choosing to model the WB as a communication channel rather than a separate process, we understand that the *principal* field will be imparted by the ether with the assumption that password verification succeeds. In the following protocol description, the participant WAA is represented as A, and the participant WLS is represented as B.

We can assume A knows, and implicitly trusts, all keys in the service set $\mathcal{S}$ which are installed when the WAA is initially set up. B signs responder messages using key K_i^{-1}, i.e. A is expected to be able to verify signed messages spoken by B using the corresponding key K_i.

$\mathcal{S} = \{K_1, K_2, ..., K_n\}$, and $K_i \in \mathcal{S} \subset K$, where K is the set of all possible keys.

We formalise the protocol as follows.

$$\begin{array}{ll} \text{Message 0} & \rightarrow A: \ B, \mathcal{S} \\ \text{Message 1} & A \rightarrow B: A, X_a, N_a, T_a \\ \text{Message 2} & B \rightarrow A: M(X_b, N_a, N_b, T_b), i, \{H(|M|)\}_{K_i^{-1}} \end{array}$$

Here, T_a and T_b are timestamps (representing fields *date* and *issue* respectively), N_a and N_b are nonces (representing fields *params* and *id* respectively), i represents field *kid*, and X_a and X_b are composed of other data (i.e. the remaining fields of the message space already described).

---

3 https://www.ietf.org/rfc/rfc3447.txt.
4 https://www.schneier.com/blog/archives/2005/02/cryptanalysis_o.html.
5 https://cabforum.org/2014/10/16/ballot-118-sha-1-sunset/.

2.4 Analysis

We are not concerned with secrecy (a channel property provided by TLS), we are only concerned with the authenticity of Message 2 (ostensibly from B), and what the message says about a 3rd party's identity (*principal*). In other words a desirable goal, in the familiar notation of the BAN-logic papers [3–5], is:

$$A \models B \models M,$$

meaning "A believes that B believes M".

The reduced protocol assumes $A \models \overset{K_i}{\mapsto} B,\ B \ni K_B^{-1}$, i.e. that A believes that the public key of B is K_i, and that B possesses the corresponding private key. Ucam Webauth provides no mechanism for key distribution, so all keys in the service set $\mathcal{S}$ must be transferred manually by a system administrator from B to A. It is assumed that this is the only way that A can accumulate knowledge of keys. It should follow by application of BAN-logic message meaning rules[6] that $A \models B \models M$:

(1)	$\dfrac{P \models \overset{K_i}{\mapsto} Q,\ P \triangleleft \{X\}_{K_i^{-1}}}{P \models Q \mid\!\sim X}$	Rule M̲M, page 238 [3]
(2)	$\dfrac{P \models Q \mid\!\sim H(X),\ P \triangleleft X}{P \models Q \mid\!\sim X}$	Rule H̲ page 266 [3]
(3)	$\dfrac{P \models \#(X),\ P \models Q \mid\!\sim X}{P \models Q \models X}$	Rule N̲V, page 238 [3]
(4)	$A \models \overset{K_i}{\mapsto} B, B \ni K_i^{-1}$	Assumption
(5)	$A \triangleleft M, \{H(\lvert M \rvert)\}_{K_i^{-1}}$	Message 2
(6)	$A \models B \mid\!\sim H(M)$	4, 5, 1 (Rule M̲M)
(7)	$A \models B \mid\!\sim M$	5, 6, 2 (Rule H̲)

At this point, we might continue by assuming the freshness of the nonce N_a.

(8)	$A \models \#(N_a)$	Assumption
(9)	$A \models B \models M$	7, 8, 3 (NV)

However, in practice, WAAs are implemented in a stateless way, and WAAs are generally satisfied with $A \models B \mid\!\sim M$ ("A believes B once said M"), provided that T_b is reasonable (clock skew is configurable for most WAAs so that they will tolerate high latency connections).

[6] It should be noted that inference rule H has been considered unjustified by Teepe, who questions the soundness of BAN logic in [7].

It should be obvious that B is not able to verify the authenticity of Message 1, which is entirely plaintext. WAAs typically accept unsolicited authentication response tokens, and most do not even include an unpredictable value for N_a, an optional challenge sent in Message 1 (contrary to the best practice advice offered in Abadi and Needham [1]).

Mapping Message 2 to the appropriate protocol instance may not be possible, e.g. it may be mapped to an older instance, or even an instance relating to another participant.

3 Attacks

3.1 Tampering with the Token Response Message

The most obvious attack vector would be for an intruder to capture and replay Message 2. This should be mitigated by the WAA making robust checks on the timestamp T_b, allowing for some minimum acceptable latency of the connection. Should the WAA fail to check T_b, then any such replay attack would allow the intruder to impersonate the authenticated user indefinitely (at least for the lifetime of the key K_i). However, this attack is considered out of scope, since we assume secrecy of the communication channels through the use of TLS.

Clearly an intruder, with only partial knowledge of $\mathcal{S}$, might spoof a message from B choosing a suitable value for i which indexes a key from the service set which they somehow control. This attack is probably only useful in practice for large $\mathcal{S}$. For the case where $|\mathcal{S}| = 1$ (which is the case for all known deployments), this attack really just means the singular service key has been compromised, which is obviously catastrophic. A scenario where this attack might be useful occurs soon after a key rollover event, at which time the old (potentially compromised) key might still reside on the target A. For this reason, old keys should be removed once they are no longer in use because the key rollover feature of the protocol also allows for key rollback. Importantly, an attacker does not need to know $\mathcal{S}$ to be able to forge messages from B. The attacker only needs to compromise one key, K_i, where $K_i \in \mathcal{S}$.

It should be clear that if an attacker has the capability to spoof credible response messages from the WLS, then they will be able to authenticate as any user to any Raven-protected resource. We discovered two ways in which an attacker can tamper with a WLS response message, and these are elaborated in the following sections.

Forging a Verifiable RSA Signature: We discovered a path traversal vulnerability existent in several WAAs with varying impacts. It was possible under certain conditions to leverage this vulnerability to specify which public key should be used by the WAA to verify a token response message from the WLS, clearly an undesirable consequence.

The *kid* field (shown as i in Message 2) should represent an integer, and is typically a single numeric character. In some WAA implementations, the *kid* field is used in an unsafe way to construct a path to a file (the RSA public key used for signature verification). By supplying a crafted *kid* field, we were able in some cases to choose any public key on the target server to use for signature verification (i.e. potentially a key outside of the service set $\mathcal{S}$), e.g.:

```
https://example.cam.ac.uk/?WLS-Response
    =3!200!!20180319T000000Z!!https://example.cam.ac.
    uk/!Test0001!current!pwd!!!/etc/ssl/certs/{
    Compromised key}!{Forged signature}
```

This vector is of course partly mitigated by the scarcity of known public/private key pairs which may be present on the target server. However, many software packages install such key pairs, perhaps for testing purposes, into well-known locations. Additionally, it may be possible for an attacker to upload their own files to the target server via other unspecified vectors (e.g. the web application itself allows file uploads and therefore presents an authenticated attacker with a privilege escalation opportunity). We found both the C-based authentication handler for Apache[7], and the PHP library[8] to be vulnerable in this way.

The C-based authentication handler for Apache did already make an attempt at mitigating path traversal, by checking for forward slashes ("/") in the user-supplied data, but of course such a mitigation was entirely ineffective when the module was deployed on Microsoft Windows platforms which prefer a backward slash ("\") as a path separator. This vulnerability was addressed with the addition of a function "is_valid_kid()"[9] which makes more robust checks, insisting on the *kid* being no more than 8 characters long, consisiting only of digits 0-9, and not beginning with the number 0.

The PHP library offered no mitigation at all, using the unfiltered *kid* field to build a file path. This implementation was patched in a similar way, again making more robust checks on the validity of the *kid* field[10]. The PHP language represents an interesting case, as it may be possible under certain conditions to prepend a "scheme://..." component to the file path passed to fopen()[11]. This language feature might have allowed an attacker to host their own public key on a secondary HTTP server, and direct the WAA to use this key when verifying the signature on a forged WLS response message. In the worst case, an attacker might have leveraged the "data://" stream wrapper[12] to supply a Base64-encoded public key inline with the WLS response message. However,

[7] https://github.com/cambridgeuniversity/mod_ucam_webauth.

[8] https://github.com/cambridgeuniversity/ucam-webauth-php.

[9] https://github.com/cambridgeuniversity/mod_ucam_webauth/commit/dd4fedbe819 2e3b147d9cfe05c8373b2fd8c195e#diff-db9058c9017dbde922e625e3be2d6557.

[10] https://github.com/cambridgeuniversity/ucam-webauth-php/commit/cd471c38612 941c213716d4b7dd2dceff607bd04#diff-48bcdf5cb926243bf258df83114dd4e9.

[11] http://php.net/manual/en/function.fopen.php.

[12] http://php.net/manual/en/wrappers.data.php.

at least for the implementation under test, this vector was mitigated by the prepending of a forward slash to the file path. Perhaps most interestingly, the wording of the Ucam Webauth protocol documentation has been updated in response to the notification of this vulnerability[13]. This update bumped the protocol version number from 3.0 to 4.0, and includes a more robust definition of the *kid* field so that WAA implementers adhering to the specification are less likely to expose the path traversal vulnerability discussed. This is a salient reminder of the importance of input data sanitisation.

This vulnerability was the first vulnerability disclosed to the Raven team in over a decade of operation. It exploited a problem with the key rollover feature of the Ucam Webauth protocol, which has never actually been used in anger during Raven's entire service history. With less than 1000 online resources making regular use of the Raven Ucam WebAuth server, one might consider disposing of the feature entirely without disagreeable impact. Because the key has not been changed since the Raven service was launched, it might be high time this feature was actually tested if it is to be retained. During the lifetime of this key it has been physically moved to a new site as the University relocated its IT services division from the New Museums Site in the centre of Cambridge to the West Site on the outskirts. We are more concerned that the private key exponent may have been physically compromised during this upheaval, than the remote possibility that an enthusiastic amateur has been able to factorise the 1024-bit modulus. It's also worth noting that 1024 bits is less than the keylength currently recommended (2048 bits) for a public authentication key by NIST [2]. NIST also recommends that an appropriate cryptoperiod in this application is 1–2 years [2]. At least the key is not "export grade" (i.e. 512 bits).

The rather obvious lesson here is to do with data sanitisation, and the fact that while the feature was designed to future-proof the protocol, in practice the extra complexity introduced a vulnerability with no practical gain.

XSS: Injecting Error Messages: For a *status* field value in the token response message from the WLS holding any value other than 200 (indicating successful authentication), it is possible to supply a more descriptive error message so that the receiving WAA may present this information to the user. This optional message is supplied in the *msg* field of the WLS response message. We discovered that the WebAuth Java Toolkit[14] did not apply robust filtering to this optional parameter, which left several online resources vulnerable to XSS-based attacks. Vulnerable online resources included the portal which University members use to retrieve a unique network access token which is required for both eduroam and VPN access. In the following example, we pass a *status* field value of 520 (meaning unsupported protocol version). We also include a crafted error message containing Javascript which will be executed by the victim's browser. The only

[13] https://github.com/cambridgeuniversity/UcamWebauth-protocol/commit/3d71cc2840ef745aed8caaf5a565e48988d39fbd#diff-90c8938be2a4fc76543eae935d1a4f2b.

[14] https://raven.cam.ac.uk/project/java-toolkit/.

other parameter we need to consider is the return URL, as this is checked for congruity by the WAA:

```
https://tokens.csx.cam.ac.uk/?WLS-Response=1!520!
    message%3Cscript%20type=%22text/javascript%22%3
    Ealert(%27XSS%27)%3C/script%3E!a!a!https://tokens
    .csx.cam.ac.uk/
```

Had this vector been leveraged in a phishing campaign, it may have been possible for attackers to exfiltrate a large number of network access tokens.

It is not necessary to forge a valid RSA signature in such cases, as the *status* field is processed before any signature verification is performed (i.e. all WLS response messages reporting error conditions are implicitly trusted by the WAA). We propose that all error-based WLS response messages be signed, and that this signature be verified by the receiving WAA. According to the current Ucam Webauth protocol documentation, such behaviour is optional (which obviously breaks the weak authentication that may otherwise have existed between the WLS and the WAA). Ideally, the WAA should believe that the WLS spoke all token response messages, not just those informing of successful authentication.

Once again, the lesson here won't come as a surprise: error messages are messages too and should be treated with the same care (in this case to ensure integrity) as any other part of the protocol.

3.2 Tampering with the Token Request Message

Unvalidated Redirects and Forwards (Open Redirects): This vulnerability should also peek the interest of any attacker who wishes to augment a phishing campaign. An open redirect allows the attacker to craft sensible looking clickable links, which then "bounce" the victim to a malicious page where they may encounter spoofed login forms, malware, or other undesirable content. Redirection is intrinsic to the Ucam Webauth protocol, and we discovered that it's in fact quite trivial to hijack the normal functioning of the WLS. In the following example, we supply an invalid value for the *ver* field (99) to engineer an error condition, at which point the WLS duly redirects the victim's browser to what it believes to be the originating online resource without stopping to verify credentials. However, the originating online resource can be any URL we like (in this example a "Rickroll"):

```
https://raven.cam.ac.uk/auth/authenticate.html?ver
    =99&url=https://youtu.be/dQw4w9WgXcQ
```

Potential mitigations might include inspecting the HTTP_REFERER header and/or the *url* field supplied in the token request message to check that it matches a registered application (or at least a service operating under the domain "cam.ac.uk"), and then perhaps redirecting the user to an intermediary warning page if an unregistered service is detected.

We were able to test the utility of the open redirect during a recent red team exercise at the University of Cambridge. We took the opportunity to spoof an e-mail from University Information Services, targeting a short list of management personnel late on a Friday afternoon. The spoofed e-mail included a link to a spoofed Raven service login page, and that link leveraged the open redirect to appear more plausible. We were successful in directly compromising a number of Raven accounts, including that of a systems administrator whose responsibilities included resetting passwords for other members of the University. We thus ended up with the capability to reset the passwords of nearly all Raven accounts. The potential impact extended to every member of the University and their data, except in a few rare cases where users had opted out of the most convenient password resetting mechanisms. The phishing campaign had lasted for less than half an hour, and compromised thousands of users. Of course our campaign was well researched and well targeted, but we caution that phishing campaigns do not need to be nearly that sophisticated to be successful.

CAS provides a service management facility which allows an administrator to configure a list of authorised services[15]. However, we discovered a number of CAS deployments have chosen not to use this feature and so these sites also exhibit open redirect vulnerabilities. This includes Yale University, the birthplace of CAS, e.g.:

```
https://auth-ldt.yale.edu/cas/login?service=https://
   youtu.be/dQw4w9WgXcQ&gateway=true
```

Specifying "gateway = true" in the above example ensures CAS will immediately redirect to the "service" URL without painting any login screen.

For some CAS deployments, we also noticed XSS opportunities in the login page presented to users (see Fig. 2). Such opportunities were exploitable by providing Javascript payloads in the "service" parameter of the CAS login URL.

This is not a problem with the CAS protocol *per se*, but highlights the apparent difficulties of ensuring a secure web authentication stack which involves many interoperating components, not just the underlying security protocol.

Stanford's WebAuth protocol ensures that the IdP only accepts requests encrypted with a pre-shared key, established when an application is registered, and so can not be manipulated in this way.

Clearly, application registration works as a mitigation, but it might also be considered too restrictive in some environments, especially those with high churn of applications where registration would add significant overhead, not to mention deployment complexity. We understand that, despite pointing out this feature as a potential vulnerability, on balance some sites may view it as an acceptable risk, and preferable to the alternative. A possible compromise would be to redirect users to a an intermediary warning page if they are about to be transported beyond their usual domain.

[15] https://apereo.github.io/cas/5.2.x/planning/Security-Guide.html#service-management.

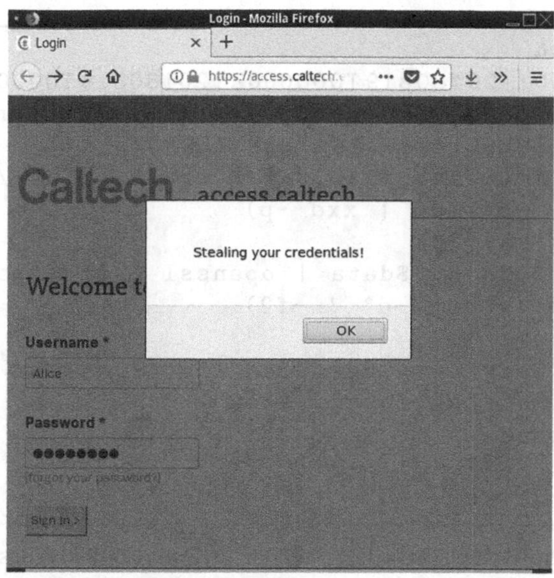

Fig. 2. XSS at Caltech

3.3 Tampering with the WAA's Session Tracking Mechanism

If an attacker has the capability to tamper with a WAA's session tracking mechanism (e.g. the session cookie used by the popular C-based authentication handler for Apache), then it is not necessary to break Ucam Webauth at all in order to target a specific application.

Brute Force Attack Against the mod_ucam_webauth MAC: Most WAAs use HMAC-SHA1 for generating a MAC, and so are not susceptible to hash collisions like those recently reported for SHA-1 in Stevens *et al.* [6]. Attackers with limited resources are unlikely to effect useful cookie tampering. However, a brute force attack may still succeed if the WAA operator chooses a weak secret key. We developed an auditing tool for the session cookies issued by the C-based authentication handler for Apache. The tool can be used to brute force the secret key used in generating the MAC appended to the cookie data, the secret key may then be used to forge a cookie containing any data the attacker wishes. It would be nice to use a class-leading tool like Hashcat[16] to perform a brute force attack. However, Hashcat imposes a limit of 50 characters on salt length, so this is not possible (cookie data length typically exceeds 50 characters). We illustrate this attack using a simple Bash script, which should be more readable than solutions presented in some other languages:

[16] https://hashcat.net/hashcat/.

```
#!/bin/bash
data="3!200!!20180319T000000Z!20180319T000000Z
   !86400!0000000000-0000-0!test0001!current!pwd!!"
raw_sig="o88E6CrefqXsgfAlmePJlE0A3Tw_"
decoded_sig=$(echo $raw_sig | tr "\-._" "+/=" |
   base64 --decode | xxd -p)
while read key; do
    sig=$(echo -n $data | openssl dgst -sha1 -hmac
        $key | cut -d' ' -f2)
    echo $sig
    if [ "$sig" == "$decoded_sig" ]; then
        echo "Key found: $key"
        break
    fi
done < wordlist
```

In the above example, the secret key "secret" is found quickly, assuming it exists in the attacker's wordlist.

The session cookie MAC can be brute-forced rapidly because HMAC-SHA1 is relatively quick to calculate. We understand that the designers may have chosen a fast algorithm for the MAC to reduce processing overhead on busy sites. However, the impact of a "heavy" algorithm would probably be inconsequential for most practical deployments. Typical Raven-protected resources are simply not that busy. Of course a fast algorithm here does help to mitigate DoS attacks, where an attacker might force the Raven-protected resource to verify thousands of cookies per second. However, such attacks may be adequately mitigated by leveraging request rate-limiting options available in the web server configuration. Such configuration options would also prevent an attacker from forcing the Raven-protected resource to verify the RSA signatures on huge numbers of token response messages too.

Allowing the WAA operator to choose a secret key clearly allows scope for human error to compromise the security of a particular web application. It would make some sense for the secret key to be chosen randomly by the WAA. In fact, the WAA could choose a new secret key for each instance during initialisation. One unfortunate consequence of this approach is that should the WAA need to be restarted, it would forget the secret key and all current user sessions would be voided requiring reauthentication. However, this consequence might easily be tolerated in many environments. Another problem is that it may be useful to be able to specify the same secret key for more than one instance of a WAA, perhaps in load balancing applications. A good compromise might be for the WAA to generate a random secret key during initialisation only if the WAA operator has not already specified a secret key as a configuration option. This is perhaps the most flexible approach. We note that some package maintainers already include post-install routines to ensure a strong secret key is added as a configuration option during installation. However, this practice is not widespread.

The lesson is to avoid leaving key choice to the end user. Especially where the key is something not intended for use by a human, autogenerating a random key could result in significantly increased security.

4 Discussion

The Ucam Webauth protocol was conceived at a time when there was scant consensus on the best way to implement a web authentication system. It has been used exclusively by The University of Cambridge, perhaps largely due to the fact that despite there being many open source WAA implementations, the source code for the production WLS has never been made public. This strategy may have afforded the flagship deployment some level of security through obscurity.

By contrast, Yale's CAS is something of a higher-ed open source success, and is deployed at hundreds of sites including universities as well as Fortune-500 companies. Released under the Apache 2.0 Licence[17] CAS is supported by an open source community that actively contributes to the project.

Stanford's WebAuth has also seen wider deployment (notably underpinning Oxford's Webauth web SSO service since 2002). However, Stanford is planning to switch from its homegrown WebAuth to the SAML 2.0 standard for web authentication in the summer of 2018[18]. This has prompted Oxford to consider the same migration path.

Raven remains useful because it is so straightforward for system adminstrators to deploy. We would not advocate its disappearance. However, it may require some development effort to stave off emerging attacks that were less well understood at the time Ucam Webauth was conceieved.

The question of whether open redirects pose an acceptable risk remains a choice for each site. Some sites will be comfortable with open redirects, which is fine as long as they understand the potential threat impact and can make an informed decision, or take other mitigating steps (e.g. providing security awareness training for users).

5 Conclusion

The original Ucam Webauth implementation offers somewhat of a case study of security failings. The ease with which it can be deployed and the longevity of its use at the University of Cambridge are contributing factors to both its success, and its weaknesses. As noted in the preceding sections, the main lessons learnt include the need to sanitise input data, ensure a consistent approach to the level of security, treat all data – especially error messages – as security-relevant, and avoid leaving unnecessary key-choices to the end-user.

Far from being the detritus of a home-built authentication experiment, we believe Ucam Webauth still represents a significant contribution to life at the

[17] http://www.apache.org/licenses/LICENSE-2.0.html.

[18] https://uit.stanford.edu/service/saml/webauth-announce.

University of Cambridge, and Raven has been a reliable and long-lived service. It is a fine example of the University's capability to cultivate in-house projects to compliment commercial off-the-shelf products. However, other universities, even those who have previously designed and implemented their own authentication systems, are converging on common well-supported solutions. If the University of Cambridge plans to continue using the Ucam Webauth protocol, it needs to continue to be able to respond to emerging threats.

In the course of our investigation, we noticed that there was no native authentication handler for the nginx web server, despite the availability of a mature C-based authentication handler for Apache. It is of course possible to use some other authentication handler implementation, perhaps the PHP library, in tandem with an nginx deployment. However, such a solution would not be optimal. We decided to develop our own native authentication handler for nginx as an nginx module (available on GitHub[19]). This development effort resulted in a lightweight implementation roughly three times smaller in terms of lines of code than the Apache module. This module has served as a testbed for new ideas, and not only fills a gap in WAA provision on the nginx platform, but has also been carefully engineered to be robust against the attacks discussed in this paper.

Acknowledgments. The authors would like to thank Malcolm Scott (University of Cambridge, Computer Laboratory) for his contribution to the further development of the prototype nginx WAA. We would also like to thank Jon Warbrick, original designer of the Ucam Webauth protocol for many useful discussions.

References

1. Abadi, M., Needham, R.: Prudent engineering practice for cryptographic protocols. IEEE Transactions on Software Engineering **22**(1), 6–15 (1996)
2. Barker, E., Barker, W., Burr, W., Polk, W., Smid, M.: Recommendation for key management part 1: General (revision 3). NIST special publication **800**(57), 1–147 (2012)
3. Burrows, M., Abadi, M.: A logic of authentication. In: Proc. R. Soc. Lond. A. vol. 426, no. 1871, pp. 233–271. The Royal Society (1989)
4. Gaarder, K., Snekkenes, E.: On the formal analysis of pkcs authentication protocols. In: Proceedings of the International Conference on Cryptology: Advances in Cryptology. pp. 106–121. Springer-Verlag (1990)
5. Gong, L., Needham, R., Yahalom, R.: Reasoning about belief in cryptographic protocols. In: Research in Security and Privacy, 1990. Proceedings., 1990 IEEE Computer Society Symposium on. pp. 234–248. IEEE (1990)
6. Stevens, M., Bursztein, E., Karpman, P., Albertini, A., Markov, Y.: The first collision for full SHA-1. In: Annual International Cryptology Conference. pp. 570–596. Springer (2017)
7. Teepe, W.: On BAN logic and hash functions or: how an unjustified inference rule causes problems. Autonomous Agents and Multi-Agent Systems **19**(1), 76–88 (2009)

[19] https://github.com/grymer/ngxraven.

Raven Authentication Service Attacks and Countermeasures (Transcript of Discussion)

Graham Rymer(✉)

Computer Laboratory, University of Cambridge, William Gates Building,
15 JJ Thomson Avenue, Cambridge CB3 0FD, UK
Graham.Rymer@cl.cam.ac.uk

Reply: presenting the paper.

Ian Goldberg: Considering the messages [see Fig. 1] the only thing that Message 2 had that came from Message 1 is N_A, which is often not used. That's a little more than slightly concerning.

Message 0	$\rightarrow A : B, \mathcal{S}$
Message 1	$A \rightarrow B : A, X_a, N_a, T_a$
Message 2	$B \rightarrow A : M(X_b, N_a, N_b, T_b), i, \{H(\lvert M \rvert)\}_{K_i^{-1}}$

Fig. 1. Protocol sequence taken from Sect. 2.3

Reply: I think you've hit the nail on the head. There's no way for B to be authenticated to A in this exchange. You can have a completely out-of-sequence Message 2 arrive at any time and A actually trusts it.

That's assuming that the application agent doesn't make use of the nonce N_A, but none of the ones that we tested do. The one which we wrote does. The feature of including a nonce has actually been in the protocol for a long time, but nobody uses it. So in practice there is nothing in the Message 2 which ties it to the first one. It seems unbelievable but it's true. If you're an application agent and you just see Message 2 arriving, you will quite happily start verifying the signatures and authenticating people. You don't really have to trust that it's part of a session.

Similar systems like CAS actually have a third back channel between the Application Agent and the Login Service and they check that the token issued is part of a legitimate request. This is probably an unnecessarily complicated way of doing it, because you can actually do it just by including some extra data in the message.

Daniel Weitzner: Is there a message log somewhere that would allow the administrators to check for these mismatched or untimed messages?

Reply: Yes, the logs exist, but in a disjointed way. There will be message logs on the Web Application Agent, and there will be message logs on the Web

V. Matyáš et al. (Eds.): Security Protocols 2018, LNCS 11286, pp. 15–23, 2018.
https://doi.org/10.1007/978-3-030-03251-7_2

Login Service. They're run by two different people and it'd probably take several days to check.

Daniel Weitzner: Have you ever looked at them all together?

Reply: I have. I haven't done an analysis to see if there is any spoofing going on in the wild. I think that would be very difficult to do because there are about a thousand application agents in the field. Really you'd want to look at the data for all of them. You can't tell just by looking at the data from the Web Login Service; you can see legitimate requests and authentication tokens issued, but you can't tell if those were actually the result of requests which originated on an Application Agent.

Daniel Weitzner: You have to match everything.

Reply: Yes, you have to get a thousand people involved in the project, essentially. Which is probably challenging.

Spoofing that Message 2 is the most obvious thing to do. And you can do that in some cases, but it's not easy. These exchanges are also protected by TLS. What we can do is tamper with the token response message and tell the application agent which key from the server set to use to verify the message. We can do this with path injection. Most Application Agents take the *kid* key ID field and they use it to index the key in the server set for verification.

Unfortunately in most implementations that key ID can be pretty much anything. Many application agents expect to see a number and they tag that on to the end of the file name and use that to look up the key on the local file system. There is a path traversal attack in many cases, so you can actually tell it to use any key that you can access on that target system to verify the message. This doesn't seem too useful to start with but when we started looking there are lots of well known key pairs that exist on computer systems. Obviously you need to know the private key as well to craft your message, but you can find key pairs conveniently distributed on computer systems, which are well known in many cases. For example OpenSSH, NodeJS, and many frameworks, include test keys for various parts of their test packages. If these keys are accessible the vulnerability may be exploitable and quite undesirable.

The other thing you can do is index other keys in the server set. This feature was built for key rollover and is an enterprise-grade feature so that if the central administration ever need to change the key all they have to do is issue everyone the new public key in advance and knock that number up by one so that everyone just immediately starts using the next key.

This sounds great, but if that server set gets too big then after a key rollover event you can do a key downgrade by indexing the previous key, assuming the administrator hasn't removed it from their system yet. So it does expose you to some pitfalls like this if you're not doing things operationally in a very tidy way.

That was one of the most interesting types of attack on this message. The fact that we were able to exploit that key rollover feature. Here's an example:

```
https://example.cam.ac.uk/?WLS-Response
    =3!200!!20180319T000000Z!!https://example.cam.ac
    .uk/!Test0001!current!pwd!!!!/etc/ssl/certs/{
    Compromised key}!{Forged singature}
```

Ian Goldberg: The exclamation point seems to be the field separator, and the 2nd-to-last field was i in Message 2. So that string starting with `/etc` was meant to be the number 3, but you changed it. But if it's being appended to a path name, then shouldn't that string there start with `../../../`?

Reply: It depends on the application engine. For some of them the string is appended to a path name, but others aren't vulnerable because they look up the key in something like a key store. There's a Java application agent which does that, and is immune to this type of attack.

There was a PHP implementation, which was great because PHP supports other types of access. It uses the `fopen()` function which supports things like HTTPS. So you can actually ask for keys on other servers.

The really good one is that it also has a data specifier, so you can add base64-encoded data inline in the message and put your key in there, and it will use that. So the PHP version is really horrible. For other implementations it depends on whether they have a hard-coded directory path, or where they build the key if they're just assuming it to be in the local directory and they're not putting any sort of path in front of it. It depends on various conditions. A lot of application agents were horribly flawed, some of them got away and fluked it, just because they used something like a certificate store, for example.

Frank Stajano: If you are aware that some application agent is happy to read the thing with the path that starts with a slash, can you use that to read any file on the system?

Reply: It may not make sense as a key, but yes, you can read any file on the system, or certainly touch any file on the system. In the case of the PHP example, you can drag any file from any HTTP server anywhere. This relies on your PHP configuration being a bit sloppy, but it does happen.

Ian Goldberg: For that HTTPS example, `cam.ac.uk` is the WAA's address, presumably? Can you do something tricky by putting exclamation points in the WAA address? Are they clever enough to escape that?

Reply: In some cases, but we'll come back to that in a bit. There are other fields in there, which are vulnerable.

That key rollover is interesting because in 15 years of operation it's never been used. It's also using a 1024-bit key, which certainly goes against NIST recommendations currently for this type of application. It's been using the same 1024-bit key since 2004. One of the horrible things about this is that the computer system which it sits on has actually been moved physically in the back of a transit van several miles from the centre of Cambridge to the West site on the outskirts of Cambridge.

I'm not really concerned that anyone's broken the 1024-bit key. I'm more concerned that it's just been left lying around on a USB stick or sitting in the back of a van at some point. In that 15-year period anything could have happened, which is why we should have short crypto-periods. It's slightly concerning that they have this feature, but they never use it. I think it's high time it was actually used, if only to upgrade that key. It would cost them nothing to do.

What can you do with the token response message? You can inject error messages, which include Javascript for example. The response message includes a message field so that if an error is encountered you can present a custom error message to the user in your own application.

Unfortunately this causes a vulnerability, certainly for the Java implementation, which backs `tokens.csx.cam.ac.uk`. This is quite an important server because that's where you get your network access tokens from to access the university via VPN or if you want to access other sorts of remote systems, and of course it's Raven-protected. We can just send it a response message, with an error code, which will prompt it to display the error message, which can have a cross-site scripting payload in it. Quite a few applications were vulnerable to this injection of Javascript into error messages. The horrible thing here is they don't verify the signature on the response message if they have an error condition. The signature is only verified if they think they're going to proceed with the access control. If they're just presenting an error message, they think, "why bother?" In fact, it turns out, sometimes it's important to trust everything in that message: certainly if you're going to start including it in your output page.

There's no signature check performed at all for any error messages on any of the Application Agents we tested. Message integrity is important even if it's an error message.

Bruce Christianson: How should you handle an error message that doesn't pass an integrity check?

Reply: You shouldn't.

Bruce Christianson: That seems a bit harsh. Just go silent?

Reply: Yes. In this context, I don't think it's harsh. So, in a broader context, certainly you might want to know that there has been some error condition potentially. But actually in this context I think its completely harmless just to drop that message completely.

Reply: A lot of people don't think open redirects are particularly important. They can be leveraged in phishing campaigns, and that sort of thing. I know Google have changed their stance on open redirects. These days if you're redirected, off site, you tend to get an intermediary page that says "you are about to be redirected to this URL, are you happy to proceed?" That's the normal way of dealing with that situation.

```
https://raven.cam.ac.uk/auth/authenticate.html?ver
    =99&url=https://youtu.be/dQw4w9WgXcQ
```

If you type the above in, you'll get a Rick Roll. This is a token request message, stating that the protocol version is 99, which is unsupported, and probably will be for the next few centuries. The URL of the Application Agent in this message can be anything we like. If the server encounters an error condition, it sends a response message, which again is vulnerable to XSS. The response message will have an error code in it and it will wing its way merrily to anywhere you tell it to, and as long as that target ignores the web login service string, which is appended to it, you can pretty much redirect anywhere with any results.

Open redirects are trivial to exploit on the Raven platform. I expect the easiest way to mitigate this would be with an intermediary page which says "are you happy to proceed?" if it's outside of `cam.ac.uk`. This would be very easy to implement. At the moment you can paste into your phishing campaign a rather neat Cambridge-looking URL that could redirect pretty much anywhere.

Yale's CAS is vulnerable to this as well. We've got people here from Yale, today, I think? I spoke to the IT team at Yale quite recently. CAS is a lot more commercially successful than Raven and is actively developed. It's a huge project, used in many universities in the United States and across Europe, as well as by commercial entities. CAS does have a feature which lets you register applications. It's entirely optional and, in fact, Yale doesn't use it. So the people who invented CAS don't use this feature themselves, which means that you can do this at Yale all day long as well, and have an open redirect to a Rick Roll:

```
https://auth-ldt.yale.edu/cas/login?service=https
    ://youtu.be/dQw4w9WgXcQ&gateway=true
```

It is a little bit of administrative overhead to register applications, if you have a lot of churn, for example. Maybe you've got thousands of website administrators adding this system all the time. However, it's actually quite easy to implement. It's basically just a database of URLs. I did speak to Yale about this and they said that they're not actually too worried about it, and it's up to the site. Some sites really don't care about open redirects, whereas others think it's a big deal. As long as you're aware of the risks, then I guess that's okay.

Fabio Massacci: That's what the administrator says. But are the users aware of the risk if they get redirected to some place where their credentials can get stolen? Is that written in the terms of service?

Reply: Highly unlikely. I think most users, non-technical users in the majority of cases, would struggle to understand the threat impact, I would think.

Fabio Massacci: Yeah but then, it's not really true that they are aware of the risks. They're sweeping the risks under the carpet.

Reply: Yes, when I said they're aware of the risks, I meant the IT department at Yale. Certainly not the users. They hope that they're being looked after.

Ian Goldberg: The danger of the one you show is that it is a Yale URL, but when you click on it, it takes you to an arbitrary offsite place. So rather than requiring a registration of every service, perhaps it can just whitelist `yale.edu`? And require a registration of any non-`yale.edu` service that for some reason is using CAS.

Reply: That's the other approach, yes. And I think with CAS that's possible to implement in a matter of seconds, with a regex. It's just missing a management decision to do this. The same is true for Cambridge: it'd be trivial to implement. A slick move, I think.

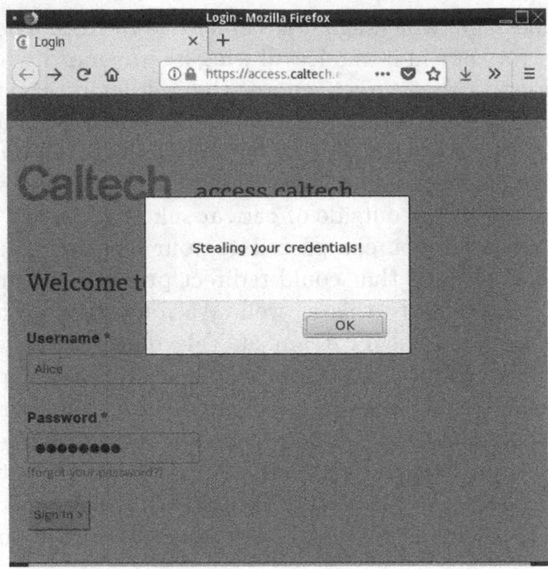

Fig. 2. XSS at Caltech

Figure 2 shows something different. We spent a little bit of time looking at all the implementations of CAS in universities in the US. Quite a few of them were vulnerable to cross-site scripting when you included payloads in the token request message. It has a feature, which will redirect you to an upstream gateway, and you can exploit that in a very similar way to inject payloads.

So actually, at Caltech for example, it's possible to inject Javascript into their main login page, which could steal login credentials. Which is nice. It probably only affects Firefox browser users, and although Firefox has only a 3% share globally you find that's slightly higher in academic environments. Chrome and Internet Explorer have quite good cross-site scripting mitigation built into the browsers. The browsers are leading the fight, because they've given up on developers actually writing proper Web sites.

Firefox still doesn't have any mitigation so you can do this sort of thing quite easily. Caltech fixed that in less than a day; they were quite proactive. Of course, what can you do with the session tracking mechanisms of sites? This isn't specific to Raven, but of course you can brute force the HMACs on the session cookies very easily. In most Web Application Agent deployments the secret key is not chosen randomly by the Application Agent. It's entered by the system administrator and they'll choose, I guess, their pet's name or whatever they feel like. This is something that could certainly be improved because it's trivial to brute force HMAC SHA1 and then start forging session cookies for the application. If you can do that then of course you can bypass Raven completely.

It's not clear exactly why they chose HMAC SHA1. If you've got a busy website you want a fast algorithm, but they could still have something which would frustrate brute-forcing efforts. I think they're worried about the processing hit on the website, but in practise, no Raven website is that busy. They get at most a couple of requests a minute, I would think, so you could get away with a much better algorithm.

Ian Goldberg: This key – the thing you're brute forcing – is not a user's password. It's the HMAC key at the WAA. So each WAA has its own HMAC key?

Reply: They each have their own session tracking mechanism, so some of them will use a PHP session ID, some of them will use a session cookie, which will have an HMAC like this.

This example was taken from `mod_ucam_webauth` which is an Apache module which does use a session cookie. Those session cookies you can brute force very rapidly. We haven't done a survey yet of the thousands of instances out there but I would expect that quite a few of them are crackable in a reasonable amount of time.

Ian Goldberg: Right, so the problem is that the WAAs are configuring to non-random passwords.

Reply: Yes exactly it's a manual option which you have to embed in the configuration file. Some people are smart enough to provide packages which do some post-processing after installation to add that field in for the user. A lot of them don't so that would be a nice feature for them to have.

There is one reason why you might want to have that manual access. In some cases you have two application engines doing load balancing, in which case they'll need to have the same key. So you can't just choose a pure random one and start up. That's quite a niche case and there are very few cases where there's enough load to actually warrant load-balancing in Cambridge.

So take key-generation away from the end user. Some of them are really good at it, some of them are too good at it, some of them are terrible at it, so user-generated keys should be avoided. Yes we can also use a slower hash algorithm to mitigate against brute force attacks, maybe as an option.

Ucam Webauth is quite niche, it's not used in many places but it is used to protect a lot of interesting things here in Cambridge. We notice of course that Yale's CAS is much more widely used. They've just had a better business model I think. Interestingly Stanford's Web Auth, which has been great, has a key distribution facility.

Martin Kleppmann: One attack that comes to mind which I'd like to discuss, is, can I set up some kind of a dodgy service for people to log into and then tell my victim to log into that service, take the token, and re-purpose that token to pass on to some other service? I didn't see anything in the protocol about tying the token to the particular destination that you're trying to log in to? That would be a fun one to cause a problem.

Reply: There is the return URL, but of course you can spoof that anyway if you have control of that service. It wouldn't allow you of course to spoof the user ID. But you could certainly recycle tokens from one service for another service.

Martin Kleppmann: Yes so you could get a token for some other user who is your victim and then use that to access whatever resource you're trying to?

Reply: I think it amounts to the same thing as intercepting and replaying Message 2.

Martin Kleppmann: Ah, yes.

Reply: So you're still limited by the time-to-live (TTL). Some systems have a 60-min TTL. If you're intentionally monitoring a site, because you want to gain access, 60 min is a long time to be able to replay a token. Stanford's Web Auth has a mechanism for loading the service set keys when you set up an application engine. You actually end up with a pre-shared, AES key. All the request messages are encrypted symmetrically. This makes it really hard to tamper with them. It's a bit of hassle of course to register applications in that way.

So Stanford's Web Auth is actually really, really robust. And it's used in other places, for example it underpins the University of Oxford's framework as well. They call it Oxford Web Auth, but it's basically Stanford's Web Auth underneath. Stanford have made the decision to deprecate Web Auth, and they're moving to a SAML-based solution in the summer this year. That's prompted Oxford to do the same thing and anyone else who is downstream, I expect, will make the same decision. I think the future of Raven – certainly Ucam Webauth – is questionable, when we have actually more robust solutions.

Ian Goldberg: You mentioned a couple of times how quick the reactions were from some people, so can you say something about your disclosure process and how all that went with the various universities?

Reply: Sure, so, simply an email chain. In the case of Caltech, I can't remember the name of the lady whom I spoke to there, but she'd been working there since she'd studied there, for many years. She thanked us immediately. She told us that she would let us know as soon as it was mitigated and a couple of hours later it was done. So that was quite straightforward. We haven't had any instances where there's been any pushback, apart from Yale.

In the case of Yale, it was very difficult to get hold of anybody who was really involved in CAS development, because that's all been shifted outside to a separate entity. It was difficult to persuade the IT team and they certainly aren't interested in doing anything about the open redirects, although most other CAS deployments do leverage the application registration feature.

I did eventually speak to the team who were developing CAS, not based at Yale anymore. They just said this isn't a vulnerability because we actually have this great feature which stops it from happening. When I explained that Yale's not using it, they said it's up to them. So Yale is the only place where we've had any pushback. I think still the message hasn't got through to anybody who is reasonably involved in policy.

In Cambridge they've been great. There's been a lot of flux in the university information services in the last couple of years, but they've still responded quickly, although the mitigations are still to happen. So I think there's some desire to implement these mitigations, but they don't have the resources or the political will to get it done in a reasonable amount of time. We're still waiting for any sort of consensus on whether open redirects are an issue in Cambridge, for example.

I'm quite happy for there to be open redirects, as long as there is some security awareness training for end users.

Ucam Webauth may be on it's way out. It's not being actively maintained anymore and it doesn't seem to be resistant to more modern Web application-style attacks, which, perhaps, weren't as well understood at the time it was developed. There are other things out there and other universities are moving towards them. There seems to be a consensus that things like SAML are better because they're just universally supported. Nobody is really scrutinising Raven so even if you have a slightly buggy solution the fact that people are looking at it is probably a good thing. Raven's just being left to rot, I'm afraid. So, who knows what the future will bring.

Your Code Is My Code: Exploiting a Common Weakness in OAuth 2.0 Implementations

Wanpeng Li[1(✉)], Chris J. Mitchell[2], and Thomas Chen[1]

[1] Department of Electrical and Electronic Engineering, City, University of London, London, UK
{Wanpeng.Li,Tom.Chen.1}@city.ac.uk

[2] Information Security Group, Royal Holloway, University of London, Egham, UK
me@chrismitchell.net

Abstract. Many millions of users routinely use their Google, Facebook and Microsoft accounts to log in to websites supporting OAuth 2.0-based single sign on. The security of OAuth 2.0 is therefore of critical importance, and it has been widely examined both in theory and in practice. In this paper we disclose a new class of practical attacks on OAuth 2.0 implementations, which we call Partial Redirection URI Manipulation Attacks. An attack of this type can be used by an attacker to gain a victim user's OAuth 2.0 code (a token representing a right to access user data) without the user's knowledge; this code can then be used to impersonate the user to the relevant relying party website. We examined 27 leading OAuth 2.0 identity providers, and found that 19 of them are vulnerable to these attacks.

1 Introduction

Since the OAuth 2.0 authorisation framework was published at the end of 2012 [8], it has been adopted by a large number of websites worldwide as a means of providing single sign-on (SSO) services. By using OAuth 2.0, websites can reduce the burden of password management for their users, as well as saving users the inconvenience of re-entering attributes that are instead stored by identity providers and provided to relying parties as required.

There is a correspondingly rich infrastructure of identity providers (IdPs) providing identity services using OAuth 2.0. This is demonstrated by the fact that some Relying Parties (RPs), such as the website USATODAY[1], support as many as six different IdPs—see Fig. 1.

As discussed in Sect. 4, the security of OAuth 2.0 has been analysed both theoretically, e.g. using formal methods, and practically, involving looking at implementations of OAuth 2.0. The research methodology used in most of this

[1] https://login.usatoday.com/USAT-GUP/authenticate/?.

V. Matyáš et al. (Eds.): Security Protocols 2018, LNCS 11286, pp. 24–41, 2018.
https://doi.org/10.1007/978-3-030-03251-7_3

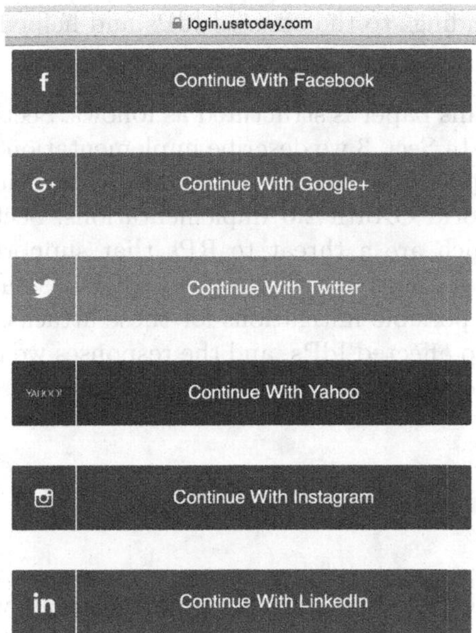

Fig. 1. The OAuth 2.0 IdPs supported by USATODAY.

work involves treating RPs and IdPs as black boxes; because of the inherent limitations of this approach, it is likely that potential implementation flaws and attack vectors exist that have yet to be found. Illustrating this, in this paper we disclose a new class of practical attacks on OAuth 2.0 implementations, which we call Partial Redirection URI Manipulation (PRURIM) attacks, that affect many leading real-world IdPs. These attacks either allow an attacker to log in to the RP as the victim user or enable compromise of potentially sensitive user information. We examined 27 leading OAuth 2.0 identity providers, and found that 19 of them are vulnerable to PRURIM attacks.

OAuth 2.0 is used to protect many millions of user accounts and sensitive user information stored at IdPs (e.g. Facebook, Google and Microsoft) and RP servers around the world. It is therefore vitally important that the issues we have identified are addressed urgently, and that IdPs take actions to mitigate the threats from PRURIM attacks. We have therefore notified the IdPs we have found to be vulnerable to these attacks.

To summarise, we make the following contributions:

- We describe a new class of practical attacks, PRURIM attacks, on OAuth 2.0 implementations. These attacks can be used to gain a victim user's OAuth 2.0 code without the user's knowledge.
- We examined the security of 27 leading OAuth 2.0 identity providers, and found that 19 of them are vulnerable to PRURIM attacks.
- We propose practical improvements which can be adopted by OAuth 2.0 RPs and IdPs that address the identified problems.

– We reported our findings to the affected IdPs and helped them fix the problems we identified.

The remainder of this paper is structured as follows. Section 2 provides background on OAuth 2.0. In Sect. 3 we describe implementation strategies that RPs use to support multiple IdPs. Section 4 summarises previous work analysing the security of real world OAuth 2.0 implementations. Section 5 describes the PRURIM attacks, which are a threat to RPs that support multiple IdPs. In Sect. 6, we report our findings and discuss why PRURIM attacks are possible. In Sect. 7, we propose possible mitigations for these attacks. Section 8 describes the disclosures made to affected IdPs, and the responses we received from them. Section 9 concludes the paper.

2 Background

2.1 OAuth 2.0

The OAuth 2.0 specification [8] describes a system that allows an application to access resources (typically personal information) protected by a *resource server* on behalf of the *resource owner*, through the consumption of an *access token* issued by an *authorization server*. In support of this system, the OAuth 2.0 architecture involves the following four roles (see Fig. 2).

1. The *Resource Owner* is typically an end user.
2. The *Resource Server* is a server which stores the protected resources and consumes access tokens provided by an authorization server.
3. The *Client* is an application running on a server, which makes requests on behalf of the resource owner (the *Client* is the RP when OAuth 2.0 is used for SSO).
4. The *Authorization Server* generates access tokens for the client, after authenticating the resource owner and obtaining its authorization (the *Resource Server* and *Authorization Server* together constitute the IdP when OAuth 2.0 is used for SSO).

Figure 2 provides an overview of the operation of the OAuth 2.0 protocol. The client initiates the process by sending (1) an authorization request to the resource owner. In response, the resource owner generates an authorization grant (or authorization response) in the form of a *code*, and sends it (2) to the client. After receiving the authorization grant, the client initiates an access token request by authenticating itself to the authorization server and presenting the authorization grant, i.e. the code issued by the resource owner (3). The authorization server issues (4) an access token to the client after successfully authenticating the client and validating the authorization grant. The client makes a protected source request by presenting the access token to the resource server (5). Finally, the resource server sends (6) the protected resources to the client after validating the access token.

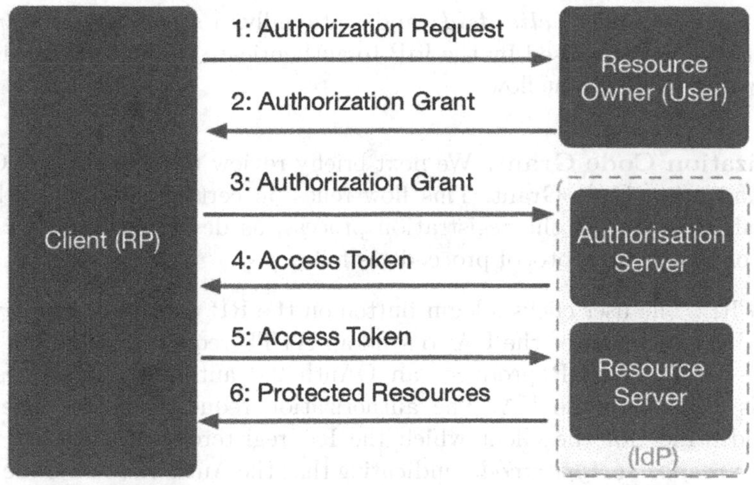

Fig. 2. OAuth 2.0 protocol flow.

2.2 OAuth 2.0 Used for SSO

In order to use OAuth 2.0 as the basis of an SSO system, the following role mapping is used:

- the resource server and authorization server together play the IdP role;
- the client plays the role of the RP;
- the resource owner corresponds to the user.

OAuth 2.0 SSO systems build on user agent (UA) redirections, where a user (U) wishes to access services protected by the RP which consumes the access token generated by the IdP. The UA is typically a web browser. The IdP provides ways to authenticate the user, asks the user to grant permission for the RP to access the user's attributes, and generates an access token on behalf of the user. After receiving the access token, the RP can access the user's attributes using the API provided by the IdP.

The OAuth 2.0 framework defines four ways for RPs to obtain access tokens, namely Authorization Code Grant, Implicit Grant, Resource Owner Password, and Client Credentials Grant. In this paper we are only concerned with the Authorization Code Grant and Implicit Grant protocol flows. Note that, in the descriptions below, protocol parameters given in bold font are defined as required (i.e. mandatory) in the OAuth 2.0 Authorization Framework [8].

RP Registration. The RP must register with the IdP before it can use OAuth 2.0. During registration, the IdP gathers security-critical information about the RP, including the RP's redirect URI, i.e. ***redirect_uri***, the URI to which the user agent is redirected after the IdP has generated the authorization response and sent it to the RP via the UA. As part of registration, the IdP issues the RP with a unique identifier (***client_id***) and, optionally, a secret (*client_secret*). If defined, *client_secret* is used by the IdP to authenticate the RP when using the Authorization Code Grant flow.

Authorization Code Grant. We next briefly review the operation of OAuth 2.0 Authorization Code Grant. This flow relies on certain information having been established during the registration process, as described in Sect. 2.2. An instance of use of the protocol proceeds as follows.

1. U → RP: The user clicks a login button on the RP website, as displayed by the UA, which causes the UA to send an HTTP request to the RP.
2. RP → UA: The RP produces an OAuth 2.0 authorization request and sends it back to the UA. The authorization request includes ***client_id***, the identifier for the client which the RP registered with the IdP previously; ***response_type=code***, indicating that the Authorization Code Grant method is requested; *redirect_uri*, the URI to which the IdP will redirect the UA after access has been granted; *state*, an opaque value used by the RP to maintain state between the request and the callback (step 6 below); and *scope*, the scope of the requested permission.
3. UA → IdP: The UA redirects the request which it received in step 2 to the IdP.
4. IdP → UA: The IdP first compares the value of *redirect_uri* it received in step 3 (embedded in the authorization request) with the registered value (how *redirect_uri* is compared is described in Sect. 3.1); if the comparison fails, the process terminates. If the user has already been authenticated by the IdP, then the next step is skipped. If not, the IdP returns a login form which is used to collect the user authentication information.
5. U → UA → IdP: The user completes the login form and grants permission for the RP to access the attributes stored by the IdP.
6. IdP → UA → RP: After (if necessary) using the information provided in the login form to authenticate the user, the IdP generates an authorization response and redirects the UA back to the RP. The authorization response contains ***code***, the authorization code (representing the authorization grant) generated by the IdP; and *state*, the value sent in step 2.
7. RP → IdP: The RP produces an access token request and sends it to the IdP token endpoint directly (i.e. not via the UA). The request includes ***grant_type=authorization_code***, ***client_id***, *client_secret* (if the RP has been issued one), ***code*** (generated in step 6), and the ***redirect_uri***.
8. IdP → RP: The IdP checks ***client_id***, *client_secret* (if present), ***code*** and ***redirect_uri*** and, if the checks succeed, responds to the RP with *access_token*.
9. RP → IdP: The RP passes *access_token* to the IdP via a defined API to request the user attributes.
10. IdP → RP: The IdP checks *access_token* (how this works is not specified in the OAuth 2.0 specification) and, if satisfied, sends the requested user attributes to the RP.

Implicit Grant. The Implicit Grant protocol flow has a similar sequence of steps to Authorization Code Grant. We specify below only those steps where the Implicit Grant flow differs from the Authorization Code Grant flow.

2. RP → UA: The RP produces an OAuth 2.0 authorization request and sends it back to the UA. The authorization request includes ***client_id***, the identifier for the client which the RP registered with the IdP previously; ***response_type=token***, indicating that the Implicit Grant is requested; *redirect_uri*, the URI to which the IdP will redirect the UA after access has been granted; *state*, an opaque value used by the RP to maintain state between the request and the callback (step 6 below); and *scope*, the scope of the requested permission.
6. IdP → UA → RP: After (if necessary) using the information provided in the login form to authenticate the user, the IdP generates an access token and redirects the UA back to the RP using the value of *redirect_uri* provided in step 2. The access token is appended to *redirect_uri* as a URI fragment (i.e. as a suffix to the URI following a # symbol).

As URI fragments are not sent in HTTP requests, the access token is not immediately transferred when the UA is redirected to the RP. Instead, the RP returns a web page (typically an HTML document with an embedded script) capable of accessing the full redirection URI, including the fragment retained by the UA, and extracting the access token (and other parameters) contained in the fragment; the retrieved access token is returned to the RP. The RP can now use this access token to retrieve data stored at the IdP.

3 Supporting Multiple IdPs

As described in Sect. 1, many RPs support more than one IdP. This recognises the fact that users will have trust relationships with varying sets of IdPs — for example, one user may prefer to trust Facebook, whereas another may prefer Google.

In this section we describe two ways in which this is achieved in practice. The first approach (using redirect URIs) gives rise to the new class of attacks which we describe in Sect. 5. The second approach (explicit user intention tracking) gives rise to the IdP mix-up attacks described by Fett et al. [7].

3.1 Using Redirect URIs

One way in which an RP can support multiple IdPs is to register a different *redirect_uri* with each IdP, and to set up a sign-in endpoint for each. It can then use the endpoint on which it receives an authorization response to recognise which IdP sent it. For example, AddThis[2] has registered the URIs

- https://www.addthis.com/darkseid/account/register-facebook-return as its *redirect_uri* for Facebook, and

[2] http://www.addthis.com/.

– https://www.addthis.com/darkseid/account/register-google-return as its *redirect_uri* for Google.

If AddThis receives an authorization response at the endpoint https://www.addthis.com/darkseid/account/register-facebook-return?code=[code_generated_by_Facebook], (in step 7 of Sect. 2.2), it assumes that this response was generated by Facebook, and thus sends the authorization *code* to the Facebook server (step 8 of Sect. 2.2) to request an *access_token*.

The *redirect_uri* in OAuth 2.0. As described in Sect. 2.2, an RP must register with an IdP before it can use OAuth 2.0. The OAuth 2.0 Authorization Framework [8] defines the following two ways in which an IdP can register *redirect_uri* for an RP.

1. The IdP **should** require the RP to provide the complete redirection URI.
2. If requiring the registration of the complete redirection URI is not possible, the IdP **should** require the registration of the URI scheme, authority, and path. This allows the RP to dynamically vary only the query component of the redirection URI when requesting authorization.

As described in §3.1.2 of the OAuth 2.0 Authorization Framework [8], the redirection endpoint URI **must** be an absolute URI. The framework requires the authorization server to match the received *redirect_uri* value against the redirection URIs registered by the RP when a redirection URI is included in an authorization request. Also, if the *redirect_uri* registered by the RP includes the full redirection URI, the IdP **must** compare the two URIs using a simple string comparison [15].

Real-World Implementations of *redirect_uri* Checks. As noted above, the OAuth 2.0 Authorization Framework [8] requires the IdP to check the two URIs using a simple string comparison if the registered *redirect_uri* value includes the full redirection URI; however, this is not always done. In practice, we have identified three approaches used by real-world IdPs to check the *redirect_uri*.

– **Checking only the origin of *redirect_uri*.** Many IdPs, including Facebook[3], Yahoo[4] and Microsoft[5], only check the *origin* part of *redirect_uri*. For example, suppose an RP registers https://www.RP.com/facebook-return as its *redirect_uri* with Facebook. When Facebook receives an authorization request generated by this RP, it only checks whether the origin part of *redirect_uri* in the authorization request matches https://www.RP.com, i.e. it ignores `/facebook-return`.
– **Checking *redirect_uri* using a simple string comparison**. Some IdPs, such as Google[6] and Amazon[7], execute a simple string comparison when performing a *redirect_uri* check (as required in [8]) on the authorization request.

[3] https://developers.facebook.com/docs/facebook-login/web.
[4] https://developer.yahoo.com/oauth2/guide/.
[5] https://msdn.microsoft.com/en-us/library/hh243647.aspx.
[6] https://developers.google.com/identity/protocols/OAuth2.
[7] http://login.amazon.com/website.

Other IdPs, such as OK[8] and Yandex[9], perform a *redirect_uri* check by executing a simple string comparison only when generating the authorization response, i.e. they accept an unauthorised OAuth 2.0 request as described in Listing 1.1, but refuse to generate an OAuth 2.0 response for such a request.

- **Issuing an IdP-generated value for *redirect_uri*.** Some IdPs, such as ebay[10], issue a *redirect_uri* value (e.g. `Jerry_Smith-JerrySmi-TestOA-pkvmjju`) to the RP when the RP registers with the IdP. When the IdP receives an authorization request generated by this RP, it first compares the *redirect_uri* (i.e. `Jerry_Smith-JerrySmi-TestOA-pkvmjju` in this example) in the authorization request with the value it has stored in its database. If the two values agree, it generates an authorization response and sends it to the redirect URI that the IdP retrieved using the *redirect_uri* value (i.e. `Jerry_Smith-JerrySmi-TestOA-pkvmjju` in this example).

3.2 Explicit User Intention Tracking

Registering a different redirection URI for each IdP is not the only approach that could be used by an RP to support multiple IdPs. An RP can instead keep a record of the IdP each user wishes to use to authenticate (e.g. it could save the identity of the user's selected IdP to a cookie).

In this case, when a authorization response is received by the RP, the RP can retrieve the identity of the IdP from the cookie and then send the *code* to this IdP. This method is typically used by RPs that allow for dynamic registration, where using the same URI is an obvious implementation choice [7].

4 Security Properties of OAuth 2.0

OAuth 2.0 has been analysed using formal methods [1–4,7,17,20]. Pai et al. [17] confirmed a security issue described in the OAuth 2.0 Thread Model [14] using the Alloy Framework [9]. Chari et al. analysed OAuth 2.0 in the Universal Composability Security framework [4] and showed that OAuth 2.0 is secure if all the communications links are SSL-protected. Frostig and Slack [20] discovered a cross site request forgery attack in the Implicit Grant flow of OAuth 2.0, using the Murphi framework [6]. Bansal et al. [1] analysed the security of OAuth 2.0 using the WebSpi [2] and ProVerif models [3]. However, all this work is based on abstract models, and so delicate implementation details are ignored.

The security properties of real-world OAuth 2.0 implementations have also been examined by a number of authors [5,10,11,13,18,21,22,24]. Wang et al. [22] examined deployed SSO systems, focussing on a logic flaw present in many such systems, including OpenID. In parallel, Sun and Beznosov [21] also studied deployed OAuth 2.0 systems. Later, Li and Mitchell [10] examined the security

[8] https://apiok.ru/ext/oauth/.
[9] https://tech.yandex.com/oauth/.
[10] https://developer.ebay.com/Devzone/merchant-products/account-management/HowTo/oauth.html.

of deployed OAuth 2.0 systems providing services in Chinese. In parallel, Zhou and Evans [24] conducted a large scale study of the security of Facebook's OAuth 2.0 implementation. Chen et al. [5], and Shehab and Mohsen [18] have looked at the security of OAuth 2.0 implementations on mobile platforms. Finally, Li and Mitchell [11] conducted an empirical study of the security of the OpenID Connect-based SSO service provided by Google.

We conclude this review by mentioning prior art that has a close relationship to the PRURIM attacks described below.

- The **cross social-network request forgery** attack was described by Bansal, Bhargavan and Maffeis [1]. It applies to RPs using third party libraries, such as JanRain or GigYa, to manage their IdPs, as these RPs use the same login endpoint for all IdPs.
- A similar attack, the **Redirection URI Manipulation Attack**, is defined in §10.6 of the OAuth 2.0 Authorization Framework; in this attack, the attacker sets the *redirect_uri* in the authorization request to that of the attacker's own website (e.g. https://www.attacker.com).
- Another attack with a similar outcome, the **IdP mix-up attack** due to Fett et al. [7], works in the context of RPs using explicit user intention tracking to support multiple IdPs, as described in Sect. 3.2. For it to work, a network attack is needed to modify the http or https messages generated by the RP in step 1 (see Sect. 2.2). Li and Mitchell [12] argued that this attack would not be a genuine threat to the security of OAuth 2.0 if IdP implementations strictly follow the standard.

5 A New Class of Attacks

We now introduce PRURIM attacks, which can be used by a malicious party to collect a *code* belonging to a victim user without the user being aware. These attacks exploit the fact that many IdPs only check the origin part of the *redirect_uri* (as discussed in Sect. 3.1). In Sects. 5.2 and 5.3 we describe two variants of the attack with differing assumptions about the capabilities of the attacker.

5.1 Adversary Model

We suppose that the adversary has the capabilities of a **web attacker**, i.e. it can share malicious links or post comments which contain malicious content (e.g. stylesheets or images) on a benign website, and/or can exploit vulnerabilities in an RP website. The malicious content might trigger the web browser to send an HTTP/HTTPS request to an RP and IdP using either the GET or POST methods, or execute JavaScript scripts crafted by the attacker.

In addition, in the first of the two variants of the PRURIM attack described in Sect. 5.2, we suppose that the adversary can set up a server which acts as an OAuth 2.0 IdP; we refer to this as a Malicious IdP (MIdP). In the second PRURIM variant (see Sect. 5.3) we assume instead that the RP website contains a Cross-site scripting (XSS) vulnerability.

5.2 Using a MIdP

We divide our discussion of the first PRURIM attack variant into three parts. We first describe the core of the attack, in which the attacker is able to obtain a victim user's *code*. We then describe two ways in which knowledge of this *code* can be used to perform unauthorised actions.

This attack applies to both the authorization code grant and implicit grant flows. For simplicity we only present the attack for the authorization code grant flow. We describe real-world examples of these attacks in Sect. 6.

Obtaining the *Code*. As described in Sect. 3.1, many IdPs only check the origin of the *redirect_uri*. If the *redirect_uri* is not fully checked, an attacker can change part of it without the change being detected by the IdP. This observation underlies the following attack.

Suppose an attacker can, in some way, cause a victim user's browser to generate (unknown to the user) an unauthorised authorization request for the target IdP (TIdP) of the form given in Listing 1.1. This might, for example, be achieved by inserting the request in an *iframe* or *img* in an apparently innocent web page, which the victim user is persuaded to visit. When it receives this request, the TIdP will assume that it is a normal authorization request generated by the RP, as it only checks the origin part of the *redirect_uri*. It then authenticates the victim user, if necessary (see step 4 in Sect. 2.2), and then generates an authorization response. This response is sent to the URL https://RP.com/MIdP-return?code=[code_generated_by_TIdP].

When the RP receives this *code*, it first constructs an access token request which includes the *code*, and then sends it to the MIdP. The attacker (MIdP) now has the user's *code*; this *code* can now be used for a range of malicious purposes. We describe below two examples of how this value might be used.

```
// a normal authorization request generated by the RP supporting
    for target IdP (TIdP)
https://TIdP.com/auth2?
client_id=[client_id_generated_by_TIdP]&
redirect_uri=https://RP.com/TIdP-return&
response_type=code

// an unauthorised authorization request crafted by the attacker
    (MIdP)
https://TIdP.com/auth2?
client_id=[client_id_generated_by_TIdP]&
redirect_uri=https://RP.com/MIdP-return&
response_type=code
```

Listing 1.1. The partial redirect URI manipulate attack

An Impersonation Attack. An attacker with access to a victim user's *code* for a particular TIdP can use it to impersonate this user in the following way. The attacker first initiates a new login process at an RP using the attacker's own browser (we suppose this RP supports SSO using the TIdP). The attacker chooses the TIdP as the IdP for this login process, and the attacker's browser is accordingly redirected to the TIdP. The attacker provides his/her own account information to the TIdP. After authenticating the attacker, the TIdP generates an authorization response containing a *code* and tries to redirect the attacker's browser back to the RP website (step 6 in Sect. 2.2).

The attacker intercepts this redirection, replacing the TIdP-supplied *code* in the authorization response with the stolen *code* for the victim user. It now forwards the modified response to the RP.

The RP next uses the supplied (stolen) *code* to retrieve an access token from the TIdP. The retrieved access token is then used to retrieve the victim user's id. The RP now believes that the attacker is the owner of the victim user's account, and issues a session cookie for this account to the attacker. The attacker is now logged in to the RP as the victim user and can access the victim user's protected resources stored at the RP.

Accessing User Data Stored by the TIdP. Suppose an attacker has the *code* for a particular victim user at the TIdP, and suppose also that the TIdP did not issue a *client_secret* to the RP (this is possible because *client_secret* is an optional parameter in the OAuth 2.0 Authorization Framework). In this case, the attacker uses the *code* to construct an access token request (see step 8 in Sect. 2.2) and sends it to the TIdP. The TIdP, in return, sends an access token for the victim user to the attacker. The attacker can now use this access token to access the victim user's protected resources stored at the TIdP.

5.3 Using an XSS Vulnerability at the RP

This second variant of the PRURIM attack again applies to both the authorization code grant and implicit grant flows. As above, we only present the attack for the authorization code grant flow.

According to the OWASP Top 10 – 2013 report [16], XSS attacks are ranked as the third most critical web application security risk. That implies that it is likely that at least some RP websites contain an XSS vulnerability.

```
// an unauthorised authorization request crafted by the attacker
https://TIdP.com/auth2?
client_id=[client_id_generated_by_TIdP]&
redirect_uri=https://RP.com/XXSVul&
response_type=code
// JavaScripts used to extract the code from the authorization
    response
<script>
var code = document.URL.replace("?", "&");
var src = "http://www.attack.com?RP=" + code;
var img = document.createElement("img");
img.src = src;
document.appendChild(img);
</script>
```

Listing 1.2. The redirect URI manipulate attack

For the purposes of describing this attack we assume that the RP has a XSS vulnerability at https://RP.com/XXSVul which is under the control of the attacker. The attacker first (by some means) causes a victim user to generate an unauthorised authorization request for the target IdP (TIdP) of the form given in Listing 1.2. When it receives this request, the TIdP assumes that it is a normal authorization request generated by the RP, as it only checks the origin part of the *redirect_uri*. It then authenticates the victim user, if necessary (see step 4 in Sect. 2.2), and then generates an authorization response. This response is sent to the URL https://RP.com/XXSVul?code=[code_generated_by_TIdP].

The script (see Listing 1.2) crafted by the attacker at `XXSVul` is assumed to be able to extract the value of https://RP.com/XXSVul?code=[code_generated_by_TIdP]; once it has done this it sends it back to the attacker. The attacker now has the user's *code*, which can now be used to conduct an impersonation attack and/or access user data stored at TIdP, as described in Sects. 5.2 and 5.2.

5.4 Discussion

As noted above, the attack variants described in Sects. 5.2 and 5.3 also apply to the implicit grant flow. Depending on the precise type of attack (and assumptions about the capabilities of the attacker), an attacker is able to obtain varying sets of sensitive values—see Table 1.

The *no state* in the table means that the attack only works if the RP fails to implement CSRF countermeasures at its MIdP sign-in endpoint. This might be made more likely if the MIdP provides sample code without the *state* parameter in the OAuth 2.0 authorization request, or configures the MIdP to not include the *state* in the authorization response before it is sent to the RP.

Table 1. Redirect URI manipulate attacks.

	Authorization code grant		Implicit grant	
PRURIM attacks	Using MIdP	Using XSS	Using MIdP	Using XSS
Attack Assumption	MIdP, web attacker, no state	XSS vul at RP, web attacker	MIdP, web attacker, no state	XSS vul at RP, web attacker
Attackers can get	*access_token*, *code*	*access_token*, *code*	*access_token*	*access_token*

5.5 Relationship to the Prior Art

We conclude this section by describing how the PRURIM attack differs from three somewhat similar attacks described in Sect. 4.

- The **cross social-network request forgery** attack, due to Bansal et al. [1], applies to RPs that use third party libraries, as these RPs use the same login endpoint for all IdPs. By contrast, the PRURIM attack works in situations

where IdPs only check the origin of the *redirect_uri*. While the Bansal et al. attack only works for a special category of RPs, PRURIM attacks apply to all IdPs not strictly checking the *redirect_uri*, and to all RPs using these IdPs.
- In the **Redirection URI Manipulation Attack**, the attacker sets the *redirect_uri* in the authorization request to that of the attacker's own website (e.g. https://www.attacker.com). The key difference between this attack and the PRURIM attacks is that, in a PRURIM attack, the attacker is not required to change the origin of the *redirect_uri*, making it a much greater threat in practice.
- The **IdP mix-up attack** due to Fett et al. [7] works in the context of RPs using explicit user intention tracking to support multiple IdPs; for it to work, a network attack is needed to modify the http or https messages generated by the RP. PRURIM attacks, by contrast, apply to RPs using different *redirect_uri* values to support multiple IdPs. IdP mix-up attacks need a **network attacker** and a MIdP to operate; PRURIM attacks only need a **web attacker** and a MIdP to work, making them a much greater threat in practice.

6 Our Findings

6.1 Summary

We examined the implementations of 27 popular OAuth 2.0 IdPs providing services in English, Russian and Chinese (see Table 2)[11]. Unfortunately, our study revealed that 19 of them (70%) are vulnerable to PRURIM attacks (see Fig. 3). Among the 19 affected IdPs, one is Russian-language, namely mail.ru; four provide services in English, namely Facebook, Microsoft, Instagram and Yahoo; and as many as 14 IdPs are providing services in Chinese, meaning that 88% of the IdPs in China in our study are vulnerable to PRURIM attacks.

6.2 Implications

As described in 3.1, in order to allow the RP to dynamically vary only the query component of the redirection URI when requesting authorization, many IdPs only require an RP to register the URI scheme, authority, and path. For example, iQiyi[12] registers http://passport.iqiyi.com/apis/thirdparty/ncallback.action (together with a varying query component) with every IdP it supports, and it uses the query component in the *redirect_uri* to determine the IdP used (e.g.

[11] Most of the English and Russian language IdPs were chosen from the login page of https://badoo.com/ and https://usatoday.com/. Most of the Chinese-language IdPs were chosen from the login page of http://youku.com, http://www.iqiyi.com and http://ctrip.com.

[12] http://www.iqiyi.com/.

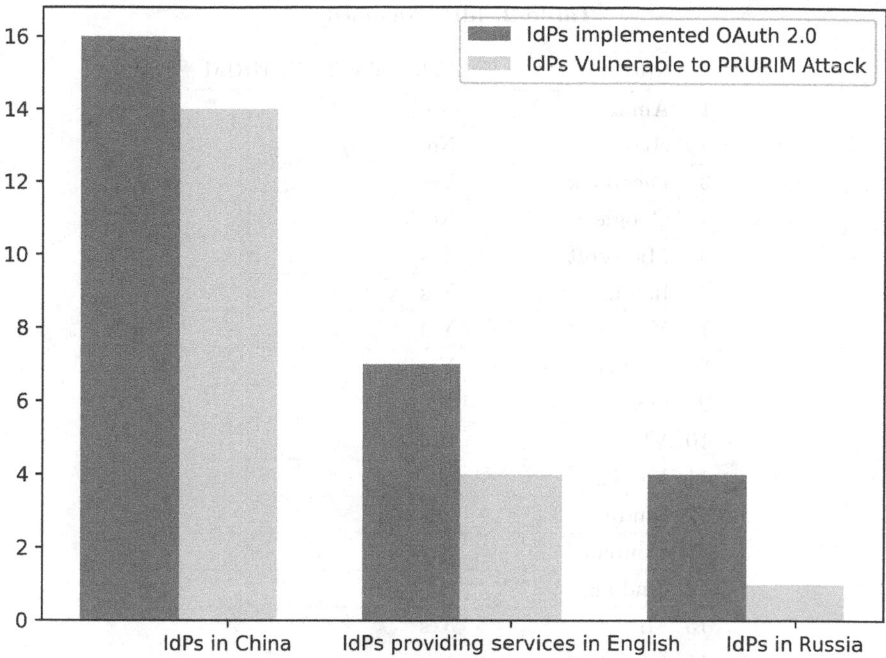

Fig. 3. IdP vulnerabilities by language of site.

http://passport.iqiyi.com/apis/thirdparty/ncallback.action?from=2 is the *redirect_uri* registered with IdP Wangyi, http://passport.iqiyi.com/apis/thirdparty/ncallback.action?from=30 is the *redirect_uri* registered with IdP Xiaomi). This reduces the effort for the RP to manage *redirect_uri* values for multiple IdPs, and gives the RP the ability to customize its OAuth 2.0 sign-in endpoint.

It is interesting to speculate why the standard does not define a single mandatory approach for the IdP to register a *redirect_uri* value with an RP; it seems plausible that this is to give maximum flexibility for RP implementations. As a result, many IdPs allow RPs to register a range of types of *redirect_uri*, and in many cases the IdP only checks the origin part of a *redirect_uri* in an authorization request. This flexibility gives rise to the attacks we have described.

7 Mitigations for PRURIM Attacks

7.1 Impose Strict Redirect URI Checking

PRURIM attacks are made possible if an IdP only checks part of the *redirect_uri*. A simple mitigation for this attack is therefore for the IdP to always check the complete *redirect_uri* using a simple string comparison [15]. However, this can cause problems for those RPs that rely on the origin of the *redirect_uri* to deliver an authorization response. In such cases, the OAuth 2.0 service would stop working if a strict check is always performed.

Table 2. IdPs examined.

	IdP	Vulnerable to PRURIM
1	Amazon	No
2	ebay	No
3	Facebook	Yes
4	Google	No
5	Microsoft	Yes
6	Instagram	Yes
7	Yahoo	Yes
8	mail.ru	Yes
9	OK	No
10	VK	No
11	Yandex	No
12	Baidu	Yes
13	Douban	No
14	Jindong	No
15	Mi	Yes
16	QQ	Yes
17	QQ Weibo	Yes
18	Sina	Yes
19	Taobao	Yes
20	Wangyi	Yes
21	Wechat	Yes
22	anonymised-site-1	Yes
23	anonymised-site-2	Yes
24	anonymised-site-3	Yes
25	anonymised-site-4	Yes
26	anonymised-site-5	Yes
27	anonymised-site-6	Yes

7.2 Implement CSRF Countermeasures

While the main reason that the MIdP-based PRURIM attack is possible is the failure to strictly check the *redirect_uri*, to make the process work the attacker also needs to use a CSRF attack to cause the victim user to visit the site serving the malicious authorization request. This means that the implementation of appropriate CSRF countermeasures by RPs (e.g. including a state value in the authorization request) would help to mitigate the threat of the PRURIM attacks described in Sect. 5.2.

However, in practice, RPs do not always implement CSRF countermeasures in the recommended way. A study conducted by Shernan et al. [19] in 2015 found that 25% of websites in the Alexa Top 10,000 domains using Facebook's OAuth 2.0 service appear vulnerable to CSRF attacks. Further, a 2016 study conducted by Yang et al. [23] revealed that 61% of 405 websites using OAuth 2.0 (chosen from the 500 top-ranked US and Chinese websites) did not implement CSRF countermeasures.

While it is up to the RP to implement CSRF countermeasures, a MIdP can make it less likely that this will happen, e.g. by not including a *state* variable in its sample code, or by not including a *state* value in an authorization response even if it is included in the authorization request.

8 Responsible Disclosure

We reported our findings to all the affected IdPs that provide services in English or Russian. However, reporting our finding to the affected Chinese IdPs was a little more difficult; since 20th July, 2016, China's biggest bug report platform Wooyun[13] has been closed. We reported the problem to the eight IdPs that have set up a security response centre in China; for the other six IdPs affected by the PRURIM attacks, for which we had no obvious way to report our findings, we have simply chosen not to disclose their identities in this paper.

We received positive responses from Yahoo, Microsoft, mail.ru, Sina and Wangyi. These IdPs all stated that they are working on a fix to the PRURIM attack. Facebook also acknowledged our report, but did not commit to making any changes. However, Tencent (the largest Chinese IdP, including QQ IdP, Wechat IdP and QQWeibo IdP) and Baidu both stated that the attack is caused by the RP redirection configuration and do not propose to take any action. Similarly, the response from Xiaomi IdP was "Xiaomi's responsibility of its OAuth 2.0 system is only to authorize user, it is the RP's responsibility to protect the authorization", and thus it seems reasonable to assume that it will not take any action to address the problem. Finally, Taobao IdP (owned by Alibaba) stated that the attacker cannot get the user's code, and hence they do not propose to take any action.

9 Conclusion

In this paper, we described the PRURIM attacks, a new class of attacks against OAuth 2.0. These attacks work against RPs supporting multiple OAuth 2.0 IdPs. We examined 27 IdPs providing services in English, Russian and Chinese. Given the fact that OAuth 2.0 has been widely adopted by IdPs around the world, our study only covers the tip of the iceberg of real-world OAuth 2.0 implementations that are potentially vulnerable to PRURIM attacks.

We have also proposed mitigations for this new attack which can be adopted by IdPs and RPs.

[13] http://www.wooyun.org.

References

1. Bansal, C., Bhargavan, K., Delignat-Lavaud, A., Maffeis, S.: Discovering concrete attacks on website authorization by formal analysis. J. Comput. Secur. **22**(4), 601–657 (2014). https://doi.org/10.3233/JCS-140503
2. Bansal, C., Bhargavan, K., Maffeis, S.: WebSpi and web application models (2011). http://prosecco.gforge.inria.fr/webspi/CSF/
3. Blanchet, B., Smyth, B.: ProVerif: cryptographic protocol verifier in the formal model. http://prosecco.gforge.inria.fr/personal/bblanche/proverif/
4. Chari, S., Jutla, C.S., Roy, A.: Universally composable security analysis of OAuth v2.0. IACR Cryptology ePrint Archive 2011, 526 (2011)
5. Chen, E.Y., Pei, Y., Chen, S., Tian, Y., Kotcher, R., Tague, P.: OAuth demystified for mobile application developers. In: Ahn, G., Yung, M., Li, N. (eds.) Proceedings of the 2014 ACM SIGSAC Conference on Computer and Communications Security, 3–7 November 2014, Scottsdale, AZ, USA, pp. 892–903. ACM (2014). https://doi.org/10.1145/2660267.2660323
6. Dill, D.L.: The murphi verification system. In: Alur, R., Henzinger, T.A. (eds.) Computer Aided Verification. LNCS, pp. 390–393. Springer, Heidelberg (1996). https://doi.org/10.1007/3-540-61474-5
7. Fett, D., Küsters, R., Schmitz, G.: A comprehensive formal security analysis of OAuth 2.0. In: Weippl, E.R., Katzenbeisser, S., Kruegel, C., Myers, A.C., Halevi, S. (eds.) Proceedings of the 2016 ACM SIGSAC Conference on Computer and Communications Security, 24–28 October 2016, Vienna, Austria, pp. 1204–1215. ACM (2016). https://doi.org/10.1145/2976749.2978385
8. Hardt, D. (ed.): RFC 6749: the OAuth 2.0 authorization framework, October 2012. http://tools.ietf.org/html/rfc6749
9. Jackson, D.: Alloy 4.1 (2010). http://alloy.mit.edu/community/
10. Li, W., Mitchell, C.J.: Security issues in OAuth 2.0 SSO implementations. In: Chow, S.S.M., Camenisch, J., Hui, L.C.K., Yiu, S.M. (eds.) ISC 2014. LNCS, vol. 8783, pp. 529–541. Springer, Cham (2014). https://doi.org/10.1007/978-3-319-13257-0_34
11. Li, W., Mitchell, C.J.: Analysing the security of Google's implementation of OpenID connect. In: Caballero, J., Zurutuza, U., Rodríguez, R.J. (eds.) DIMVA 2016. LNCS, vol. 9721, pp. 357–376. Springer, Cham (2016). https://doi.org/10.1007/978-3-319-40667-1_18
12. Li, W., Mitchell, C.J.: Does the IdP mix-up attack really work? (2016). https://infsec.uni-trier.de/download/oauth-workshop-2016/OSW2016_paper_1.pdf
13. Li, W., Mitchell, C.J., Chen, T.: Mitigating CSRF attacks on OAuth 2.0 and OpenID Connect. CoRR abs/1801.07983 (2018). https://arxiv.org/abs/1801.07983
14. Lodderstedt, T., McGloin, M., Hunt, P.: RFC 6819: OAuth 2.0 threat model and security considerations (2013). http://tools.ietf.org/html/rfc6819
15. Masinter, L., Berners-Lee, T., Fielding, R.T.: RFC 3986: uniform resource identifier (URI): Generic syntax (2005). https://www.ietf.org/rfc/rfc3986.txt
16. OWASP Foundation: Owasp top ten project (2013). https://www.owasp.org/index.php/Top10#OWASP_Top_10_for_2013
17. Pai, S., Sharma, Y., Kumar, S., Pai, R.M., Singh, S.: Formal verification of OAuth 2.0 using Alloy framework. In: Proceedings of the International Conference on Communication Systems and Network Technologies, CSNT 2011, pp. 655–659. IEEE (2011)

18. Shehab, M., Mohsen, F.: Securing OAuth implementations in smart phones. In: Bertino, E., Sandhu, R.S., Park, J. (eds.) Fourth ACM Conference on Data and Application Security and Privacy, CODASPY 2014, 03–05 March 2014, San Antonio, TX, USA, pp. 167–170. ACM (2014). https://doi.org/10.1145/2557547.2557588
19. Shernan, E., Carter, H., Tian, D., Traynor, P., Butler, K.: More guidelines than rules: CSRF vulnerabilities from noncompliant OAuth 2.0 implementations. In: Almgren, M., Gulisano, V., Maggi, F. (eds.) DIMVA 2015. LNCS, vol. 9148, pp. 239–260. Springer, Cham (2015). https://doi.org/10.1007/978-3-319-20550-2_13
20. Slack, Q., Frostig, R.: Murphi analysis of OAuth 2.0 implicit grant flow (2011). http://www.stanford.edu/class/cs259/WWW11/
21. Sun, S.T., Beznosov, K.: The devil is in the (implementation) details: an empirical analysis of OAuth SSO systems. In: Yu, T., Danezis, G., Gligor, V.D. (eds.) the ACM Conference on Computer and Communications Security, CCS 2012, 16–18 October 2012, Raleigh, NC, USA, pp. 378–390. ACM (2012)
22. Wang, R., Chen, S., Wang, X.: Signing me onto your accounts through Facebook and Google: a traffic-guided security study of commercially deployed single-sign-on web services. In: IEEE Symposium on Security and Privacy, SP 2012, 21–23 May 2012, San Francisco, California, USA, pp. 365–379. IEEE Computer Society (2012)
23. Yang, R., Li, G., Lau, W.C., Zhang, K., Hu, P.: Model-based security testing: An empirical study on OAuth 2.0 implementations. In: Chen, X., Wang, X., Huang, X. (eds.) Proceedings of the 11th ACM Asia Conference on Computer and Communications Security, ASIA CCS 2016, 30 May–3 June 2016, Xi'an, China, pp. 651–662. ACM (2016). https://doi.org/10.1145/2897845.2897874
24. Zhou, Y., Evans, D.: SSOScan: automated testing of web applications for single sign-on vulnerabilities. In: Fu, K., Jung, J. (eds.) Proceedings of the 23rd USENIX Security Symposium, 20–22 August 2014, San Diego, CA, USA, pp. 495–510. USENIX Association (2014). https://www.usenix.org/conference/usenixsecurity14/technical-sessions/presentation/zhou

Your Code Is My Code: Exploiting a Common Weakness in OAuth 2.0 Implementations (Transcript of Discussion)

Wanpeng Li(✉)

Department of Electrical and Electronic Engineering City, University of London, London, UK
Wanpeng.Li@city.ac.uk

Jean Martina: Maybe the attack here would be more interesting if you think of the service provider trying to get more information about you than you shared with one of the internet providers. For example, with Google I may only share my name and my email, but with Facebook I may share my friends list. So I it's played by the service provider so that he can force you to use another account; you click Google but then it gets a token from Facebook and then gets all your information back. Wouldn't that work?

Reply: This is an interesting question. Because you are a service provider as an attacker, you totally control the authentication means. If you provide two ways for the users to authenticate, the user is able to choose between these two IdPs. So you can actually do the attack by putting a login button pretending to be Google, but actually it's Facebook. But in your case, the service providers can always track all of the users activities, no matter which IdP the user is using. At the same time, the attacker can get access tokens from all the identity providers and retrieve user information from the identity providers using these access tokens.

The attack described in the paper is that the attacker is not a service provider. It's just a web attacker, but he successfully implements a malicious identity provider. Maybe we regard Google as benign because we trust it, but Google has the ability to log into your USA Today website using your Facebook account.

So what I mean here is that if the website supports two identity providers, let's say Facebook and Google, because Facebook only checks part of the *redirect_uri*, for example, the origin, if there is one guy at Google who controls Google's server he can use the user's Facebook account to log in to the relying party.

Mark Lomas: When the user clicks the Google button, if it's the first time in that session they will get a login dialogue. I can't help feeling history is repeating itself. We design systems with what we call a secure attention sequence to make sure that you are genuinely talking to the authentication service. But what you're describing here, I think you are not having that guarantee that you're actually talking to the authentication service that you think you are talking to.

V. Matyáš et al. (Eds.): Security Protocols 2018, LNCS 11286, pp. 42–44, 2018.
https://doi.org/10.1007/978-3-030-03251-7_4

Reply: I think I mentioned in the paper, but I didn't mention in the talk, that here we assume that the user has logged in to the system using, for example, Facebook or Google, in advance. Real world identity providers such as Facebook and Google implement an automatic authorization granting feature. If it is the first time that the user chooses one of the IdPs to log in to the RP, they will get a login dialogue and also an authorization page; this page will display useful information (such as the RP that is going to access your email, first name, and phone number from Google), and the page will allow the user to either grant or deny authorization for the RP. But if the user has already signed in his identity provider account, for example if you have already signed in your Google account, the authorization procedure will happen silently, and the user might not notice the authorization procedure.

Mark Lomas: Yes. I'm less worried about the second authentication, because I know that I initiated the connection with Google, but if it's the first time in this session, I'm essentially being asked to type a password into a dialogue where I have no idea where the service is.

Reply: Yes, you are right. In that circumstance, the user will notice this and say that "I didn't click this login button, why should I grant access for it?" In our attack, we suppose the relying party did not implement any cross-site request forgery protections. An attacker can generate this attack authorization request, he can put the request in one of the websites he controls, and wait for victim users to visit the website. One way to do that is for the attacker to put the request into the *src* attribute of an *img* tag. If the victim user visits this web page, the authorization procedure happens automatically because of the automatic authorization granting feature.

If it is the first time that the user chooses one of the IdPs to log in to the RP, the user will be asked for grant authorization and will notice the attack.

Mark Lomas: Okay. Thank you.

Patrick McCorry: I'm just wondering, so if you're a malicious IdP, let's just say I'm WeChat. How do you use WeChat to spy on Facebook in order to spy on the user and see their Facebook information?

Reply: Yeah, WeChat is vulnerable to this attack so you are able to get a code from WeChat and then use this code. Maybe if the user is trying to use WeChat to log in to some services, you can get this code and pretend to be the user on the services. WeChat is vulnerable to this attack and we reported this to them, but they said, "It's not our problem, it's the relying party's problem." They just ignored us.

Patrick McCorry: Could attackers abuse this?

Reply: It depends. We trust most real world identity providers such as Google and Facebook. But identity providers might originate from different countries. For example, WeChat belongs to China, and Facebook belongs to the U.S. Attackers at a nation level might use the attack we described in the paper to get the code from identity providers from another country, and get unauthorized access to the accounts on the RP.

Fabio Massacci: When you have the statistics of the 19 that were vulnerable, how many of them actually said, "Well it's not our problem?" Because from your examples it seems a lot of them said it's somebody else's problem.

Reply: Yeah, I think it is described in the paper in the disclosure part. China has a social media platform called Weibo. We reported to them and they are really active, and they fixed it in around one week. But for several other identity providers from China, they just claimed that, "this is not our problem, it belongs to the relying party, because the relying party did something wrong in the registration procedure." I will share with you one of the responses from one of the relying parties. The IdP claims that the relying party only registers the domain name with it. But if the relying party submits an authorization request whose redirect_uri contains not just the domain name, the IdP does not block the request and still believes it is a benign OAuth 2.0 authorization request because the IdP does not employ a strict string comparison to check the redirect_uri. But the IdP claimed it's the relaying party's problem and ignored our report.

I reported to another identity provider in Russia and they claim that they are trying to fix this problem. I think the problem now has been fixed because they have an upgrade plan, some kind of maintenance. They said, "it's our plan; we are going to fix this." Facebook also acknowledged our report, but did not commit to making any changes. And Google is not vulnerable to this attack. Thank you very much. Thank you very much.

Non-monotonic Security Protocols and Failures in Financial Intermediation

Fabio Massacci[1(✉)], Chan Nam Ngo[1], Daniele Venturi[2], and Julian Williams[3]

[1] University of Trento, Trento, Italy
{fabio.massacci,channam.ngo}@unitn.it
[2] Sapienza University of Rome, Rome, Italy
venturi@di.uniroma1.it
[3] Durham University Business School, Durham, UK
julian.williams@durham.ac.uk

Abstract. Security Protocols as we know them are *monotonic*: valid security evidence (e.g. commitments, signatures, etc.) accrues over protocol steps performed by honest parties. Once's Alice proved she has an authentication token, got some digital cash, or casted a correct vote, the protocol can move on to validate Bob's evidence. Alice's evidence is never invalidated by honest Bob's actions (as long as she stays honest and is not compromised). Protocol failures only stems from design failures or wrong assumptions (such as Alice's own misbehavior). Security protocol designers can then focus on preventing or detecting misbehavior (e.g. double spending or double voting).

We argue that general financial intermediation (e.g. Market Exchanges) requires us to consider new form of failures where honest Bob's actions can make honest good standing. Security protocols must be able to deal with *non-monotonic security* and *new types of failures* that stems from rational behavior of honest agents finding themselves on the wrong side.

This has deep implications for the efficient design of security protocols for general financial intermediation, in particular if we need to guarantee a *proportional burden* of computation to the various parties.

Keywords: Security protocol · Non-monotonicity · Honest failure
Proportional burden · Failure-by-omission

1 Introduction

Thirty years ago, popular security protocols were essentially authentication protocols. A protocol could have various degree of complexity (e.g. Kerberos [17] vs TLS [6] vs IKE [8]) but essentially two parties tried to authenticate each other (possibly with the help of a trusted third one). There was no question that an honest party could invalidate the evidence of *the* other honest party and there

V. Matyáš et al. (Eds.): Security Protocols 2018, LNCS 11286, pp. 45–54, 2018.
https://doi.org/10.1007/978-3-030-03251-7_5

was no issue of computational load because (i) each party's main goal was actually receiving the other party security evidence and (ii) they participated equally to the protocol.[1]

In the past decade, with the emergence and practical deployment of multi-party-computation the *number of parties* participating to a protocol has massively increased.[2] These parties do not talk to each other, they talk to the ensemble *and* some parties might be far more active than others. Yet they potentially share the same burden in computational effort in generic MPC.

At this point there are some interesting questions to make:

- Is security evidence always monotonic as the number of honest parties increases? What type of failures can materialize if this is not the case?
- If some application requires non-monotonic security are there design implications if some parties are more active than others?

As an example *e-cash or voting protocols are essentially monotonic* in terms of legitimacy of digital assets: valid security evidence (e.g. commitments, blinded signatures, etc.) accrues over protocol steps performed by honest parties. Alice's security evidence for a correctly casted vote is not impacted by Bob's correctly casted vote, no matter how many Bobs join, and what they votes. Bobs may tip the balance of the election but not make Alice's vote invalid. This monotonic accumulation of the security legitimacy of digital assets is visible in the security proofs for cash fungibility in ZeroCash [19], or vote's eligibility in E2E [9]. We illustrate this technically in Sect. 2.

In contrast, *general financial intermediation is not monotonic*: Alice's asset might be proven *cryptographically* valid by Alice (given the current market price her inventory is above her debts) and later made *economically* invalid by the honest Bob who, by just offering to sell assets and thus changing the market price, can make Alice bankrupt without any action on her side. We illustrate this technically in Sect. 3.

This means that *new type of failures* are possible: *honest failures and failures by omission*. The former, are managed by Exchanges in the current centralized intermediation. The Exchange makes sure Alice deposits enough cash in advance, may eventually suspend trading and eventually absorb Alice's honest losses (acting as a sort of insurance). In a distributed system implementing financial intermediation nobody can absorb Alice's 'honest losses'. Hence the protocol might need to consider mechanisms to manage this (not unlikely) possibility.

Failures by omission are more critical, especially for non-monotonic protocols. In the example above, as no one but Alice can prove the validity of her standing,

[1] Obviously the server would have had more load than a client, but this only happens because the server participates to several authentications with several clients at once.

[2] The largest claimed example is the Danish sugar beet auction where 1229 Danish farmers auctioned their production [3]. However, an actual technical reading of the paper reveals that there were only three servers performing MPC over the secret shares generated by the 1200 bidders. As we will illustrate in Sect. 3 it is actually a good example of a monotonic security protocol.

whenever a new order arrives and changes the market price she has to publish some (cryptographic) proofs for her valid inventory.[3] If she discovers that her inventory is not valid and learns that she cannot benefit from participating in the protocol anymore, she would simply stop joining the step and any multi-party-computation protocol in the all-but-one security model hang waiting for her messages.

One might argue that a well designed protocol might *fail safe* so that nothing is disclosed and the parties could restart as if nothing happened. From the perspective of the other traders this would rather be *fail uselessly* as there cannot be a market if you can walk abruptly away as soon as you are unhappy with the likely outcome, irrespectively of what you promised to do.

2 Monotonic Security Behavior

To define monotonicity of security credentials we focus on a single legitimate protocol run that comprises of multiple steps (and potentially never stops).[4] Clearly, the security evidence in a step must be valid immediately after the step completed. In the next steps, other *honest* parties may perform some actions. If such actions do not invalidate the security evidence, a protocol is monotonic. Otherwise it is non-monotonic.

For example, a single run of ZeroCash [19] starts with initiating a genesis block and continues to expand the chain to include transactions (The protocol never stops). To make a transaction, a payer simply broadcast the payment information (encrypted and its correctness is proven in zero-knowledge) and the miners find a Proof-of-Work [18] to converge on the transaction result. To do so, the miners first must verify the payment information's correctness by checking the zero-knowledge proofs provided by the payer: (i) the spending coin belongs to an unspent set of coins maintained as a Merkle Tree [16]; (ii) the payer knows a secret parameter (ρ) to unlock the aforementioned coin; and (iii) the transfer amount is well within availability. Another transaction (except for double-spending in which the same coin is paid twice), which would claim another coin, cannot invalidate any of the above proofs.

Similarly, in E2E voting [9], a voter will receive from the Election Authority a vote card giving the voter an authentication code and a vote code. A vote is only valid with the correct authentication code and well-formed vote code. Hence its eligibility (the authentication code and the vote code's correctness) cannot be changed by another vote which claims another authentication code (again, except for double-voting in which the authentication code is used twice) as the other votes yield no direct effect against such vote.

The same phenomenon happens for privacy-preserving reputation systems (e.g. [21]) which evaluate information quality and filter spam by providing linkage

---

[3] See an additional discussion in [15] and a concrete implementation in [14].

[4] Security evidence created during a protocol run should not extend beyond the protocol run. Several protocol failures are indeed due to protocol design errors where a credential could be used across sessions [1].

between user actions and feedback. In such systems, Alice's reputation, once gained, cannot be affected by Bob's actions to gain his own reputation. Hence security evidence for reputation grows monotonically over honest traders actions.

3 Security of Financial Intermediation is Non-monotonic

A financial intermediation service provider, which acts as a counter-party for other participating parties, can be as simple as an auction house, a voting system or a reputation system to be as complex as a futures exchange. Table 1 summarizes the monotonic versus non-monotonic steps in the example of an auction house and a futures exchange [2].

Table 1. Monotonicity vs non-monotonicity

Auction house		
Steps	Monotonic	Non-monotonic
Authenticate a bidder (optional)	X	
A bidder makes a bid	X	
A bidder proves to have money	X	
Determine winner (in multiple rounds)		X
Voting system		
Steps	Monotonic	Non-monotonic
Authenticate voter	X	
Authenticate vote	X	
Determine winner	X	X
Reputation system		
Steps	monotonic	Non-monotonic
Accrue reputation	X	
Prove reputation	X	
Futures exchange		
Steps	Monotonic	Non-monotonic
Authenticate a trader	X	
Make a quote (in a round)	X	
Prove valid order	X	
Prove inventory validity		X
Match a trade	X	
Mark to market		X

In the first scenario, multiple bidders join the auction with a pre-defined balance. Each bidder will take turn to make bids by raising the highest price until the winner is identified (as the one who bids the highest). Security requirement in an auction house only includes checking the balance of the bidder's account to be able to satisfy the bids (authentication is only optional, an anonymous auction requires no identity to make a bid). There is no other way to change the validity of a bid once it has been proven except when the owner changes the price to be higher than the available cash in a new bid. Hence this security requirement is monotonic.

To determine the highest bid by bidding against a fixed price is mostly monotonic as shown in this case (only the proclaim winner step needs to be non-monotonic as the winner can change after each bid, hence Alice's proof to be the owner of the highest bid can be invalidated by Bob once he makes a bid that is higher in the next round).

The famous Danish Sugar Beet auction [3] was actually an example of a monotonic bidding against fixed prices. There were 400 fixed price levels and everybody bidded the amount of product they would like to buy (or sell) at each price level. Bob's bid (cryptographically represented as three secret shares) would not make Alice's bid invalid (which were three other independent shares). The three servers (each receiving one share by each bidder) would then perform a MPC computation to add up the quantities at each price level and determine the mid price (where supply would equal demand). Everybody who had bid at that price would actually have to sell/buy. Similarly, in an e-voting system (e.g. [9]), to authenticate a voter and a vote is monotonic while determine winner *might be* non-monotonic if the result is determined by multiple rounds of voting. A reputation system (e.g. [21]) is fully monotonic.

Differently, in a futures exchange [2], such as Chicago Mercantile Exchange, multiple traders participate with an initial margin to trade futures contracts, a standardised legal agreement between two parties to buy or sell an underlying asset at specified price agreed upon today with the settlement occurring at a future date [20]. Traders take positions (accumulating contracts in inventory) by posting buy and sell orders which effectively changes the market price and directly affects the validity of all trading inventories[5]. Thus the security requirement now involves all parties after an action made by a party. Once an order has been proven valid by a trader, other traders have to come in and prove their inventory valid regarding the new order as their old proofs are discarded when the market price changes. As a result, the security requirement for a futures exchange is non-monotonic: an action made by a trader upon changing the market price immediately invalidates (economically) all validity proofs of other traders[6].

A futures exchange is a good example of a non-monotonic protocol. In the next sections we will discuss the non-monotonic behavior's effect against the new failures and design implications of such non-monotonic protocol.

[5] A formal definition of a Futures Market is given in [15] (Sect. 4).

[6] See additional discussions on non-monotonic security in [14] (Sect. 5, Remark 1).

4 Design Implication of Non-monotonicity: The "Proportional Burden" of Computation

All security protocols implicitly satisfy a *Proportional Burden:* Each computation should be mainly a burden for the party benefiting from it (e.g. Alice is expected to do more work to cast her vote than when Bob is casting his vote). Other parties should join the protocol only to avoid risks (e.g. failed solvency or protect anonymity). This is a *practical* constraint, and not a *security* one. Such constraint is immaterial in classical security protocols such as user authentication (every user gets the token he ask for), or multi party computation applications such as auctions where everybody makes one bid, or e-voting when everybody casts one vote.

This is definitely not true for security protocols implementing general financial intermediation. In a stock market, most "retail traders" make few quotes, but "algorithmic traders" (typically speculators) make and cancel *thousands* of quotes. For example, the empirical study in [13] showed that retail and institutional investors are 71% of traders in the TSX market but only make 18% of the orders. Traders responsible for the bulk of the over 300 K orders per day were algorithmic traders who, in 99% of the cases, only submitted limit orders that would never be matched in an actual trade. Any implementation should reflect this practical constraint. Indeed, Centralized Exchanges charges differently based on the number of quotes.

The same thing happens in the Bitcoin network. A transaction from a payer to a payee has to leave some (small) amount to be collected as transaction fee. A miner in the Bitcoin network is compensated for their effort with those transaction fees upon finding the Proof-of-Work to extend the longest chain [18]. As a result, the more transactions a payer makes the more fees he has to pay.

Monotonic security allows efficient optimizations [21] as a costly multi-party computation (MPC) with n interacting parties may be replaced by n independent (possibly zero-knowledge) non-interactive proofs or secret shares. The sugar beet auction did exactly that: instead of having 1200 bidders performing an MPC operation all together it had only three servers doing MPC. Each bidders actually submitted only three secret shares to the three servers. Monotonicity of the underlying financial model made it possible to implement it with a monotonic security protocol.

This replacement is also possible when a party only need to make changes to their old secret values based on some public information and prove the correctness in zero-knowledge. This happens in ZeroCash transaction's correctness [19]. It makes it possible for a party to stay off-line and only connect on demand as well as allowing public verification (the proof of payment in ZeroCash can be verified by any party, even the newly arrived ones).

In the general case, the financial intermediation system corresponds to a security reactive functionality [4] and changes its internal state because an agent performs a valid move which updates the public information and her own private information. If an agent's legit move can unpredictably make another agent's state invalid the system as a whole as a whole must transit to a new state where the legit move is accepted and the invalid state is fixed. This is intrinsically not monotonic as the arrival of one security credential might make economically invalid all the other security proofs cumulated so far.

The solution would be to implement the whole functionality as MPC. Let alone any efficiency consideration[7], this would be unacceptable given the large variance in trading efforts: some traders only make few operations, others can make gazillions of them. In the cited example [13], it is hard to believe that retail investors would be willing to pay CPU and network resources so that speculators could securily and anonimously make their 245.000 vacuous bids against the actual 5000 trades.

A solution would be to require each trader to prove the constraint satisfaction of the economic validity of the order again when new order arrives. However this conflicts with the market's anonymity requirement in case *only one* party cannot prove the validity. This leads to dangerous seconomic vulnerabilities such as price discrimination attack [15].

Hence, the challenging part of the protocol construction is to identify the minimal core of the state of the reactive security functionality implementing the financial intermediation service provider that would account for its non-monotonic behavior in the legitimacy of traders and assets.[8] This is the only part where MPC needs to be used.[9] As shown in [14], this approach can reduce the total burden of computation by retail traders by several orders of magnitude heavier comparing to the generic MPC implementation.

Table 2. MPC performance (adopted from [14])

MPC functionality	Size			Time		
#Parties	3	5	10	3	5	10
Range check	425 MB	709 MB	1.4 GB	14 s	24 s	67 s
Positive check	212 MB	354 MB	708 MB	7 s	13 s	36 s

Table 2 (from [14]) reports the size of the bytecode and the corresponding running times for 3, 5 and 10 traders using generic MPC. The memory requirement for the compilation of the MPC functionalities using SHA-256 commitments crashed after 10 traders by exceeding 120 GB. The dynamic memory requirement is typically 100x the final bytecode size. In addition, the simulation in [14] employs the futures trades in the first quarter 2017 for the Lean Hog futures market from the Thomson Reuters Tick History database[10]. As shown in Fig. 1

[7] The 1229 parties full MPC variant is still out of reach for the foreseable future as experimental papers typically reported MPC with less than 10 parties [5].

[8] See Sect. 7 of [14].

[9] This does not violate the proportional burden requirement as each trader has the responsibility to prove the solvency if s/he still wants to be in the game.

[10] https://tickhistory.thomsonreuters.com.

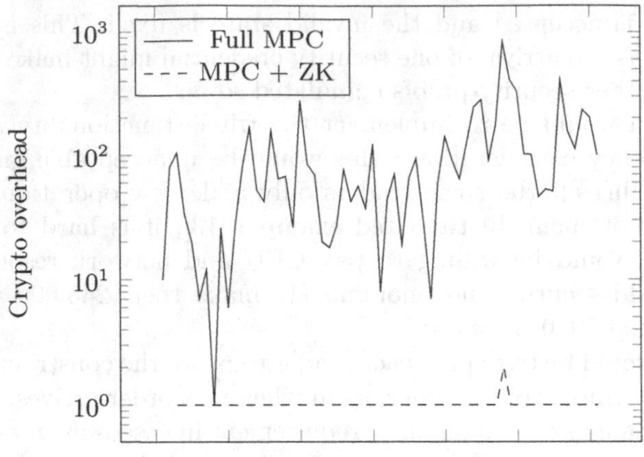

Fig. 1. Crypto overhead by retail traders (adopted from [14])

(also from [14]), retail traders would need to devote significant computational resources in a generic MPC implementation for allowing speculators to indeed speculate.

5 Design Implications of Non-monotonicity: Failures by Omission

From a security perspective, the above design is only secure-with-abort as an adversary can abort the protocol by simply not participating in a joint MPC step. The protocol *fails by omission.* It is true that from a security perspective one can design the protocol to be fail-safe [7], but this is hardly acceptable in practice. Which speculator would join the TSX market mentioned above if any retail investor disconnecting its computer could fail safe to nothing happend and thus avoid being thoroughly shaved? Would institutional or retail investors ever join if any glitch by mistake or mischief by an algorithmic trader could fail safe to nothing done a day of costly MPC computation?

A preliminary observation is that in practice one cannot initialize a market with a self-claimed account. The cash that get deposited into the market must be backed by a verifiable source where a debit is acknowledged by every market participants, e.g. ZeroCash. Hence, such source must be able to publicly verify the validity of the transactions resulting from the market's operation at the end of the day to credit each the account with the corresponding amount.

An approach to penalize a faulty participant upon aborting in an MPC with digital cash is to make the adversary lose some digital cash. The works in [11] and [12] require the adversary to make deposits and forfeit them upon dropping out. Technically the parties have to stake *increasing deposit in a fixed order* since order of revelation is important (the see-saw mechanism, [11, p. 7]) for the aforementioned penalty mechanism to work[11] To participate in a game where x is at stake, the first trader completing the protocol deposits $n \cdot x$, the second trader deposits $(n-1) \cdot x$, and the n-th trader deposits x.

Unfortunately those protocols are not usable in any practical scenario when deposits are actually meaningful (i.e. x is truly money and not a LaTeX symbol) as they are *economically unfair*. This is due to the difference in financial capability of traders. Consider a real futures market: the single smallest contract has a value of 1 million (real) dollars. In a low-frequency market (lean-hog futures) there are only few tens of traders but still the trader completing first would have to deposit assets 35x times the stake of the trader completing last, and in large markets more that 500 times larger. It is true that this money would be returned at the end of the protocol, yet while the protocol is in execution the first completing trader would have to borrow 500million dollars for its deposit to make an order worth 1 million...

A better solution against omission is the mechanism of Hawk [10, Appendix G, §B] in which private deposits are frozen and the identified aborting parties cannot claim the deposits back in the withdraw phase. This requires that the protocol must be able to provide security tokens of successful completion and provide identifying evidence not only in case of misbehavior but also in case of aborts. We refer the reader to Sect. 10 of [14] for additional discussion.

6 Conclusions

In this paper we have argued that the increasing number of (honest) parties that participate to security protocols makes it possible to distinguish between monotonic and non-monotonic security protocols.

Non-monotonic security implies novel failure modes and novel design challenges for protocol designers. Yet, we have also shown that some of them could actually be addressed.

References

1. Abadi, M., Needham, R.: Prudent engineering practice for cryptographic protocols. IEEE Trans. Software Eng. **22**(1), 6–15 (1996)
2. Allen, F., Santomero, A.M.: The theory of financial intermediation. J. Bank. Finance **21**(11–12), 1461–1485 (1997)
3. Bogetoft, P., et al.: Secure multiparty computation goes live. In: Dingledine, R., Golle, P. (eds.) FC 2009. LNCS, vol. 5628, pp. 325–343. Springer, Heidelberg (2009). https://doi.org/10.1007/978-3-642-03549-4_20
4. Canetti, R., Lindell, Y., Ostrovsky, R., Sahai, A.: Universally composable two-party and multi-party secure computation. In: ACM Symposium on Theory of Computing, pp. 494–503. ACM (2002)

[11] In some cases this fixed order might interfere with the security goal, if the order of actions may leak some information on who started the process.

5. Damgård, I., Keller, M., Larraia, E., Pastro, V., Scholl, P., Smart, N.P.: Practical covertly secure MPC for dishonest majority – or: breaking the SPDZ limits. In: Crampton, J., Jajodia, S., Mayes, K. (eds.) ESORICS 2013. LNCS, vol. 8134, pp. 1–18. Springer, Heidelberg (2013). https://doi.org/10.1007/978-3-642-40203-6_1
6. Dierks, T., Allen, C.: The TLS Protocol Version 1.0 (1999)
7. Gong, L.: Fail-Stop Protocols: An Approach To Designing Secure Protocols (1994)
8. Harkins, D., Carrel, D.: The internet key exchange (IKE), Technical report (1998)
9. Kiayias, A., Zacharias, T., Zhang, B.: An efficient E2E verifiable e-voting system without setup assumptions. IEEE Secur. Priv. (2017)
10. Kosba, A., Miller, A., Shi, E., Wen, Z., Papamanthou, C.: Hawk: the blockchain model of cryptography and privacy-preserving smart contracts. In: IEEE Symposium on Security and Privacy, pp. 839–858. IEEE (2016)
11. Kumaresan, R., Moran, T., Bentov, I.: How to use bitcoin to play decentralized poker. In: ACM SIGSAC Conference on Computer and Communications Security, pp. 195–206. ACM (2015)
12. Kumaresan, R., Vaikuntanathan, V., Vasudevan, P.N.: Improvements to secure computation with penalties. In: ACM SIGSAC Conference on Computer and Communications Security, pp. 406–417, ACM (2016)
13. Malinova, K., Park, A., Riordan, R.: Do retail traders suffer from high frequency traders (2013). SSRN 2183806
14. Massacci, F., Ngo, C.N., Nie, J., Venturi, D., Williams, J.: FuturesMEX: secure, distributed futures market exchange. In: IEEE Symposium on Security and Privacy, pp. 453–471. IEEE (2018)
15. Massacci, F., Ngo, C.N., Nie, J., Venturi, D., Williams, J.: The seconomics (security-economics) vulnerabilities of decentralized autonomous organizations. In: Stajano, F., Anderson, J., Christianson, B., Matyáš, V. (eds.) Security Protocols 2017. LNCS, vol. 10476, pp. 171–179. Springer, Cham (2017). https://doi.org/10.1007/978-3-319-71075-4_19
16. Merkle, R.C.: A digital signature based on a conventional encryption function. In: Pomerance, C. (ed.) CRYPTO 1987. LNCS, vol. 293, pp. 369–378. Springer, Heidelberg (1988). https://doi.org/10.1007/3-540-48184-2_32
17. Miller, S.P., Neuman, B.C., Schiller, J.I., Saltzer, J.H.: Kerberos authentication and authorization system. In: Project Athena Technical Plan (1987)
18. Nakamoto, S.: Bitcoin: a peer-to-peer electronic cash system (2008)
19. Sasson, E.B., et al.: Zerocash: decentralized anonymous payments from bitcoin. In: IEEE Symposium on Security and Privacy, pp. 459–474. IEEE (2014)
20. Spulber, D.F.: Market microstructure and intermediation. J. Econ. Perspect. **10**(3), 135–152 (1996)
21. Zhai, E., Wolinsky, D.I., Chen, R., Syta, E., Teng, C., Ford, B.: AnonRep: towards tracking-resistant anonymous reputation. In: USENIX Symposium on Networked Systems Design and Implementation, pp. 583–596 (2016)

Non-monotonic Security Protocols and Failures in Financial Intermediation (Transcript of Discussion)

Fabio Massacci(✉)

University of Trento, Trento, Italy
fabio.massacci@unitn.it

Frank Stajano: A question about your notation: does Bob 1, Bob 2, Bob 3 mean the same Bob in different rounds of the same protocol or different people?

Reply: They are different people. For example here, the server authenticates Bob 1 to the routing service, and [Bob 2] is authenticated to the routing service, and [Bob 3] is authenticated to the routing service, and so on. The Bobs are all other good guys beside Alice. There is not only one Bob. Typically we have Sam, the server, and Alice talks to Sam and Bob talks to Sam. If want to cope with general financial intermediation and you believe in blockchains and all that... then you want to get rid of Sam and you want to have Alice and all the Bobs talking by themselves.

So what can normally go wrong? Some good guys does the wrong thing (he is fooled into doing so), or some good guy is not so good. Nothing else can happen. Consider e-voting: try double voting, stuffing the ballot box, double spending, etc. But anyhow, these are not good guys, technically. They're good guys turned bad. They did good things once, and then decided they wanted to cheat. If they were good, they would not try double voting.

So now the question for you is, what does this to do with non monotonic security? Look at what Alice actually does when she ran the protocol. At very high level she creates some security evidence, whatever this evidence is... she submits this evidence to Sam (if she has a server) or to the Bobs (if she has a broadcast channel or if she uses a ledger). Then our fellas, the good guys, either Sam the middleman or the Bobs, they verify the security evidence from Alice. If she's good, they said oh yes, this vote is correct; we take it. Then you have Bob 1st doing the same, and Bob 2nd doing the same, and Bob 3rd doing the same. Until Bob 8th does it... and you repeat [for other Bobs].... For instance, if that was an auction, then some crypto magic happens at the end. After everybody has voted, multi-party computation happens and, low and behold, there's a winner. The question that I have for the audience is: What happened to Alice when Bob the 8th has done something?' To Alice's credential, to Alice's proof? Alice, she's a good lady. What happens to her?

Mansoor Ahmed: Nothing. Stays the same, credentials don't change.

Reply: Exactly. Nothing happens. This is a good property of the protocol, from a theoretical perspective... Nothing happens to Alice and her security credentials. Because she's in a good standing. Her vote was good, she had good cash in the pocket... Nobody needs to go again and check-in on Alice. From the

V. Matyáš et al. (Eds.): Security Protocols 2018, LNCS 11286, pp. 55–62, 2018.
https://doi.org/10.1007/978-3-030-03251-7_6

perspective of the Bobs, this is monotonic: each new guy that does something in the protocol is accruing valid credentials.

Ian Goldberg: So that's not true with all e-voting protocols. There are e-voting protocols where in order to achieve non-coercibility, you're allowed to vote, possibly under coercion, and then later you're allowed to vote again and that would prove that your first vote was invalid. If you hadn't voted again, your first vote would have been in fact a valid vote.

Reply: I agree with you, but this is nothing to do with the fact that *other* people's vote will impact on your vote. In your very example, if you vote, you can vote again: "This vote was bad", "My new vote", but if Virgil votes, nothing touched you, right?

Ian Goldberg: Fair.

Virgil Gligor: What you are saying makes very good sense if you're talking about one protocol. If you have multiple protocols that compose, monotonicity may not hold. For example, you may have revocation of credentials. In which case Alice is out of luck: she get her credentials revoked whilst doing nothing.

Reply: Agreed. When you have composition, all kinds of messy thing can happen, but we're really thinking of one single protocol. The anti-coercion mechanism mentioned by Ian is really a good example. You may vote two times, it is acceptable. Still, the 2nd guy who votes has no impact on your vote. The 3rd good guy who votes has no impact on your vote...

Ilia Shumailov: This is not necessarily true, suppose that I vote and then ask: "Who doesn't want to vote now?" Imagine a situation which I want to only vote given that the other Bob hasn't voted yet. Or other similar situations.

Reply: Agreed. These are more sophisticated and not so popular protocols.

Virgil Gligor: The class of problems Ilia is talking about belong to a class of problems where the protocol has *obligations*, not just permissions. Here we are talking of permissions. If you insert obligations in a protocol things change.

Reply: At the moment we're only talking about permission. Normal protocol that we design are all based on permission... And this is visible in the proofs.

Mansoor Ahmed: What about cases where the good guys are also in charge of maintaining the integrity of the system itself as in the blockchain? There the good guys are also in charge of the consistency of the systems.

Virgil Gligor: This would be, again, a composition of protocols.

Reply: Letting composition aside, why is monotonicity technically important? Suppose you have Alice and the Bobs, a protocol, and Sam as a middle man. You can get rid of Sam by using blockchains or similar things. You can say that since Sam doing the intermediation is gone, we want to do multiparty computation. But multiparty computation is costly, a lot more than you think.

To bypass these costs a commonly used trick is the following one [3]: replace some steps of MPC with zero knowledge proofs. What are you going to do? Alice proves on zero knowledge that she's in a good standing. Bob the 1st proves on zero knowledge that he's in good standing. And so does Bob the 2nd, and so on and so forth. All these things can be verified asynchronously and you minimize multiparty computation to what I called the crypto magic at the end: you verify that there is a majority of votes in favor of candidate A versus candidate B, that A is the highest bidder etc. It's a lot more efficient of course if you can do some steps in zero knowledge, to you prove your good standing. But it needs monotonicity because it works as in the example of coercion: Bob the 8th will not make Alice's claim invalid. In most of the protocols, it is a reasonable assumption.

So let me now focus on simple general financial intermediation. Remember that the fat cats, as they used to call them in England, so the intermediation man, like the Chicago Mercantile Exchange, London Stock Market... They are gone. If you look at blockchain, it's all about getting rid of the middle man.

So the only people left are Alice and the Bob's. And Alice trades in buyers of oil. And in the typical future market, what's going to happen is that she promises "I'm going to buy 25 barrels of oil at the end of the day, whatever the price is." Given today's price, she has the cash to buy them and meet her promises[1]. Then some people will actually take her offer and say, "I'm here to sell them. Promise." Of course there's a risk in this, because the price can go up, and the price can go down. But they all did this through Sam (the futures exchange). And all is good, everything works fine.

So why should we worry about that? What happens if good Bob the 8th—I should've probably said Henry the 8th because we have his picture just at the end of the room—makes an offer to buy more oil? Because he makes this offer, the price sky rockets: there's more people buying oil, and then of course the price goes up. Now the point is what happens to Alice? Does she have money anymore? Because she made a cryptographic proof in zero knowledge that she has enough money in the pocket to buy it. Of course nobody knows how much money it is, you want to be confidential otherwise there can be lots of problem. We discussed about that in a last year paper, it's called Price Discrimination. This is a problem because of what can happen at the end of the day. If the good ol' Sam, the Chicago Mercantile Exchange was there, there would be one guy calling her. Now they have an API called `margin call`, but in the old days it was actually one guy calling you, "Hey, the price of oil is above this money, you're off luck. Please pour other money into your account at the Mercantile Exchange to meet your promises, otherwise you're off."

At some point Alice said "I promise to buy some barrels of oil". She did so at $1 a barrel. Now the price of oil is $2 a barrel. You don't have money here to meet your promises, Alice. What are you going to do? Sam is gone. There's no Sam. Only the Bobs. Who's going to get the money from Alice if she only committed an amount of money to buy 20 barrels at $1, and now the barrels are $2? Who's going to give to Bob 3rd his money? Sam normally would, but Sam's gone. There's no Sam, there are only the Bobs. Alice can't foot the bill, Bob wants the money, so we have a problem. This is essentially the problem of

[1] Note that in a Futures Market you have a pile of cash and a pile of promises (future contracts) about selling or buying at some future time some underlying goods such as barrels of oils or pork. You buy and sell promises and must be able to fulfill the promises you hold at the end of the day [2].

general financial interpretation and this has introduced something that didn't exist before.

Frank Stajano: In the previous slide, you said that while Sam was still around he would foot the bill. So is Sam making a loss in there whenever the price goes up? Is Sam eventually giving Bob 3rd the money because Alice is gone bankrupt? He covers for everybody who had bid while the price was low? Does Sam like doing that?

Reply: Albeit everything goes through the Exchange, Sam is ultimately taking the money from Alice *before* she went into red. He will liquidate and force her out of the market if she can't cope. As soon as Sam is seeing that the price is going down, he's going to call Alice and say, "Hey Alice, you don't have enough money. Pour money there." And if Alice says, "Well I don't have any money, sorry about that." Then Sam will liquidate Alice position and tell the Bobs, "Sorry Bobs, that's the money you're going to make it." Of course I'm simplifying it here, but Sam makes sure he is up to no losses: he is just a middleman.

Basically, there's a promise from Alice and before Alice went into red (suppose Alice can still fulfill her pile of promises when the price of the barrel is 1.5) we make her fulfill her promise at that point, and then we keep going.

Mark Lomas: You already have this risk, even if the price doesn't move. Let me explain Alice's risk. There was a German bank, and it was so long ago, this was when they were still dealing in Deutsch Marks... Herstadt Bank specialized in converting between Deutsch Marks and US dollars. Because they had large amounts of this money flowing, they could get a better exchange rate. So anyone who wanted to exchange Deutsch Marks to dollars would go to Herstadt, would hand over a certain amount of Deutsch Marks, and subsequently get back US Dollars. The problem was that their banking license got revoked in the middle of a trading day, and therefore all of the people who were converting Deutsch Marks to US Dollars lost their Deutsch Marks. It wasn't that the market moved, Herstadt had the money, but the regulator basically shut them down.

Reply: This corresponds to shutting down Sam midway. I agree the problem of the regulator shutting down Sam is an interesting one, but our scenario is that the Bobs and Alice want to get rid of Sam, from a security protocol perspective.

Daniel Weitzner: This is a wonderful distinction you're exploring, but you're pretending as if these are both security protocols. The market is really a risk management system. If you take any of the traditional fully monotonic security protocols and look at how they're actually used in any sensible system, they are actually used in a non-monotonic way.

In other words, they have risk management wrapped around them in various ways. You check whether users are behaving as you would expect and similar things. I really do like the distinction, but the observation should be that monotonic protocols never actually work right within human systems, unless you do other things of the sort that financial markets do.

Reply: I agree with your observation. My additional claim is that if you want to have security protocols for financial intermediation this [risk management] need really go in the theory.

In this futures market protocol Alice was honest and Bob was honest. There was no dishonest action happening: Bob the 8th just made an honest offer. And what happens is we have a honest failure. Because Alice at the beginning crafted a perfectly valued zero knowledge proof. Everything is valid except that Bob 8th bankrupted Alice. So all Alice proof... they were all cryptographically valid then, but they become economically invalid now, and therefore you need to redo everything again from the protocol perspective. And because monotonicity is destroyed you can't do what other papers normally do - the mentioned privacy preserving reputation paper [3] is a good example in which you replace MPC steps with zero knowledge proofs - They would be broken. You can't do this. Now what a cryptographer will do is what I call the armchair cryptographer solution: 'What's the problem? You run general MPC and you're done."

So for every step you run the big multiparty computation and we know from the Sugar Beet Danish Auction [1] that MPC can stand thousands of parties. In theory it would be possible to run the entire Chicago Mercantile Exchange on multiparty computation and be done.

Let me ask you a question. Who actually read the Danish Auction paper [1]? How many Bobs were in the multiparty computation? 1,229 were the farmers who participated, but how many technical parties of MPC were in the protocol?

Ian Goldberg: I think it was five...

Reply: Three. So one thing is running a multiparty computation with three, one thing is with 100. The correct title of the paper should have been "Secret Sharing goes lives", not"Secure Multiparty Computation goes live".

Why is this important? When we tried to implement it for the Chicago Mercantile Exchange – Nam, the Phd student, was actually implementing it [4]. Every time his machine crashed, we used the top notch implementation of MPC and ZK [pointing to the slide] and we said, "Your implementation is wrong because your machine crashes all the time." Instead... Table 2[2] shows the final size of the circuits, you've seen published in some MPC papers. This is the offline computation, and nobody talks about the offline computation in their papers because it's offline. If you look here, this is 256 MB that was part of the computation for SHA1 we needed to do it. But then the offline part was something like 65 GB. Now 65 GB of offline computation... It's a lot. Even on Amazon, there's only few machines that can actually have this amount of memory. And we had to actually buy one in order to have some plots that the reviewers from the Security and Privacy symposium conference wanted to see. We had to buy one specific machine with this amount of memory. Why is this important? it's offline. If you only vote once and you only bid once, then it's offline. But if you have to run that part for the multiple, Bobs each time Bob 8th makes an offer, and Bob 9th makes and ... Then it's not offline anymore because you can't recycle any offline part. You have to generate it fresh each

[2] The table is in the main paper.

time. And therefore, wow, it's bad. It's a gigantic effort. Figure 1[3] in our paper shows some computation based from the Chicago Mercantile Exchange data. Each tick is an order of magnitude. This is the average overhead of our protocol and this is the generic MPC: it's a factor of 1,000. And Lean Bacon is one of the least traded markets. It is a factor of 1,000 if you run multiparty computation on ten parties, not even 100 parties. This means it just can't run. You can run a hybrid protocol like ours but it needs to be designed ad hoc. You cannot say, "We just use multiparty computation." You need to look at very complicated things to avoid that honest Bob is going to bankrupt honest Alice.

So let me go through the most funny things. Okay, MPC is expensive. There's a recent Communication of the ACM of electronic traded market paper recently claiming that it's a price for getting rid of middleman Sam: we're all in the same boat, we get rid of the middleman Sam, and we share his bounty.

So then you take a different market, the data showed in the slide is DTSX market in New Zealand. It's one of the few markets in which you have actually the identifier of the traders available. They get 300,000 orders per day. Imagine running this in MPC. The Lean Hog that I showed you is in the thousands per day, and already MPS is a factor of 1,000 overhead. So 71% are retail traders and 29% are what's called algorithmic traders. So you see that some Bobs are not the same Bobs as the others. We have frantic Alice and the sleepy Bobs. This is the number of traders, but if you look at the proportion of orders, 82% of the 300 K are by algorithmic traders. And 99% of those orders are limit orders[4]. They're almost never going to be matching into actually a trade. Basically they're just making fuss.

But in multiparty computation everybody does the same. Everybody casts one vote... Maybe they cast two votes, but that's it. If you look at the overhead [Pointing at a slide] this is an incredible burden of computation of the poor retail trader to let these other algorithm traders do their trading. It's crazy: they will have to participate at a factor of 100 to participate in a trade in which they're doing very little. And this is the hybrid algorithm we specifically designed.

So when you go to the conclusion. You have honest failures now, you have non-monotonic security. It will change the way we think about security. In a sense, we'll have to design more and more ad hoc protocols. The traditional way of implementing a MPC, taking some part of MPC and splitting some parts as zero knowledge protocols, it's not so easy anymore.

Maybe fat cat Sam is there to stay and most things about distributed financial market are not going to happen. If they happen, they are going to happen very differently from the way we think they will.

Petra Sala: I'm not sure I understand this source of uncertainty. If Alice committed to something before the prices went up, what kind of commitment is it? Maybe it's a contract or something similar. Then, if it's a form of a contract

[3] The figure is in the main paper.

[4] Limit orders are order with higher sell requests and lower buy bids than the current market price. Limit orders are at the fringes of the order book and actually matched buy and sell orders meet at the middle.

or at least some binding words, then this contract should be honored at that moment the conditions were like that and she should get the barrels for the money she committed to. Maybe it's too black and white as far as I see. I agree that the conditions changed but then from that moment from when the condition changed, then another party will pay another price.

Reply: You have a source of uncertainty because the agreement is about the future. Basically you have to think Futures Market as a casino. You buy a number of chips, you start bidding, and sometime you run out of chips.

Daniel Weitzner: This uncertainty happens because she's given credit. So you must verify if she's still worthy of the credit. It's just because she's not making a one time transaction that's banded only by the current knowledge, she's making a transaction based on credit and the transaction is in the future. The market extends her some credit, so they have to figure out whether she's actually credit worthy given the state of the market.

Virgil Gligor: In real life, her bid is not even taken into account by the market unless she deposits the money. For example when you trade through Fidelity, or through whoever trades on your behalf, they have your money already. Whether that your trade will go through by the end of the day is unclear because it depends on the market. And if you have a limit order it might never go through. So the point is more that Alice is denied the execution the protocol, but she'll never keep losing money. I'm not sure what your point is here because if the price of oil fluctuates she may not get her barrel, but she should never end up paying more and more money.

Reply: In these markets you hold both money and promises. At the end of the day you should be able to honor your promises. If you promised to buy something, those promises should eventually be marked at market price.

Virgil Gligor: If you have a limit order, you might not get what you want, but you should not be forced to execute an order. It wasn't clear to me from the beginning that you don't only have limit orders here.

Daniel Weitzner: These commodities markets don't have those kinds of limits. This is the whole point. So they have to do a risk assessment...

Reply: At the end of the day, every promise gets liquidated at the mid market price. This is the way the Chicago Mercantile Exchange works. So at the end of the day, you may run out of money because every promise has to clear. The purpose of Sam is exactly to make sure that this goes smoothly.

Daniel Weitzner: It seems like your claim about the applicability of being able to boot out Sam in favor of completely decentralized system is limited by the kind of market.

Reply: Exactly. Depending on the type of market, maybe getting Sam out is going to be extremely hard, or the protocol is becoming extremely challenging.

Virgil Gligor: When you have arbitrage, it's not clear that your protocols are monotonic to start with so...

Peter Roenne: I had an idea: have you ever heard of tropical geometry and how that could be used to make this multiparty computation more efficient?

Reply: No, we didn't. We will check if we can run it. Thank you.

References

1. Bogetoft, P., et al.: Secure multiparty computation goes live. In: Dingledine, R., Golle, P. (eds.) FC 2009. LNCS, vol. 5628, pp. 325–343. Springer, Heidelberg (2009). https://doi.org/10.1007/978-3-642-03549-4_20
2. Spulber, D.F.: Market microstructure and intermediation. J. Econ. Perspect. **10**(3), 135–152 (1996)
3. Zhai, E., Wolinsky, D.I., Chen, R., Syta, E., Teng, C., Ford, B.: AnonRep: towards tracking-resistant anonymous reputation. In: USENIX Symposium on Networked Systems Design and Implementation, pp. 583–596 (2016)
4. Massacci, F., Ngo, C.N., Nie, J., Venturi, D., Williams, J.: FuturesMEX: secure, distributed futures market exchange. In: IEEE Symposium on Security and Privacy, pp. 453–471 (2018)

HoneyPAKEs

José Becerra[1], Peter B. Rønne[1], Peter Y. A. Ryan[1(✉)], and Petra Sala[1,2]

[1] University of Luxembourg, Esch-sur-Alzette, Luxembourg
[2] École Normale Supérieure, Computer Science Department, Paris, France
{jose.becerra,peter.roenne,peter.ryan,petra.sala}@uni.lu

Abstract. We combine two security mechanisms: using a Password-based Authenticated Key Establishment (PAKE) protocol to protect the password for access control and the Honeywords construction of Juels and Rivest to detect loss of password files. The resulting construction combines the properties of both mechanisms: ensuring that the password is intrinsically protected by the PAKE protocol during transmission and the Honeywords mechanisms for detecting attempts to exploit a compromised password file. Our constructions lead very naturally to two factor type protocols. An enhanced version of our protocol further provides protection against a compromised login server by ensuring that it does not learn the index to the true password.

1 Introduction

In this paper we propose combining two existing security mechanisms in order to obtain the benefits of both. On the one hand, Password-based Authenticated Key Establishment (PAKE) style constructions have been used as a way to protect the password during the execution of an access control protocol. The password is thus protected by the protocol rather than having to rely on the establishment of a secure channel, e.g. SSL, with the attendant dangers of Phishing attacks, etc. On the other hand, Juels and Rivest proposed in [1] the idea of *Honeywords*, as a way of raising an alert when an attacker tries to exploit a stolen password file. The idea here is, rather than just storing the (hash of the) password for each user, it is stored at a random position in a list of (hashed) decoy *honeywords*. The indices indicating the position in the list of the real password is stored in a separate, hardened device called the *Honeychecker*. Someone obtaining the password file does not know which is the real password and so if he tries to login as the user, he will have to take a guess as to which is the real password. If he guesses wrong, this is detected and is a clear indication of compromise of the password file and alerts can be raised and remedial actions taken, i.e. updating passwords etc.

Achieving a combined protocol gives rise to the idea of a secondary password, which in turn leads to a very natural, two-factor instantiation. A further elaboration of the protocol serves to counter the corrupted login server problem, i.e. prevents the server learning the Honey-index.

V. Matyáš et al. (Eds.): Security Protocols 2018, LNCS 11286, pp. 63–77, 2018.
https://doi.org/10.1007/978-3-030-03251-7_7

1.1 Our Contribution

Building on the idea of Juels and Rivest [1] we propose a new protocol model called *HoneyPAKE*, by merging the design of PAKE with Honeywords, with a goal to add an additional shield for passwords. The proposed protocols are not trying to prevent an attacker compromising the server and stealing the file of hashed passwords, but to detect such malicious behavior and act accordingly, e.g. raising the silent alarm to the administrator. The alarm raiser would be an additional, secure, simple hardware, *Honeychecker*.

1.2 Organization of the Paper

The rest of the paper is organized as follows: in Sect. 2, we introduce PAKE protocols and a motivation for proposed models and describe the case of access control based on PAKE protocol with an example. In Sect. 3 we give definitions and descriptions of honeywords along with the importance of properly generating them and define a role of a honeychecker. In Sect. 4 we lay out the security model and discuss possible constructions of HoneyPAKEs. Section 5 gives an example of how to include authentication of the login server to the client. Finally in Sect. 6, we conclude our work.

2 Password-Based Authenticated Key Establishment Protocols

Here we briefly describe the design principles of PAKE protocols. A comprehensive survey of PAKEs can be found in Chap. 40 of [2]. Many PAKEs are based on the Diffie-Hellman or similar key-establishment mechanism, with the difference that the resulting session key is a function not only of the fresh random values, but also of the shared password. Thus, if the two parties do indeed share a common password then the resulting keys computed by both parties should agree. Such protocols have to be carefully designed to avoid introducing possibilities of off-line dictionary attacks, i.e. providing an attacker, either active or passive, with enough information to test guesses at the password off-line, at his leisure.

The key establishment with a PAKE is often followed by a form of key confirmation, which will provide explicit authentication if the codes agree. For access control we will need such a mechanism at any rate to authenticate the client to the server. It may be useful to also authenticate the server to the client.

PPK

A rather elegant protocol, and the one that we will base our construction on, is the PPK protocol due to MacKenzie and Boyko [3], here in simplified form for illustration (H denotes a suitable mapping from the password space to the DH group):

$$A \to B: \quad X := H(s_A) \cdot g^x$$
$$B \to A: \quad Y := H(s_B) \cdot g^y$$

A computes $K_A := (Y/H(s_A))^x$ and B computes $K_B := (X/H(s_B))^y$. These keys match in an honest run if the passwords s_A and s_B match.

On-line guessing attacks are of course always possible against PAKEs, but observe that here if an active attacker masquerading as one of the parties makes an incorrect guess at the password then the key computed by the legitimate party will be masked by a non-identity term raised to the DH random. This foils off-line dictionary attack against terms observed during the protocol, and any subsequent key confirmation steps or communications encrypted by the legitimate parties.

2.1 PAKE-Based Access control

PAKEs were principally designed as a way to establish secure channels, but the underlying mechanism can be used to protect the password during transmission in an access control protocol. The key confirmation mechanism can be used to authenticate the client to the server.

Thus, for example we might adapt PPK to provide authentication of C to S:

$$\begin{aligned} C \rightarrow S: &\quad Req_C\,;\, X := H(s_A) \cdot g^x \\ S \rightarrow C: &\quad Y := H(s_B) \cdot g^y \\ C \rightarrow S: &\quad H_2(K_C) \end{aligned}$$

S confirms that $H_2(K_S) = H_2(K_C)$, where H_2 is a hash function from the group to a compression space.

Notice that we inherit the off-line dictionary attack resistance of the PAKE when we base access control on a PAKE. Thus an attacker masquerading as the login server S will not gain any useful information about the password. This is in contrast to a conventional login protocol where the user's password, possibly hashed, will be revealed to such an attacker.

Remark. In the client-server scenario, the server stores the file F containing password related information. It is desired that the passwords in F are hashed with a random salt to prevent attacks where the pre-computation of possible passwords immediately discloses the passwords in clear after the leakage of the file F, e.g. using previously computed rainbow tables. However, since integrating salted passwords with PAKEs is not entirely straightforward, either (i) PAKEs do not use salted passwords or (ii) the server sends the salt value in clear to the client during the login. Recently Jarecki et al. [4] proposed a general transformation of PAKE protocols to make them secure against pre-computation attacks using an Oblivious PRF. This method could also be applied in our setting.

3 Honeywords

Stealing a password file clearly compromises any access control mechanism that uses it. The first step to counter this threat is the well-known idea of storing not the raw passwords but rather crypto hashes of the passwords. Now, when the AC server receives an access request for a user with a password it computes the hash of the given password and checks that this agrees with the stored hash. The effectiveness of this counter-measure has diminished as password cracking tools have become more powerful, such as the use of rainbow tables and increasing number of brute-forcing algorithms. Incorporating salt into the hashes and using slower hash functions helps a bit but still does not prevent a determined attacker who obtains a password file from extracting the passwords. It thus seems inevitable that password files will be compromised.

Ways to distribute shares of the passwords across several remote servers have been proposed in [5,6] as a way to make the compromise of such files harder, but even this will not guarantee the security of the passwords. Additionally, it would require network infrastructure for password management, and in this paper we want to omit such difficulty.

The first ones who tackled the problem of password file theft were Bojinov et al. in [7] where the mention of *honeywords* first appeared. Honeywords were decoys of passwords proposed to set a trap for the attacker who steals a database of passwords to obtain users credentials. The authors in [7] built a theft-resistant system that generate decoy password sets and forces the attacker to perform a great deal of on-line attempts, which major websites would detect and inhibit.

Where Bojinov *et al.* left off, Juels and Rivest continued in [1] and came up with a very simple but effective way to mitigate the effects of password file compromise: not to prevent but rather to detect and perhaps deter exploitation of such a compromise. Instead of storing just the single, correct password, *sugarword*, against the user Id, we store it alongside a number of decoy *honeywords*. Together sugarword and honeywords are called *sweetwords*. The real password will be placed at an arbitrary point in the list and this position is not stored in the file.

Logging in is similar to the standard mechanism: the user C provides a putative password and the Server (S) computes the hash of this, but now it tries to match this against each of the stored hashes. If the proffered password is valid then the server should find a match and it now sends the index of the matching term to the *Honeychecker* (HC). If S finds no match, it will typically notify C that the password is incorrect. The HC should be a separate device linked only to S by a *minimal channel* able to carry only values of type *Index*. HC stores the correct index for each user and if the index provided by S is correct for the user it will authorize access. If the index is incorrect then this indicates that, most likely, an attacker is attempting to login as C using information obtained from a compromised password file. The protocol is thus not fail-safe, but upon intrusion we can let it fail-deadly. Figure 1 illustrates the original Honeywords proposal of Jules and Rivest.

The proposal of Juels and Rivest requires the following assumptions:

- A *secure channel* between Client and Server to prevent an eavesdropper from obtaining the client's password during the authentication phase. In practice, this is typically implemented via TLS connection, however, it is vulnerable

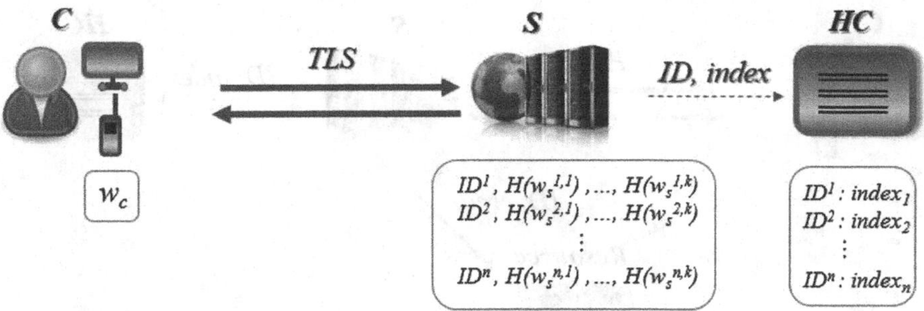

Fig. 1. The Honeywords system of [1] is composed of the Honeychecker, the server and client.

to phishing attacks. In this work we aim to eliminate this requirement with the help of PAKE-based access control mechanisms.

- *Flatness* on the honey words to ensure that they look plausible alternatives to the real password, i.e. an attacker trying to exploit a stolen password file does not have a better than $1/k$ chance of guessing the true password, where k is the number of sweetwords for that user. We refer to [1,7] for further details about honeywords generation.

4 HoneyPAKE

Consider the scenario where a client C would like to login to server S using his password as means of authentication. We introduce a mechanism that integrates a PAKE protocol into the Honeywords proposal of Juels and Rivest as shown in Fig. 2. The resulting system benefits of the security guarantees offered by underlying primitives. More concretely, the idea is (i) to detect whenever the password file stored at the *Server* has been compromised and (ii) protect the client's password during its transmission to the Server.

4.1 The Naive Approach

Incorporating the honeywords idea into PAKEs is not entirely straightforward because S does not know which (hashed) honeyword to use when running the protocol. The simplest way to address this is simply to have S not inject any password hash term into the exchanged terms:

$$C \rightarrow S: \quad Req_C$$
$$S \rightarrow C: \quad Y_S := g^y$$

C now computes $K_C := (Y_S)^x$ and $Z_C := H_2(K_C)$ and sends the following back to S:

$$C \rightarrow S: \quad X_C := H(w_C) \cdot g^x \ , \ Z_C$$

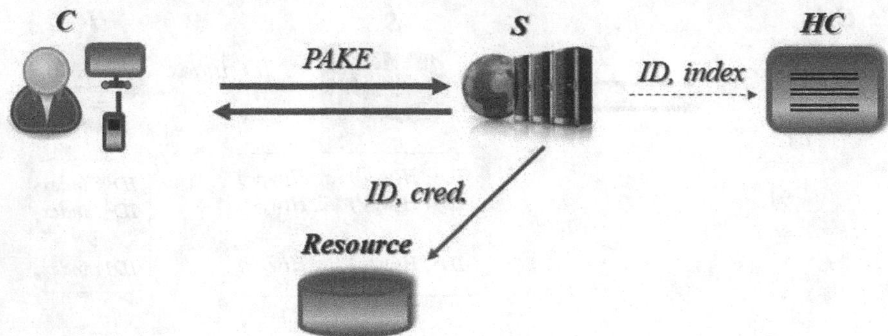

Fig. 2. HoneyPAKE system. The client wants to use the Resource. After running the HoneyPAKE protocol with the login server S, the client can access the resource. The credential shared between the Resource and C can be the output of the HoneyPAKE.

Now S computes, for $i \in \{1, \cdots, k\}$

$$W_i := H_2((X_C / H(w_S^i))^y)$$

and compares with Z_C to find the correct hashed password.

However, this allows an attacker masquerading as S to launch an off-line dictionary attack: computing W_i for guesses at the password w_S^i until he finds a match. A slightly less naive approach is to just run the PPK protocol k times and find a match in one of the runs. This is clearly rather inefficient, tedious for the user and could leak the index.

We consider an alternative approach: we introduce a secondary password known to both parties.

4.2 Technical Description of Components

We consider a system with three components: Clients, Server and Honeychecker which we describe next.

Client. A legitimate user who would like to connect to server S. Let $\mathcal{C} = \{C_1, \ldots, C_n\}$ be the set of clients. Each client C_j holds two passwords: a *primary* password and a *secondary* password, which we simply denote by w_C and w'_C and we assume they are chosen uniformly at random from password dictionaries $\mathcal{D}$ and $\mathcal{D}'$ respectively.

Server. It is a system in charge of handling clients' login requests. The server S has access to file F storing the clients' passwords. More specifically, the file F stores one entry *per client*, each entry containing the secondary password followed by k *potential* passwords, i.e.:

$$F[C_j] = H(w'_S), H(w_S^1), \ldots, H(w_S^k)$$

where for each client $C_j \in C$ holding w_C and w'_C as primary and secondary password, it holds that $H(w'_S) = H(w'_C)$ and $\exists\ i$ s.t. $H(w^i_S) = H(w_C)$. The correct index i is not stored by S.

Honeychecker: This is an auxiliary and simple device whose only goal is to detect whenever the password file F has been compromised. It maintains a list L storing the correct index i per client C_j, i.e. $L[C_j] = i$. It accepts two commands:

- Set (C_j, i): Sets $L[C_j]$ to value i.
- Check (C_j, i'): Checks whether $L[C_j]$ equals i'. It outputs a $r = 1$ if $L[C_j] = i'$ and $r = 0$ otherwise.

The connection between S and HC is a *minimal channel* which we assume secure. The idea is to run a PAKE protocol between C and S in such a way that it will allow S to identify the index i such that $H(w^i_S) = H(w_C)$. Subsequently, S queries the HC with Check(C,i) and the latter will check against its records whether the index i is associated to client C or not. If $r = 1$, it is an indication that a legitimate client is attempting the login and therefore access to the requested resource should be granted. However, $r = 0$ signals a possible compromise of the password file. In the next paragraph we detail how a *passive* or *active* HC may react to each scenario.

Login Access. As described in Fig. 2 the client wants access to a Resource e.g. an email service, which may or may not be co-located with the login server. The HoneyPAKE protocol between the client and the login server will in the end output a shared key which the server can forward to the resource as a credential for the service (or the established secure PAKE-channel can be used to create a new credential). We do not explicitly write these extra steps in the protocols below, since they may depend on context.

The HC can enter this login access passively and just log the login requests and corresponding correct or wrong indices. The administrator can then periodically check if an alarm was raised, or be alerted immediately. Alternatively the HC can also play a more active role, see Fig. 3, and contribute to the decision whether access is granted or not. The advantage is that malicious attempts to gain access via honeywords will immediately be bounced, however the downside is need for a more active HC. The possible cases for login attempts are

- with a a correct password i.e. the sugarword
- with a false password, which is a honeyword
- with a false password, which is not in the honeyword list.

The first case will always result in login, while the last possibility will always be blocked by S. The outcome of the second possibility will depend on whether the HC is active or passive.

4.3 Security Model

In the security model for the HoneyPAKE system, we will in general consider the HC as being incorruptible. The reasoning behind this assumption is that

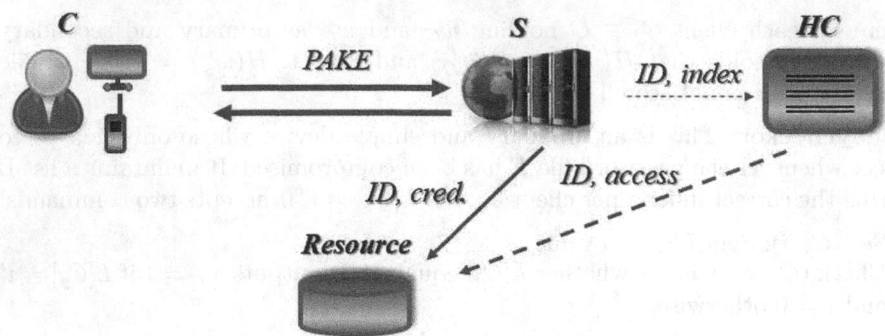

Fig. 3. Login access granted by resource

the HC is a very simple piece of hardware only having to handle simple indices. It only has minimal external channels, it only needs a minimal memory storing indices and only needs to be able to handle simple comparisons of indices. On the other hand, the security model does allow the adversary to corrupt S, but only in the form of stealing the password file F. We will discuss stronger forms of corruption below.

One could speculate in extending this model and allow the attacker to compromise either S or HC, but not both, and indeed this will also be secure since the information stored on HC is minimal and would not allow an attacker to compromise security. Indeed, in case HC is compromised, it should not jeopardize the security level of communication between client and server as it is protected by the PAKE protocol. In the worst case scenario, the security level of HoneyPAKEs, even with a corrupted HC should be at the same security level of any PAKE protocol [3].

We will however stay in the model above which is more closely related to the Honeyword idea and argument of a simple incorruptible HC.

Next we describe the attack scenarios that we consider in this proposal:

1. Compromised File F: As result from a security breach, the adversary $\mathcal{A}$ might get access to the password file F. Regardless of how the passwords are stored in F, e.g. plain text, hashed or hashed and salted, it is reasonable to assume that $\mathcal{A}$ can obtain the passwords in clear by brute forcing F and then try to masquerade as C to S [8].
2. Standard Operation: We consider an adversary who has full control of the communication C between S, different to [1], where they assume the existence of a secure channel. However in this scenario the attacker does not have access to the password file F.

Discussion: The first attack scenario is considered by Juels and Rivest in [1] by introducing the HC as a secondary server. The motivation in [1] is not to prevent the leakage of F but detect whenever such event occurs.

The underlying idea is that whenever F gets compromised, $\mathcal{A}$ may observe at most k *potential* passwords per client, but only one is the correct one. Furthermore F contains no information about the index position of the correct password. Then the adversary can only select one candidate password at random when trying to masquerade as C to S. In such a case, the leakage of F could be detected by the HC with probability $(k-1)/k$ for each attempt of $\mathcal{A}$ and subsequent security measures can be taken e.g. trigger an alarm informing about compromise of F and asking the server to *reject* the login attempt.

In this work we augment the proposal of Juels and Rivest by removing the requirement for a secure channel between C and S. The proposal is to run a PAKE-style protocol between C and S, after which S can identify if C holds one of the k potential hashed passwords $H(w_S^1), \ldots, H(w_S^k)$ and ii) the *potential* index i s.t. $H(w_C) = H(w_S^i)$. Then S proceeds as described in [1], by querying the HC which checks if i is the *correct* index or not. The construction guarantees that if the password file F is compromised, an active adversary $\mathcal{A}$ has at most $1/k$ chances of masquerade as C without being detected, while if F is not compromised, $\mathcal{A}$ can masquerade as C with success probability at most $1/|D|$, where D is the password dictionary.

The second scenario above, called standard operation, is close to the standard PAKE model and the attacker can be active masquerading as either S or C. However, we do not allow the password file to be compromised in this scenario. The reason is that an adversary knowing the honeyword list of passwords, can actively masquerade as S towards C and do a binary search for the correct password. This would be detectable from the client side, but might not be practical in the real world. We will discuss this below.

It is reasonable to question why one could not simply store the password file in HC or split it between S and HC and benefit from the assumption that HC is incorruptible. The reason is that the HC is by design an extremely simple component with minimal external channels as mentioned above. In particular, it is not meant to compute hashes, nor to compare or retrieve passwords.

4.4 HoneyPAKE Construction

We will now consider our suggestion for a HoneyPAKE protocol. Remember that C holds the two passwords w'_C, w_C and S stores the corresponding password list $H(w'_S), H(w_S^1), \ldots, H(w_S^k)$. The login protocol now runs as follows:

$$C \rightarrow S: \quad Req_C$$
$$S \rightarrow C: \quad Y_S := H(w'_S) \cdot g^y$$

C now computes $Y = (Y_S/H(w'_C))$ $K_C := Y^x$ and $Z_C := H_2(Y, g^x, K_C)$ and sends the following back to S:

$$C \rightarrow S: \quad X_C := H(w_C) \cdot g^x \ , \ Z_C$$

Now S computes, for $i \in \{1, \cdots, k\}$

$$W_i := H_2((X_C/H(w_S^i))^y)$$

If $W_i \neq Z_C \; \forall i$, then the login request is rejected directly by S. If $W_i = Z_C$ for some i, then:

$$S \rightarrow HC : i$$

HC checks if i agrees with the stored value i^* for C, and if $i \neq i^*$ then an alarm is raised.

Notice that if we are using this construction purely for access control then it appears that it may be possible to drop the second hash function H_2 as we will not be using the session key subsequently, but this needs to be confirmed by a full analysis and changes the group security assumption from CDH to DDH. Of course if we want to keep open the option of later using the session key for a secure channel, perhaps to communicate a credential or ticket to C, as described above, we need to retain H_2 to conceal K_C.

4.5 HoneyPAKE Security Analysis

In this section we make a brief and sketchy security analysis. The security of the HoneyPAKE relies on the intractability of the CDH problem in group $\mathbb{G}$. Similar to other security proofs for PAKE protocols in the random model [3,9], in order to construct a CDH reduction, the confirmation code K_C has to be associated with the identity of the session for which it was computed.[1] This can be easily achieved by making the following changes in the the HoneyPAKE protocol: The client sets $Z_C := H_2(Y, g^x, K_C)$ instead of $Z_C := H_2(K_C)$, while the server sets $W_i := H_2(g^y, X_i, X_i^y)$ with $X_i = X_C/H(w_S^i)$ instead of $W_i := H_2((X_C/H(w_S^i))^y)$.

We proceed to analyze the security of the HoneyPAKE protocol for *passive* adversaries and sketch a reduction to CDH problem. For *active* adversaries, we give only intuition of the security guarantee and leave the full security proof for future work. We consider the following scenarios:

Scenario 1. Security against eavesdropper adversaries who may have access to password file F.

Claim. Honest executions of the protocol between C and S do not leak password information under the CDH assumption.

Proof. Let P_0 be the original protocol. We demonstrate that it is possible to simulate P_0 such that i) no password information is included in the protocol and ii) an eavesdropper $\mathcal{A}_E$ can not distinguish the original protocol from the simulation except with negligible probability. Let P_1 be such simulation as follows:

$$\begin{aligned} C \rightarrow S :& \quad Req_C \\ S \rightarrow C :& \quad Y_S := g^y \\ C \rightarrow S :& \quad X_C = g^x, Z_C \end{aligned}$$

[1] Typically the session ID is defined as the concatenation of the messages exchanged between C and S without the confirmation code.

where $Z_C = H(g^x, g^y, g^z)$ and $x, y, z \xleftarrow{\$} \mathbb{Z}_q$.

By inspection it follows that P_1 does not contain password information. Let E_0 be the event where $\mathcal{A}_E$ queries the random oracle for $H(g^x, g^y, g^{xy})$ such that i) the term g^x and g^y generated respectively by C and S in an honest protocol execution. Then obviously P_0 and P_1 are identical unless the event E_0 occurs, let $Pr[E_0] = \epsilon_0$. We build a CDH-solver $\mathcal{B}^{\mathcal{A}_E}$ whose advantage is ϵ_0/n_{ro}, where n_{ro} is an upper bound to the number of random oracle queries made by $\mathcal{A}_E$. Then it simply follows that P_0 and P_1 are indistinguishable under the CDH assumption.

Scenario 2. Security against active attackers with no access to password file F.

Let $\mathcal{A}$ be an adversary against the HoneyPAKE protocol who fully controls the channel between C and S and does not have corruption capabilities. The construction of the HoneyPAKE intrinsically protects the client's password during the authentication phase even for hostile networks. It also limits $\mathcal{A}$ to only online dictionary attacks, where she has to guess the primary and secondary password for a client of her choice. Let E_2 be the event where $\mathcal{A}$ successfully logs into server S without the HC raising an alarm.

Claim. For all adversaries $\mathcal{A}$, $\Pr[E_2] \leq 1/(\mathcal{D} \cdot \mathcal{D}') + \epsilon(\lambda)$, where $\mathcal{D}$ and $\mathcal{D}'$ denote the password dictionaries, ϵ is a negligible function of the security parameter λ.

Scenario 3. Security against active attackers with access to password file F.

In this scenario we allow $\mathcal{A}$ to compromise the server S and obtain the password file F, i.e. for each client, she knows the secondary password w'_C and the list of k potential primary passwords $w^1_C \cdots w^k_C$. Let E_3 be the event where $\mathcal{A}$ successfully logs into server S without the HC raising an alarm.

Claim. For all adversaries $\mathcal{A}$ with corruption capabilities, $\Pr[E_3] \leq 1/k$.

We do not provide proofs for these claims, but they should follow via standard methods for PAKEs.

Remark. As mentioned above, an adversary, who manages to obtain the password File F and controls the communication between C and S, could try to masquerade as S to C, run the HoneyPAKE protocol and use the client C to obtain the i-th position such that $H(w_C) = H(w^i_S)$. Even though our protocol does not prevent such situations to happen, such attack could be detected by the client who could raise an alarm. Therefore, for our security definition, we assume that an adversary can only compromise the password file but not masquerade as the server.

4.6 Variations on a Theme

There are several possibilities for handling the secondary password, that we describe here. We also mention an alternative approach which avoids the need for the secondary password but at a penalty in terms of efficiency. This latter approach does however have some interesting features such as not directly revealing the correct index to S.

Naive Approach: The simplest option is simply to store the hash of the secondary password on the server side and either have the user input it each time or store it on the user's device. The former is obviously inconvenient for the user, while the latter makes the protocol device dependent.

Derived Secondary Password: Rather than having to store or re-input each time the secondary password, it could be computed as a short hash H^* of the $H(w_i)$, where the honeywords for a given user are chosen such that they all yield the same short hash value. This of course means that there will be a small loss of entropy, a few bits, with respect to the already rather low entropy of the usual passwords, but this is probably acceptable.

Secondary Password as Nonce: In place of the secondary password $H(w'_C)$ in the protocol above we could use a nonce generated by a token for a two factor type authentication. We assume that each user is provided with a hardware token that will generate short nonces in sync with a similar generator at the server side, as is done for many internet banking protocols. Such nonces will typically be quite short, low-entropy and easy for the user to type in, so maybe six digit strings.

The purpose of the secondary password, or nonce, is to counter an attacker masquerading as S from launching offline dictionary attacks. Suppose that such an attacker has managed to guess this value correctly, then this will cancel the value injected by C in computing Z_C. Knowing y, the adversary can now test guesses at the password at leisure by checking for guesses at w_Y:

$$H_2((X_C/H(w_Y))^y) = Z_C$$

It is enough then that the nonce space be sufficiently large to make the chance of guessing correctly reasonably small. This is analogous to the way that we have to accept that there will be non-negligible chance of a successful on-line guessing attack against a PAKE. The protocol is as above with the nonce replacing the hash of the shared password.

4.7 HoneyPAKE Without Secondary Password

As remarked earlier, the use of a secondary password may impact usability. We can avoid introducing a secondary password, and we discuss some constructions in this section. The setup is as before but without the secondary password.

$$C \to S: \quad Req_C$$

$$S \to C: \quad X_1 := (H(w_S^1))^y, \cdots, X_k := (H(w_S^k))^y$$

C now computes for $i \in \{1, \cdots, k\}$ $Y_i := X_i^x$, and $Y_{k+1} := H_2((H(w_C))^x)$ and sends the following back to S:

$$C \to S: \quad Y_1, Y_2, \cdots, Y_{k+1}$$

S now checks if $H_2(Y_i^{1/y}) = Y_{k+1}$ for some i, and if true then:

$$S \to HC : \; i$$

This version is less efficient than those presented above and does allow an adversary masquerading as S to have k guessing attempts per faked login, but it does avoid the need for the secondary password.

4.8 Index-Hiding HoneyPAKE

To reduce the scope of online guessing attacks in last subsection, we can reintroduce the nonce mechanism as above. Further, if C cyclically shifts the terms in the list, we can prevent an honest, but curious, S from learning which is the correct password. This addresses a further threat scenario which is discussed in [10]: that of the login server being corrupted and simply recording and later replaying the correct index, perhaps triggered by a cryptic knock.

Of course we have to communicate the shift to HC in order for it to check if the index is correct. We thus assume that the nonces can be broken into two concatenated pieces, $Nonce = Nonce_1 || Nonce_2$ such that C sees the full string but S sees only $Nonce_1$ and HC sees only $Nonce_2$. $Nonce_1$ protects against online attacks and $Nonce_2$ disguises the index and both can be low entropy as above.

$$C \to S : Req_C$$

$$S \to C : X_1 := H(Nonce_1) \cdot (H(w_S^1))^y, \cdots, X_k := H(Nonce_1) \cdot (H(w_S^k))^y$$

C now computes for $i \in \{1, \cdots, k\}$ $Y_i := (X_i / H(Nonce_1))^x$, and $Z_c := H_2((H(w_C))^x)$, and cyclically shifts the indices:

$$Z_i := Y_{i+Nonce_2 \; (mod \; k)}$$

and sends the following back to S:

$$C \to S : Z_1 \, , \, Z_2 \, , \, ..., \, Z_k \, , \, Z_c$$

Now S checks if, for some $j \in \{1, \cdots, k\}$

$$H_2(Z_j^{1/y}) := Z_c$$

If so, then:

$$S \to HC : j$$

Finally HC will remove the $Nonce_2$ shift: $j' := j - Nonce_2 \; (mod \; k)$ and check if j' agrees with the stored index.

Note that this does not prevent an active adversary who controls S to learn the correct password by replacing passwords in the honeyword list, and check if login is still possible, however we could make this statistically detectable and auditable by adding an extra round of confirmation codes to be checked by C. An advantage of this protocol over the one in Sect. 4.4, is that an adversary guessing or knowing $Nonce_1$ cannot launch an offline dictionary attack against the password. It follows that if a client accidentally types a password for another service, a malicious S cannot derive this password. A drawback of the protocol in this and the previous subsection is that a malicious client can purposely trigger the honeychecker alarm by changing the order of the returned terms. This could be countered in more advanced, but less efficient, versions of the protocol.

The security of these protocols are based on the CDH or DDH assumption depending on the type of attack to be prevented. The proofs need a subtly different model than standard PAKE due to the use of secondary passwords. Session Ids and Ids in general have been omitted above, but can easily be added for the security proofs.

5 Authentication of the Server

In the above we have focused on authentication of C to S, as befits an access control mechanism. However it seems wise in certain situations to also authenticate S to C. Our protocols with ephemeral nonces are ready transformable to versions in which S is authenticated to C first, allowing C to abort early if authentication fails. To achieve this C supplies a masked DH term along with the initial request. S can now compute a confirmation code derived from the putative session key which is transmitted back to C in the second message.

To illustrate, let us consider a transform of the previous protocol where S also authenticates to C via the shared nonce. The round efficiency is preserved by appending new cryptographic data to the first message which previously only contained the logon request:

$$C \rightarrow S : Req_C\,,\ V := H(Nonce_1) \cdot g^z$$

S calculates the confirmation term $X_{-1} := H_2((V/H(Nonce_1))^y)$ and sends it back along with

$$S \rightarrow C : X_{-1}\,,\ X_0 := H(Nonce_1 + 1)g^y\,,\ X_1 := H(Nonce_1 + 1) \cdot (H(w_S^1))^y,$$
$$\cdots, X_k := H(Nonce_1 + 1) \cdot (H(w_S^k))^y$$

C now confirms that $X_{-1} = H_2((X_0/H(Nonce_1 + 1))^z)$ and then proceeds exactly as before:

$$C \rightarrow S : Z_1\,,\ Z_2\,,\ \ldots,\ Z_k\,,\ Z_c$$

with Z_i as above except 1 is added to $Nonce_i$. And finally S can check whether $H_2(Z_j^{1/y}) := Z_c$ for some $j \in \{1, \cdots, k\}$.

6 Conclusions

We have presented a way of merging PAKE-based access control with Honeywords to get the benefits of both:

- Intrinsic protection of the password during login phase.
- Detection of attempts to exploit the compromise of a password file.

We have also presented a variant that incorporates a two-factor mechanism in a very natural way, where the token-generated nonce plays the role of the secondary password. Further, we presented a variant of the protocol in which the honey server S does not directly learn the index of the correct (hashed) password. Finally, we briefly discussed how S can also authenticate itself to the client via the shared nonce while preserving the number of rounds, making masquerading detects detectable early in the protocol.

Acknowledgments. We would like to thank Marjan Skrobot for helpful discussions. We would like to thank the Luxembourg National Research Fund (FNR) for funding, in particular PBR was supported by the FNR INTER-Sequoia project which is joint with the ANR project SEQUOIA ANR-14-CE28-0030-01, and JB was supported by the FNR CORE project AToMS.

References

1. Juels, A., Rivest, R.L.: Honeywords: making password-cracking detectable. In: Sadeghi, A., Gligor, V.D., Yung, M. (eds.) 2013 ACM SIGSAC Conference on Computer and Communications Security, CCS 2013, Berlin, Germany, 4–8 November 2013, pp. 145–160. ACM (2013)
2. Vacca, J.R., Vacca, J.R.: Computer and Information Security Handbook, 2nd edn. Morgan Kaufmann Publishers Inc., San Francisco (2013)
3. Boyko, V., MacKenzie, P., Patel, S.: Provably secure password-authenticated key exchange using Diffie-Hellman. In: Preneel, B. (ed.) EUROCRYPT 2000. LNCS, vol. 1807, pp. 156–171. Springer, Heidelberg (2000). https://doi.org/10.1007/3-540-45539-6_12
4. Jarecki, S., Krawczyk, H., Xu, J.: OPAQUE: an asymmetric PAKE protocol secure against pre-computation attacks. In: Nielsen, J.B., Rijmen, V. (eds.) EUROCRYPT 2018. LNCS, vol. 10822, pp. 456–486. Springer, Cham (2018). https://doi.org/10.1007/978-3-319-78372-7_15
5. Boyen, X.: Hidden credential retrieval from a reusable password. In: Proceedings of the 4th International Symposium on Information, Computer, and Communications Security, ASIACCS 2009, pp. 228–238. ACM, New York (2009)
6. Ford, W., Kaliski, Jr, B.S.: Server-assisted generation of a strong secret from a password. In: Proceedings of the 9th IEEE International Workshops on Enabling Technologies: Infrastructure for Collaborative Enterprises, WETICE 2000, pp. 176–180. IEEE Computer Society, Washington, DC (2000)
7. Bojinov, H., Bursztein, E., Boyen, X., Boneh, D.: Kamouflage: loss-resistant password management. In: Gritzalis, D., Preneel, B., Theoharidou, M. (eds.) ESORICS 2010. LNCS, vol. 6345, pp. 286–302. Springer, Heidelberg (2010). https://doi.org/10.1007/978-3-642-15497-3_18
8. Bonneau, J., Herley, C., van Oorschot, P.C., Stajano, F.: Passwords and the evolution of imperfect authentication. Commun. ACM **58**(7), 78–87 (2015)
9. Abdalla, M., Pointcheval, D.: Simple password-based encrypted key exchange protocols. In: Menezes, A. (ed.) CT-RSA 2005. LNCS, vol. 3376, pp. 191–208. Springer, Heidelberg (2005). https://doi.org/10.1007/978-3-540-30574-3_14
10. Genc, Z.A., Lenzini, G., Ryan, P.Y.A., Sandoval, I.V.: A security analysis, and a fix, of a code-corrupted honeywords system (2017)

HoneyPAKEs (Transcript of Discussion)

Peter Y. A. Ryan(✉)

Luxembourg City, Luxembourg
peter.ryan@uni.lu

Frank Stajano: Just to clarify what you said. The axiom of the system is that the bad guy can steal the password file, but cannot steal the index file?

Reply: Yes. So the index file is assumed to be stored on this honey checker-

Frank Stajano: And you could not store the password file on this more secure honey checker thing?

Well, the assumption is that the login server has to be outward facing to the internet, so it's hard to secure. And the beauty of this architecture is that the honey checker just has a very simple link to the login server, which really just carries an index value, nothing else.

Frank Stajano: Why would it not be possible to put the whole password file on the other side of this very simple link, and only send back, over the simple link, the answer about that particular password?

Reply: Well, maybe you should ask Ari and Ron (joking).

Frank Stajano: I mean, there seems to be some magic dust about this thing cannot be hacked and this one can, but I'm not sure I see the conceptual difference between why one can and why one can't.

Reply: The point is that the architecture is designed such that the Honey Checker is linked to the Login Server through this very trivial channel, which can only carry an index value. The Honey Checker can be minimal in its functionality too: just checking equality of indices and raising an alarm when they don't match. Precisely how these things are implemented, I'm not too sure. But something has to be outward facing and has to run a full API, receive the passwords, compute and compare the hashes etc.

Frank Stajano: I guess my question is why couldn't the password file be in the secure part, and just give the Boolean answer, yes the password is good or is not good.

Reply: Well, I think you would have to pass a lot more over that internal channel. The beauty of this is that this channel is minimal. I think that's the point, but-

Frank Stajano: Alright. I'll let you continue.

Ilia Shumailov: Just to answer your question, I think the idea is, that if an attacker actually breaks into your system and steals the database with passwords, he will not at the same time have access to the indexes which he accesses in real time. Right? So that implies that the attacker actually needs to break into both of those systems to effectively do anything.

Reply: Well, it's certainly true that you have to break two things. But I think also the point is it's much harder to break into the honey checker than the login server.

V. Matyáš et al. (Eds.): Security Protocols 2018, LNCS 11286, pp. 78–83, 2018.
https://doi.org/10.1007/978-3-030-03251-7_8

Frank Stajano: Yes. I still don't quite get why it would not be possible to put the password file into the one that's harder to hack into.

Virgil Gligor: But what if you are saying is true, then you can come up with an equally good protocol that doesn't use honey words. Because you have two servers. I remember working on one some years ago. And basically, you cannot break into the system unless you break into both independently, so-

Reply: Well, there are systems that secret share the password, so there are approaches which do that too. But that's a different approach. And by the way, the beauty of this is that if someone steals your password file, they shouldn't know what is the correct index. So if they try and exploit it, they have to guess which is the correct password. So if they send in the wrong one, that raises alarms. The honey checker finds a mismatch in the index, and that's a fairly clear indication that someone's stolen your password file and is trying to exploit it. So I think that's one of the beauties of this, which was perhaps not stressed enough on the slides. Okay. Was that okay? In which case I can get onto the nub of the matter.

Ilia Shumailov: Can you please explain one more time, where does actually index comparison happen? Which part?

Reply: In the honey checker.

Ilia Shumailov: And what happens then?

Reply: Yes. Perhaps I was skipping things fairly quickly 'cause I thought people were familiar with it. So the login process for honeywords is: the users send in their password, the server will hash that, and will try to find a match in the list. If it finds a match it sends off the index of that match to the honey checker across this minimal channel. And the honey checker stores the correct index, and it does the check. And if they match, then it approves-

Ilia Shumailov: Where does it happen? The check itself.

Reply: In the honey checker.

Ilia Shumailov: So you give the hash... sorry, you give the index to the honey checker and then it says true or false?

Reply: Yes. Peter, do you want to add something?

Peter Roenne: Yes. I just want to say, the honey checker is very, very simple, it only stores indices, right? So it only has a user name and an index, and all it will do is compare whether the index and the user name that it gets will fit that index that has been stored. It's a very simple system, it could be a smartcard or something. And a very minimal channel. So you don't want to store hashes on your honeychecker. It's very simple. So you make it much harder to hack.

Ilia Shumailov: Wait, wait, wait. Did you say you don't store hashes?

Reply: On the honey checker, you don't.

Ilia Shumailov: Wait, wait, wait. But what is the index associated with?

Peter Roenne: There's a client and an index. In the honey checker. That's all. Client and index. Client and index.

Ilia Shumailov: You have a client and a hash?

Peter Roenne: In the honey checker. Not in the server. The server has the hashes. The honey checker has a column of user names, and a column of true indices.

Ilia Shumailov: Can you explain one last thing? What's the actual trusted computing base? Is it only the link to your honey checker? If it is, then what's the actual point of this, if I can see it before the link, and say, okay, everything then is true? If I break into your non-trusted environment, which has this list of hashes, why should I not change the behaviour of this, to eliminate this link and always assume that it's true?

Reply: Oh, okay. So you're talking about if you corrupt the login server, I think? We'll come to that. That is an issue. It's an issue that Ari and Ron didn't address, but I think left as an open question in their paper. We have a previous paper which tried to address that in a different way. But if I get to it, we've got a protocol which tries to address that, toward the end. Is that? So, good point.

Fabio Massacci: In the original paper, is there a minimum number of k you need? Because the server is doing this, right? So the server will have to go through a number of tests. And so you have a limit or upper bound, lower bound on k, for which...

Reply: Well, in the original protocol of course, you mean the Juels and Rivest? Well, I mean that wasn't as complicated. So computationally, I don't think...

Fabio Massacci: No, no. The number k, because you're now making the server do all this computation, right? 'Cause it doesn't know a priori, which is the right one.

Reply: Yes. Yes. Well, what is a typical k? I think the suggestion is it's perhaps 10 or 20 or something. The point is to give a fairly low chance of the attacker guessing the index correctly, but without having to store too many hashes and do too much computation.

Ilia Shumailov: One thing to mention too. Who populates those things into a database? This additional list of passwords.

Reply: Who populates them?

Virgil Gligor: Trusted individual.

Reply: A trusted individual. Exactly, Virgil. Thank you.

Ian Goldberg: Sorry. But if the server's corrupted, why is it talking to the HC at all?

Reply: Well, I think the idea would be that the HC that actually controls whether the access is granted or denied, login server ... And ordinarily, a login server would control the access.

Ian Goldberg: Well then it doesn't sound like a smartcard thing. Like what is it doing to actually say, yes grant access?

Reply: Well, I presume it sends some signal, again over a minimal channel to whatever's controlling the access control. And maybe it's-

Ian Goldberg: Which is usually the login server.

Reply: Which is usually the login server. But...

Ian Goldberg: Which could be potentially corrupted. Like if your HC is a smart card, like you said, it's not actually talking to the database or ... It's just sending one bit "Yes, grant access." But it's just telling it to the corrupted server, which says, "Thank you for your opinion."

Reply: Right, right. Well, I am assuming that it would send an approve login directly to the resource or something.

Ilia Shumailov: The only way that could work. So this is no longer a login server. This is basically your mechanism to say whether a particular password is actually a legitimate one, or somebody just found a hash collision. Right? So the only way this would become a login server, if your server, the original one has actually zero knowledge about which one of those passwords is the real one. And then it performs some sort of computation on this password, and returns it back. And then the server performs some computation or something happens, and gets to the honey checker, and then the honey checker performs some sort of computation on top of it, and then gives it back to the client. And the client does something with it. Because otherwise, there's no connection between the actual person who's trying to, as you say, authenticate. And what's using the output of this authenticator is as...

Reply: Well, we can talk about the various intricacies, as to exactly how the access control is granted in the background.

Ilia Shumailov: But this is not a login server.

Reply: Well, this is really a protocol. I haven't really described all the details of the architecture and the background. And I think, to be honest, we haven't worked out all the details. I'm not sure that Ron and Ari worked out all the details on what happens in the background.

Jeff Yan: I want to ask a little clarification. When actually we use PAKE protocols, do we have to store passwords in the server at all? If actually there's no passwords stored in the server at all, why do we need to actually use this honey words concept? Because as I understand-

Reply: Well, there are augmented PAKEs that store the hash of the password, rather than the password on the server site, if that's what you mean. That already exists. But again, it's vulnerable to someone stealing that file.

Fabio Massacci: So how does the honey checker get the $Nonce_2$ at all?

Reply: Ah. Well, okay. We're assuming that there's another server, which is running the nonce generation on, if you like, the server side. Which is separate from the login server and the honey checker. And it will supply $Nonce_1$ to the login server, on request.

Fabio Massacci: No, but $Nonce_2$. I'm worried about $Nonce_2$. Because $Nonce_2$ is apparently calculated by the client, right?

Reply: It's calculated... So the client has one of these tokens, yes.

Fabio Massacci: Okay. So there is some way in which the client has to give $Nonce_2$ to the honey checker. Otherwise, the honey checker is stuck. Completely stuck.

Reply: Yes. So exactly. So that was what I was coming to. So we have another device which is generating these nonces on the server side. And it communicates $Nonce_1$ to the login server, and $Nonce_2$ to the honey checker.

Fabio Massacci: I'm not sure I buy this.

Reply: And again, it's a minimal channel, because you're just supplying a few bits. But we can argue about the details later.

Fabio Massacci: You have a separate channel, actually, right? 'Cause the meaning... you need trusted channel between the server and the honey... so the client and the honey checker. Through the second server, you have that.

Reply: It's a channel if you like. It's one of these tokens, right? Which is supposed to generate synchronised nonces on the two sides. So that's a sort of channel, if you like. But it's not-

Mark Lomas: I suspect we need to be clear about what the threat model is. And I think that the threat model that the original protocol was supposed to cope with is the attacker has a copy of the back-up tape from the server. They haven't actually broken into the server itself.

Reply: Yes. For the honey words, that's the model. Yes.

Mark Lomas: And it's key to understanding the discussion. To know that that was the threat model.

Reply: That was the original model but, as was raised, you can go to a stronger threat model-

Mark Lomas: You can. But the moment you assume that you can corrupt it, all you need is to corrupt it in such a way, it just doesn't bother talking to this tamper-evident device, the honey checker.

Reply: It doesn't bother talking to it? So somehow bypass-

Mark Lomas: Yeah. Because the honey checker merely sends a yes or no. So basically, you just hardwire it, so it always accepts a yes.

Peter Roenne: Let me to just throw in something quick here. So we actually have several models for the honey checker. One thing is that it could always say, yes or no, grant access or not. But you can also have, and I actually like that model more, it just runs in the background, gets these indices, and then raises an alarm at some point later. So you can have it as a log, and you can later go and check whether these indices actually fit or not and compare with the log of the server. So there, you really need to get the right passwords or indices.

Reply: So there's a lot of discussions we can have about the sort of architecture, which you build in the background. At the moment, we are mostly focused on the protocol on the front end.

Ian Goldberg: I have a totally other concern now. So in this protocol, the hashes don't serve to hide the password at all, right? You don't have to brute force any hashes, because if you get the back-up tape, and you have the hash of the first honey word, the second honey word, the third... You don't need to reverse the hashes to figure out what the honey words are. You can just use the hash of the honeywords in your protocol, right?

Reply: That's probably true, of this one.

Ian Goldberg: You never need to actually reverse the hash, right? So it's... All the hash is doing here is a map from strings to the group, but it's in no way supposed to be a one-way function. So basically, the server is storing clear text passwords, not hashed passwords.

Reply: At least in this protocol, yes I think that's true.

Ian Goldberg: Which seems a poor choice.

Virgil Gligor: Speaking about hashes. How do you get those hashes, which map into the group. I'm talking about real hashes, not just string to output transformations. You divide by the hash. So the hash of any group cannot be zero.

Ian Goldberg: It's in a group. There's no zero in a group.

Virgil Gligor: Well, yeah. But how do you get those? I mean, generally if you have a hash of that sort, somewhere there is an assumption that they are uniformly distributed-

Reply: Yes, such things exist.

Ian Goldberg: There are lots of maps. You can use Elligator or something like that if you're in an elliptic curve group.

Reply: They exist. Yeah.

Virgil Gligor: You're talking about real hashes?

Ian Goldberg: Yeah. Real hashes that map to a uniform string, and then a map like Elligator changes uniform strings into the group.

Frank Stajano: So the more we hit on the same issue, the more I think it matters what is your trusted computing base. This is something you need to address in your revised paper, before you do any other protocols etc. And this would also cover my earlier question of, if you have something that's automatically guaranteed not to be hackable, then why can't you put the password file there? So once you tell us what exactly your threat model and your trusted computing base is, we know which parts couldn't be hacked, which parts can be hacked. And then at that point, you should have a justification for why we cannot put the password file in the trusted computing base.

Reply: I agree. We have to elaborate the threat model and the analysis. If I ever get to my conclusions, that's one of the remarks.

Entropy Crowdsourcing – Protocols for Link Key Updates in Wireless Sensor Networks

Lukas Nemec(✉), Radim Ostadal, Vashek Matyas, and Petr Svenda

Faculty of Informatics, Masaryk University, Brno, Czechia
{lukas.nemec,ostadal}@mail.muni.cz, {matyas,svenda}@fi.muni.cz

Abstract. In this work, we propose a completely different design of key distribution protocols for ad-hoc networks of nodes with restricted resources, wireless sensor networks (WSNs). Earlier research on so-called secrecy amplification (SA) for WSNs went with the discrete "take it or leave it" design – either the newly transferred key components got to their destination securely, or the attacker learned their values. And as the SA measures are probabilistic and preventive in nature, no-one but the attacker knew what the attacker learned (and when Mallory learned a key component, she obviously did not push for the fail-deadly trigger). We propose to combine vanilla secrecy amplification with key extraction from the radio channel, coming up with a novel method to produce and deliver key updates to individual link keys.

1 Introduction

Key distribution is an essential part of any secure network. Our work is focused on one of the areas where symmetric cryptography (due to its efficiency) is preferred over public-key cryptography: wireless sensor networks (WSNs) and internet of things (IoT) systems. These usually come with many hardware limitations and focus on energy conservation. To add even more complexity, we are assuming a mesh-type network, therefore point to point communication may require multiple hops and neighbours are not known in advance, only after the network deployment.

The aim of our research is to improve the overall security of such a network, in the best case scenario even continually through the whole lifetime of the network. We are assuming use of link keys (every link in the network has its own key) and a potential compromise of a fraction of link keys. Using a combination of two known techniques: secrecy amplification and key extraction from the radio channel, we provide a method to produce and deliver key updates to individual link keys.

1.1 Key Extraction from Radio Channel (KEx)

Key extraction from radio channel uses random properties of wave propagation, shared in between both parties communicating over such radio channel, for gen-

V. Matyáš et al. (Eds.): Security Protocols 2018, LNCS 11286, pp. 84–92, 2018.
https://doi.org/10.1007/978-3-030-03251-7_9

eration of a secret shared bit sequences. Although the communicating parties do not obtain exactly same data, KEx algorithms are designed to minimalise errors and match correlated values into exactly same outputs.

The underlying idea is following: two nodes send each other messages repeatedly over a public channel and both upon reception record received signal strength (RSS) of received messages. Both nodes then transform series of RSS measurements into a bit string using quantization algorithm; example of such is shown in a Fig. 1. Follows the information recognition phase, which ensures both parties produce the same bit string, again using only discussion over a public channel. Successful execution of KEx, therefore, results in bit string shared between two parties, produced only via public channel, and known only to these two parties. Comparison of several algorithms for KEx can be found in [4].

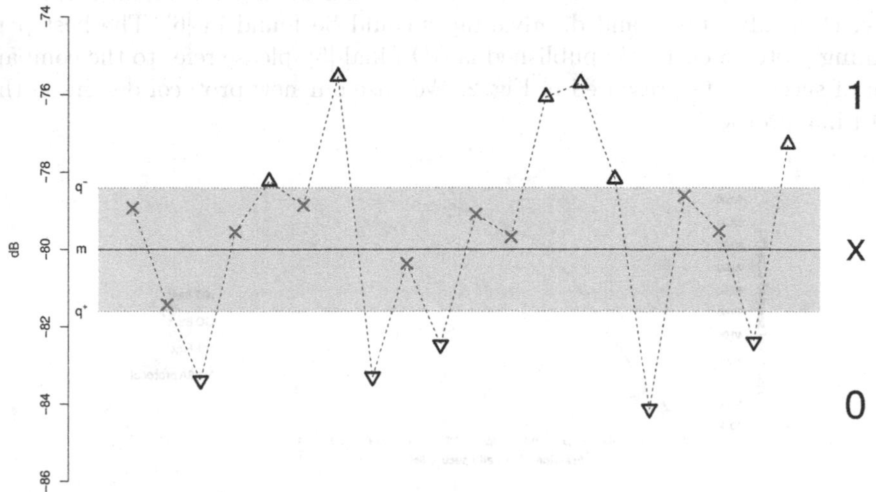

Fig. 1. Example of quantization algorithm, points in the graph represent a sequence of RSS measurements. Two thresholds q^+ and q^- are on the border of greyed out area. Measurements in between these thresholds are dropped, values above are converted to ones, values below are converted to zeroes. In this particular case, the outcome sequence would be: 01100111001.

Such approach may look like a silver bullet for most of the key distribution problems, however, there is one major pitfall. Static networks in undisturbed areas produce low amounts of entropy, even over long periods of time. Therefore rendering common KEx useless in such conditions.

1.2 Secrecy Amplification (SA)

Secrecy amplification protocols were firstly introduced in [1] as an improvement for plaintext key establishment, but could be used for partially compromised networks as well. A secrecy amplification protocol defines a way how a group of neighbours cooperate to re-secure a previously compromised part of the network using a non-compromised paths to deliver key updates. The number of such paths could be very large and it is not feasible to try all of them. SA protocols need to balance a trade-off between consumed resources by the SA protocol (e.g., energy or number of messages transmitted) and an improvement of security (number of secure links).

Previous work [7] presented the ability of SA protocols to increase a fraction of secured link keys from 50% of compromised link keys to 90% of secure keys after the SA protocol execution. The exact results depend on a particular attacker model, the initial key establishment protocol, and the particular SA protocol being used. Different SA protocols are suitable for different scenarios.

There are three different types of SA protocols – node-oriented, group-oriented, and hybrid designed protocols. A detail description of each protocol type, their advantages and disadvantages could be found in [6]. The best performing protocol currently published is HD Final [5], please refer to the comparison of success rate presented in Fig. 2. We base our new protocol design on the HD Final protocol.

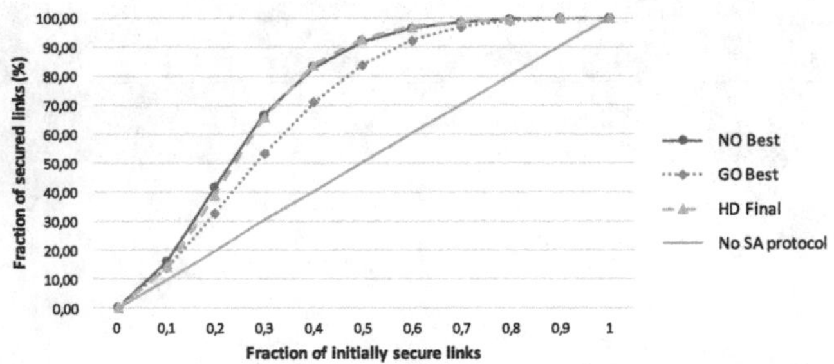

Fig. 2. NO Best and GO Best represent the best node - and group-oriented protocols respectively. Increases in the number of secured links after the secrecy amplification protocols are executed. A strong majority of secure links (>90%) can be achieved using a secrecy amplification protocol, even when 50% of all network links are initially compromised. The performances of the node-oriented and hybrid designed protocols are comparable, and both significantly outperform the group-oriented protocol.

1.3 Proposed Solution

Our goal is to utilise basic concepts of SA and combine entropy gathered by KEx on multiple links into a key update for a single link. Using entropy from multiple links allows us to produce and deliver the key update in a shorter time while using KEx only might not produce any key update at all.

We demonstrate our algorithm using 3 nodes from our network (named A, B, and C), all mutually neighbours. Every link has established link key K, such key is unique for every particular link in the network. KEx is executed on all 3 links in between nodes A, B, and C; we refer to the resulting KEx bit string as a En, which is shared between two nodes[1].

2 Attacker Model

We assume a global passive attacker, with the initial network compromise as introduced in [3]. With respect to the KEx part, we limit the attacker position so that the KEx would not be vulnerable to the passive attacker (attacker has to be over $\frac{\lambda}{2}$ away from legitimate nodes). In addition we assume that the attacker is able to brute force any key with entropy lower than 80 bits.

3 Push Protocol

Let the gathered entropy within a bitstring En for every link be over half of a defined *threshold*. All messages during the protocol execution are encrypted using the already present link keys, in addition to any other encryption provided by the Push protocol.

Node A generates a random nonce N to update the link key K_{AC} with node C using the Push protocol (with intermediate node B). Node A encrypts the nonce N using the En_AC as a key and sends the resulting value $E_{En\_AC}(N)$ to the node B. Intermediate node B encrypts the received value using the En_BC as a key and sends the resulting value $E_{En\_BC}(E_{En\_AC}(N))$ to the node C. Since node C knows both En_AC and En_BC, it is able to recover the original nonce N. Nodes A and C then proceeds with the key update procedure as in any other SA protocol and create a new link key K'_{AC}. Graphic visualisation of the Push version can be seen in Fig. 3.

3.1 Security Analysis in Brief

We can inspect several outcomes based on previous states of individual links, note that already secure links remain secure (same as in original SA).

Link Key K_{AC} is compromised. We rely on the nonce N to secure the link. If both link keys K_{AB} and K_{BC} are secured, the result is equivalent to the usual SA. When both link keys are compromised; the attacker has both messages $E_{En\_AC}(N)$ and $E_{En\_BC}(E_{En\_AC}(N))$ and is able to brute force both En_AC and En_BC consecutively. Therefore the attacker is able to get the nonce N and the updated key K'_{AC}.

Also in a case of K_{AB} being compromised and K_{BC} secured, the attacker has message $E_{En\_AC}(N)$, which he is able to brute force and therefore get the nonce N and the updated key K'_{AC}.

Finally, in a case of K_{AB} being secured and K_{BC} compromised, the attacker has the message $E_{En\_BC}(E_{En\_AC}(N))$, where the combined entropy of En_AC

[1] The individual bit string is denoted as En_AB for nodes A and B.

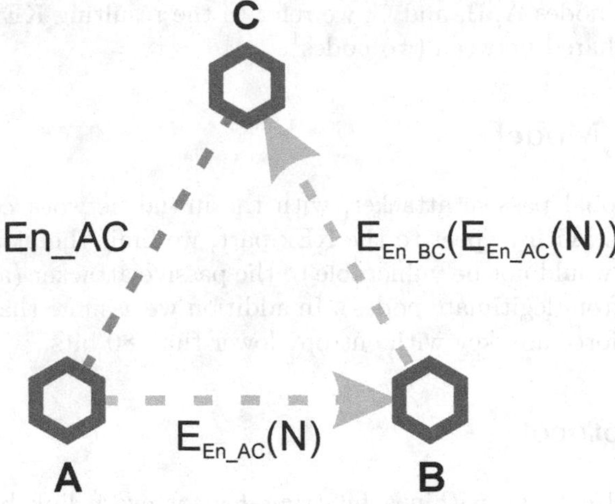

Fig. 3. Visualisation of the push version.

and *En_BC* exceeds our threshold, therefore the attacker is not able to get N by brute force. Thus once we use the nonce N to produce updated key K'_{AC}, the link becomes resecured.

When compared to usual SA, we can see the benefit that only one link has to be secure, more specifically it has to be the link from the initiating node to the intermediate node.

4 Pull Protocol

As introduced in [2], in a Pull version of SA protocols the key update is initiated by the intermediate node. Same as in the previous case, node B shares *En_AB* with node A and *En_BC* with node C, in addition, node A also shares *En_AC* with node C.

Node B sends messages $E_{En\_AB}(En\_BC)$ to node A and $E_{En\_BC}(En\_AB)$ to node C (both encrypted by the already present link keys). Node A then decrypts *En_BC* and node C decrypts *En_AB* from the received messages. Now nodes A and C can use all three values *En_AB*, *En_AC*, and *En_BC* to create a key update, producing a new link key K'_{AC}. Graphic visualisation of the Pull version can be seen in Fig. 4.

4.1 Security Analysis in Brief

In all cases, we add *En_AC* to the key update and since *En_AC* is never send in any message, we consider it to be secure. Granted the sufficient entropy contained within *En_AC* we improve the security of the link key only by using *En_AC* in the key update.

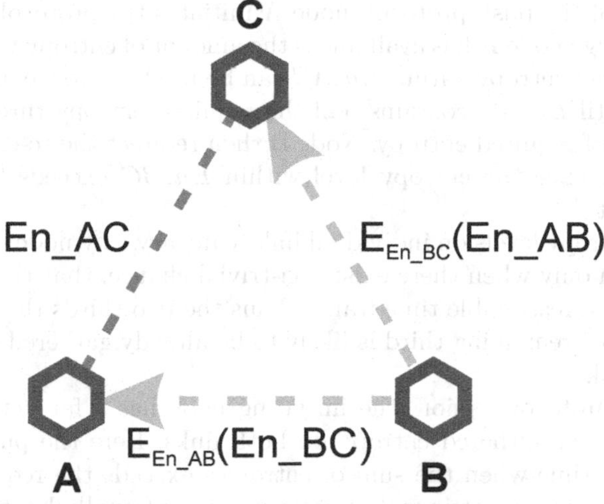

Fig. 4. Visualisation of the pull version.

We rely on the three values *En_AB*, *En_AC*, and *En_BC* to resecure the link. We are only concerned about the confidentiality of values *En_AB* and *En_BC* since these values are sent over possibly compromised links.

Therefore, if both link keys from node B (keys K_{AB} and K_{BC}) are secure, values *En_AB* and *En_BC* will be transferred over corresponding links without any issues and the key update can be successfully made. In case of one link compromised (the issue is symmetrical to either side) attacker obtains message $E_{En\_AB}(En\_BC)$, but he has nothing to brute force the *En_AB* value against, rendering the update successful.

In the event of both link keys being compromised, the attacker can brute force both messages $E_{En\_AB}(En\_BC)$ and $E_{En\_BC}(En\_AB)$ against each other, receiving a majority of the key update sources.

When we compare the pull version (of our new protocol) to the traditional SA, again only one link has to be secure to produce a successful key update. Compared to the push version, both require at least one link to be secure. However, the pull version will benefit from any link being secure[2].

5 Entropy Tresholds

Considering simplified examples presented in Figs. 3 and 4 with three nodes, one of these three nodes initiates the selected protocol. However, such node has only limited knowledge of gathered entropy amounts (two out of three links to be exact).

[2] The push version requires the link from the initiating node to the intermediate node to be secure.

In the case of the push protocol, node A initiates the protocol and the only relevant knowledge node A has available is the amount of entropy within En_AC. Since the gathered entropy within En_AC can be used only once, node A should wait at least until En_AC contains half the required entropy threshold, ideally over two-thirds of required entropy. Node B then redirect the re-encrypted message to node C, once the entropy level within En_BC exceeds the remaining required amount.

Since the entropy levels on individual links can vary, any node should initiate the push version only when there exist non-trivial chance, that the protocol will be completed in a reasonable time frame. Thus the two-thirds threshold is more beneficiary, as the remaining third is likely to be already gathered on the second participating link.

In the pull protocol version, the initiating node has a far better stance, as it knows amount of gathered entropy on both links. Here the pull version can be initiated any time when the sum of entropies exceeds the required amount. Depending on the initial settings, the protocol can optionally be initiated before the required amount of entropy is collected, as we add to the final key update also the entropy collected over the third link.

6 Previous Work

Assuming we have enough entropy gathered on fraction of individual links in the network, we have no need to combine entropy over multiple links. However, we can still benefit from combination of both approaches.

6.1 Naïve Combination

The naïve way to combine SA and KEx would be to employ both without any interaction in between these. In such combination, KEx would be executed through the whole lifetime of our network, with occasional execution of SA. Employing both SA and KEx at the same time should come with greater benefit, as both provide an increase in the number of secure links.

Even though this approach uses combination of SA and KEx, the benefit from using both techniques is not that significant. As both approaches require non-trivial amount of resources, deploying them in such naïve combination would be quite short-sighted.

6.2 Entropy Driven Secrecy Amplification

To utilise advantages from employing both SA and KEx, we proposed entropy driven secrecy amplification. Same as in the case of naïve combination, KEx is executed through the whole lifetime of our network, gradually gathering the secret shared bits in between neighbours. Naturally, links with a high volume of traffic will collect more bits than others.

Using the results from KEx, we can guide the intensity of SA on every link. Therefore on some links, SA will not be executed (reducing the amount of messages required), while on other links we execute the preferred SA protocol of choice. Using this combination we can reduce the amount of messages required for successful SA execution and by saving communication we ultimately save energy.

7 Conclusions (Preliminary)

In this paper, we have presented a protocol for link key updates, utilising two different concepts and combining them together. Our work is based on secrecy amplification protocols, which we enhanced with the key extraction from radio channel fading. We propose two versions of our new protocol: push and pull approaches.

Using the KEx, we gather entropy on all links in the network. In the push approach, we send a random nonce N to the intermediate node, encrypting the message with a key derived by KEx through the link to the destination node. The intermediate node re-encrypts the nonce N using its key derived from KEx on the link to the destination node and sends it to the destination.

In the pull approach, the update is initiated by the intermediate node that sends opposite results from KEx to the destination nodes, encrypting it using the complementary KEx results on respective links.

Compared to the classical SA approach, both versions require only one link to be secure.

Choice between these two options should be made during the network operation, based on entropy estimates on KEx results, as the different levels of gathered entropy on individual links will favour either push or pull approach.

We have following open questions:

- Both versions (push & pull) have their advantages. At which time should we select which one to use; prior to network deployment or in ad-hoc fashion during the network operation?
- In the push version of the protocol, since node A does not know the amount of entropy collected on link between nodes B and C, at what entropy level should certain node initiate the protocol?
- Has the concept of adding entropy from multiple sources (some possibly compromised) been used in other protocols proposed for some other environments/contexts?

Acknowledgements. Czech Science Foundation project GBP202/12/G061 partly supported this work.

References

1. Anderson, R., Chan, H., Perrig, A.: Key infection: smart trust for smart dust. In: 12th IEEE International Conference on Network Protocols, pp. 206–215. IEEE (2004)
2. Cvrcek, D., Svenda, P.: Smart dust security key infection revisited. Electron. Notes Theor. Comput. Sci. **157**(3), 11–25 (2006). Proceedings of the First International Workshop on Security and Trust Management (STM 2005)
3. Eschenauer, L., Gligor, V.D.: A key-management scheme for distributed sensor networks. In: 9th ACM Conference on Computer and Communications Security, Washington, DC, USA, pp. 41–47. ACM (2002)
4. Jana, S., Premnath, S.N., Clark, M., Kasera, S.K., Patwari, N., Krishnamurthy, S.V.: On the effectiveness of secret key extraction from wireless signal strength in real environments. In: Proceedings of the 15th Annual International Conference on Mobile Computing and Networking, MobiCom 2009, pp. 321–332. ACM, New York (2009)
5. Oštádal, R., Švenda, P., Matyáš, V.: Attackers in wireless sensor networks will be neither random nor jumping – secrecy amplification case. In: Foresti, S., Persiano, G. (eds.) CANS 2016. LNCS, vol. 10052, pp. 552–561. Springer, Cham (2016). https://doi.org/10.1007/978-3-319-48965-0_34
6. Oštádal, R., Švenda, P., Matyáš, V.: On secrecy amplification protocols. In: Akram, R.N., Jajodia, S. (eds.) WISTP 2015. LNCS, vol. 9311, pp. 3–19. Springer, Cham (2015). https://doi.org/10.1007/978-3-319-24018-3_1
7. Švenda, P., Sekanina, L., Matyáš, V.: Evolutionary design of secrecy amplification protocols for wireless sensor networks. In: Second ACM Conference on Wireless Network Security, pp. 225–236 (2009)

Entropy Crowdsourcing – Protocols for Link Key Updates in Wireless Sensor Networks (Transcript of Discussion)

Lukas Nemec(✉)

Faculty of Informatics, Masaryk University, Brno, Czechia
xbukac@fi.muni.cz

Ilia Shumailov: Could you explain, what's the trusted environment model in here?

Reply: The protocol is executed on separate nodes, separate devices, and they communicate which each other, just send messages one to another, and these messages contain the sequence number of the particular message.

Ilia Shumailov: How do I know when his message started?

Ian Goldberg: What do you mean, when his message started?

Ilia Shumailov: How do I know when I should start recording?

Ian Goldberg: Oh, you mean how do you know to expect to receive the message?

Reply: This I would consider being a rather low-level radio control, which we do not deal with in the protocol design. We expect to have software provided with the radio, which, depending on the system design, can either trigger an event or set some flag, which you have to check periodically. All the values, e.g., message payload, or RSS, are then provided by the radio software.

Jean Martina: Can't you just synchronise clocks, and out of synchronised clocks try to derive when it's time to record and when it's time to expect an incoming message?

Ian Goldberg: Yes, but that way lies madness.

Reply: Let's go to the secrecy amplification: the basic idea is that we start with a partially compromised network; some links in the network are compromised, some links are secure, and we use our neighbours to transfer key updates. I will show you an example how this is done. We have our network; some links are compromised, some links are secure, and if these two nodes want to secure the link in between them, they send a key update over using their neighbour to secure the link.

Frank Stajano: Do you know which of your links are secure and which are compromised? How do you know that?

Reply: We don't know which of the links are secure, which are not, and we don't care. We just try enough times to increase the security of our network.

So, now let's talk about the attacker model. We assume the global passive attacker during the operation of our protocol, and we assume that there was some initial network compromise; therefore some links are compromised, some links are secure.

V. Matyáš et al. (Eds.): Security Protocols 2018, LNCS 11286, pp. 93–95, 2018.
https://doi.org/10.1007/978-3-030-03251-7_10

From key extraction, we take the condition that the attacker is located more than half the wavelength away from regular nodes. Thus the attacker records different RSS values than the legitimate nodes, and these values are of no use to him. We also assume that attacker is able to brute force any key which has a lower amount of entropy than the set threshold. In our case, we set the threshold for 80 bits.

What was the motivation for our protocol?

When we played with the key extraction, we realised that it generates some amount of entropy, but on static networks, it generates quite low amounts of entropy. So, we decided to use principles from secrecy amplification to combine multiple entropies over multiple links into one single key update.

So our setup for our protocol is that we have three nodes: Alice, Bob, and Cecil. There are link keys over every connection, possibly compromised, and we assume that key extraction over every link guarded at least half of the required entropy for the threshold. So in our case, 40 bits.

Ian Goldberg: You're getting individual measurements; you're getting a fraction of a bit from one measurement.

Reply: We can get approximately 40 bits from a sequence of thousands of measurements.

Ian Goldberg: Right, so you do a sequence of thousands of measurements, and you can get 40 bits, but you're not willing to do two thousand measurements to get 80 bits; you'd rather do this complicated protocol.

Fabio Massacci: The antenna is what costs. If I talk to some of my colleagues that do wireless sensor networks: computation, it's as much crypto as you want; but antenna is what costs. Especially because antennas have to be on when they listen and transmit, so this is what really costs them. They don't worry about computation.

Reply: Thank you for the explanation.

And now to the protocol itself. This is the Push version of the protocol, and it's initiated by Alice, who generates a random nonce and sends it to Bob; encrypted with the key extraction result that Alice shares with Cecil. Bob obviously cannot decrypt this message, but he can encrypt it once again with what he shares with Cecil, and send it to Cecil. Therefore, Cecil can decrypt both layers of encryption and get to the random nonce. So this is the protocol itself and now to the analysis of it.

Let's say we have both links secure; then the result is the same as in case of unmodified secrecy amplification; we get a successful key update without caring about our encryption added to the origin of link keys.

In the case of both links being compromised; our attacker then, therefore, can brute force these values consecutively, because he has both of these messages and can get to the random nonce, once the nonce is used somewhere in communication.

The next option: if only the first link is compromised and the second one is secure, then still attacker can brute force this value because the first layer contains less than 80 bits, and once the nonce is used, he can get to the right value.

But in case of only second link being compromised, the cumulative encryption with two values is stronger than 80 bits, and the attacker cannot brute force this value.

Thus we require only one secure link, compared to regular secrecy amplification. This was the push protocol; in the proceedings is also the Pull version of this protocol, which is quite similar.

We also tried other approaches to combine these two techniques, and one of them is what we call entropy driven secrecy amplification, and the idea here is that we employ both of these techniques at once, and we use the results from key extraction as a parameter for secrecy amplification. Some links are then directly secured by key extraction, while on the others we execute secrecy amplification. We also tried this in an experiment with our network of 20 nodes and 70 links in between them; we were able to secure six links directly using key extraction, and then because of this, we were able to save 144 messages out of, quite a lot actually, but saving energy for secrecy amplification part.

Now let's go to the conclusions. We have our protocol, which requires only one secure link to transfer key updates securely in a network, compared to regular secrecy amplification, which requires at least two secure links to transfer a key update. The combination of these two is very dependent on a network environment. So in the areas of dynamic networks, there will be quite a lot of disturbances, and key extraction will be able to secure most of the links on its own. However, in areas of static networks, the key extraction will struggle to produce any entropy at all.

Ian Goldberg: Is there a way for the node to measure how much entropy it has?

Reply: Sure; You get the resulting bit string from the key extraction, and you can run the min-entropy estimates; there are several functions how to do it. For example, how much you can compress the bit string.

I will end now with some open questions. The first one: whether you know of a similar concept of adding entropy together being used in different areas, contexts. And the second one, in a push protocol the node A doesn't obviously know how much entropy is over the second connection from node B to node C, so when should be the right time to execute a protocol? Should it be when on the link from node A to the node C (the first encryption layer) is half of the required entropy? Should it be when there are two thirds? We don't know yet, so if you have any comments on this one.

Jean Martina: Have you tried anything over an ad hoc network? Because then your measurements on the amount of energy you're using there may be much less because you're already using nodes to route and then you can collect all this entropy, or you can keep feeding the entropy with time.

Reply: Yes, definitely. In our experiments, we are collecting the RSS measurements from the regular traffic, so if the nodes are routing the regular traffic, they are measuring the RSS values and collecting the entropy.

Daemones Non Operantur Nisi Per Artem

Daemons Do Not Operate Save Through Trickery: Human Tailored Threat Models for Formal Verification of Fail-Safe Security Ceremonies

Taciane Martimiano and Jean Everson Martina(✉)

Programa de Pós-Graduação em Ciência da Computação, Departamento de Informática e Estatística, Universidade Federal de Santa Catarina, Florianópolis, SC, Brazil
tacianeemartimiano@gmail.com, jean.martina@ufsc.br

Abstract. In this paper we argue that we must impoverish (or enrich in a different sense) threat models in order to be able to verify fail-safe security protocols that include human peers (a.k.a. security ceremonies). Some of the threat models we use nowadays for establishing the security of communication protocols are far too much concerned with failing deadly and do not encompass subtleties of the real world. Security is then maintained at all costs, especially in the presence of human constraints and expectations. Our position is that we must assume omnipresent and omnipotent evil beings (daemons) do not exist in order to be able to verify fail-safe security protocols that include human peers. We show how a popular security ceremony could be made fail-safe assuming a weaker threat model and compensating for that with usability. We also discuss the impact of our work for formal verification techniques and how they can be expanded for security ceremonies.

Keywords: Threat models · Security ceremonies
Formal verification · Fail-safe security ceremonies
Human-peer security protocols

1 Introduction

In the past we discussed how important it is to establish the goals of security protocols in the presence of human constraints and in the real environment where they will be used [9]. Security protocols fail too often, and mostly due to misunderstandings at design time. These misunderstandings have to do with misconceptions in preconditions and/or in environmental assumptions. Sometimes protocols assume strong assumptions or twist the environmental conditions where they execute so that a worst case scenario threat model can be addressed.

We also argued in the past [5] that Dolev-Yao's [6] threat model, the "de facto" standard used in protocol design and verification is powerful but not suited to be used as-is when we are trying to encompass human interactions

V. Matyáš et al. (Eds.): Security Protocols 2018, LNCS 11286, pp. 96–105, 2018.
https://doi.org/10.1007/978-3-030-03251-7_11

with protocols. In our paper [5] we break down Dolev-Yao's attacker capabilities into atomic actions and create an adaptive way of using them. In that paper we argued that some of Dolev-Yao's capabilities are not present when we have human-to-human interactions, such as the fabrication or blocking capabilities. Furthermore, allowing such things which do not respect the laws of physics in the presence of humans is equivalent to assume omnipresent, omnipotent evil beings (daemons) exist.

More recently we went deeper into the relation of threat models and the subtleties they entail on the formal verification process of security protocols in the presence of humans [8]. We started to symbolically evaluate security ceremonies in the presence of multiple attackers which are constrained in their capabilities depending on the layer of execution they are attacking [4]. We try to leave the daemons out of the equations and to construct more human friendly interactions with security protocols. This experimentation taught us that to represent the reality where humans and protocols co-exist we must take into account potentially uncountable threat models. This is a requirement if we want to make protocols fail-safe to the human peer behind the screens.

We have also seen that this topic of human interaction with security protocols has been fully discussed in the last couple years. We can cite Roscoe's detection of failed attacks on human interactive protocols [11]. He proposes a method to test and design security protocols that have human interactions where attacks can not be misdiagnosed as communication failure. In his work he introduced the concept of protocols being auditable for humans and the fact that transformations are time-dependent. Our position is that Roscoe's work can be reinterpreted taking a different view on threat models. We believe that Roscoe's work can be extended in the sense of transforming communication failures into fail-safe scenarios for users.

Bella [3] argue that security should encompass human beings while remaining invisible. They introduce various security protocols that can be constructed involving human peers and advocates that making security less present can help the user to participate more willingly. He also brings to attention that integration of security protocols that involve human peers need to be done with other socio-technical facets of the task that the user is trying to accomplish. Our position regarding Bella's work is that to properly integrate human interaction with security protocols, we need to be able to assess its security in more formal manner. To do so we need threat models to establish whether security is available or not. We can, by establishing plausible threat models for security ceremonies, enter the realm of verifying fail-safe characteristics of such human-protocol interactions and deliver the invisibility proposed by Bella et al.

Finally our position is that to properly design security ceremonies in a systematic and secure way to fail-safe, we need to understand and adapt threat models to presence of human peers. We also defend that this can ultimately be done using theoretical tools such as First-Order Theorem provers with standard protocol verification techniques.

This paper is organised with this introduction, followed by a background Sect. 2 to present some concepts we used to develop our verification framework. Then, we describe our mechanisation strategy in Sect. 3. Section 5 has our Bluetooth case study ceremony, alongside with our justification for threat modelling choices. Finally, Sect. 6 brings our final thoughts and conclusions.

2 Background

To be able to demonstrate our strategy for the design and verification of security protocols in the presence of human peers (a.k.a. security ceremonies), we need to present some of the background work on that field (Sect. 2.1). We also present some threat models for symbolic evaluation (Sect. 2.2) by giving a historical context, and classifying threat models regarding capabilities.

2.1 Security Ceremony Layers

Bella et al. argue that a ceremony can be layered and analysed on specific sections of its description. For that, the Concertina approach establishes security and privacy in the presence of humans. By doing so, they present a ceremony model which links technology to society through five layers, ranging from computer processes to user personas [2], as follows:

- Layer 1 (L1) - Informational: stands for the insecure network, where we have the protocol running between processes on the communicating devices;
- Layer 2 (L2) - Operating System: intermediate level between the protocol (executing on behalf of the user) and the process that runs the interface for that user;
- Layer 3 (L3) - Human-Computer Interaction: socio-technical protocol whereby a user interacts with a user interface. This layer is crucial for the protocol to reach its end, and achieve its goals;
- Layer 4 (L4) - Personal: related to the user expressing a given persona while interacting to the interface;
- Layer 5 (L5) - Communal: shows the society influence over the user behaviour.

From all five layers, protocols just focus on the first layer once they only handle network traffic. Ceremonies enable us to study layers 2 and 3 as well. Thus, we cover layers L1 through L3 in our work (being the layers related to computer science research). As stated in the work of Bella et al. [2], layers L4 and L5 are strongly related to social science (which is out of our scope), as such layers deal with the non-deterministic nature of the human being itself. Layer 4 concerns the mindset of the user when interacting with the system, while layer 5 represents the influence of the society over the user's behaviour.

2.2 Threat Models

In Ellison's words: "A ceremony can be designed and analysed with variants of the mature methods already in use for a network protocol."[7]. As such we need threat models to enable such symbolic evaluation. We start with the Dolev-Yao (DY) which is the "de facto" standard attacker model for security protocol design and symbolic evaluation.

A Dolev-Yao attacker controls the network channel, being capable of altering, copying, replaying and creating messages [6]. However, the attacker is not allowed to perform cryptanalysis and guessing random numbers. A protocol considered secure against such attacker is also considered secure against less powerful ones.

In addition to the DY model, we have one of its variants: the Multi-Attacker (MA) model [1]. This model allows each participant protocol to behave maliciously, intercepting and forging messages. Nevertheless, each agent of this model neither colludes nor shares knowledge with any other agent, bringing insights such as retaliation and anticipation attacks [1].

We use in our verification framework MAs (besides the well-known Dolev-Yao) to exemplify attackers acting in more than only one channel. As standard for protocol messages, a DY only acts on messages being transmitted through the network (namely L1 only). It is convenient to emphasise that both models do not allow the attacker to share information with any other attack in the system.

Alongside attacker types DY and MA, we use Martimiano and Martina's Distributed Attacker (DA) [8]. They consider that each layer can have more than one attacker associated to it, so several attackers are allowed to be distributed throughout the layers of the ceremony. The distinction among the three attacker types we used is summarised in Table 1 [8].

The DY attacker has fixed capability set and appears only in layer 1 (network). It is possible for MAs to control several layers, however their set of capabilities must not change. As for DAs, they can also be in several layers, with the differential of possible distinct capability sets for each one of them.

Table 1. Comparison among attacker types

Attacker type	Share knowledge	Fixed capabilities	Different layers
DY	No	Yes	No
MA	No	Yes	Yes
DA	Yes	No	Yes

The DA approach is most unique for its sharing feature: an DA may share knowledge with other DA attackers, attempting to corrupt the system by himself and/or colluding with others. In contrast, a DY never shares his knowledge as it would contradict its own rules. Similarly, MAs cannot share either.

In real life, DAs who share information stand for different attackers being in distinct places (attacking a network from home and eavesdropping the user on the street, for instance). Those DAs who do not share can be seen as waiting for the opportunity to share. Such behaviour is encouraged in order to demonstrate the power of sharing, mainly when human peers are considered.

Regarding the attacker's capabilities our verification framework uses Carlos et al. ideas [5]. If we overestimate the attacker's capabilities in a ceremony, we will probably end up designing complex ceremonies which tend to be more complicated and not followed by users. On the other hand, if we underestimate the attacker, we might have a flawed ceremony. They proposed an adaptive threat model approach for security ceremonies, which we based our framework upon. In their model, the designer can remove capabilities from the whole DY capability set in order to make the attacker more realistic. They define the DY set as containing *Eavesdrop* (E), *Initiate* (I), *Atomic Break Down* (A), *Block* (B), *Crypto* (C), *Fabricate* (F), *Spoof* (S), *Re-order* (O), *Modifying* (M) and *Replaying* (R). Over the network, they set the standard DY threat model as it is its default setting [5].

2.3 Notation Syntax

The notation chosen started with the early paper from Needham and Schroeder [10]. Showing each step of the protocol in numbered lines, it has the sender on the left of the arrow denoting the flow of information and the receiver on its right. The message contents are shown after the receiver.

Martimiano [8] added the Ceremony Concertina layers in order to have a more detailed view of the information pathway. The idea here is to pinpoint the layers being crossed by each message as it is sent from one end to the other of the communication parties.

Furthermore, Martimiano [8] related each layer of the Concertina methodology to one or more attackers, and their correspondent capability set, accordingly to the threat models mentioned in the previous subsection.

The steps now are numbered in a dot separated version to represent the crossing of subsequent Concertina layers by each message. For example, step "2.1" stands for the first layer of the second message of the ceremony. Sender and receiver remain each on either side of the arrow just as in the protocol syntax. Nevertheless it is below the arrows that layers L1, L2 and L3 were added for the ceremonies description. The threat model (capability set) and attacker type (DY, MA or DA) are beside the layer contents in each step. Lastly, the messages come out at the rightmost part of each step [8].

The capability set for each attacker is either the full Dolev-Yao set of capabilities or a subset of such set - accordingly to the adaptive threat model of Carlos et al. [5].

Martimiano defines four different threat models for a Concertina layer [8]:

- "N": represents safe model, meaning the absence of threat model (no attacker);
- In case of a subset (of the DY full set of capabilities) with just one capability, we write it in capital letter (e.g. "E"). In this case, the attacker has only such capability;

- In case of a subset of capabilities with size greater than one, we use the symbol "+" to split the notation of the capabilities. For instance, "E + B" stands for the attacker subset of capabilities containing Eavesdrop and Block.
- "DY": full set of the DY attacker capabilities; in other words, an active attacker. Mainly used for the network layer.

A DY attacker is always linked to the DY full capability set, and never to a subset of these capabilities. On the other hand, MAs and DAs may have varied capability sets. More importantly, they can appear in more than one layer throughout the ceremony. For this reason, we give each MA and DA a number to serve as their unique identification (e.g. MA_1).

3 Mechanisation Strategy

We developed our verification framework as a set of scripts in Python that parses ceremonies in .tex format following Martimiano's syntax to the input format .dfg of the theorem prover SPASS [12]. As we displayed the ceremonies in LaTeX throughout this paper we as well use it as input of our program.

TexReader is our class responsible for parsing the tex, via regular expressions, and creating a ceremony object properly initialised with its contents. Our Ceremony class stores all needed information about the scenario in case so that it is clear what a writer should receive. In our case, our writer is SpassWriter, which passes through all the agents, threat models and messages to create all the formulae specified in the SPASS syntax, such as predicates and conjectures.

Our code is easily adaptablc to other formats, though. The reader and writer classes (or even methods, if one prefers) can be programmed to translate a ceremony, say, in JSON to some other theorem prover once provided all needed ceremony info. This information, mentioned as attributes of class Ceremony, regards basically ceremony agents (senders and receivers of messages, besides attackers), message steps themselves, layers and threat models in the order occurred.

Our main method arranges for the list of ceremonies to be parsed and run in SPASS in order. The produced files have the same name of the original one, only the extension changes. We follow Martimiano and Martina's ceremony basic model for SPASS [8], so each new ceremony .dfg file starts with as a copy of this model and is incremented through the iterations of the writer. All our scenarios in tex and its corresponding generated files, as well as our code is available at: https://github.com/tacianem/SpassModel.

In the list of conjectures we can test the possibilities of sharing among the DAs for each scenario, or to test different scenarios to find the best solution for a specific problem, such as failing-safe.

4 The Devil Lies in Details

Carlos et al. [5] believe an over-powerful attacker to be unrealistic in certain cases, especially those related to the human peers. Having an attacker that may overcome the laws of physics, and interfere with human speech or direct human action is usually above reason for ceremonies. We go even further, in that assuming such threat models to be possible is equivalent to allow for daemons (omnipotent, omnipresent and evil being) to dictate how we design security protocols and ceremonies.

Thus, the adaptive threat model of Carlos et al. is also part of our solution, since we assume attackers only capable of attacks reasonable from a human perspective. This is in fact one of the main characteristics of our verification framework. It also allows us to design and verify security ceremonies with reasonable attacks from the user perspective, enabling us to easily encompass security features that enable fail-safe situation in the execution for security ceremonies.

5 Bluetooth Fail-Safe Security Ceremony

We now describe the design and verification process to add a fail-safe strategy to the Bluetooth pairing protocol, adapting it from the work of Carlos et al. [5] by adding the non-diabolic threat models. We also show how it can be proven to fail-safe securely in the presence of reasonable attacker using our security ceremony verification framework.

1	B	$\xrightarrow[L2_{(N)}, L1_{(DY)_{DY}}]{}$	A :	$C_b = f1\ (PK_B, PK_A, N_b, 0)$
2	A	$\xrightarrow[L2_{(N)}, L1_{(DY)_{DY}}]{}$	B :	N_a
3	B	$\xrightarrow[L2_{(N)}, L1_{(DY)_{DY}}]{}$	A :	N_b
4	A	$\xrightarrow[L2_{(N)}, L3_{(N)}]{}$	U_A :	$V_a = g\ (PK_B, PK_A, N_a, N_b)$
5	B	$\xrightarrow[L2_{(N)}, L3_{(N)}]{}$	U_B :	$V_b = g\ (PK_B, PK_A, N_a, N_b)$
6	U_A	$\xrightarrow[L4_{(N)}]{}$	U_B :	V_a
7	U_B	$\xrightarrow[L4_{(N)}]{}$	U_A :	V_b

Fig. 1. Scenario 1 - default bluetooth ceremony

Figure 1 is our ceremony adaptation for phase two of the Bluetooth secure simple pairing (SSP) using the Numeric Comparison (NC) mode from Carlos et al. work, where we apply the Concertina layers instead of the DD (device-device), HD (human-device) and HH (human-human) channels as presented in their work. As we simply put it as a protocol, we have the standard DY attacker for the network and safe environment for the remaining layers. Besides, we have compressed layers as it is even suggested by Bella et al. [2] in their proposal of the Concertina methodology, once it is simpler to analyse what is happening at each step.

Essentially, the first three messages start on each device's own operating system and cross to the other device via Internet. Messages 4 and 5 also start on the operating system of devices A and B, and reach the user interface (layer L3). Finally, messages 6 and 7 are related to the users' interaction in order for the ceremony to achieve its goals, and be completed. For more details on the contents of each message payload, see [5].

$$
\begin{array}{llll}
1 & B & \xrightarrow[L2_{(E)DA_1}, L1_{(DY)DY}]{\hspace{6em}} A : & C_b = f1\ (PK_B, PK_A, N_b, 0) \\
2 & A & \xrightarrow[L2_{(E)DA_1}, L1_{(DY)DY}]{\hspace{6em}} B : & N_a \\
3 & B & \xrightarrow[L2_{(E)DA_1}, L1_{(DY)DY}]{\hspace{6em}} A : & N_b \\
4 & A & \xrightarrow[L2_{(E)DA_1}, L3_{(N)}]{\hspace{6em}} U_A : & V_a = g\ (PK_B, PK_A, N_a, N_b) \\
5 & B & \xrightarrow[L2_{(E)DA_1}, L3_{(N)}]{\hspace{6em}} U_B : & V_b = g\ (PK_B, PK_A, N_a, N_b) \\
6 & U_A & \xrightarrow[L4_{(N)}]{\hspace{3em}} U_B : & V_a \\
7 & U_B & \xrightarrow[L4_{(N)}]{\hspace{3em}} U_A : & V_b
\end{array}
$$

Fig. 2. Scenario 2 - Eavesdrop on both devices

For our second scenario (Fig. 2) we only vary the threat model for the first three messages, considering a DA attacker on the devices operating system. Such attacker has only the subtle yet powerful capability of Eavesdrop, as it is already sufficient enough for him to get all information computed and processed in each device. In here, the attacker is not able to actually modify any contents, however.

$$
\begin{array}{llll}
1 & B & \xrightarrow[L2_{(E)DA_1}, L1_{(DY)DY}]{\hspace{6em}} A : & C_b = f1\ (PK_B, PK_A, N_b, 0) \\
2 & A & \xrightarrow[L2_{(E)DA_1}, L1_{(DY)DY}]{\hspace{6em}} B : & N_a \\
3 & B & \xrightarrow[L2_{(E)DA_1}, L1_{(DY)DY}]{\hspace{6em}} A : & N_b \\
4 & A & \xrightarrow[L2_{(E)DA_1}, L3_{(E)DA_2}]{\hspace{6em}} U_A : & V_a = g\ (PK_B, PK_A, N_a, N_b) \\
5 & B & \xrightarrow[L2_{(E)DA_1}, L3_{(E)DA_2}]{\hspace{6em}} U_B : & V_b = g\ (PK_B, PK_A, N_a, N_b) \\
6 & U_A & \xrightarrow[L4_{(N)}]{\hspace{3em}} U_B : & V_a \\
7 & U_B & \xrightarrow[L4_{(N)}]{\hspace{3em}} U_A : & V_b
\end{array}
$$

Fig. 3. Scenario 3 - Eavesdrop on both devices and on users' environment

Next, Fig. 3 brings our third scenario, we bring another DA attacker, now on the same environment as the users ("shoulder-surfing" them). Such physical intrusion can compromise significantly the insurance of several ceremonies once most people do not watch their back while entering critical credentials in their devices, for instance.

Given that we expect both users to meet and exchange messages 6 and 7, we set our second DA to be around both users (which are not distant from each other themselves), hence controlling two different communication channels over the same layer (L3).

Similarly to DA_1, the second DA is only able to observe at best (in this case, the users' devices screens) and does not alter anything. The two of them are capable of sharing their knowledge (as explained in [8]), if they both agree.

It is worth noting that we are not varying the threat model of layer L4 as it is out of computer science scope and therefore we limit ourselves to assessment of layers L1 up to L3 solely. Our code for the ceremony scenarios above is in: https://github.com/tacianem/SPW18

6 Conclusions

During the formal verification and specification of security ceremonies for the Bluetooth pairing protocol we were able to detect that some actions could be included in the security ceremony to make it fail safe.

With a reasonable (non-diabolic) threat model we can design a ceremony where the user can be advised to execute the pairing in a specific setting. For example for devices that execute numeric comparison, but that do not have a good interface for showing the numbers (or use fixed numbers), we could change the protocol so that before pairing a precondition is to scan the Bluetooth spectrum trying to find other devices around. This can be used to either interrupt the pairing because it could lead to a possible man-in-the-middle attack from the other device, or at least to let the user know that he is in this somewhat insecure setting.

Having an automated verification framework where realistic, fine grained threat models can be easily tested for security ceremonies, allowed us to come with a series of ceremonies which aim to avoid that the human-being behind the device fall in an insecure setting which could jeopardise his secure communication effort. This is one of our main contributions for this work.

As future work we plan to embed more threat models to our security ceremony verification framework, as well as creating a more usable interface and to make the proof interpretation process easier for the ceremony designer.

References

1. Arsac, W., Bella, G., Chantry, X., Compagna, L.: Multi-attacker protocol validation. J. Autom. Reason. **46**(3–4), 353–388 (2011)
2. Bella, G., Curzon, P., Giustolisi, R., Lenzini, G.: A socio-technical methodology for the security and privacy analysis of services. In: COMPSACW (2014)

3. Bella, G., Christianson, B., Viganò, L.: Invisible security. In: Anderson, J., Matyáš, V., Christianson, B., Stajano, F. (eds.) Security Protocols 2016. LNCS, vol. 10368, pp. 1–9. Springer, Cham (2017). https://doi.org/10.1007/978-3-319-62033-6_1
4. Bella, G., Coles-Kemp, L.: Layered analysis of security ceremonies. In: Gritzalis, D., Furnell, S., Theoharidou, M. (eds.) SEC 2012. IAICT, vol. 376, pp. 273–286. Springer, Heidelberg (2012). https://doi.org/10.1007/978-3-642-30436-1_23
5. Carlos, M.C., Martina, J., Price, G., Custodio, R.F.: An updated threat model for security ceremonies. In: Proceedings of the 28th Annual ACM Symposium on Applied Computing, SAC 2013, pp. 1836–1843. ACM, New York (2013)
6. Dolev, D., Yao, A.C.: On the security of public key protocols. IEEE Trans. Inf. Theory **29**(2), 198–208 (1983)
7. Ellison, C.: Ceremony design and analysis. Cryptology ePrint Archive, Report 2007/399, October (2007)
8. Martimiano, T., Martina, J.E.: Threat modelling service security as a security ceremony. In: 2016 11th International Conference on Availability, Reliability and Security (ARES), pp. 195–204, August 2016
9. Martina, J.E., Carlos, M.C.: Why should we analyse security ceremonies? In: First CryptoForma workshop, May 2010
10. Needham, R.M., Schroeder, M.D.: Using encryption for authentication in large networks of computers. Commun. ACM **21**(12), 993–999 (1978)
11. Roscoe, A.W.: Detecting failed attacks on human-interactive security protocols (transcript of discussion). In: Anderson, J., Matyáš, V., Christianson, B., Stajano, F. (eds.) Security Protocols 2016. LNCS, vol. 10368, pp. 198–205. Springer, Cham (2017). https://doi.org/10.1007/978-3-319-62033-6_22
12. Weidenbach, C.: SPASS input syntax version 1.5. Max-Planck-Institut fur Informatik (2007)

Daemones Non Operantur Nisi Per Artem

Daemons Do Not Operate Save Through Trickery: Human Tailored Threat Models for Formal Verification of Fail-Safe Security Ceremonies (Transcript of Discussion)

Jean Everson Martina(✉)

Programa de Pós-Graduação em Ciência da Computação,
Departamento de Informática e Estatística, Universidade Federal de Santa Catarina,
Florianópolis, Santa Catarina, Brazil
jean.martina@ufsc.br

Ian Goldberg: So this reminds me of a talk I saw Frank introduced at Usenix Security[1] some number of years ago, where the speaker was a magician I think and the idea was that there's an adversary who really can trick you in real life into seeing things that aren't real, and interfering with real life communication through sleight of hand and trickery and things like that. So by supposing such a demon doesn't exist, perhaps you're opening a door to that ab nihilo attack where I deceive you in real life and through sleight of hand in order to disrupt your ceremony.

Reply: Frank?

Frank Stajano: An interesting observation. I had a completely different one, which is that, if you start your investigation by saying, "I think that the formal verification of just the network part of the protocol is insufficient. I need to do it end to end where the ends are the actual human beings," then I fully agree with the assessment. Formal verification to a machine to machine part is insufficient. On the other hand, I believe that the reason why it fails is because it is impossible accurately to model the things that humans do. So as soon you start saying formal verification, and then you say all the things done by the humans, I think that's going to be where it fails.

Reply: Sort of, and I'll have some slides later on explaining how we sliced the problem. We didn't get to the human part yet, but we realised that there are some places where it fails and the verification can be easily mechanised. For example, when I have my protocol running, should I assume that the machine running is controlled by a virus or a worm? What happens to my protocol if that happens? What happens with my protocol if I have a two factor authentication, and my phone is Chinese, and my operating system is American? Will they cooperate to exchange information just to overthrow me? We don't know and we don't test that! What we are trying to do in these early stages is not to get to that human to human part because we also believe that this may not be work for computer scientists alone. This is work for social scientists, and we need a

[1] Frank Stajano and Paul Wilson. 2011. Understanding scam victims: seven principles for systems security. Commun. ACM 54, 3 (March 2011), 70–75. DOI:https://doi.org/10.1145/1897852.1897872.

V. Matyáš et al. (Eds.): Security Protocols 2018, LNCS 11286, pp. 106–113, 2018.
https://doi.org/10.1007/978-3-030-03251-7_12

lot of interaction to start grasping on that. But there are some things like the layers that Giampaolo and Lizzie Coles-Kemp[2] came with three or four years ago, and how we can interleave things in there.

Frank Stajano: I think the core of my objection is that it is formal methods that are incompatible with the ultimate human part, which is what I understood at the beginning of your introduction was your ultimate aim to get at. I think that anytime you try to model that, in the modelling you will lose something where a smart attacker would be able to insert an attack.

Reply: When we touch the human part, the formal verification of the human part, in fact we were inspired by a talk from Ross here in 2010, about the hats, that people when doing things keep changing hats.

Frank Stajano: I was the coauthor of that with Ross who gave the talk[3].

Reply: Great! Maybe we cannot grasp specific human behaviour, but we can test the ceremony against those hats, right? We can formally model a guy that will click everything. And that happens a lot! The guy just wants to achieve his goal, he doesn't read what's on the screen, he will click next. This is very easy to model because it's an erratic behaviour where the guy will just go through to achieve the goal, and will not actually encompass the problems that are in between. To me it is still not clear we will be able to get to the humans. But we see that there are some research that show that problems tend to happen because people have some pattern of erratic behaviour. And if we can at least demonstrate that our ceremonies can survive those problems, it's much better than not looking to them at all. We can already do some things with first-order theorem provers and get answers out of that. I agree that there may be some tricks, but assuming that the person tricking you is present all the time is also an overshot. So the idea here is, okay, it may be insecure under certain domains, under certain circumstances, but we can alert you on that. We can design the protocol to alert when you get into some situation that you may be tricked. So that's where we based our ideas. Giampaolo and Lizzie came with this idea of a security ceremony concertina where we have layers, and in all these layers, we have what they called "informational layer" that is the security protocol that we are used to. We then have OS, HCI, personal, and communal layer. Basically what we are trying to do so far is to reach this point between HCI and personal, because we believe that this part can be actually treated with formal methods. We don't know how these other parts here will be, if they will ever be. But it's much more looking to that here than only the security protocol. And we can find assumptions that can actually be fulfilled, or can actually be checked in execution time, and can give the guarantees of the proof

---

2 Bella G., Coles-Kemp L. (2012) Layered Analysis of Security Ceremonies. In: Gritzalis D., Furnell S., Theoharidou M. (eds) Information Security and Privacy Research. SEC 2012. IFIP Advances in Information and Communication Technology, vol 376. Springer, Berlin, Heidelberg.

3 Anderson R., Stajano F. (2014) Its the Anthropology, Stupid!. In: Christianson B., Malcolm J. (eds) Security Protocols XVIII. Security Protocols 2010. Lecture Notes in Computer Science, vol 7061. Springer, Berlin, Heidelberg.

that we ended up creating with the formal method. Another thing that we did was to evolve the idea of threat models. We have the classic Dolev-Yao, that does not share information because it is only one almighty powerful attacker. And for us it works only on the protocol layer, so it cannot shift from one layer to another, and it has a fixed set of capabilities. Then there is some work on symbolic evaluation threat models, that was presented in here some time ago, that is the Multi-Attacker[4]. In the Multi-Attacker we have different Dolev-Yao attackers that do not share information among themselves. And then you can, with this threat model, get to retaliation attacks. You can detect and retaliate an attack that you were suffering. And you can demonstrate that using formal methods. And then we came out with the Distributed Attacker (DA), because in our setting, Dolev-Yao is a Cold War threat model. You have another, a very powerful nation that is against you, it is polarised, then you see just the other guy as the bad guy and that's how it works. But after Cold War, we had seen multiple attackers. What does it mean? There are a series of states that do not share information among themselves and that see all the others as evil, and then that's how it works. Giving sense to the Multi-Attacker. But then, since 2012 with Snowden, we've seen that this is actually not true because there may be the case where the British and the Americans share information to achieve some goal. And then when we design our protocols and our ceremonies, we need to be aware that our execution architecture should be conflicting, right? So if my phone is Chinese and my software is British, I might have guarantees that the attack will not work. But if I use my phone and my computer is within the five eyes countries that share the information among them for counter terrorism I'm not secure against that. So we had to tailor this idea of threat models to bring it to our reality right now, where we are not against an almighty powerful state, and we are not against a series of states that do not cooperate, but we can have this exchange. And if we want to be secure, we need to compensate for that.

Mansoor Ahmed: So in your second model, wouldn't the cluster of knowledge sharing entities just eventually become equal to a single country in an MA model? Is there some sort of incentive modelling them in the knowledge sharing cluster?

Reply: Yes. In the Distributed Attacker they will only share when they gain something, it's not sharing everything, so they do not become a single country in MA mode. The confusion comes when someone say: "Okay, if you have two of these guys cooperating, then it is another MA that is more powerful than the others, or that has more coverage." But in the DA case, they choose what to share. They may share or may not. And then what we do in our formal verification framework is to test what happens if they share, and if they do not share. At design phase of my protocol or ceremony I may be trying to find something that is powerful enough to counteract this sharing.

---

[4] Arsac, W., Bella, G., Chantry, X. et al. J Autom Reasoning (2011) 46: 353. https://doi.org/10.1007/s10817-010-9185-y.

Mansoor Ahmed: Wouldn't network effect just essentially make it so that you end up with one entity being the biggest knowledge sharing entity? And then everyone has to join that network to acquire knowledge.

Reply: If we look back to Dolev-Yao, there is a paper[5] where there is a demonstration that if you use multiple Dolev-Yaos, you end up with a single one, and only one is as powerful as having many. But what we want is to uncover subtleties when doing formal verification, because if we assume that there is only that powerful attacker, all the problems will end up in a single basket. And what we want to see is a series of baskets, and see where is the problem. I want to understand why I'm not achieving this goal. The answer may be I'm not achieving this goal because two states may cooperate. So I'll have to change my design to cope with that or live with it. I may need to alert the user. In our case here, what we are proposing is that we may get to an HCI specification where we need to tell the user, "Look, this is secure assuming that you use technology that has conflict of interest between who is monitoring it." We assume that you are always monitored for example in all layers.

Patrick McCorry: I'm just wondering, do you have any other examples of when they wouldn't share information to get a positive gain? You're saying here that there's multiple parties, and they'll only share information when they get a deal from doing that. But do you have any good examples of when they won't share information?

Reply: When it's strategic or commercially important. For example, you have countries that record everything you do online. The sharing usually has the purpose of going against terrorism, but there are still commercial disputes between those nations. And they will not share information where they will lose the edge on something that can put them in front economically, for example. So they will balance between the gains of counteracting terrorism and the financial gains that it can have on their economy. So that's how it conflicts. The information may be available for example here in Britain, but it's not shared with the US because that information is in a strategic sector of the economy in here that will take out the edge of the British peers against the Americans. So the government may choose not to share. So that's a scenario. Then what we started doing was we went to study Bluetooth, because we realised that on the original specification of Bluetooth there was a ceremony. That happened back in 2012 when I was working with Geraint Price and one of his students. Bluetooth was conceived as a protocol for pairing devices. But if you read the specs, there are loads of details on how human interaction should happen on that. And basically for our formal verification framework we started augmenting some things. In the work with Geraint, we realised that we could break down Dolev-Yao into some atomic actions. For example, eavesdropping, or replaying, or breaking down messages, composing new messages out of previous knowledge we learned from the execution. We basically get our specification, and we translate it to a set of first-

[5] Jonathan Herzog. 2005. A computational interpretation of Dolev-Yao adversaries. Theor. Comput. Sci. 340, 1 (June 2005), 57–81. DOI=http://dx.doi.org/10.1016/j.tcs.2005.03.003.

order horn classes, and smash it with a first-order theorem prover to extract security properties automatically.

Ilia Shumailov: Can you explain please, does your model allow an observation of information flow between the different layers?

Reply: Yes. We can model a layer without any threat model and basically ignore it from the verification point of view. In this sense it is a straight flow. If we compress all but the informational layer we are actually verifying a protocol and not a ceremony.

Frank Stajano: Just a technical question. Why do some things have two subscripts in succession?

Reply: This is the attacker and the capabilities that the attacker has. In this full ceremony where, for example, I have a Distributed Attacker that has only eavesdrop capability, he cannot add new things, he can only listen passively to what's going on. This may represent that there is something on the operating system that is recording what's going on. It is a reasonable scenario for me, keeping in mind that in the network we still have full Dolev-Yao happening. But if I have a worm that actively interferes with my things, then I would say that this guy has more capabilities, such as eavesdrop and probably fabrication or replaying, and then I add those to the ceremony. In our formal model, instead of having a full set that create the rules for what the Dolev-Yao can do, to get to the full Dolev-Yao, I need to turn on each one of the capabilities, and then I can turn them on and off during the verification. This helps me to see different baskets. And it is interesting to see we are doing this verification assuming, for example, that when we have on the operating system one Distributed Attacker, so one nation that has embedded something into your operating system, we then have some other Distributed Attacker that is shoulder surfing the user, for example. On layer three, there is eavesdropping on the HCI, so we can encode for the equivalent of shoulder surfing. If these two guys are different attackers, then they may not share information. And what happens is that I may be secure. This would not be captured by a full Dolev-Yao. We did some other example with two-factor authentication. We assumed that it is secure because we have two different devices that are under different threat models. If we take a mobile phone, for example, and assume that it has exactly the same threat model as my computer, it doesn't make sense to have two-factor authentication. So I have to assume that they are under slightly different threat models, and probably controlled by different attackers. Then a two-factor authentication can be demonstrated secure. If I assume that the attacker is the same person, so it's full Dolev-Yao, then the guy will get my one time password and my user name and password on the computer.

Ilia Shumailov: Coming back to the question I had earlier. Practice has shown that the side channels exist in every layer of the computer operational stack. In this case for example, you are saying there is some level three eavesdropping meaning HCI eavesdropping. That eavesdropping could actually say something about the operating system, like how fast, how responsive your system is. It could actually say stuff about the underlying operations within the operating system, or even smaller network players. And so I don't see this being reflected in here, because in here each of the layers don't mention any other layers. Eavesdropping through side channels, this is the common way to actually steal information.

Reply: Right. In fact, that's the proposition. This is still under development and that's why it was submitted to this workshop. And we're trying to give a minimal coverage right now, but we know that some things will have to be expanded in the future. So I agree with you, we'll have to, in some way, look for side channels, and to encode that on the ceremony description.

Peter Roenne: Could you remind me what is the layer four? And why is there no eavesdropping?

Reply: Layer four is human-to-human communication. It's the idea that we have two phones, two devices, two Bluetooth devices with screens that pair, and then they show a number that one user should tell the other. So this is the user A reading the value that was generated by his device to user B, and then user B reading it back so that there is confirmation that they generated exactly the same number.

Peter Roenne: Yes, but why no eavesdropping?

Reply: We haven't touched layer four yet, because then we have to think about how to formally encode human behaviour. So we are giving one step at a time. And actually, I agree with Frank. I don't know if it will be possible. But we started doing some experiments with this idea of the hats I mentioned earlier. Keeping with the presentation, we did some tweaking on the Bluetooth protocol. We didn't change the protocol, we just changed the ceremony that is described with it. We realised, for example, that if you have devices with no screens, we may change the protocol so that the device helps the user to know if the threat model is in favour of him or against him. So for example, we did some trials where we changed the protocol so that before letting the user pair their phone with their headphones, it scans Bluetooth around to see if there is someone with the radio on. Or it turns on GPS to know if he is at home or at a public location. And then you can alert the user saying, "Look, this is not secure under these circumstances. Do you want to go through?" So the idea here is that we are trying to design the ceremonies to be fail safe, or to help the user to fail safely. And that's why the theme of the workshop was spot on for what we were doing. And about mechanisation, now we have a series of Python scripts that get all that description and translate them into first-order horn clauses. And it's then pushed to SPASS, that is a first-order prover. We have a parser that parses straight from Latex that description, and then writes all the ceremony data, peers, layers, messages, and everything in First Order Clauses, automatically. We then push this in the form of predicates, axioms, and conjectures into SPASS for each scenario. We get the information out and we parse it back to human readable information.

Ross Anderson: Yeah, you get this in many human ceremonies. Some things could be done only in particular places, weddings can only be conducted at premises licensed for the purpose, some kinds of transactions need witnesses, and so on. So perhaps the thing to do is drive it from a human layer rather than from a formal layer, a means of describing the circumstances in which particular ceremonies are acceptable.

Reply: I agree, in fact we base most of our work from that human part, but I don't know if this is work for computer scientists. In fact we've been talking to psychologists and to crime specialists and it's very difficult to get something that will bind these two different worlds of computer protocol security with the real world. But I agree it makes sense. My final remarks: during formal verification specification of security ceremonies for the Bluetooth, we were able to detect that some actions could be included into the ceremony so that it makes it fail safe, that's the message. So we can help the user to detect that the threat model is not safe for him at that very moment. And it would be good if people started doing that for other protocols.

Daniel Weitzner: I agree, you're never going to be able to perfectly bind these two worlds, because they don't speak in the same terms. But I was very encouraged by your effort to move into the HCI zone. More than the benefit of possibly verifying some protocols, which I think you're going to have too many unknowns in them, I actually think you could help the interface designers quite a bit to reflect what the security assumptions are, even if they don't understand them perfectly.

Reply: What we are doing is that. We are actually writing down what the HCI designers need to care about. And when people design protocols, this is never written. So that's one thing that I believe can start helping in the short term. But the long term goal would be trying to find human weaknesses, because that's what drives most of the effects these days.

Ilia Shumailov: So just a suggestion, maybe the way to think about that would be the bandwidth of information flow. Humans are very limited in the amount of information they can observe over time, and the amount of information they can process over time. Similarly for side channels, or actually any sort of eavesdropping, it will be limited by the bandwidth.

Reply: We have that encoded on this idea of the dynamic threat model. In our early paper[6], for example, one thing that we do not assume is that human channels would have crypto, because humans cannot encrypt their communication on the fly. They can tweak it a little bit, but we would not get the strength of the encryption that exist on the computer channel. So in some sort of way, we already have this idea in there. It's not well-developed, but we already have this idea that there are different bandwidths within the communication.

Virgil Gligor: How many people out of the entire population of users of computers do you believe understand any threat model?

Reply: They do not, but they understand their own world. I'm transferring the actual decision that is very specialised and very complex, even to ourselves that are specialised on that subject, to a design of the HCI, or the interaction that the person will have with the device so that the device can assist the person in

[6] Martina, J.E., dos Santos, E., Carlos, M.C. et al. Int. J. Inf. Secur. (2015) 14: 103. https://doi.org/10.1007/s10207-014-0253-x.

saying: "Okay, look, it may not be a good idea to pair your headphones with your phone if you are inside Heathrow Terminal 5 and there are another 20 Bluetooth devices in range, because someone could do a man-in-the-middle attack on that." I should not use those words, but I can just tell them, "Look, it's not a good idea. Would you like to try to do this at home, or do you need it now?"

Daniel Weitzner: It means you could make a mistake. You don't have to say man-in-the-middle, you could just say something could go wrong, right? The risk is higher.

Reply: We didn't get to that language, but we are sure that we can embed something in the protocol where at least it gets enough information to give the user the power of choice, because today he will pair it, and he actually is subject to that threat model.

Virgil Gligor: But the user might not even know that that protocol exists.

Reply: But he wants to listen to music! His main goal is to listen to music. So should I listen to music here? And is it secure for that? Maybe he doesn't care even about security, but we should give him the possibility of knowing that it may not be a good idea to do that at that very moment. Then the wording that we will use is unclear to me. It is subject to more research. But what we cannot do is say, "Okay, it's fine, pair wherever you want. And then if someone is in the middle, fine." And then the protocol fails badly. We are trying to make it fail safe.

Peter Roenne: Maybe a more technical question. So in the approach of David Basin of modelling humans[7], just say they can do everything except a few secure routes that they will follow, and they do this in Tamarin. Would it be possible to do something like that in SPASS, which is Horn-clause based?

Reply: I don't know, it's very likely that we have to move to higher order, to encode that. But then to move to higher order we have another problem, we don't have full mechanisation, we have guided proving.

[7] D. Basin, S. Radomirovic and L. Schmid, "Modeling Human Errors in Security Protocols," 2016 IEEE 29th Computer Security Foundations Symposium (CSF), Lisbon, 2016, pp. 325–340. https://doi.org/10.1109/CSF.2016.30.

Intentionality and Agency in Security

Kat Krol(✉), David Llewellyn-Jones, Seb Aebischer, Claudio Dettoni, and Frank Stajano

Department of Computer Science and Technology, University of Cambridge, Cambridge, UK
{kat.krol,david.llewellyn-jones,seb.aebischer,claudio.dettoni, frank.stajano}@cst.cam.ac.uk
https://mypico.org

Abstract. In this paper we explore the tension between automatic security and intentionality. During a user trial of Pico we offered two proximity authentication modalities: scanning a QR code, or pressing a button in the Pico app that is available only when the user is in Bluetooth range of a machine they can authenticate to. The feedback from this trial provides an insight into users' expectations with regard to intentionality. We discuss how this relates to the Pico authentication solution, how it has informed future Pico design decisions, and we suggest some ways in which security and usability researchers could address the issue of intentionality in future security design.

1 The User Experience of Security

Weiser [22] said that "the most profound technologies are those that [just blend in and] disappear". Security software has been at odds with this principle because it attempts to attract user attention whenever possible—it has been largely designed to be *visible* to the user and ask them to *take action*. For example, anti-virus software proudly tells the user how many viruses it has stopped, while websites display padlocks and security seals. Users are disrupted in their work by security notifications; they are asked to read warnings and decide whether they want to heed or ignore them.

One may question the motives behind software wanting to be more visible and requiring user action. Arguably, the best security experience would be that nothing bad ever happens, therefore good security should mitigate threats in the background and never be visible to the user. However, the parties offering security products aim to sell their offerings, and informing the user how effective they are is part of their sales strategy. Users should be satisfied that buying a security product to protect their devices is the right thing to do, and that they're not just wasting money on software that might not be doing anything at all. Vendors therefore design their products to make users aware of what the product is doing. At the heart of designing security software there has always been a conflict between truly effective security and business interests, as highlighted by Anderson [1].

V. Matyáš et al. (Eds.): Security Protocols 2018, LNCS 11286, pp. 114–125, 2018.
https://doi.org/10.1007/978-3-030-03251-7_13

More practically, when it comes to user actions, security software sometimes requires a decision from the user because it may not be ready to handle all situations. Often this boils down to a question of liability—by ignoring a warning, the user is forced to concede they are not making the company liable for any damage that might occur to their machine.

This sad state of affairs has led security researchers to argue that demanding more user attention and effort cannot be the way forward. Herley [8] emphasises that rejecting security advice may be rational from an economic point of view because certain security mechanisms are broken. For example, most certificate warnings are false positives and heeding them may cost users time and thus result in unfinished work. Elsewhere, Herley [9] calculates that, if every one of the two billion online users spends five seconds a day entering a password, this will result in a cost of 1,389 person-years of human effort per day. He stresses that human effort is a valuable resource and should be used wisely.

There has been a persistent view that "security has to be hard to be effective" and for many years now there has been a movement to blame failed security on a failure to educate users. As a consequence of this, people now feel their involvement in the security process is an intrinsic requirement for maintaining security. Users feel the need to perform certain tasks—security rituals, if you will—to ensure their active participation in the security process, even though in practice these tasks don't improve security in any tangible way, as shown in a study on 2-factor authentication in online banking by Krol *et al.* [12]. There remains a tension between automatic security and intentionality, which the security community must understand empirically if it is to truly achieve seamless security. In this paper, we will explore this tension, how it relates to the Pico authentication solution, and some of the ways security and usability researchers can attempt to address this in future security design.

2 Authentication and Agency

The user experience of passwords has not been great. Users today are asked to create a strong, long and unique password for various devices, websites and services. They are asked not to reuse passwords and to have a Chinese Wall in their head not mixing personal and work-related passwords. Despite passwords being a user experience disaster, alternatives have not taken off. Passwords are still superior on several security, usability and deployability fronts. Passwords are very flexible and alternatives might not offer enough control. It might be, for example, because some password alternatives do not support the features of passwords that users like, such as delegation: while it is easy to share your Facebook password with your best friend as a sign of trust, it is impossible to do so with something that is secured by biometrics. Users might be uncomfortable trusting a third party with access to all their accounts.

One of the fundamental considerations of human-computer interaction (HCI) is that there is a tension between human agency and computer agency—between how far the user has to express their intention as opposed to the computer anticipating user needs and taking action on their behalf.

Agency is related to the concepts of *automaticity* and *intentionality*. As devices and systems are becoming smaller and more pervasive, the user cannot keep making choices all the time and expressing their actions because it would be too time consuming, and it would require a user interface that isn't available, so there is a gradual shift towards more automaticity. There are many ways in which the user can indicate intentionality. Jia *et al.* [11] discuss the notions of *human and object agency* for Internet of Things (IoT) devices saying these can adopt more intuitive modalities such as input relying on movement and other natural actions. The authors bring up the example of E-ZPass tags which are active RFID transponders attached to a car that facilitate the collection of toll tax. As the car passes by a toll booth, the presence of a unique radio signature is registered and the driver is charged for the use of the motorway. The presence of the E-ZPass tag is sufficient for the car to be charged. There are alternative models across the world, commonly with gates where the user has to stop at a booth, queue until it's their turn, pay the toll by cash or card and only then can continue on their journey. Research by Currie and Walker [4] has demonstrated that E-ZPass has improved traffic fluidity, led to reduced congestion and air pollution, and improved health for those living in proximity of the collection areas. However, the E-ZPass has also attracted criticism from civil liberty campaigners [10] because a government agency has deployed E-ZPass readers throughout Manhattan at many more locations than needed for paying road tolls. Location data coming from the E-ZPass has also been used against the intended purpose. Ulatowski describes its regular use as evidence in civil lawsuits [21] for example; as often happens, we see here a tension between convenience and security/privacy.

Another example of intentionality in automatic payment is the deployment of contactless cards where the user only taps their card on a reader and no longer has to slot their card into a Point of Sale machine and enter their PIN. While contactless cards have a usability advantage in that the number of steps to make a payment has been reduced and the user no longer has to recall and enter their PIN, users have been worried about making accidental purchases without realising as shown in a study on payment methods by Krol *et al.* [13]. For example, Transport for London (TfL) allows passengers to pay for travel using either a dedicated travel smartcard—the Oyster card—or a contactless bank card. If the user taps their wallet containing both cards at an entry point to the London transport network, they might be charged on the card they did not intend to pay with. As a result, TfL [20] has been advising passengers to touch only one card on their card reader instead of a whole wallet in order to avoid a card clash. In terms of security, contactless cards have been demonstrated to be easy to attack as illustrated by Emms and colleagues [5,6] so users not only worry about accidental payments but also about attackers stealing their money.

There are similar problems in other mechanisms, for example in the case of smart keys for cars. When using a traditional key, the user expresses their intention to unlock the car (and *that* particular car) by taking their key out, putting it in the keyhole, turning it and opening the door. With a smart key, the user can just approach the car, keeping the key in their pocket, and the doors unlock and the engine starts without them having to touch their key. However, this great convenience and presumed intentionality can have security implications. Relay attacks have been demonstrated both in academic research by Francillon *et al.* [7] and real-life cases as publicised by the media [3]. If more intentionality was required and the user had to press a button on the key, the type of attack where someone else unlocks the car while the victim was otherwise concerned and didn't intend to unlock any car at all would be far less likely to succeed. What does this mean for computer security?

3 Intentionality and Pico

During the design of Pico [14,19], we have always worked from the assumption that users would want to explicitly express their intention as to whether they would like Pico to log them in or not. We first worked on Pico as a dedicated physical device and envisioned the user could express intentionality in different ways. In his talk at USENIX 2011 [18], Frank Stajano suggestioned that the user express intentionality by pointing the Pico's camera at a QR code and pressing a button (see Fig. 1). Since then, the idea has evolved from a physical device to a smartphone application.

Fig. 1. Ways of expressing intentionality for login with Pico as proposed by Frank Stajano in his USENIX 2011 talk [18]. On the left, a drawing of a Pico device shows a camera and a main button. On the right, scanning a QR code was proposed as a way of expressing the intention to log in.

3.1 Our Study

Between October 2016 and March 2017, we conducted a trial of the Pico smartphone application in our immediate environment, the University of Cambridge Computer Laboratory. It consisted of a four-week pilot with five participants and a ten-week main deployment with 13 participants using Pico to log in to their computers, periodically completing questionnaires and participating in a debriefing interview at the end. The login interaction was designed with intentionality in mind: in order to log in, the user had to take out their phone, unlock it, open the Pico app and then scan a QR code or tap a button (shown in Fig. 2).

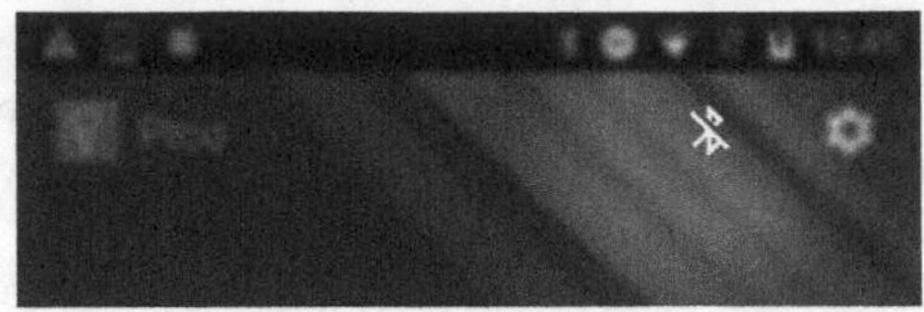

Fig. 2. A Bluetooth button inside the Pico app at the time of the study (blur added for emphasis).

3.2 Procedure

Participants were recruited through a department-wide call for participants sent to staff and students of the Computer Laboratory. We asked them to complete a pre-screening questionnaire to make sure Pico could be installed on their devices. At that time, we supported Windows (8 and higher), Ubuntu (16.04) and Android phones (4.4 and higher). We received 39 responses. After excluding those who were ineligible or did not respond to our emails, we obtained a final sample consisting of 13 participants and we were able to conduct interviews with 10 of them.

Once we established a participant's eligibility, we sent them an information sheet and a consent form that they were asked to read and sign. In the forms, they had the option to request access to the source code of the Pico software. We also encouraged participants to ask questions. They could hand in their signed consent form by either visiting our office or sending a scanned document by email. Before starting the trial, we offered every participant a Bluetooth dongle in case their computer did not already have Bluetooth hardware.

Once we ascertained eligibility and consent, we sent installation instructions to every participant via email. Two days after this, they received a feedback questionnaire asking them about the installation process and their experiences with Pico so far. Another questionnaire followed three weeks later and a final questionnaire another three weeks later. During this time, we could be contacted via email with any issues participants might have had. Depending on a participant's availability, they were invited for a feedback interview around 10 weeks after the installation. After the end of the trial, participants were free to continue or stop using Pico.

The study received an ethics approval from the Ethics Committee of the University of Cambridge Computer Laboratory (approval number: 404).

3.3 Research Aims

Our goal was to explore the user experience with Pico when used to log in to a computer, either Linux or Windows. We offered our participants two ways of logging in, both involving the Pico app for Android—they could either open the Pico app on their phone and scan the QR code displayed on their computer screen or press a button within the app. Using the QR code option to log in required an Internet connection on both devices, while pressing a button inside the app required a Bluetooth connection between the computer and the phone as well. These two methods of logging in varied in terms of the interaction they required (scanning *vs* pressing a button) and the type of connection needed (Internet *vs* Bluetooth). User behaviour with QR codes has been studied academically before, for example by Shin *et al.* [17], and the results showed user acceptance to be strongly influenced by interactivity, meaning users saw scanning a QR code as a way to interact and engage with others. More broadly, one could interpret the result to mean that users were willing to scan QR codes if they saw them useful in achieving a certain goal. Using Bluetooth for login is a fairly new idea. At the moment, at least three commercial products use phone-based Bluetooth for authentication: SAASPASS lets the user log in using their phone [15], Apple Watch can be used to unlock a Macbook [2] and Windows offers a feature to lock your computer when your phone is absent [23]. However, we were unable to find any academic research studying user perceptions of and experiences with such solutions. Our study is therefore valuable in gauging participants' willingness to use Bluetooth to log in. While entering a password is very tangible because it requires cognitive and physical effort, scanning a QR code is less tangible and pressing a button even less so. Hence, our goal was to explore the user experience of these less tangible ways of expressing intentionality to log in.

3.4 Findings

In what follows, we present the qualitative and quantitative results of our study. While we do not present the quantitative results of the pilot study as we used preliminary versions of our questionnaires, we do include some of the participant quotes.

Overall Perceptions. There was a general perception that participants liked the 'coolness' of Pico. P01 (Windows)[1] explained: *"Overall, I liked it. [...] It was quite fancy, you scan a barcode and everything just turns on."* and later said: *"you need to open the app so it probably even takes more time but on the other hand, it is just cooler to do that."* P03 (Windows) stated *"It was mostly fun."* and went on to discuss some connectivity issues and bugs they encountered. PP2[2] (Ubuntu) told us: *"It's different from passwords, it's a fun thing to use."*

Experience of Using Pico with QR Codes and Bluetooth. We received 13 responses to the post-installation questionnaire. Out of these 13 participants, seven were able to set up Pico to work with Bluetooth, which in practice meant going through the normal Pico setup procedure and then Bluetooth pairing their

[1] With each new mention of a participant, we report the operating system they used Pico on.

[2] For quotes from pilot participants, we use the format of PPX, that is "pilot participant" followed by a number.

computer and phone through the standard interfaces on their devices. Three participants stated that they had not tried it yet. Two stated that it did not work for them, citing problems such as *"Do not know how to setup bluetooth on Xubuntu."*[3] (P09, Xubuntu) and *"I couldn't Bluetooth pair my phone with my computer."* (P05, Kubuntu). One participant stated that they preferred not to use Bluetooth, later explaining in their interview that the use of Bluetooth increased the number of channels through which their devices could be compromised, and that having Bluetooth on would drain their battery quicker.

We also asked participants who switched between login modalities (QR code and Bluetooth) about what influenced their choice of interaction. P03, who stated they used both modalities "50-50", explained: *"I don't know. I just sometimes would put the camera up. Sometimes... It depends. If my phone is already in my hand, I feel there is the Bluetooth button at the top."* PP3 (Ubuntu) preferred Bluetooth, saying: *"I'm using the Bluetooth a lot more than the scanning because the scanning is fiddly. Slightly fiddly to line this up on the screen get it to... It takes up to 10 seconds wobbling the phone around to get it to recognise the QR code but the Bluetooth is really good."* PP2 preferred scanning a QR code as they enjoyed the tangibility of the login process:

> *"I used the scan version more often than the Bluetooth one. I think because there is more physical action to doing it so... there is something more responsive about scanning than just press the button, I think. [...] because there is the physical action involved of you picking up and scanning the screen rather than pressing the button and sort of waiting for a little bit for the computer to respond."*

Later in the interview, PP2 and the interviewers speculated that a preference for QR codes or Bluetooth might be due to reliability—if the user's camera scans the QR code reliably, they would prefer this option, while if their Bluetooth is reliable, they might prefer that. PP2 elaborated: *"With Bluetooth, you are just pressing a button but there is no feedback as to what is going on. But I guess for people, for whom scanning doesn't work reliably, it's still better."*

Problems Using Pico. In all three questionnaires, we asked participants to report on any problems they had experienced while using Pico. All but one participant reported experiencing problems. In six out of 12 cases, the problems were related to connectivity; in most cases the participant did not have an Internet connection on their phone (but probably didn't notice it until they attempted to log in), while in isolated cases it was down to failure of the Bluetooth connection. It's worth mentioning that at this stage in Pico's development, an Internet connection was required in order to authenticate, independent of the use of Bluetooth. P03 explained their laptop had problems connecting to some WiFi networks:

[3] Any participant quotes coming from questionnaires are reproduced as written by our participants.

"If I come up here [to the Computer Laboratory] and my laptop wants to connect to Eduroam, the first time it turns on, it won't automatically log on. [...] You can try to connect to Eduroam but the laptop won't do it because you have not logged in yet."

Other problems could have had something to do with connectivity but they were mentioned in their own right. Two participants mentioned app crashes. Three participants felt Pico was slow to log them in. Another three participants mentioned a bug in our software whereby the password field would keep refreshing when their computer did not have an Internet connection.

Expressing Intentionality. Although a small-scale trial with computer scientists as participants, a large proportion of our participants felt the expression of intentionality that we required was too much—they didn't like to take out their phones, enter a PIN, go to the app and press a button to be logged in. P07 (Windows) explained:

"It would be better if it could work automatically. The requirement to press the button on my phone for the computer to unlock makes it more effort than a password."

PP1 (Ubuntu) would have preferred a login mechanism that did not require them to take their phone out of their pocket:

"It would be better if I would be able to just not even have to click or choose maybe. Like, I feel it's alright if I rely on my Bluetooth sensitivity and say it's around a couple of metres from my machine and then and I'm fine to use it like that and I don't have to press anything. And once I get back in my room with my phone in my pocket, it unlocks."

PP1 then immediately reflected on the security of this approach and explained that there are many parts to an attack:

"It is really hard to talk about these things, there is so many scenarios we can think about, like sometimes you have to balance, you have to trade off ease of use between actual need of security between how disciplined people are. [...] If I leave my phone like this and someone steals my phone, they can get into my account, these kinds of things. Then what happens once he gets to my computer? [...] But on the other hand, if he steals my phone and he already has access to my emails... You see, there are all sorts of different parts."

This implies that every user would need to take the decision whether to use an automatic login based on their personal circumstances and context of use. P02 (Windows) explained in their interview that they would not like automatic login because of the particular threat model they have:

> *"The 'Log me in automatically as I approach' I actually don't want. I think this is the danger of you just walking past your computer and it unlocking. I don't really want that. It would also mean that somebody that stole my laptop out of my bag in a coffee shop, could sit behind me and use my laptop."*

3.5 Subsequent Development of the Pico App

Even in a small sample like ours, we saw a great diversity in terms of preferences for expressing intentionality. These might have had to do with universal personal preferences but also with the risk levels the individuals perceived. When subsequently developing the Android application, we introduced three Bluetooth login modes that varied how much intentionality the user had to express (see Fig. 3):

- *Automatic*: The user will always be automatically logged in when their phone is in range of a Pico-enabled computer.
- *Manual with notification*: When the user's phone is within range, Pico puts up a notification that appears in their phone's notification tray, with an accompanying vibration. The user can tap the notification to log in, without having to switch application.
- *Manual*: Each time the user wants to log in, they need to open the Pico app and press a button inside the app. In this case there is no notification, so the user makes their own assessment that they are within range of a Pico-enabled computer.

In the case of *automatic*, there is no action or intent required from the user. This means less effort for the user to log in, but with the associated risk that the user may be logged in to a machine without being aware. In the cases of *manual with notification* and *manual*, the user must make an explicit action on their phone, which may involve having to remove it from their pocket, and so comes with additional effort. However, the risk of the user being logged in to a machine without being aware of it is greatly reduced. The distinction between the two manual cases rests on whether the user wants to be made explicitly aware that a usable machine is nearby. In some cases this may be obvious for the user based on context (for example, if the user always logs in to the same machine at the same desk) and so no notification is needed. Indeed, notifications in this case may simply be an annoyance. However, in other cases, such as where a user is moving between machines, the notification may provide value. In both cases the user has chosen to require the affirmative action of tapping a button on their phone to log in.

A further mode, where the user is authenticated automatically but notified in a passive manner, such as through vibration, would address the case where the user is made aware, but only has to take action to reverse an unwanted authentication. This was not included in our trial, but would make an interesting topic to explore in future work.

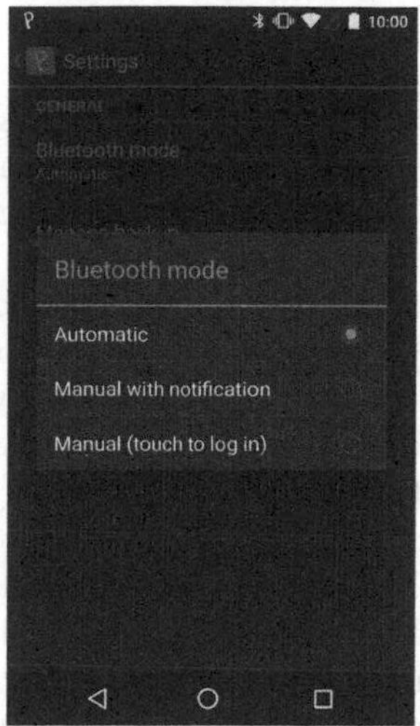

Fig. 3. A screenshot of the Pico app for Android showing the three login modes, varying the level of intentionality the user has to express to be logged in.

4 Designing Secure and Usable Systems

In common with Sasse *et al.* [16], we hold the belief that security designers should strive for products that excel in terms of both security and usability, avoiding any security-usability tradeoffs. However, the different login modes and ways of expressing intentionality highlight the tension between security (awareness and control over each login event) and usability (logging in without having to intervene manually) and allow the user to select the combination that best matches the risk context (logging in to a personal machine at home *vs* logging in to a hotdesking machine in an open plan office).

Although this provides flexibility, some will consider any request for user input as a cop-out: it pushes responsibility onto the user to decide and, if the security software can't figure out the appropriate response, the question being asked will sound like gobbledygook to the user, who will not be in a position to make an informed decision. If the designer wanted to choose ahead of time on behalf of the user, the dilemma is therefore whether to push the slider towards security (protecting but annoying the user) or towards usability (seamless operation but greater risk of attacks). We believe the slider should be set by default towards greater usability but also that people who, rightly or wrongly, don't feel secure without the added ritual should be offered the option to express their intentions more explicitly and to be notified of (and given a chance to block) any actions that are taken automatically on their behalf. There remains the question of how much responsibility the designer bears if a user falls prey to an attack when the default was set to favour usability. Avoiding such liability is probably one of the main reasons why most commercial software still pushes the choice onto the user.

5 Conclusion

Although only a small-scale trial, the feedback highlighted a number of interesting differences between participants. We allowed users the flexibility to authenticate either by scanning a QR code, or by touching a button in the Pico app that appears when in Bluetooth range of a Pico-enabled machine. There was no clear-cut overall preference for one or the other, but we could conclude that the expressed desire was towards a more seamless experience than towards more overt or demanding modes of expressing intentionality. The subsequent design of Pico has been adjusted based on these results and, as discussed above, we have identified four levels of intentionality that apply. Fully automatic login based on proximity remains the most controversial option, and we hope can be the subject of future work to identify where the appropriate balance lies between seamless usability and expression of intentionality. In particular, our hope is that future work will find the relationship between usability, intentionality and security as it applies to authentication and software security more generally.

Acknowledgments. We thank the European Research Council (ERC) for funding this research through grant StG 307224 (Pico).

References

1. Anderson, R.: Why information security is hard—An economic perspective. In: Computer Security Applications Conference (ACSAC 2001), pp. 358–365. IEEE (2001)
2. Apple Support: How to unlock your Mac with your Apple Watch, January 2018. https://support.apple.com/en-us/HT206995
3. BBC: ‘Relay crime’ theft caught on camera, November 2017. http://www.bbc.co.uk/news/av/uk-42132804/relay-crime-theft-caught-on-camera
4. Currie, J., Walker, R.: Traffic congestion and infant health: Evidence from E-ZPass. Am. Econ. J.: Appl. Econ. **3**(1), 65–90 (2011)
5. Emms, M., Arief, B., Freitas, L., Hannon, J., van Moorsel, A.: Harvesting high value foreign currency transactions from EMV contactless credit cards without the PIN. In: Conference on Computer and Communications Security (CCS), pp. 716–726. ACM (2014)
6. Emms, M., van Moorsel, A.: Practical attack on contactless payment cards. In: HCI2011 Workshop—Health, Wealth and Identity Theft (2011)
7. Francillon, A., Danev, B., Capkun, S.: Relay attacks on passive keyless entry and start systems in modern cars. In: Network and Distributed System Security Symposium (NDSS) (2011)
8. Herley, C.: So long, and no thanks for the externalities: The rational rejection of security advice by users. In: New Security Paradigms Workshop (NSPW 2009), pp. 133–144. ACM (2009)
9. Herley, C.: More is not the answer. IEEE Secur. Priv. **12**(1), 14–19 (2014)
10. Hirose, M.: Newly Obtained Records Reveal Extensive Monitoring of E-ZPass Tags Throughout New York, April 2015. https://www.aclu.org/blog/privacy-technology/location-tracking/newly-obtained-records-reveal-extensive-monitoring-e-zpass

11. Jia, H., Wu, M., Jung, E., Shapiro, A., Sundar, S.S.: Balancing human agency and object agency: An end-user interview study of the Internet of Things. In: ACM Conference on Ubiquitous Computing, pp. 1185–1188. ACM (2012)
12. Krol, K., Philippou, E., De Cristofaro, E., Sasse, M.A.: "They brought in the horrible key ring thing!" Analysing the usability of two-factor authentication in UK online banking. In: NDSS Workshop on Usable Security (USEC) (2015)
13. Krol, K., Rahman, M.S., Parkin, S., De Cristofaro, E., Vasserman, E.: An exploratory study of user perceptions of payment methods in the UK and the US. In: NDSS Workshop on Usable Security (USEC) (2016)
14. Payne, J., Jenkinson, G., Stajano, F., Sasse, M.A., Spencer, M.: Responsibility and tangible security: Towards a theory of user acceptance of security tokens. In: NDSS Workshop on Usable Security (USEC) (2016)
15. SAASPASS: About: What is SAASPASS? February 2018. https://saaspass.com/about.html
16. Sasse, M.A., Smith, M., Herley, C., Lipford, H., Vaniea, K.: Debunking security-usability tradeoff myths. IEEE Secur. Priv. **14**(5), 33–39 (2016)
17. Shin, D.-H., Jung, J., Chang, B.-H.: The psychology behind QR codes: User experience perspective. Comput. Hum. Behav. **28**(4), 1417–1426 (2012)
18. Stajano, F.: Pico: No more passwords! Talk at USENIX Security (2011). https://www.usenix.org/conference/usenix-security-11/pico-no-more-passwords
19. Stajano, F.: Pico: No more passwords! In: Christianson, B., Crispo, B., Malcolm, J., Stajano, F. (eds.) Security Protocols 2011. LNCS, vol. 7114, pp. 49–81. Springer, Heidelberg (2011). https://doi.org/10.1007/978-3-642-25867-1_6
20. Transport for London: Card clash, February 2018. https://tfl.gov.uk/fares-and-payments/oyster/using-oyster/card-clash
21. Ulatowski, L.M.: Recent developments in RFID technology: Weighing utility against potential privacy concerns. J. Law Policy Inf. Soc. **3**, 623 (2007)
22. Weiser, M.: The computer for the 21st century. Sci. Am. Spec. Issue Commun. Comput. Netw. **265**(September), 94–104 (1991)
23. Windows Support: Lock your Windows 10 PC automatically when you step away from it, April 2018. https://support.microsoft.com/en-gb/help/4028111/windows-lock-your-windows-10-pc-automatically-when-you-step-away-from

Intentionality and Agency in Security (Transcript of Discussion)

Kat Krol(✉)

University of Cambridge, Cambridge, UK
kat.krol@cst.cam.ac.uk

This screenshot shows what the Android app currently looks like. We have three different Bluetooth modes: *automatic*, *manual with notification*, and *manual*. The authentication protocol can happen over the Internet, but it currently happens over Bluetooth. In the *automatic* mode, as the name implies, you have your computer, you have your phone in your pocket, you approach the computer, an authentication protocol happens, and you are logged in (or the computer unlocks, depending on the previous state). Then you have a *manual with notification* option: when you approach your computer and you are within Bluetooth range, your phone vibrates, you are shown a notification, and you can tap on it to be logged in. The third option is *manual*, which is the one we tested. You approach the computer, you have to take the phone out of your pocket, there is a button inside the app, you tap it and you are logged in.

Another option that we are thinking of implementing is where you would be automatically logged in, but you would still get a notification on your phone just to make sure you are aware that you were logged in. This is to avoid the situation where you are facing away from your computer and you are logged in without realising. The notification is accompanied by a vibration, which is physical feedback telling you that you have been logged in.

Ian Goldberg: I'm not sure of the difference between the second and third one? Oh, in the second case it's a notification and you have to tap it. In the third case, you have to open the app and tap it.

Reply: Yes, precisely. So, for example, if you don't like notifications, your phone buzzing and these alerts popping up all the time, you would say, "Oh, on the rare occasion that I actually want to log in, I would prefer to go to the app and do it, rather than be bothered all the time".

Ilia Shumailov: Can you expand a little bit on *automatic*? Is there some distance requirement? And in what way does it do discovery? How is the Bluetooth connection initiated?

Reply: For the Android app we're discussing here, this is based on standard Bluetooth, as opposed to on the iPhone app that we are developing, where it's based on Bluetooth Low Energy (BLE). With BLE, you can get RSSI[1] values and the user can set RSSI thresholds for when they will be logged in or out. For example at home you might be more liberal with it, but in an open plan office, where you can potentially log in to multiple computers because you have accounts on all of them, you would probably want to set the threshold higher to

[1] Received Signal Strength Indication.

V. Matyáš et al. (Eds.): Security Protocols 2018, LNCS 11286, pp. 126–131, 2018.
https://doi.org/10.1007/978-3-030-03251-7_14

require you to be closer to the computer. David, would you like to talk about discovery?

David Llewellyn-Jones: Oh, discovery. The computer sends out beacons—

Ilia Shumailov: So the computer initiates?

David Llewellyn-Jones: The computer initiates, the program picks that up, and that's what triggers the notification.

Ross Anderson: Shouldn't that slide mean *automatic with notification*, rather than *manual with notification*? And more importantly, what's going to be the default? Because that's what most people will go with. Will it be *automatic with notification*? Or would it be *silent automatic*? Or would it be *manual touch to log on*?

Reply: To answer your first question: how we distinguish it is that the login would not happen automatically. The notification happens automatically, but the login you have to approve, I think that's the distinction. Does this make sense?

Ross Anderson: Well the natural way for me to implement that would be to make it automatic login, but with a buzz.

Reply: That's the part that would be *automatic with feedback*.

Ross Anderson: Yes, rather than automatic silent login that you never get to know about. But, in my use of language, "manual login" would be something where I have to do something, and so to say "manual with notification" would, as a user interface point, be overkill, I think.

Reply: Okay, interesting. And your second question was referring to the default. Yes, we've been thinking about defaults a lot, and currently it's set to *manual*. At some point, we had it set to *automatic*, and... Obviously we have not had many users, but yes they were aware of it, and some of them went to change the setting to another one they preferred. I cannot give you statistical significance on any of these findings because we haven't had that big of a userbase, especially for the Android app.

Frank Stajano: I think that, as designers of the system, and also as security engineers, we have clear ideas on what should be "the right thing". But we are letting ourselves be guided by what users actually want before taking our own decisions, and we have an ongoing trial with a government agency at the moment, and we are trying to have more trials with commercial clients to understand what it is that they want, and what it is that annoys them among the options. This is why, at the moment, we haven't finalised a default, and we want to choose one not based just on what *we* think is right, but based on what users actually want. If we need to nudge them in a certain direction, we'll do that after we see what they want to do.

Graham Rymer: Just an observation: these are the same three modes that web authentication frameworks like Raven have used for a long time. The default in that situation is manual, and if you set it to automatic it basically translates to "cross-site request forgery, please", which is a poor option. This is something that is common to web authentication frameworks.

Reply: So the most interactive level is entering your Raven password again, and then the middle one is confirmation, saying "Yes, I want to log in to this service", and then automatic is you never actually see that anything is happening, correct?

Graham Rymer: Yes, it just transparently logs you in to new services.

Reply: Interesting.

Daniel Weitzner: As I listen to this, I find myself asking "Logging in to what?" I understand the model is logging in to a traditional desktop or mobile thing that has a full-fledged operating system. But, out in the commercial world, there are lots of apps and other devices floating around that we authenticate to, and it amounts to giving a certain kind of authorisation that we often don't understand. I get very uncomfortable with this mode, and it partly goes to Ross's question about what sort of notification, or what sort of user direction, but I think for users the problem now is: what are you authenticating to? And what are you authorising? Because I think those have been completely conflated. You could live in a world of pure authentication here, but I have a feeling the environment is moving beyond that. So I just wondered about how you think about that in the design here.

David Llewellyn-Jones: It didn't apply in this trial, but people can log in and authenticate to lots of different services, and these settings are independent of those services, so you may want to choose a different approach for different types of login, which might also be different authorisations on the same computer.

Fabio Massacci: I have the same question that he asked: logging in to what? In your studies, did all the people have essentially individual rooms, or would it be three people in a room or something like this? Was it basically a small office?

Reply: Yes, the study was conducted in the Computer Laboratory. Most of the participants were postgraduate students or researchers, so they mostly had shared offices. They could have been by themselves or with up to three or four other office members.

And to anticipate what you might say: yes, these people already have their practices, like how they currently lock the computer, they trust these people, they know them, etc., so we wanted them to behave as naturally as possible, and they kind of discussed that. They said, for example: "Oh, I never actually lock my computer, so while using Pico I did it exactly the same way."

Fabio Massacci: So just to continue on this, because Frank said you had a plan for different experiments, do you have something in which you have, say, students in a class where they can have different laptops, or people with very different delegations of authority like doctors and nurses, or a similar setup? But not just friends or coworkers in a small office?

Reply: Yes, currently we're developing such studies. Obviously what you are mentioning would be very valuable usable security research that has not been done sufficiently. Currently we are developing Pico towards our customers, and we are studying and physically looking at what kind of working spaces they are in. So currently the customer that Frank mentioned, they have hot-desking, and they all have their own laptops, so for example they might want to adjust the RSSI thresholds to reflect that, to ensure that they are not accidentally logged in to somebody else's computer they have an account on, etc.

Fabio Massacci: So they don't have their own computer, right?

Reply: They all have their own laptops, and they might still have an account on other devices in the room, so they would basically have to adjust RSSI values based on that.

Mark Lomas: Can I suggest an example that may help you? I think we're being misled by the word "login". We did some experiments a number of years ago with active badges in the Computer Laboratory, and a lot of the useful features were essentially authenticating the user but *after* the login. For example, I wrote a program called `abprint`, Active Badge Print, where you could say "Print this document, but only do it when my badge is next to the printer." The point is, I'd already logged in and it had authenticated me, but it says, "Don't actually complete this action until I'm there." The reason I give that example is because it's not a login *per se*, it's authorisation.

Reply: Interesting.

Diana Vasile: Just a quick question: you mentioned users having to fiddle with the RSSI values, but that's a bit too fiddly, isn't it? You assume a certain level of knowledge for them... And also, just another side question, you also mentioned the fiddling of the RSSI values depending on where you are. Would they have to do this always? Would they be prompted to say, "You've just logged in to a new WiFi, would you like to have it set by default? Or would you like to preset?" How would that work? How do you envision that working?

Reply: These are all very valid questions, and the iPhone app that actually has the RSSI values that you can adjust is something that we have been only developing recently, so we have not actually addressed any of these questions, but they are absolutely very valid. Your physical circumstances change, and even how many people in the room is going to affect RSSI values, so there's going to be all sorts of settings problems.

Virgil Gligor: This is all great work, I really enjoyed listening to your talk. I do have a question about how Pico, in this instance, would be integrated into the larger world of computing, when in fact a lot of services require passwords. So yes, this does help a great deal with my devices, but if I go to a lot of remote services, I still have to have passwords, and I still have to go through the same pain and agony of remembering them, writing them down and so on. So what's your reaction? How would Pico penetrate that world, if at all?

Reply: I think this is very much a question for Frank.

Frank Stajano: In this presentation today, we have shown the Pico for logging in to a physical device: a computer. In a previous presentation a few years back[2], we introduced our solution to how to log in to something across the web, which ultimately would depend on the verifier on the other side of the

[2] F. Stajano et al., "Bootstrapping Adoption of the Pico Password Replacement System", Proc SPW 2014, LNCS 8809.

web agreeing with us to run a complete Pico protocol. But it's unrealistic to convince all these people upfront, so in the meantime we had decided to man-in-the-middle the situation (in a benign way) by inserting what we called the 'Pico Lens' in the web browser. That transformed non-cooperating websites into ones that looked to the user as if they were already Pico-enabled, and looked to the website as if a user were typing a super complicated unbreakable password. So we have this technology, it's not what's being described in this talk, but that's in the bag already, and that is a step on the way towards the sites then running a full Pico protocol where you can add extra security features if you want. As for compatibility mode, we can run without the cooperation of the other end.

Virgil Gligor: Even if they require two-factor authentication, on a specific phone and ...?

Frank Stajano: Well, it depends how willing we are to make *ad hoc* adjustments for things that are popular. If there is one thing that everybody uses, then we are going to program something for it; if it's something that only one site uses, probably we are not going to bother.

If I may go back to the question about RSSI, the design intention is to offer a slider that lets the user say, "I want to be logged in when I'm within one metre (or five, or...)". However, the reality of measuring distance with signal strength is that it's not at all that straightforward. If we give the user a slider in metres, that's a lie: I put the slider at one metre, then it never works, because when I'm facing towards the computer it feels like one metre, but when I'm facing the other way, the same distance maybe feels like 10 m from the RSSI. Therefore, instead of saying something allegedly user-friendly (metres) that would annoy users for not working as advertised, we are saying the more technical thing (RSSI), which is less comprehensible, but at least it's closer to what is happening, until we manage to find a way to make the technology work better than it does now.

Ilia Shumailov: So the question I have is with the *automatic* and general notification delivery. In your study, did anybody reflect on those notifications? Was there a preference for receiving the notification before you log in, or once you're logged in? Or do you actually want to receive two of them? Because for example, in my private usage, when I designed my own benign man-in-the-middle (as Frank called it), I usually send myself two notifications, once when I am attempting to, and the second one when I am successful, so that I actually know that somebody attempted to do something.

Reply: Just to remind you, this development was after the study, so we have not empirically evaluated this with many participants yet. But yes, this is a very valid point, thank you.

Peter Ryan: I assume that you have to place a lot of trust in this device or app. But also—I'm generalising—I suspect the more transparent you try and make security, the greater the trust you have to place in some kind of device or component, and so on.

Reply: Yes, the more invisible something becomes, the more you have to trust that things are being done right, and people elaborate on that. So for example, not with Pico, but with other mechanisms that I studied before in research[3], what happened is that users made the inference that if a technology had been around for long enough, then they said "Oh, it must be okay". If it's a big multi-billion dollar company, then "Oh, it must be okay." So they are making all these inferences based on trust, which are very human and a way to reduce complexity. But yes, absolutely, there is a lot of trust in the technology that is invisible.

Thank you.

[3] K. Krol, S. Parkin and M. A. Sasse, "Better the devil you know: A user study of two CAPTCHAs and a possible replacement technology", Proc NDSS Workshop on Usable Security (USEC 2016).

Incentives in Security Protocols

Sarah Azouvi, Alexander Hicks, and Steven J. Murdoch(✉)

University College London, London, UK
{sarah.azouvi.13,alexander.hicks,s.murdoch}@ucl.ac.uk

Abstract. Real world protocols often involve human choices that depend on incentives, including when they fail. We look at three example systems (the EMV protocol, consensus in cryptocurrencies, and Tor), paying particular attention to the role that incentives play in fail-safe and fail-deadly situations. In this position paper we argue that incentives should explicitly be taken into account in the design of security protocols, and discuss general challenges in doing so.

1 Introduction and Background

Many real-world systems involve human interaction and decisions that impact the security protocols involved. Protocols can fail, sometimes due to the human side of the system, because of mistakes or malicious behaviour. A way to understand such failures is to look at incentives, as these can determine the human choices involved. Equally, protocol designers can structure incentives to avoid failures of the overall system. Despite the importance of incentives, security proofs very rarely (if ever) explicitly consider the role of incentives as part of the protocols, treating incentives separately. This is unfortunate as in many cases of failure, the human side of the system is blamed and considered to be one of the weakest components, while with properly aligned incentives it may become one of the strongest.

Incentives come in many shapes and forms. Economic incentives are commonly discussed, following work by Anderson [8], but usually in the context of economic analysis of security problems rather than protocol design. Non-economic incentives also exist, in systems designed to provide privacy and anonymity properties, and that do not involve transactions or handle valuable assets. Differentiating between positive and negative incentives, such as fines or rewards, which serve to discourage or encourage some behaviour can also be useful as they may be perceived differently. Incentives can also be internal (inherent to the protocol) or external (due to factors like legislation) and explicit or implicit if they are derived from other factors, sometimes unexpectedly.

Fail-safe and *fail-deadly* protocols provide good examples of protocol instances involving incentives, as they handle various types of behaviour. We refer to the standard definitions of fail-safe and fail-deadly, whereby we mean that an instance of a protocol failing will cause minimal or no damage (fail-safe) or that an instance of the protocol failing is deterred (fail-deadly). These are

V. Matyáš et al. (Eds.): Security Protocols 2018, LNCS 11286, pp. 132–141, 2018.
https://doi.org/10.1007/978-3-030-03251-7_15

to some extent two sides of the same coin, where one side aims to protect the victims of a failure, while the other aims to deter those who might cause it. With this in mind, we look at three examples, the EMV protocol where incentives were added after the design of the protocol, consensus in cryptocurrencies that explicitly consider incentives, and Tor that may benefit from incentivisation schemes. We highlight for each example some failings in the understanding of the role played by incentives, their application or the models used, before discussing general challenges in designing protocols that incorporate incentives.

2 Incentives in Existing Systems

2.1 EMV

The EMV protocol is used for the vast majority of smart card payments worldwide, and also is the basis for both smartphone and card-based contactless payments. Over the past 20 years, it has been gradually refined as vulnerabilities have been identified and removed. However, there is still considerable fraud which results, not from unexpected protocol vulnerabilities, but from deliberate decisions that participants can make to reduce the level of security offered. Such decisions include the bank omitting the cards' ability to produce digital signatures (making cards cheaper but easy to clone), the merchant omitting PIN verification (making transactions faster, but stolen cards easier to use), or the payment network not sending transaction details back to the bank that issued the card for authorisation when the card is used abroad (reducing transaction latency, but making fraud harder to prevent).

Fraud exploiting such decisions is not strictly speaking a protocol failure but, if unchecked, could be financially devastating for participants and reduce trust in the system. The way in which the payment industry has managed the risk is through incentives: firstly, reducing fees for transactions that use more secure methods, and secondly, assigning the liability for fraud to the party which causes the security level to be reduced [9]. Any disputes are handled as specified by the relevant contracts, whether in court or through arbitration.

Looking at the EMV ecosystem as a whole, this serves as a fail-safe overlay on top of a protocol which is optimised for compatibility rather than security. While any individual transaction could go wrong, over time, parties will be encouraged to either adopt more secure options or mitigate fraud in other ways, for example through machine-learning based risk analysis. However, there is little indication that the EMV protocol was designed with the understanding that incentives would play such a central role in the security of the system.

Where this omission becomes particularly apparent is that during disputes, it may be unclear how a fraud actually happened, leading to a disagreement as to who should be liable. This is because communication between participants is designed to establish whether the transaction should proceed, rather than which party made which decision. Importantly, the policies on how participating entities should act are not part of the EMV specification. Even assuming that all participants in a dispute are acting honestly, it can be challenging for experts to reverse-engineer decisions from the limited details available [31].

This suggests that where incentives are part of the fail-safe mechanism, the protocol should produce unambiguous evidence showing not only the final system state, but how it was arrived at. This evidence should also be robust to participants acting dishonestly, perhaps through use of techniques inspired by distributed ledgers [32]. Currently only a small proportion of the protocol exchange has end-to-end security, but because payment communication flows are only between participants with a written contract (for historical, rather than technical reasons) this deficiency is somewhat mitigated. We know how to reason about the security of protocols, but what would be an appropriate formalisation that would indicate whether evidence produced by a system is sufficient to properly allocate incentives?

2.2 Consensus Protocols in Cryptocurrencies

We move on to consider cryptocurrencies (e.g. Bitcoin, Ethereum), public distributed ledgers relying on a blockchain and consensus protocol. Originating from the rejection of any centralised authority, these are a rare example of systems whose security inherently relies on incentive schemes, unlike the EMV protocol above. Transactions are verified and appended to the blockchain by miners incentivised by mining rewards and transaction fees defined in the protocol to encourage honest behaviour in a trustless, open system.

This has had notable success, but does not address every possible issue as attacks on Bitcoin mining exist [12,14,17,18,30,36], suggesting that the incentives defined in the Nakamoto consensus protocol do not capture all possible behaviours. Despite all these attack papers discussing incentives, few other papers focus on them [4,28,29,33], and security oriented papers consider them separately [11,27,34].

These papers also focus on standard game theoretic concepts like Nash equilibria [11,27,33] and assume rational participants, whilst distributed systems aim for security properties like Byzantine Fault Tolerance to tolerate a subset of participants arbitrarily deviating. (This is with the exception of recent work by Badertscher et al. [10] that considers mining in the setting of rational protocol design.) Some attacks are also not appropriately studied from the point of view of Nash equilibria, as they are often on the network layer of the protocol, as in the case of selfish mining [18]. The fact that papers considering incentives tackle these attacks separately also points to the fact that Nash equilibria are not well suited for this context. Indeed, there is a mismatch between the idea of a Nash equilibrium, which exists in the context of finite action games involving a finite set of participants, and systems such as consensus protocols where the set of actions is theoretically unlimited as one could try to build alternative chains or broadcast their blocks at any time.

Examples of incentive based fail-safe and fail-deadly instances of the consensus protocol can be found in forking mechanisms, which can be used to incorporate new rules or revert to a previous state of the blockchain. Soft forks are an example of a fail-safe mechanism as even in the case of a disagreement amongst network peers, they are backwards compatible and allow peers to choose what software to run without splitting the network. When no such compatibility can be found, the network can implement a hard fork where every peer has to comply with the new rules. On the other hand, if a hard fork is implemented without the consent of the whole network, it may split like Ethereum after the DAO hack [37]. Due to part of the network having clear incentives to roll back, a hard fork was organised to reverse the state of the blockchain to a moment before the hack. This caused controversy, as some considered it to go against the ideology of decentralisation, causing part of the network to split and create a new currency, Ethereum Classic [1], in which the hack remained. Nonetheless, forking and splitting up the network could lessen its utility (Ethereum Classic is now worth much less than Ethereum [15]), which gives a fail-deadly case since miners would risk losing mining rewards and the cost of creating a block if their fork is not supported.

Finally, there is the case of protocols added on top of the system such as the Lightning off-chain payment channel system [35] which allows two or more parties to transact offline, publishing only two on-chain transactions: a deposit which locks funds and a final balance which settles the payment. Although this involves cryptography, the security is largely based on incentives: parties are disincentivised from cheating (by publishing an old transaction to the blockchain) as the honest party could then broadcast a revocation transaction (signed by the cheating party) and receive the deposit of the cheating party. This fail-deadly case is not unlike the EMV protocol case, where robust evidence may deter dishonest behaviour.

2.3 Incentives in Non-economic Systems

The above examples illustrate systems involving transactions, but what of systems which do not involve transactions or valuable assets? We consider this case by looking at the anonymity system Tor, whose security relies on the number of participants and servers in the network. Whilst there may be incentives for many (perhaps not all) users of the Tor network, there is less incentive to host a Tor server. Nevertheless, the network has grown to around 4 million users and 6 thousand servers as of January 2018.

Clearly, the lack of economic incentives does not prevent the existence of Tor but perhaps they could motivate users to participate and host servers. The economics of anonymity have been studied, dating back to at least the early 2000s [6] and proposals to reward hosting servers have been made [20,25] but not implemented. Performance based incentives were also considered by Ngan et al. [16]. Incentives to avoid security failures like sending traffic through a bad node could also be considered, as robust evidence of a node's status would provide a fail-safe (participants could avoid sending traffic through it) and fail-deadly (by punishing the host) mechanism.

But whilst adding incentives may improve the performance and security of the network, it may also produce unexpected results. A relevant study is the

Table 1. Summary of incentive types, enabling mechanisms and models mentioned in this paper.

Incentive Types	Enabling mechanism	Models
Economic & non-economic	Evidence	Nash equilibrium & extensions
Internal & external	Trusted third party	BAR model
Implicit & implicit	Consensus	Rational cryptography
Reward & punishment		Prospect theory & further game theory

work of Gneezy and Rustichini [21], who looked at the effects of implementing incentives (fines in their case) to parents at a nursery who did not collect their children on time. This resulted in parents coming even later, a change which was not reverted once fines were removed. They concluded that adding incentives to a system could irreversibly damage it. Simulating the reaction of network participants is very challenging (compared to network performance [24]), which is likely the reason we have seen little experimentation around incentives.

3 Discussion

The previous section serves to illustrate the role incentives can play in the security of a system. From what we've discussed, there are three important aspects to consider: incentive types, mechanisms that enable them and models to reason about them.

Incentive types are divided into economic or non-economic, external and internal, explicit and implicit, and rewards and punishments (see Table 1). For most real world examples, economic incentives may seem like a natural choice of an exchange of valuable services, goods or currency but that is not always the case. However, non-economic incentives can also be required but it is much less clear how their utility can be evaluated, especially by the parties meant to be enticed. To evaluate the utility of an incentive, it should also be explicit. Implicit incentives are more likely to end up being exploited, as described in many of the attacks on mining. These are also linked to internal incentives that are easier to abuse, rather than external incentives that might require convincing an external party to collude. Thus the type of incentive might have an impact not only on the utility derived from incentives, but also on the security of the system if they are more likely to be exploited. Rewards and punishments are also to be considered, to incentivise honest behaviour, or disincentivise dishonest behaviour, depending on which is costlier or applicable to the context.

In order for incentives to work, they must be reliable in the sense that any party can expect (or rather, be guaranteed) to receive the related pay-off. For all of the examples we considered, evidence is used by parties to ensure an incentive's pay-off can be obtained. It is natural to expect evidence would be required; decisions are made based on information and as pay-offs are enforced by external parties (e.g. the justice system in the EMV case, or the network in cryptocurrencies) which should not reward or punish anyone without verifiable evidence. Nonetheless, it would be interesting to determine if other mechanisms could be used in place of, or on top of evidence to make incentives reliable and ensure agents in the system do not ignore them.

Once a type and enabling mechanism is chosen, it is necessary to have a framework that allows us to reason about them. The main challenge is obtaining a framework that allows reasoning about incentives on a level similar to security protocols. Standard game theoretic concepts like Nash equilibria, which only consider up to one participant deviating, are not enough when dealing with distributed systems that tolerate far more, as well as information asymmetry, asynchronicity and cost of actions. Such issues are discussed by Halpern [22], who provides an overview of extensions of the Nash equilibrium. Appendix A provides informal definitions for these concepts (as well as a few others). For example, (k, t)-robustness combines k-resilience (tolerating k participants deviating) and t-immunity (participants who do not deviate are not worse off for up to t participants deviating). Introduced by Abraham et al. [2], in the context of secret sharing and multiparty computation, this better fits the fail-safe guarantees (e.g. Byzantine Fault Tolerance) we expect from systems. Solidus [4] uses this concept to provide an incentive-compatible consensus protocol, although they address selfish mining separately from the rest of the protocol.[1] We've also considered fail-deadly cases, which are usually addressed through deterrence. A good fit for these are (k, t)-punishment strategies, where the threat of t participants enforcing a punishment stops a coalition of k participants from deviating. These definitions are only a start to bridging the gap between Game Theory and Computer Security settings. Other work in that direction includes the BAR model [7], which combines Game Theory and Distributed Systems and considers three types of participants (Byzantine, Altruistic and Rational) and the field of Rational Cryptography [10,13,19] that combines Game Theory and Cryptography by using cryptographic models with rational agents. It is also important to consider the cost of computations in the system, an aspect not usually considered in the Game Theory literature. Halpern and Pass showed that many standard notions like Nash equilibria do not always exist in games involving computation [23], leaving open the question of what the ideal solution concept is. On the other hand, taking computation into account, they find equivalences between cryptographic (precise secure computation) and game theoretic (universal implementation) notions, which motivates further work on bridging both fields.

Although the above does not capture all we could want from a system, we may now wonder what a security proof involving incentives would look like. In many ways, the current standard of security proofs involves games and probabilistic arguments. This is not far removed from game theoretic proofs concerned with strategies (especially in incomplete information games), although it requires bridging the differences in settings explored in the last paragraph. Evaluating

[1] Although included in the first version of the pre-print, the published version [5] states that rigorous analysis of incentives is left to future work.

the assumptions underlying incentives, and not only their impact, would be necessary. For example in the EMV protocol and Lightning network, both rely on evidence generated by the protocols for their fail-deadly uses. Incentives would also have to be weighted by the robustness of the mechanisms they relate to. For example, evidence based deterrence in fail-deadly instances is only as good as the evidence generated. Whilst proving robustness of the evidence is realistic for cryptographic evidence, legislation or other factors (social, moral, economic) are much harder to formally evaluate (although Prospect Theory [26] may provide some tools) even if assumptions about altruistic behaviour can clearly be made in cases such as Tor.

Acknowledgments. We thank the attendees of the workshop for the discussion. Alexander Hicks is supported by OneSpan (https://www.onespan.com) and UCL through an EPSRC Research Studentship; Steven J. Murdoch is supported by The Royal Society [grant number UF160505].

A Glossary

For completeness, we add a glossary of terms and definitions appearing in the main content of the paper, particularly in the discussion section. Note that we keep the definition fairly informal so that they can easily be referenced during the discussion. More formal definitions can be found work referenced in the main sections of the paper [2,3,7,13,19,22,26].

Nash equilibrium: In a game of n players with corresponding strategy sets and pay-off functions for each strategies, the strategy profile is the tuple of strategies selected by each player. A strategy profile is a Nash equilibrium for the game if no unilateral deviation by any single player is profitable for that player. Note that this presumes players have knowledge of the game and possible strategies for all players in the game. Moreover, it is only concerned with single players deviating rather than multiple (independent or colluding) players deviating.

k-resilience: A Nash equilibrium is said to be k-resilient if a coalition of up to k players cannot increase their utilities by deviating, given that the rest of the players do not deviate.

Nash equilibrium: In a game of n players with corresponding strategy sets and pay-off functions for each strategies, the strategy profile is the tuple of strategies selected by each player. A strategy profile is a Nash equilibrium for the game if no unilateral deviation by any single player is profitable for that player.

t-immunity: A strategy profile is said to be t-immune if players who do not deviate are no worse off for up to t players deviating.

(k,t)-robustness: A strategy profile is said to be (k, t)-robust if it is both k-resilient and t-immune. Note that a Nash equilibrium is $(1, 0)$-robust, and for $(k, t) \neq (1, 0)$ there does not generally exist a (k, t)-robust equilibrium. Aside from equilibria, (k, t)-robust strategies do exist in certain games, particularly when a *mediator* can be considered as in the case of a Byzantine agreement where the mediator relays the preference of the general to the soldiers (including t traitors). More generally, a mediator could be implemented through gossiping between players although this depends on the number of players as well as the parameters (k, t) [22] and can depend on a (k, t)-punishment strategy.

(k,t)-punishment: A (k, t)-punishment strategy is such that if k players deviate, they do not increase their utility as long as t players enforce the punishment.

BAR model: In Distributed Systems, the BAR model was introduced [7] to incorporate rational participants as in game theoretic models. Traditionally, the Distributed Systems literature considers good and bad processes in (for example) crash fault tolerant or Byzantine fault tolerant settings. The BAR model differs by considering player of three types: Byzantine players that act randomly, altruistic players that comply with the protocol and rational players that maximise their expected utility.

Rational Cryptography: The field of Rational Cryptography [13,19] incorporates incentives within traditional cryptographic systems. They consider each party in the protocol as an agent trying to increase their expected utility. Rational Protocol Design is another variant of this, introduced by Garay et al. [19], that considers a cryptographic protocol as a zero-sum game between the protocol designer and the adversary.

Forks and chain splits: In a blockchain based distributed ledger, forking can happen in two situations. Either when two blocks are found by different miners at the same time or in the case of a change in the protocol. Note that this definition is different that the one traditionally used in open source systems. *Soft-forks* are backward compatible changes, meaning that if a node in the system decides to not update their software and stay with the unchanged protocol, their blocks will still be accepted by other nodes. On the other hand a *hard fork* is not backward compatible, meaning that every node in the system needs to run the updated software following the fork. In the case where a subset of nodes decide to not update their software, a *chain-split* may occur, resulting in a split network.

References

1. Ethereum Classic. https://ethereumclassic.github.io/
2. Abraham, I., Dolev, D., Gonen, R., Halpern, J.: Distributed computing meets game theory: robust mechanisms for rational secret sharing and multiparty computation. In: Proceedings of the Twenty-fifth Annual ACM Symposium on Principles of Distributed Computing, pp. 53–62, PODC 2006. ACM, New York (2006). https://doi.org/10.1145/1146381.1146393
3. Abraham, I., Dolev, D., Halpern, J.Y.: Lower bounds on implementing robust and resilient mediators. In: Canetti, R. (ed.) TCC 2008. LNCS, vol. 4948, pp. 302–319. Springer, Heidelberg (2008). https://doi.org/10.1007/978-3-540-78524-8_17

4. Abraham, I., Malkhi, D., Nayak, K., Ren, L., Spiegelman, A.: Solidus: an incentive-compatible cryptocurrency based on permissionless Byzantine consensus. CoRR abs/1612.02916 (2016). http://arxiv.org/abs/1612.02916
5. Abraham, I., Malkhi, D., Nayak, K., Ren, L., Spiegelman, A.: Solida: A blockchain protocol based on reconfigurable Byzantine consensus. In: OPODIS (2017). https://eprint.iacr.org/2017/1118
6. Acquisti, A., Dingledine, R., Syverson, P.: On the economics of anonymity. In: Wright, R.N. (ed.) FC 2003. LNCS, vol. 2742, pp. 84–102. Springer, Heidelberg (2003). https://doi.org/10.1007/978-3-540-45126-6_7
7. Aiyer, A.S., Alvisi, L., Clement, A., Dahlin, M., Martin, J.P., Porth, C.: BAR fault tolerance for cooperative services. SIGOPS Oper. Syst. Rev. **39**(5), 45–58 (2005). https://doi.org/10.1145/1095809.1095816
8. Anderson, R.: Why information security is hard - an economic perspective. In: Annual Computer Security Applications Conference, pp. 358–365 (2001)
9. Anderson, R., Murdoch, S.J.: EMV: why payment systems fail. Commun. ACM **57**(6), 24–28 (2014). https://doi.org/10.1145/2602321
10. Badertscher, C., Garay, J., Maurer, U., Tschudi, D., Zikas, V.: But why does it work? A rational protocol design treatment of Bitcoin. Technical report, Cryptology ePrint Archive, Report 2018/138 (2018). https://eprint.iacr.org/2018/138
11. Bentov, I., Pass, R., Shi, E.: Snow white: provably secure proofs of stake. IACR Cryptol. ePrint Arch. **2016**, 919 (2016)
12. Bonneau, J.: Why buy when you can rent? In: Clark, J., Meiklejohn, S., Ryan, P.Y.A., Wallach, D., Brenner, M., Rohloff, K. (eds.) FC 2016. LNCS, vol. 9604, pp. 19–26. Springer, Heidelberg (2016). https://doi.org/10.1007/978-3-662-53357-4_2
13. Caballero-Gil, P., Hernández-Goya, C., Bruno-Castañeda, C.: A rational approach to cryptographic protocols. CoRR abs/1005.0082 (2010). http://arxiv.org/abs/1005.0082
14. Carlsten, M., Kalodner, H., Weinberg, S.M., Narayanan, A.: On the instability of Bitcoin without the block reward. In: Proceedings of the 2016 ACM SIGSAC Conference on Computer and Communications Security, pp. 154–167, CCS 2016. ACM, New York (2016). https://doi.org/10.1145/2976749.2978408
15. CoinMarketCap: Cryptocurrency market capitalizations. https://coinmarketcap.com/. Accessed 15 Jan 2018
16. "Johnny" Ngan, T.-W., Dingledine, R., Wallach, D.S.: Building incentives into tor. In: Sion, R. (ed.) FC 2010. LNCS, vol. 6052, pp. 238–256. Springer, Heidelberg (2010). https://doi.org/10.1007/978-3-642-14577-3_19
17. Eyal, I.: The miner's dilemma. In: IEEE Symposium on Security and Privacy (2015)
18. Eyal, I., Sirer, E.G.: Majority is not enough: Bitcoin mining is vulnerable. In: Financial Cryptography and Data Security (2013)
19. Garay, J., Katz, J., Maurer, U., Tackmann, B., Zikas, V.: Rational protocol design: cryptography against incentive-driven adversaries. Cryptology ePrint Archive, Report 2013/496 (2013). http://eprint.iacr.org/2013/496
20. Ghosh, M., Richardson, M., Ford, B., Jansen, R.: A TorPath to TorCoin: proof of bandwidth altcoins for compensating relays. Technical report NRL (2014)
21. Gneezy, U., Rustichini, A.: A fine is a price. J. Legal Stud. **29**(1), 1–17 (2000)
22. Halpern, J.Y.: Beyond Nash equilibrium: solution concepts for the 21st century. CoRR abs/0806.2139 (2008). http://arxiv.org/abs/0806.2139
23. Halpern, J.Y., Pass, R.: Game theory with costly computation. arXiv preprint arXiv:0809.0024 (2008)

24. Jansen, R., Hopper, N.: Shadow: running Tor in a box for accurate and efficient experimentation. In: Proceedings of the 19th Symposium on Network and Distributed System Security (NDSS). Internet Society, February 2012
25. Jansen, R., Miller, A., Syverson, P., Ford, B.: From onions to shallots: rewarding Tor relays with TEARS. Technical report NRL (2014)
26. Kahneman, D., Tversky, A.: Prospect theory: an analysis of decision under risk. In: Handbook of the fundamentals of financial decision making: Part I, pp. 99–127. World Scientific (2013)
27. Kiayias, A., Russell, A., David, B., Oliynykov, R.: Ouroboros: a provably secure proof-of-stake blockchain protocol. In: Katz, J., Shacham, H. (eds.) CRYPTO 2017. LNCS, vol. 10401, pp. 357–388. Springer, Cham (2017). https://doi.org/10.1007/978-3-319-63688-7_12
28. Kothapalli, A., Miller, A., Borisov, N.: SmartCast: an incentive compatible consensus protocol using smart contracts. In: Brenner, M., et al. (eds.) FC 2017. LNCS, vol. 10323, pp. 536–552. Springer, Cham (2017). https://doi.org/10.1007/978-3-319-70278-0_34
29. Kroll, J.A., Davey, I.C., Felten, E.W.: The economics of Bitcoin mining, or Bitcoin in the presence of adversaries. In: WEIS (2013)
30. Luu, L., Teutsch, J., Kulkarni, R., Saxena, P.: Demystifying incentives in the consensus computer. In: Computer and Communications Security, CCS 2015, pp. 706–719. ACM, New York (2015). https://doi.org/10.1145/2810103.2813659
31. Murdoch, S.J.: Reliability of chip & PIN evidence in banking disputes. Digital Evid. Electron. Signat. Law Rev. **6**, 98 (2009)
32. Murdoch, S.J., Anderson, R.: Security protocols and evidence: where many payment systems fail. In: Christin, N., Safavi-Naini, R. (eds.) Financial Cryptography and Data Security, vol. 8437, pp. 21–32. Springer, Heidelberg (2014). https://doi.org/10.1007/978-3-662-45472-5_2
33. Park, S., Pietrzak, K., Kwon, A., Alwen, J., Fuchsbauer, G., Gai, P.: SpaceMint: a cryptocurrency based on proofs of space. Cryptology ePrint Archive, Report 2015/528 (2015). https://eprint.iacr.org/2015/528
34. Pass, R., Shi, E.: Fruitchains: a fair blockchain. In: Proceedings of the ACM Symposium on Principles of Distributed Computing, pp. 315–324. ACM (2017)
35. Poon, J., Dryja, T.: The Bitcoin lightning network: scalable off-chain instant payments. Technical Report (draft) (2015)
36. Sapirshtein, A., Sompolinsky, Y., Zohar, A.: Optimal selfish mining strategies in bitcoin. In: Grossklags, J., Preneel, B. (eds.) Financial Cryptography and Data Security, pp. 515–532. Springer, Berlin Heidelberg, Berlin, Heidelberg (2017)
37. Siegel, D.: Understanding the DAO attack, June 2016. https://www.coindesk.com/understanding-dao-hack-journalists/

Incentives in Security Protocols (Transcript of Discussion)

Steven J. Murdoch(✉)

University College London, London, UK
s.murdoch@ucl.ac.uk

Steven Murdoch: Whenever there is a risk of a security problem, the person who caused that security problem to take place should be the one who actually takes the risk. If the merchant skips PIN verification, the merchant takes more of the risk, and if the card-scheme does stand-in authorization, the card scheme takes more of the risk. In this way, they try to encourage everyone to move to a more secure system. There are problems with that; this is called liability shifting. If one party is able to move much faster than the others then you have the issue that suddenly risk gets dumped on one party, who is not necessarily acting any less securely, but is just acting less quickly.

Daniel Weitzner: Can you give an example of liability shifting in the EMV case?

Steven Murdoch: The particular problematic case is right at the start of the roll out of EMV. The rule was that if a terminal is capable of a chip transaction and the card is a magnetic stripe card, the bank pays the fraud, but if the terminal is only magnetic stripe capable and the card has a chip, then the merchant pays the fraud. But it turns out the banks were able to very rapidly roll out semi-functional chips that weren't really useful (they were very slow and buggy). However, it was enough to trigger this liability shift. The merchants were much slower about rolling out their terminals because a terminal would last three years or more, whereas a card would only last one or two years, and suddenly the merchants had a huge amount of fraud that they were then having to cover even though this wasn't really their fault. Even more problematic is when liability is being shifted onto the customer, because when liability gets shifted to the bank they find some contractual way to dump it onto the customer, even though the customer is not in a position to make things more secure. This sort of liability engineering can be effective, but it is only going to be effective if there is actually sufficient evidence in the system that allows the liability to be fairly assigned to the right party, and in EMV that is generally not the case.

There are logs, but these are debugging logs for developers and there is a number of problems with that. The first is that if there is any disagreement between different aspects of the system, say because of an attack or failure, one side sees one aspect of a transaction. Say that the PIN was verified correctly and the other side sees that the PIN verification was skipped, debugging logs will only tell you one side of that story. Because the debugging logs are not actually parts of the functional requirements of the system, often it is not written down what

V. Matyáš et al. (Eds.): Security Protocols 2018, LNCS 11286, pp. 142–149, 2018.
https://doi.org/10.1007/978-3-030-03251-7_16

aspects of the system they are showing. The second thing is that these debugging logs are not very good for presenting in court, even though ultimately a jury or a judge is going to have to interpret them. When I was an expert witness in one of these cases, it was simply the hexadecimal code ten and then the bank expert said that this shows that the customer is liable, and it just says ten [laughs]. There was no documentation explaining why ten is actually an explanation for this, it was fairly unconvincing but that was the only evidence that was available. Then yet another issue is that this evidence can be tampered with; it is just stored on the developer's machine for whatever reason that they need. It is not going to go through the same chain of custody that you would expect for evidence that is actually deciding hundreds of thousands of pounds of money being transferred from one party to another. It is not actually a complete disaster but this is more through historical accident than by design.

When the banking payment system was set up, cryptography was expensive. You had to use expensive and slow line encryptors. You needed to deal with all the key management and so rather than doing end to end encryption, which is what you would do for say, Internet payments, the way it works is that communications are on a point to point basis and each side of this communication has some sort of contractual agreement. The customer talks to the merchant and they have an implicit contract. The merchant talks to the acquiring bank and they have a contract. The acquiring bank talks to the card scheme and they have a contract. The card scheme talks to the issuing bank and they have a contract and then the issuer deals with the customer again, and then they have a contract. Because these legal contracts are set up, you can sort of get away with not doing encryption because you do have some assurance that people are not acting completely maliciously.

Daniel Weitzner: I feel like there is something behind this claim that this was a historical accident. I have a hard time accepting that at face value. I can understand your point that there were some technical constraints, which shaped the way the parties aligned their liabilities but I am not sure why you think that is an accident. That just seems like an adaptation and so you are saying it would be better if the liabilities were aligned differently or if there were more options available?

Steven Murdoch: Okay, I will clarify what I think I mean, which is that the fact that the evidence is somewhat reliable is a historical accident that comes from a particular architecture, which is designed for good reasons, which were valid at the time and are still valid. If however, there was no such arrangement and instead communications just went over the Internet, straight from the customer's phone to the merchant's phone, did not involve intermediaries and had end-to-end encryption to deal with security, then the quality of the evidence would not be as good because everything would be encrypted. There would be no clear-text logs that someone can show, so in the case of the number ten saying the customer is liable, at least someone who wasn't a party to the dispute had that number then. If it was end to end encrypted, even that would not exist.

Daniel Weitzner: It sounds like you think that is a bug. It sounds like a feature. I am just not sure what we are supposed to conclude from the fact of this accident. Is it that you couldn't use these in any legal scheme, which seems obviously to be the case. I am not sure what your solution is for this.

Steven Murdoch: It is a bug and a feature. It is a feature because at least there is some evidence that you can show. It is a bug in the sense that the design of the system for creating evidence was not very well thought through, so the evidence is somewhat poor. So we're somewhere in the middle, we have got evidence and it is sort of okay most of the time but not really. If the system was designed in a different way, there would be a realisation that there is no evidence whatsoever so we need to build an evidence overlay and then reach the other extreme where actually the evidence is very good. We're in this sort of middle where it is not great and it is not a disaster and I think that is the historical accident.

Ian Goldberg: You said the customer has a contractual relationship with the issuing bank, the merchant has a contractual relationship with the acquiring bank and the banks have relationships with the card scheme. The latter one I buy, the banks certainly have contractual relationships with the card scheme. The relationship between the merchant and the acquiring bank somewhat so, but the relationship between the customer and the issuing bank really is a contract of adhesion. There is no negotiating this contract on the customer side. The customer is just presented with "you want to use this card, here's your 10 pages of terms of service that you have to agree to because if not, you do not get a card", and certainly when they rolled out the chip cards in Canada, you basically had no choice. They said when your card expires the next one you get will have a chip and these are the terms that come with it and it involves all the liability shifts from the bank or merchant to the customer, but the customer of course had no say in this. These contractual relationships that you might want to lean on to decide where the liability goes, maybe morally shouldn't even be considered that because the customer has no say in it. If the contract shifts liability onto them, it is really not their fault.

Steven Murdoch: Yes, the situation is not good. I've acted as an expert witness in both dealing with customer cases and merchant cases and you are right, there is no real negotiation here.

Daniel Weitzner: But hold on, your complaint is with the bank regulators, because it is the bank regulators who ultimately either affirmatively consent to whatever these new terms are or just aren't. Or they are asleep at the switch, intentionally or otherwise.

Ian Goldberg: Captured regulators?

Daniel Weitzner: No, no, but seriously you look around the world and there are very different arrangements. Specifically about consumer liability, U.S. law has a couple of different rules and they make these judgments. I think you can dig down deeper and there are some contractual terms that maybe the regulators do not initially need to pay attention to, but it is still not quite a fair bargain. But I think as to these broad liabilities for failures of whatever sort, that is squarely up to regulators. The question is whether they are doing their job or not.

Steven Murdoch: Yes, so from my perspective the U.S. regulators are mostly doing their job well. But that really came from Jimmy Carter, when he was president. He set down some rules and those are still the rules, which roughly say that the customer is never liable. There is some 50 dollars, 150 dollars, but in most cases that is waived. The UK is somewhere in between because there is a Payment Services Directive, which is written moderately well with a couple of bugs, enforced quite badly in the UK, better elsewhere, and Canada is actually the worst in my experience, but it is because the regulator basically said the banks can do what they want.

Okay, so that was one example, EMV. Another one is on cryptocurrencies, we have all heard of cryptocurrencies. These are distributed, decentralised to a certain extent, and because you do not actually have any contractual relationship between anyone really, it is purely functioning on the basis of incentives. That makes it a little bit fragile, because if the incentives are not aligned properly then you have problems. The protocols that are designed for cryptocurrencies are often reasoned about in the ways that we reason about security protocols nowadays. We use formal models, we use proving techniques and model checkers and all these sorts of things. But when it comes to reasoning about incentives, it is sort of like being back in the 1980's for protocol design where, if someone proposes a protocol, they think that they are not able to break it, they show it to a room like this and nobody is able to break it, then it is good to go and they ship it. They start putting billions of dollars through the thing and this is fragile, this is problematic and you do actually have failures. For example, one set of failures, for example selfish mining, come from assumptions that Nash equilibria are the right way to think about incentives. Nash equilibria make a whole bunch of assumptions to do with parties being asynchronous and parties actually acting rationally and then when these assumptions go wrong you have attacks that are going to be possible. The other place that incentives have a role to play are to do in the fail-safe and the fail-deadly aspects. An example of a fail-safe incentive model is, you need to make some change to the software for whatever reason but you can do this in a backwards compatible way, so that the people who are possibly in a failure state because they are running the buggy version of the software are still able to interoperate with the other clients, which are running the more correct version of the software.

Ian Goldberg: Okay so this is something I do not get about soft forks in blockchain type things. This may be a little tangential but maybe by explaining what exactly you mean by this, this will clear this up for me. There was just a talk at Financial Cryptography a couple weeks ago, where they talked about soft forks, hard forks, velvet forks and I do not know, tiramisu forks or something. But when you do this fork, the set of valid transactions changes between the old software and the new software. In a soft fork, the old software will still produce transactions and blocks recognised by the new software, but it might reject blocks produced by the new software. As soon as the first block is mined by an upgraded client, what happens to the old client? The old clients, they are still mining. They see a block and they are like, "that is not valid, throw it away", and they are still mining on the old thing and now you have an actual fork in the chain. How is that fail-safe?

Steven Murdoch: I think that is the intention of the fail-safe, the reality may not be. I do not know if Sarah or Paddy or anyone wants to say something.

Patrick McCorry: I can say something about that. The whole point of the soft fork is that the miners are enforcing the new rules and I am not convinced it is actually incentive aligned. One of the incentives of the network is that you can verify everything yourself, but what you are doing in the soft fork is that when you create this new block, with the new set of consensus rules, you did it in such a way where you trick the old clients. All they see is an empty transaction was sent, they cannot validate the rules at all. You rely on the miners validating the rules and over 51% of the network enforcing it. Only operating clients can see the new rules, that is the soft fork. It relies on the fact that the miners are enforcing the new rules and you can trick old clients, and the fact is that there is some trickery there, maybe your comment earlier with the decisions and you do a magic trick, a sleight of hand, I do not know if the incentives are fully aligned for that.

Sarah Azouvi: Did that answer your question?

Ian Goldberg: Sure.

Steven Murdoch: Yes, that is the intention behind the fail safe even though it might not work, and then the sort of fail deadly approach is you have a chain split. For example, if Ethereum is splitting from the Ethereum Classic. Value does get destroyed for some people and you would hope that the incentives are aligned such so that people who suffer are the ones who have the money taken off them. Although, I am not actually convinced that going to be the case there.

Mansoor Ahmed: I am just wondering if it is even possible to design an incentive compatible system where there could be a theoretically infinite number of nodes. For example, many alt-coins claim to have an incentive compatible system, but then we see alt-coin infanticide where Bitcoin miners just decide to kill that alt-coin even though it is not incentive compatible. In a system where anyone can join, is it even possible to have some sort of a consistent incentive structure?

Steven Murdoch: That is a good question, I do not know. Paddy do you have a thought on that?

Patrick McCorry: I have one more comment, it is sort of like a tragedy of the commons. Joe Bonneau highlighted that, all of the miners have a long term interest in the health of the ecosystem and the blockchain itself. But in the short term, if they can boost their short term profits i.e., killing an alt-coin or mining an alternative cryptocurrency because they get more money, we have seen that with Bitcoin and Bitcoin cash, they are actually going to do that.

Alexander Hicks: One thing with something like incentive compatibility, usually you read the paper and they say their protocol is incentive compatible, but that is for incentives in the protocol, which might not relate to people outside the protocol that then decide to kill the coin, which is the problem you have a lot, the tragedy of the commons. People are going to compete to make their coin the most valuable. We'll get to incentive design later on, but it is worth taking time to point out that when people talk about incentives, they usually take into account only incentives in the protocol they designed rather than incentives for all, which is where a lot of problems arise.

Mansoor Ahmed: But if you have an open membership list, does it even make sense to talk about incentives within your protocol without looking at incentives for the whole world.

Alexander Hicks: Yes exactly, that is a failure of the models that are used now.

Steven Murdoch: It is actually linked to the next and final example, which is Tor. For those of you that do not know Tor, this is an anonymity technology. You send your traffic via three intermediaries and then your traffic comes out through the other end in such a way that it cannot be traced back to where it came from. The people who run these servers are volunteers, they do not get paid for it. A handful get some bandwidth reimbursement through a government scheme but most do not. There are 6 000 out there who are not actually getting any economic benefit from it. Looking from the fail-safe and fail-deadly aspect, the fail safe approach is that some of these may be malicious but there are three of them so unless the first node and the last node are colluding or being observed, you should still be safe. The idea behind fail-deadly would be that if a node is detected to be misbehaving, and there is active scanning for this. Then you could kick them out and then prevent them coming back. But there is Mansoor's point about what happens when there is an indefinite amount of people in the system. Also, what happens if you are not able to identify the people operating these servers? The person will probably just come back again and they will be throttled for a while, but eventually they will go back to the previous state, under a new identity. The other interesting aspect about Tor is that there are concerns about introducing monetary incentives. The example that is sometimes given is that there was an economic experiment done in an Israeli nursery scheme where the problem they were trying to address is that parents were coming late to pick up their children, so they introduced a fine if you came late to pick up your children. It turned out that parents started coming later because you'd moved a social punishment of just feeling bad and maybe getting into trouble, into an economic punishment and they just considered this is the price of extra childcare and they are very happy to pay that fine as a price for extra childcare. At the end of the experiment, the nurseries removed this fine but still the parents came late. By shifting from a non-economic to economic incentive scheme, you've actually permanently damaged the system and that is why things are not changed.

Mansoor Ahmed: I understand why you would not want to do monetary incentives but are there trepidation incentives. Is there a leader-board where we can say "oh I contributed this much bandwidth"?

Steven Murdoch: I've got a Master's project on exactly that so maybe we should talk about that. Currently there is a leader-board but it is fairly simplistic. So the idea behind this Master's project is to actually take a little bit of psychology, game design and marketing and then use this to make it a bit more fun to run a Tor node.

We have already had some good discussion, here are some other points that we could consider to get things started, I do not know how much time we have left. How do you reason about security protocols from the incentives perspective? How do you choose the right kind of incentive? There is a categorization in the paper where we can look at different incentive schemes and different enforcement mechanisms How do you actually enforce them? Do you need to have a regulator? Do you need to have strong evidence? How do you actually do that and then should you use things like Nash equilibria, there is the BAR model, rational cryptography. When do you use a particular model in the particular context?

Ian Goldberg: I actually have a question about a figure in the paper, which did not appear in your talk. Right at the end of the paper, figure two in the pre-print [removed from final version], you have this Venn diagram here where you have different models by field. You have three circles, Game Theory, Cryptography and Systems, and you have things filled in a bunch of places. Notably the cryptography and systems intersection is completely empty. Why? Is there really no intersection between Cryptography and Systems?

Frank Stajano: Theory and practice people?

Steven Murdoch: What would you put in there?

Ian Goldberg: I mean, there are a lot of things that touch both Cryptography and Systems. Any real protocol design for example, will have both cryptographic aspects and systems aspects.

Virgil Gligor: I will cover one of those.

Ian Goldberg: Sure, yes. Like when we built Off-The-Record, there were very specific design choices we had to make to make it both cryptographically correct, but also there was a maximum message size that some networks supported. We had to make sure that instead of sending this message in message one, we have to send a commitment to it in message one and then reveal it in message three and things like this. I think protocol design certainly sits in the intersection of cryptography and systems for example in many cases.

Sarah Azouvi: In this diagram, what we wanted to put are the formal models that people are using to reason about security. There are a lot of protocols that combines cryptography and distributed system, and blockchain is one of them, but what you see is, for example for blockchain, what they use in order to prove formal models is more from the cryptographic literature or more from the distributed systems literature. What we are saying is that maybe we need new formal models that can encompass this better, because these models have failed to encompass a lot of attacks.

Ian Goldberg: But what about things just like Dolev-Yao and pi-calculus. These things definitely look at both the cryptographic side and thee distributed systems side and model the actors and model their messages. I think these things would fit in this section here.

Virgil Gligor: Just a comment. What has happened here is that Steven drew a boundary, which is reasoning about these protocols. There is always some other mechanism below the boundary that of course is not addressed in here. Indeed there is an intersection between Cryptography and Systems but at a much lower level than these, so in that sense the diagram reflects this abstract level as opposed to more concrete systems level.

Too Big to FAIL: What You Need to Know Before Attacking a Machine Learning System

Tudor Dumitraş(✉), Yiğitcan Kaya, Radu Mărginean, and Octavian Suciu

University of Maryland, College Park, USA
tdumitra@umd.edu

Abstract. There is an emerging arms race in the field of adversarial machine learning (AML). Recent results suggest that machine learning (ML) systems are vulnerable to a wide range of attacks; meanwhile, there are no systematic defenses. In this position paper we argue that to make progress toward such defenses, the specifications for machine learning systems must include precise adversary definitions—a key requirement in other fields, such as cryptography or network security. Without common adversary definitions, new AML attacks risk making strong and unrealistic assumptions about the adversary's capabilities. Furthermore, new AML defenses are evaluated based on their robustness against adversarial samples generated by a specific attack algorithm, rather than by a general class of adversaries. We propose the **FAIL** adversary model, which describes the adversary's knowledge and control along four dimensions: data **F**eatures, learning **A**lgorithms, training **I**nstances and crafting **L**everage. We analyze several common assumptions, often implicit, from the AML literature, and we argue that the **FAIL** model can represent and generalize the adversaries considered in these references. The **FAIL** model allows us to consider a range of adversarial capabilities and enables systematic comparisons of attacks against ML systems, providing a clearer picture of the security threats that these attacks raise. By evaluating how much a new AML attack's success depends on the strength of the adversary along each of the **FAIL** dimensions, researchers will be able to reason about the real effectiveness of the attack. Additionally, such evaluations may suggest promising directions for investigating defenses against the ML threats.

Keywords: Machine learning · Adversary model

1 Introduction

Machine learning techniques increasingly drive the success of a wide range of applications, including autonomous driving, computer vision, biomedical research, financial fraud detection, defenses against malware and cyber attacks, or crime prediction for informing parole and sentencing decisions. In a supervised learning setting, an ML classifier starts from a few *labeled instances* in the

V. Matyáš et al. (Eds.): Security Protocols 2018, LNCS 11286, pp. 150–162, 2018.
https://doi.org/10.1007/978-3-030-03251-7_17

training set. The classifier uses a *training algorithm* to learn a *model* that maps an instance (e.g. an executable program) to a label (e.g. malware or benign sample), without needing a predetermined specification of what constitutes malicious behavior. The model makes this *classification* by considering multiple *features* of the instance (e.g. the system calls that the program invokes). We can then apply the model on new instances from a *testing set*, which consists of unknown programs, to predict their maliciousness.

ML models are inherently vulnerable to attacks. First, machine learning systems have a large attack surface including the training algorithm, the training data, and the feature extraction process. Second, ML models have started outperforming humans in tasks such as lip reading [9], or image recognition [29], which makes it difficult to confirm that they are operating correctly. Adversaries can exploit this situation to influence the model to their own advantage. Research in adversarial machine learning has demonstrated attacks that satisfy a variety of adversarial goals and that appear to be very effective. In evasion [4,11,14,20,24], model stealing [20,27,34], or model inversion [12], adversaries attack a trained model during testing time; in poisoning [2,5,31], the attack is directed toward the training process. Moreover, such attacks can be conducted in the real-world, for example, by generating hidden voice commands, which are unintelligible to human listeners, but interpreted as commands by device's voice recognition interface [6]; or by printing a pair of eyeglass frames to attack facial biometric systems allowing the adversary to evade recognition or to impersonate another individual [28].

The practical implications of ML attacks call for a realistic security assessment. Most testing time attacks investigate adversaries with full white-box access to the victim classifier [7,32], while in many training time attacks [15,17,19,37] adversaries assumed to fully control the labeling of training set instances and the training process. These assumptions are often unrealistic and might not reflect the capabilities of practical adversaries. For example, recent work on attack *transferability* from a limited local model trained by the adversary to target model mostly focuses on adversaries with imperfect knowledge of the training algorithm [18,25]. These adversary models do not reflect real-world practices such as relying on undisclosed features instead of algorithmic secrecy [8,16,33]. Prior work has also analyzed adversaries limited in training set knowledge [19] or knowledge of the features [36], but these adversary definitions are incomplete since they each focus on a single dimension of the adversary's knowledge.

To understand the security threat introduced by attacks against a machine learning system, we must accurately model the capabilities and limitations of realistic adversaries. To this end, we propose the **FAIL** model, a general framework for analyzing the effectiveness of ML attacks for a broad range of adversaries. **FAIL** defines four dimensions of adversarial knowledge and control: **F**eatures, **A**lgorithms **I**nstances, and **L**everage. In Fig. 1, we demonstrate a practical Android malware detection task, and how the **FAIL** framework models realistic adversaries. The detector uses Android binaries in public Drebin data set [1] as the training set. The choice of using an open-source data set would result in a realistic adversary with full knowledge along **I** dimension. From binaries, detector extracts features using a proprietary program analysis tool. In consequence, a realistic adversary can only have a limited knowledge along **F** dimension. It combines these features with third-party rating scores coming from Android App markets. Even though rating scores can be manipulated, it requires additional challenges, therefore, the adversary ends up with a partial **L**everage of using these features to attack the detector. Finally, the detector uses a standard linear SVM algorithm to train the model. The adversary can easily guess the algorithm without knowing the exact parameters, therefore would have a limited knowledge along **A** dimension.

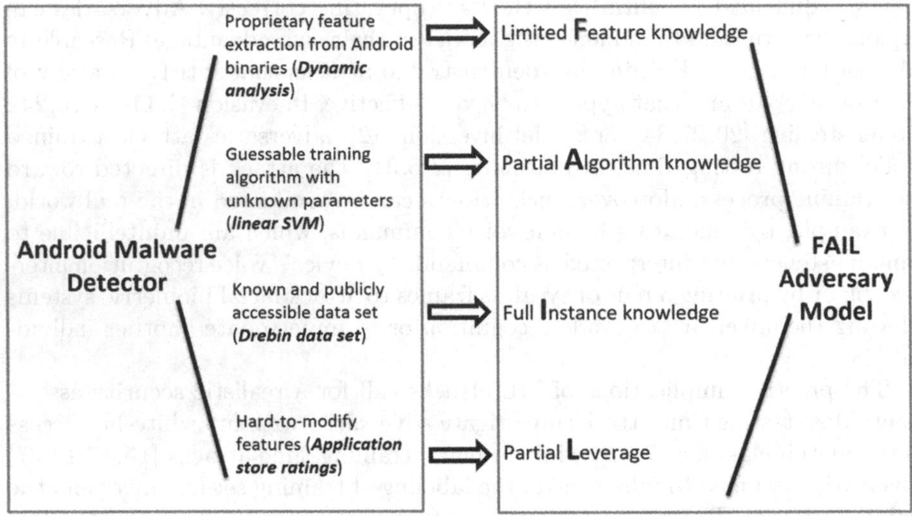

Fig. 1. Applying **FAIL** framework to define realistic adversaries against an ML-based Android Malware detector.

The **FAIL** adversary model makes the assumptions about adversarial capabilities explicit, and it enables a more comprehensive assessment of the expected effectiveness of ML attacks in realistic scenarios. For example, evaluating an attack under the **FAIL** model would generalize the transferability property—which assumes algorithmic secrecy (**A** dimension)—by considering multiple ways to limit the knowledge of the adversary. In consequence, attacks that are believed to be transferable may not be as effective under the generalized transferability defined by the **FAIL** model. Moreover, analyzing attack effectiveness within the **FAIL** model can suggest promising research avenues for defense strategies by highlighting how constraints along each of the **FAIL** dimensions affect the adversary's success rate.

In this work, we make the following contributions:

- In the adversarial machine learning literature, we identify a gap between knowledge and capabilities of a realistic adversary and the previous threat

models. To bridge this gap, we propose the **FAIL** model, a general framework for systemically modeling realistic adversaries and evaluating their impact.
- Our **FAIL** model generalizes the transferability of attacks against ML systems across various dimensions of adversarial knowledge and capabilities. Generalized transferability captures the industry practices and realistic adversaries than previous definitions more accurately.
- Using the **FAIL** model, we categorize existing attacks and defenses. In the prior work, the FAIL framework exposes implicit assumptions that can compromise security, and also captures explicit assumptions about the adversaries.

The rest of this document is structured as follows. Section 2 provides a detailed description of the problem we address. Section 3 introduces the **FAIL** framework for modeling adversaries against ML systems. In Sect. 4, we apply the **FAIL** model to existing work and highlight our findings. Finally, we conclude our study in Sect. 5.

2 Problem Statement

There are few provable security guarantees for machine learning. Existing attacks appear to be very effective, and defensive attempts are usually short-lived as they are broken by the follow-up work [7]. This arms race leaves the impression that attacking a model is easier than defending it, as the models have a wide attack surface that is difficult to defend robustly.

Existing attacks define various adversary models in a spectrum of adversarial capabilities. However, the lack of a unifying model capturing the dimensions of adversarial knowledge caused existing work to diverge in terms of adversary specifications. [25] and [36] both define black-box adversaries, however former attributes access to full feature representation, whereas latter only grants access to the raw data before feature extraction. These models are usually too rigid to account for the realistic adversaries. This elevates the disadvantage of defenders, they are required to evaluate these unrealistic definitions when employing defenses. Clear definitions that can accurately reflect the capabilities of real-world adversaries can help defenders mitigate attacker advantage. To this extent, we aim to provide a general framework to *systematically define adversaries based on realistic assumptions about their capabilities*.

In AML, an adversary crafts samples that will be mislabeled by a trained model (*evasive samples*) or samples that will be included in the training set and cause the classifier to learn a skewed model (*poison samples*). The adversary may have to craft the poison instances without knowing key details about the classifier under attack, such as the other instances from the training set, the classification algorithm, or the features used in the model. Existing work demonstrates attacks succeed when conducted by strong adversaries. Evaluating unrealistic adversaries does not improve our understanding of the security of these models. Systematically defining realistic adversaries provides us with insights, and allows us to answer the question *How much damage can a realistic adversary inflict by poisoning a machine learning system?*.

Transferability of an attack is an important benchmark for attack success, as it allows adversaries with limited knowledge of the target model to conduct effective attacks. Transferability also hinder defenses by rendering secrecy ineffective. Existing work on transferability investigates a single dimension, limiting the adversary's knowledge of the training algorithm [25]. This weak notion of transferability limits the understanding of attack impact on the real systems and overshadows potential defensive avenues. We aim to define a realistic adversary model, also to provide a more insightful concept of *generalized transferability*, across a wide spectrum of adversaries.

Attacks Against Machine Learning. Adversarial attacks can be categorized based on the *goals*, *strategies* and *capabilities* of the attacker. Testing time *evasion* attacks aim to exploit the vulnerabilities of the trained model, without altering the training process. Evasion attacks use intentionally designed adversarial examples to cause the model to make a mistake. In this setting, several targeted *sample crafting* algorithms have been proposed, allowing the adversary to modify the feature vectors of instances from the test set to evade classifiers [4,7,14,20,23,24,36]. In a training time *poisoning* attack, the adversary manipulates the training set, by either crafting new training instances, or by strategically modifying a subset of existing training samples [5,22]. An important question is whether attack instances are *transferable* [25,27], i.e. if instances crafted against a substitute model trained and controlled by the adversary, are also effective against the target model. In a *white-box* attack, the adversary crafts samples with full knowledge of the model under attack. In a *black-box* attack, the adversary trains a surrogate model, which approximates the behavior of the model under attack and takes advantage of the transferability property.

ML attacks can be further classified, based on the adversary's goals, into *indiscriminate* and *targeted* attacks. In an indiscriminate attack, the adversary aims to increase the overall error rate of the victim model, while in a targeted attack the goal is to induce a misprediction on a specific instance, or a small set of such instances, from the testing set. Even though existing work proposed defenses against both poisoning [2,3,10], and evasion attacks [26], most defenses are proven to be ineffective by follow-up work [7].

3 Modeling Realistic Adversaries

Against machine learning systems, adversaries start from their goals—forcing model to misclassify a target or hurt the model performance—and devise a strategy to achieve the goal. Figure 2 demonstrates different goals, and resulting attack strategies. In Fig. 2a and b, the goal is to force the model to misclassify a target instance. Former attack achieves the goal by performing an evasion, whereas latter achieves the same goal by conducting a targeted poisoning. In Fig. 2c, the goal is to reduce model performance as much as possible, which is achieved by performing an indiscriminate poisoning attack.

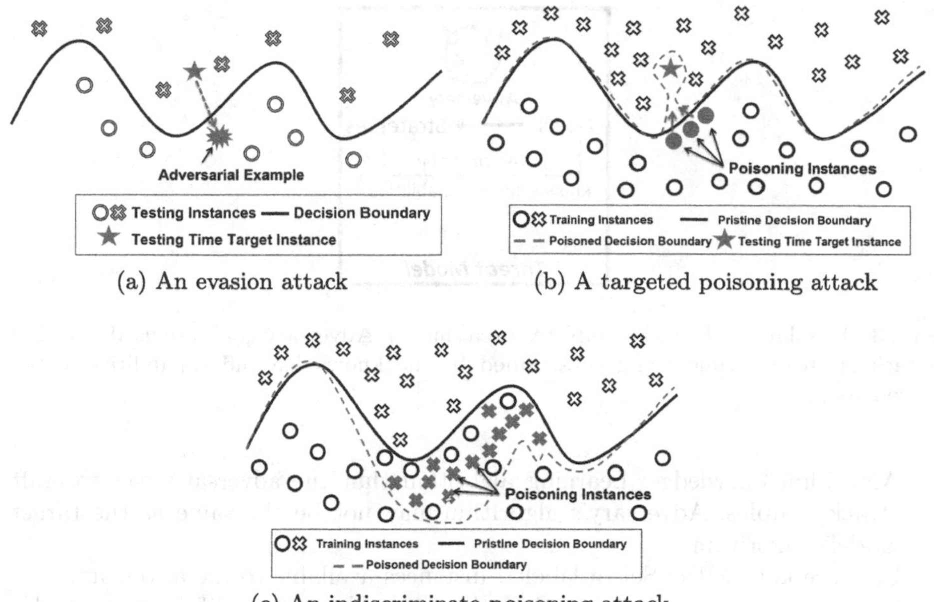

(a) An evasion attack (b) A targeted poisoning attack

(c) An indiscriminate poisoning attack

Fig. 2. Example attacks against machine learning. In evasion attacks (a), and targeted poisoning attacks (b), adversaries have different strategies to achieve the same goal, causing a specific misclassification of a test time target instance. Whereas in indiscriminate poisoning attacks (c), the goal is to distort decision boundary as much as possible to reduce model performance.

A threat model can be viewed as a combination of *adversary's goals*, *adversary's knowledge and capabilities* and *adversary's strategies*. As Fig. 3 demonstrates, adversaries devise attack strategies in line with their goals, while being constrained by their knowledge of the target model, and respective capabilities. In consequence, a threat model that does not accurately reflect adversary capabilities will not provide a realistic security assessment.

We propose the **FAIL** framework to formalize adversary's knowledge and capabilities in the context of adversarial machine learning. **FAIL** is not a complete threat model, however, it aims to bridge the existing gap connecting adversary's goals to attack strategies.

Knowledge and Capabilities. The capabilities and limitations of an adversary have an important impact on the attack effectiveness and on the realistic threat assessment. We formalize this in the **FAIL** attacker model, which describes the adversary's knowledge and control along 4 dimensions:

- Feature knowledge: Subset of features used in the target model, known to the adversary.

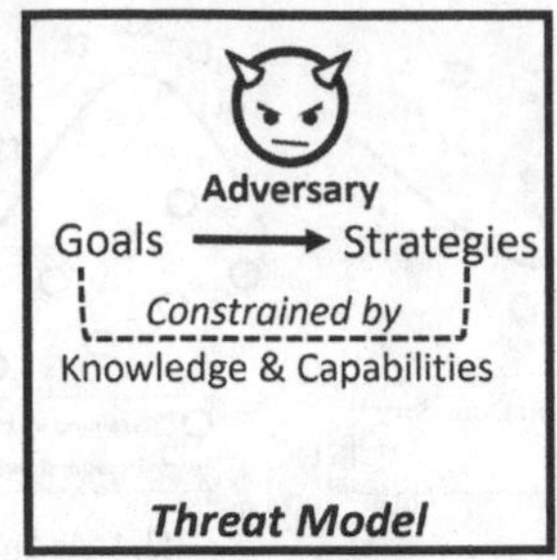

Fig. 3. Template to define a complete threat model. Adversary goals are used to define attack strategies while being constrained by the knowledge and capabilities of the adversary.

- **A**lgorithm knowledge: Learning algorithm that the adversary uses to craft attack samples. Adversary's algorithm may not be the same as the target model's algorithm.
- **I**nstance knowledge: Set of labeled instances available to the adversary.
- **L**everage: Subset of features that the adversary can modify. Leverage also defines the range a feature can be modified within.

The **F** and **A** dimensions constrain the attacker's understanding of the hypothesis space, the set of all possible models can be learned by the victim. Without knowing the target training algorithm, the attacker would have to select an alternative learning algorithm and hope that the poison samples crafted for alternative algorithm transfer to target algorithm. Similarly, if some features are unknown (i.e., partial feature knowledge), the model that the adversary uses is an approximation of the original classifier. For classifiers that learn a representation of the input features (such as neural networks), limiting the **F** dimension would result in a different, approximate internal representation. The **I** dimension affects the accuracy of the adversary's view of the instance space. Instances known to the attacker might or might not be in the training set of the target model. Finally, the **L** dimension affects the adversary's *ability* to craft poison sample—the set of modifiable features restricts the regions of the feature space where the crafted instances could lie.

Implementation of FAIL Dimensions. FAIL framework provides a systematic way to model weaker adversaries, however, it does not specify how to simulate them. Performing empirical evaluations of attacks and defenses within the **FAIL** model requires further design choices that depend on the application. To this end, we propose the following questionnaire to guide the design of experiments focusing on each **FAIL** dimension.

- **F** dimension: *What features could be kept as a secret?* and *Could the attacker access the exact feature values?*
- **A** dimension: *Is the algorithm class known?*, *Is the training algorithm secret?* and *Are the classifier parameters secret?*

- **I** dimension: *Is the entire training set known?*, *Is the training set partially known* and *Are the instances known to the attacker sufficient to train a robust classifier?*
- **L** dimension: *Which features are modifiable by the attacker?* and *What side effects do the modifications have?*

Transferability. FAIL model extends transferability property, and it can be applied to measuring the transferability of both training and testing time attacks. Generalized transferability covers a broader range of adversaries along the FAIL dimensions. The prior work on transferability [25] focused on the **A** dimension, and only in the context of the evasion attacks. However, this may not be the most important dimension. ML-based systems often employed in the security industry (for example, [8] uses proprietary reputation scores for malware detection) often rely on undisclosed features to render attacks more difficult. The resilience against adversaries with partial knowledge along the **F** dimension has not been evaluated systematically. Under the generalized transferability defined by the **FAIL** model, attacks that are believed to be transferable, such as [18,25] might not be transferable.

4 From Adversary Definitions to Security Properties

Discordant threat model definitions result in implicit assumptions about adversarial limitations, some of which might not be realistic. The FAIL model allows us to systematically reason about such assumptions. To demonstrate its utility, we evaluate a body of existing studies by means of answering two questions for each work.

To categorize existing attacks, we first inspect a threat model and ask: *AQ1–Are bounds for attacker limitations specified along the dimension?*. The possible answers are: *yes, omitted* and *irrelevant*. For instance, the threat model in Carlini et al.'s evasion attack [7] specifies that the adversary requires complete knowledge of the model and its parameters, thus the answer is *yes* for the **A** dimension. In contrast, the analysis on the **I** dimension is *irrelevant* because the attack does not require access to the victim training set. However, the study does not discuss feature knowledge, therefore we mark the **F** dimension as *omitted*.

Our second question is: *AQ2–Is the proposed technique evaluated along the dimension?*. This question becomes *irrelevant* if the threat model specifications are *omitted* or *irrelevant*. For example, Carlini et al. evaluated transferability of their attack when the attacker does not know the target model parameters. This corresponds to the attacker algorithm knowledge, therefore the answer is *yes* for the **A** dimension.

Applying the FAIL model reveals implicit assumptions in existing attacks. An implicit assumption exists if the attack limitations are not specified along a dimension. Furthermore, even with explicit assumptions, some studies do not evaluate all relevant dimensions. We present these findings about previous attacks within the FAIL model in Table 1.

Table 1. FAIL analysis of existing attacks. For each attack, we analyze the adversary model and evaluation of the proposed technique. Each cell contains the answers to our two questions, *AQ1* and *AQ2*: *yes* (✓), *omitted* (✗) and *irrelevant* (∅). We also flag *implicit assumptions* (*) and a *missing evaluation* (†).

Study	**F**	**A**	**I**	**L**
Test time attacks				
Genetic evasion [36]	✓, ✓	✓, ✓	✓, ✗†	✓, ✓
Black-box evasion [27]	✗, ∅*	✓, ✓	✓, ✓	✗, ∅*
Model stealing [34]	✓, ✓	✓, ✓	✓, ✓	✗, ∅*
FGSM evasion [14]	✗, ∅*	✗, ∅*	∅, ∅	✗, ∅*
Carlini's evasion [7]	✗, ∅*	✓, ✓	∅, ∅	✗, ∅*
Training time attacks				
SVM poisoning [5]	✗, ∅*	✓, ✗†	∅, ∅	✗, ∅*
NN poisoning [21]	✓, ✗†	✓, ✓	✓, ✓	✗, ∅*
NN backdoor [15][a]	✓, ✗†	✓, ✓	✓, ✗†	✓, ✓
NN trojan [19]	✓, ✗†	✓, ✓	✓, ✓	✓, ✓

[a]Gu et al.'s study investigates a scenario where the attacker performs the training on behalf of the victim. Consequently, the attacker has full access to the model architecture, parameters, training set and feature representation. However, with the emergence of frameworks such as [13], even in this threat model, it might be possible that the attacker does not know the training set or the features.

When looking at existing defenses through the FAIL model, we aim to observe how they achieve security: either by hiding information or limiting the attacker capabilities. For defenses that involve creating knowledge asymmetry between attackers and the defenders, i.e. secrecy, we ask: *DQ1–Is the dimension employed as a mechanism for secrecy?*. For example, feature squeezing [35] employs feature reduction techniques unknown to the attacker; therefore the answer is *yes* for the **F** dimension.

In order to identify hardening dimensions, which attempt to limit the attack capabilities, we ask: *DQ2–Is the dimension employed as a mechanism for hardening?*. For instance, the distillation defense [26] against evasion modifies the neural network weights to make the attack more difficult; therefore the answer is *yes* for the **A** dimension.

These defenses may come with inaccurate assessments for the adversarial capabilities and implicit assumptions. For example, distillation limits adversaries along the **F** and **A** dimensions but employing a different attack strategy could bypass it [7]. On poisoning attacks, the RONI [22] defense assumes training set secrecy, but does not evaluate the threat posed by attackers with sufficient knowledge along the other dimensions. This implicit assumption has been shown to allow attackers to bypass the defense while remaining within the secrecy bounds [31]. The results for the evaluated defenses are found in Table 2.

Table 2. FAIL analysis of existing defenses. We analyze a defense's approach to security: *DQ1* (secrecy) and *DQ2* (hardening). Each cell contains the answers to the two questions: *yes* (✓), and *no* (✗).

Study	**F**	**A**	**I**	**L**
Test time defenses				
Distillation[26]	✗, ✓	✗, ✓	✗, ✗	✗, ✗
Feature squeezing[35]	✓, ✓	✗, ✗	✗, ✗	✓, ✓
Training time defenses				
RONI[22]	✗, ✗	✗, ✗	✓, ✗	✗, ✗
Certified defense[30]	✗, ✗	✗, ✗	✓, ✓	✗, ✗

A systematic exploration of the **FAIL** dimensions for previous attacks and defenses can provide insights into the importance of each dimension towards an adversary's goals. For example, such an analysis can indicate whether the industry practice of maintaining feature secrecy provides a better resilience against attacks than the algorithmic secrecy explored in the recent academic literature. Moreover, the **FAIL** adversary model is applicable to an entire spectrum of attacks against machine learning systems. Future research may utilize this framework as a vehicle for reasoning about the most promising directions for defending against evasion and poisoning attacks.

5 Conclusions

We propose the **FAIL** model, a general framework for evaluating attacks against machine learning. The **FAIL** model aims to fill a gap in the threat models from previous work on adversarial machine learning by providing a systematical way to model the knowledge and capabilities of adversaries. This represents a step toward complete adversary definitions for machine learning. Additionally, the **FAIL** model generalizes the notion of attack transferability and allows us to evaluate the effectiveness of attacks conducted by more realistic adversaries. Moreover, **FAIL** analysis of attacks along multiple dimensions of adversarial knowledge and control can highlight promising dimensions for future defensive strategies.

References

1. Arp, D., Spreitzenbarth, M., Hubner, M., Gascon, H., Rieck, K.: DREBIN: effective and explainable detection of android malware in your pocket. In: 21st Annual Network and Distributed System Security Symposium, NDSS 2014, San Diego, California, USA, 23–26 February 2014 (2014). https://www.ndss-symposium.org/ndss2014/drebin-effective-and-explainable-detection-android-malware-your-pocket
2. Barreno, M., Nelson, B., Joseph, A.D., Tygar, J.D.: The security of machine learning. Mach. Learn. **81**, 121–148 (2010)
3. Biggio, B., Corona, I., Fumera, G., Giacinto, G., Roli, F.: Bagging classifiers for fighting poisoning attacks in adversarial classification tasks. In: Sansone, C., Kittler, J., Roli, F. (eds.) MCS 2011. LNCS, vol. 6713, pp. 350–359. Springer, Heidelberg (2011). https://doi.org/10.1007/978-3-642-21557-5_37
4. Biggio, B., et al.: Evasion attacks against machine learning at test time. In: Blockeel, H., Kersting, K., Nijssen, S., Železný, F. (eds.) ECML PKDD 2013. LNCS (LNAI), vol. 8190, pp. 387–402. Springer, Heidelberg (2013). https://doi.org/10.1007/978-3-642-40994-3_25
5. Biggio, B., Nelson, B., Laskov, P.: Poisoning attacks against support vector machines. arXiv preprint arXiv:1206.6389 (2012)
6. Carlini, N., et al.: Hidden voice commands. In: USENIX Security Symposium, pp. 513–530 (2016)
7. Carlini, N., Wagner, D.A.: Towards evaluating the robustness of neural networks. In: 2017 IEEE Symposium on Security and Privacy, SP 2017, San Jose, CA, USA, 22–26 May 2017, pp. 39–57 (2017). https://doi.org/10.1109/SP.2017.49
8. Chau, D.H.P., Nachenberg, C., Wilhelm, J., Wright, A., Faloutsos, C.: Polonium: tera-scale graph mining for malware detection. In: SIAM International Conference on Data Mining (SDM), Mesa, AZ, April 2011. http://www.cs.cmu.edu/~dchau/polonium/polonium_kdd_ldmta_2010.pdf
9. Chung, J.S., Senior, A., Vinyals, O., Zisserman, A.: Lip reading sentences in the wild. arXiv preprint arXiv:1611.05358 v2 (2016)
10. Cretu, G.F., Stavrou, A., Locasto, M.E., Stolfo, S.J., Keromytis, A.D.: Casting out demons: sanitizing training data for anomaly sensors. In: IEEE Symposium on Security and Privacy, SP 2008, pp. 81–95. IEEE (2008)
11. Dalvi, N., Domingos, P., Sanghai, S., Verma, D., et al.: Adversarial classification. In: Proceedings of the Tenth ACM SIGKDD International Conference on Knowledge Discovery and Data Mining, pp. 99–108. ACM (2004)
12. Fredrikson, M., Lantz, E., Jha, S., Lin, S., Page, D., Ristenpart, T.: Privacy in pharmacogenetics: an end-to-end case study of personalized warfarin dosing. In: 23rd USENIX Security Symposium (USENIX Security 2014), pp. 17–32 (2014)
13. Dowlin, N., Gilad-Bachrach, R., Laine, K., Lauter, K., Naehrig, M., Wernsing, J.: Cryptonets: applying neural networks to encrypted data with high throughput and accuracy. In: International Conference on Machine Learning, pp. 201–210 (2016)
14. Goodfellow, I.J., Shlens, J., Szegedy, C.: Explaining and harnessing adversarial examples. arXiv preprint arXiv:1412.6572 (2014)
15. Gu, T., Dolan-Gavitt, B., Garg, S.: Badnets: identifying vulnerabilities in the machine learning model supply chain. arXiv preprint arXiv:1708.06733 (2017)
16. Hearn, M.: Abuse at scale. In: RIPE 64, Ljublijana, Slovenia, April 2012. https://ripe64.ripe.net/archives/video/25/

17. Koh, P.W., Liang, P.: Understanding black-box predictions via influence functions. arXiv preprint arXiv:1703.04730 (2017)
18. Liu, Y., Chen, X., Liu, C., Song, D.: Delving into transferable adversarial examples and black-box attacks. arXiv preprint arXiv:1611.02770 (2016)
19. Liu, Y., et al.: Trojaning attack on neural networks. Technical report 17-002. Purdue University (2017)
20. Lowd, D., Meek, C.: Adversarial learning. In: Proceedings of the eleventh ACM SIGKDD International Conference on Knowledge Discovery in Data Mining, pp. 641–647. ACM (2005)
21. Muñoz-González, L., et al.: Towards poisoning of deep learning algorithms with back-gradient optimization. In: Proceedings of the 10th ACM Workshop on Artificial Intelligence and Security, pp. 27–38. ACM (2017)
22. Nelson, B., et al.: Exploiting machine learning to subvert your spam filter. In: Proceedings of the 1st USENIX Workshop on Large-Scale Exploits and Emergent Threats, LEET 2008, pp. 7:1–7:9. USENIX Association, Berkeley (2008). http://dl.acm.org/citation.cfm?id=1387709.1387716
23. Papernot, N., McDaniel, P., Goodfellow, I., Jha, S., Celik, Z.B., Swami, A.: Practical black-box attacks against deep learning systems using adversarial examples. arXiv preprint arXiv:1602.02697 (2016)
24. Papernot, N., McDaniel, P., Jha, S., Fredrikson, M., Celik, Z.B., Swami, A.: The limitations of deep learning in adversarial settings. In: 2016 IEEE European Symposium on Security and Privacy (EuroS&P), pp. 372–387. IEEE (2016)
25. Papernot, N., McDaniel, P.D., Goodfellow, I.J.: Transferability in machine learning: from phenomena to black-box attacks using adversarial samples. CoRR abs/1605.07277 (2016). http://arxiv.org/abs/1605.07277
26. Papernot, N., McDaniel, P.D., Wu, X., Jha, S., Swami, A.: Distillation as a defense to adversarial perturbations against deep neural networks. In: IEEE Symposium on Security and Privacy, SP 2016, San Jose, CA, USA, 22–26 May 2016, pp. 582–597 (2016), https://doi.org/10.1109/SP.2016.41
27. Papernot, N., McDaniel, P.D., Goodfellow, I.J., Jha, S., Celik, Z.B., Swami, A.: Practical black-box attacks against deep learning systems using adversarial examples. In: ACM Asia Conference on Computer and Communications Security, Abu Dhabi, UAE (2017). http://arxiv.org/abs/1602.02697
28. Sharif, M., Bhagavatula, S., Bauer, L., Reiter, M.K.: Accessorize to a crime: real and stealthy attacks on state-of-the-art face recognition. In: Proceedings of the 2016 ACM SIGSAC Conference on Computer and Communications Security, pp. 1528–1540. ACM (2016)
29. Simonyan, K., Zisserman, A.: Very deep convolutional networks for large-scale image recognition. CoRR abs/1409.1556 (2014). http://arxiv.org/abs/1409.1556
30. Steinhardt, J., Koh, P.W.W., Liang, P.S.: Certified defenses for data poisoning attacks. In: Advances in Neural Information Processing Systems, pp. 3520–3532 (2017)
31. Suciu, O., Marginean, R., Kaya, Y., Daume III, H., Dumitras, T.: When does machine learning FAIL? Generalized transferability for evasion and poisoning attacks. In: 27th USENIX Security Symposium (USENIX Security 2018), pp. 1299–1316. USENIX Association, Baltimore (2018). https://www.usenix.org/conference/usenixsecurity18/presentation/suciu
32. Szegedy, C., et al.: Intriguing properties of neural networks. arXiv preprint arXiv:1312.6199 (2013)
33. Tamersoy, A., Roundy, K., Chau, D.H.: Guilt by association: large scale malware detection by mining file-relation graphs. In: KDD (2014)

34. Tramèr, F., Zhang, F., Juels, A., Reiter, M., Ristenpart, T.: Stealing machine learning models via prediction APIs. In: 25th USENIX Security Symposium (USENIX Security 2016). USENIX Association, Austin, August 2016. https://www.usenix.org/conference/usenixsecurity16/technical-sessions/presentation/tramer
35. Xu, W., Evans, D., Qi, Y.: Feature squeezing: Detecting adversarial examples in deep neural networks. arXiv preprint arXiv:1704.01155 (2017)
36. Xu, W., Qi, Y., Evans, D.: Automatically evading classifiers. In: Proceedings of the 2016 Network and Distributed Systems Symposium (2016)
37. Yang, C., Wu, Q., Li, H., Chen, Y.: Generative poisoning attack method against neural networks. arXiv preprint arXiv:1703.01340 (2017)

Too Big to FAIL: What You Need to Know Before Attacking a Machine Learning System (Transcript of Discussion)

Tudor Dumitraş(✉)

University of Maryland, College Park, USA
tdumitra@umd.edu

Ilia Shumailov: I might have misunderstood something. So why do black-box models grant too little?

Reply: So, for example, you assume that the adversary does not know that you are using a linear model... which may be easy to guess.

Ilia Shumailov: From what?

Reply: Just by probing the classifier.

Ilia Shumailov: But this is an active area of research, approximating the model and trying to figure out its parameters or structure.

Reply: Right. So figuring out the parameters is a little bit more challenging, but the black-box model assumes that you don't even know that it's a linear model.

Ilia Shumailov: Yeah, but this is fairly common practice. For example, a very common scenario right now having a fusion of models to not allow people to approximate your models. The fusion does a rotation of different models, such that they keep producing new samples representative of different models altogether, so you can't approximate it efficiently.

Reply: Right, so, you're talking about a defence. In this case, and I'll give a scenario where you don't use an ensemble like you're describing, you just use one model, and you're assuming that the adversary doesn't know anything about that model.

Ilia Shumailov: Right, tell me if I understand correctly. What you are trying to say, is that there are some occasions in which you have additional information and that in such occasions, black-box models don't actually provide you with enough information.

Reply: Yes, and in fact, what we would like to know is how much the adversary's information in different areas; so about the model, about the hyper-parameters, about the features; how much does this contribute to the success of the attack? Because this can actually suggest some promising directions for defences, for how to constrain the adversary. So let's take a look at an example. In this case, the malware detector extracts a variety of features, it provides static or dynamic analysis, and there's a really long history of work in binary analysis, and there's a huge amount of features that could potentially be extracted. If you don't know exactly what features the model is extracting, you may not be

V. Matyáš et al. (Eds.): Security Protocols 2018, LNCS 11286, pp. 163–165, 2018.
https://doi.org/10.1007/978-3-030-03251-7_18

able to guess them all. In this case, the adversary would have limited feature knowledge. Again, the algorithm, it's not an ensemble, it's a linear SVM, so you may be able to guess that it's a linear SVM- but you may not know all the parameters, right? So again, you have some partial algorithm knowledge in this case, or you may need to approximate the parameters through some sort of model extraction attack. You have a full instance knowledge because the training set for the algorithm is public. Some of the features may be difficult for the adversary to modify even if it's his own app because, for example, some of the features include ratings in the app store. So the adversary may have a hard time controlling that.

Daniel Weitzner: I'm curious about how would your model react to all the various efforts that I'm sure you're aware of, to try to make various neural networks that have social significance be more interpretable, explainable... subject to assessments, fairness, bias... So, I'm wondering whether all these efforts are adversaries for you and how they might relate.

Reply: That's a great question, and it's orthogonal to this. Interpreting neural networks and machine learning is a very interesting research direction, and we do have some work in this... but it's mostly orthogonal to what I'm talking about.

Daniel Weitzner: I understand that the research is orthogonal, but it strikes me that your model might pick out some of those efforts as manifesting adversarial behaviour. I mean the extent to which you wanted to try to interrogate either a trained neural network, the training data associated that builds the model; or you try to figure out how you could prune the model... I'm just wondering, do these end up looking like adversaries?

Reply: I see. I definitely think that there is a connection. If you try to explain the model, you're basically kind of like an adversary, so you're trying to understand something about how it works. Conversely, you may be able to evade the model by taking advantage of the fact that it actually learned something that's an artefact of the training data rather than the meaningful concepts. So you might not even need to go through the attacks I talked about. There's definitely a connection. Alright, in terms of the adversary models, the adversary goal, in this case, is to bypass the detection of our Android apps, so this is a targeted attack. This is captured by the classic taxonomy. Our contribution lies in modeling, more precisely, the knowledge and capabilities of the adversary through the FAIL dimensions. And then, the adversary strategies; while at the high level, this is an evasion attack, the adversary tries to modify the app in order to evade detection. There is a variety of actual strategies, of concrete attacks, and this is actually something where more work is needed to actually capture entire classes of adversary strategies. But our work is trying to fill this gap- the knowledge and the capabilities. We looked at some of the prior work, in both poisoning and evasion, and model inference attacks. We tried to categorise it. Basically what we found is that many of these papers make implicit assumptions. So, for example, defensive papers would make an implicit assumption about how to constrain the adversary- what is the best way to constrain the adversary.

If you think about it, distillation defence assumes that you want to hide the model, so you want to act on the A dimension. In practice, if you look at the security industry, they very often publish the algorithm, so they say, "This is an SVM model." But they don't publish all the features, so they try to constrain the adversary in this way. So far we haven't had a way to compare these... these two dimensions- how important they are for the adversary. The FAIL model allows us to evaluate machine learning attacks by systematically modelling, not just the strongest adversary, but also a whole range of weaker adversaries. If you're proposing an attack, it doesn't make sense to just evaluate it with the strongest adversary. That's not a very interesting attack. You want to show that the attack is effective even if the adversary is not that strong. For defences, like I mentioned, this allows us to compare the importance of each of the four dimensions for achieving the adversary's goals. This may suggest the best ways to constrain the adversary. Finally, the FAIL model is just abstract. In order to implement it, in an actual evaluation, on an actual application, you probably have to make application dependent decisions. We have a questionnaire that can help with these decisions. In summary, the problem that I tried to address is the lack of a common set of definitions for adversaries in machine learning. And we proposed the FAIL adversary model, which focuses on the knowledge and capability aspects of the adversary model. It is not a complete adversary model, but it's a step towards precise and rigorous adversary models for machine learning. This provides a framework for evaluating both attacks and defences.

Fabio Massacci: After you have done the table that shows the implicit assumptions that prior work makes, do you think that some of the results that were shown by the prior authors will be different if they consider a different model?

Reply: Absolutely. We actually have looked at that and if you look at some of the black-box attacks, they are effective even if you don't know all the details of the algorithm. We show that in some cases for certain applications, they are less effective if you instead of hiding the algorithm, you hide the features. And I'd say definitely attacks that appear strong when evaluating only in one dimension may not be as strong overall if you consider the broader landscape of knowledge that the adversary needs to have.

How Does Match-Fixing Inform Computer Game Security?

Jeff Yan(✉)

Linköping University, Linköping, Sweden
jeff.yan@liu.se

Abstract. Match fixing is an increasingly popular phenomenon in eSports, namely competitive computer gaming between professional players. We first revisit the notion of security for computer games in the context of match fixing, which was never considered before. Then we offer a security economics analysis, and discuss potential countermeasures for addressing this threat. We propose a novel crowd-sourcing method for match-fixing detection. Our approach is incentive-compatible and it works for both traditional sports and eSports. We expect to raise awareness of these new issues and encourage further academic research.

Keywords: Security economics · Incentives
Crowd-sourcing for fraud detection · Security notions
Online game security

1 Introduction

As an interesting recent development, competitive computer-gaming, or eSports, has become a new spectator sport. It attracts a global audience of about 400 million a year. Popular eSports competitions between professional game players are physically viewed in big stadiums, televised by major TV channels, or streamed online over the Internet[1].

In sport, if a match is played to a completely or partially pre-determined result, it is match fixing. This is a dishonest practice of determining the outcome of a match before it is played. According to a recent article in The Economist [1], matching fixing is a big growing problem in sports, and it mostly remains undiscovered. Criminal groups launder a huge sum by match-fixing and illegal betting each year. Match-fixing can bend legitimate sport betting and rip off a large number of gamblers, too.

As eSports become popular, match-fixing goes digital, too. The first confirmed matching-fixing scandal in eSports occurred in 2010. One of the biggest

[1] I spent several months visiting Microsoft Research (Beijing) in 2004. During the visit, a project which we conceived and investigated in the Systems Group was to support online game spectating via a peer-to-peer infrastructure. This vision has become reality for years.

V. Matyáš et al. (Eds.): Security Protocols 2018, LNCS 11286, pp. 166–170, 2018.
https://doi.org/10.1007/978-3-030-03251-7_19

names in eSports was banned for life in 2016 in South Korea because of his role in a series of fixes in StarCraft II. According to The Economist [2], the eSports industry is estimated to be worth $700 m annually and expected to rise to $1.5 bn by 2020. Betting on eSports has an annual turnover of about $40 bn, and this figure is expected to exceed $150 bn a year by 2020. Many more match-fixings in eSports are to come, discovered or not.

Security can mean different things in different contexts. A context change warrants a revisit of established security notions for the new context. For example, the Needham-Schroeder public-key protocol was secure in the original setting which the protocol was proposed for, but when insider threats were considered, the protocol could be broken by a sophisticated attack. The emerging phenomenon of match-fixing in eSports raises an opportunity to revisit the notion of security for computer games, and to discuss how this new phenomenon informs computer game security.

2 Computer Game Security: A Revisit

Security for computer games has been an evolving concept. It was largely concerned with copy protection in the early days of single-player games.

With the emergence of networked or online computer games, security became an inherent design issue for games, just like graphics and artificial intelligence. What security meant the most for these games was fairness enforcement, i.e. making the play fair for each user (player) so that one does not have any unfair advantage over opponents [4,5].

The social norms and structures for either preventing or discouraging cheating in the non-electronic world were no longer in place for networked games. It was security that became an alternative but necessary mechanism for fairness enforcement [4,5]. Some years later, Bruce Schneier in 2012 echoed this view and generalised it to formulate a thought-provoking perspective on how trust is enabled in socio-technical systems via moral, reputational, institutional and security mechanisms [3].

We say that the focus of games security, previously, was on dealing with players cheating to beat their opponents unfairly. Now with match-fixing emerging in the scene, we should *also* explicitly address the issue of players cheating or underperforming to lose the games for illicit gains outside of the virtual worlds, such as manipulating gambling results in the real world.

Another interesting change in the context is the following. In the past, we considered security as concerning only game players, developers and operators. That is, security was a matter merely between gamers, and between gamers and developers/operators. Now, a lot more stakeholders get involved; newcomers include gambling sites, as well as a large number of people who bet on eSport results. A lot more stakeholders than before desire the fairness of game play enforced, rather than games rigged in one way or another.

Therefore, security for online games is still about fairness enforcement. This overall observation formulated more than fifteen years ago remains valid.

3 The Road Ahead

Match-fixing goes digital; countermeasures should go digital, too. Otherwise, scalability will become a serious issue that impedes effective countermeasures, given the stunning number of eSport games played every day. Let alone the lack of resources (including human power), which is already a serious problem for match-fixing detection and investigation in traditional sports.

A possible technical solution for match-fixing detection is to track, profile, analyse the performance of each player (or team) per play meticulously. Brief and coarse versions of these are available in some computer games but ineffective in dealing with match-fixing. Technically, game developers are best positioned to develop new tools and algorithms, since they have access to the games' data structure and access to players' in-game behaviour data and can interpret them expertly.

These new tools arguably should become a part of standard security toolboxes for eSport games, at least in theory. But we argue that game developers might not have sufficient incentives to do it, since they would be better off by investing in other elements of a game, e.g.

- Game play, special effects and AI and so on that help to attract a big player base which the developers can cash in. The experience of the player in a game, i.e. in-game experience, used to be the only priority for developers.
- Dedicated eSports features that support high level competition. Many successful eSports games such as StarCraft II, League of Legends and DOTA have all been designed for professional competition play.
- Enhanced spectator support that offers dedicated and convenient observing features for the benefit of spectators. These features attract spectators and increase eSports' stickiness.

On the other hand, if the game developers beef up a match-fixing detection system, the stakeholder that benefit the most would be gambling sites. Little gain for the game developers themselves by offering a sophisticated technology. A misaligned incentive, isn't it?

Instead, both gambling sites and sport gamblers have a stronger incentive to mitigate match-fixing than game developers do.

Thus, a third-party solution look like the best for match-fixing detection, since this way it is easier to make it incentive-compatible.

For example, an independent service that analyses betting patterns and the fluctuations of game odds is a useful approach for match-fixing detection. However, it has its limitations. For example, it faces issues like false positives and false negatives, the same as any other anomaly detection systems. And bad guys can evolve to stay just below the detection threshold.

Here we propose a new solution that is incentive-compatible and thus looks promising. It is a crowdsourcing platform which supports a range of functions for match-fixing detection. They include archiving key match data (such as gameplay videos, bet patterns and fluctuations of game odds), supporting game replay and review, recording whistle-blowing and suspicion reporting, correlating suspicions in gameplay and anomalies in betting patterns and game odds, summarizing confirmed evidence, and etc. A large number of gamblers have a stake in it and therefore they will be willing to contribute to the crowdsourcing efforts. The more such eyeballs, the better the crowdsourcing platform performs.

Also, a key point here is that this crowdsourcing service, together with dedicated gamblers, will spot suspicious behaviours that suggest match fixing, and will establish incriminating patterns based on these behaviours. On the contrary, occasional spectators cannot achieve this by viewing a game or two in the field; otherwise it cannot explain why a majority of match-fixing in sport remains undiscovered. On the other hand, a one-off fix of a single game might be virtually impossible to spot, and the evidence collected from the single game will be circumstantial at most.

Another key point here is that things that are not computationally tractable can be handled by human brains. For example, some tale-telling behaviour patterns can be entirely unknown at the beginning, and thus they cannot be described and programmed into code at all. However, human brains can abstract these behaviour patterns into useful heuristics that can be applied and shared. This is another power of crowd sourcing.

We note that our proposal appears to work for both traditional sports and eSports. In traditional sports such as football, match-fixing can be implemented via corrupting referees or tampering with the appointment of referees[2]. However, this does not invalidate our proposal.

We also note that our solution should take care to cope with and mitigate malicious users in the crowd whose interest is to mislead or wreck our system.

As a startup idea, a good crowd-sourcing platform for match-fixing detection will likely be financially supported by gambling sites; eventually it will likely be acquired by them, too.

4 Concluding Remarks

Fairness enforcement appears to remain as the main security issue for online computer games, even if the new threat of match-fixing is taken into consideration. When we first conceived this security notion for computer games many

[2] In 2012, several high-profile referees were convicted for fixing football matches in China [6]. At least the following contributed to their arrests and convictions. First, the referees' judgement calls and decisions had repeatedly triggered controversy and anger. The referees were either addicted to the easy money from match fixing, or blackmailed by the fixes they did before; they cheated again and again but did not stop after a single fix. Their behaviours exhibited somehow systematic suspicious patterns that smelled fishy even to outsiders and spectators. Second, whistle-blowers and suspect-turned-prosecution-witnesses offered substantial incriminating evidences. These Chinese cases appear to suggest that it is likely to catch the fixers without correlating suspicious behaviours (of players, referees or both) to betting patterns and game odds in some circumstances.

years ago, the recent emerging match-fixing phenomenon in eSports did not exist. However, our revisit suggests that it is unnecessary to revise the security notion to address match-fixing.

Match-fixing is a big and realistic problem for regulators and the society at large. It is also an interesting research problem calling computer scientists for novel research. Our security economics analysis suggests that a crowd-sourcing approach appears to be promising for detecting match-fixing both in traditional sports and in eSports, since it is incentive compatible, and since it can make good use of the power and flexibility of human brains to tackle pattern recognition problems that are computationally hard or intractable.

Acknowledgements. I thank Ross Anderson, John Chuang, Dah Ming Chiu and the workshop attendees for their input and stimulating discussions. This work was supported by the Knut and Alice Wallenberg Foundation.

References

1. The Economist, Match-fixing is more common than ever - regulators need to up their game, 23 September 2017. https://www.economist.com/news/international/21729427-regulators-need-up-their-game-match-fixing-more-common-ever
2. The Economist, Match-fixing goes digital, 21 September 2017. https://www.economist.com/news/international/21729428-esports-are-likely-see-much-more-corruption-coming-years-match-fixing-goes
3. Schneier, B.: Liars and Outliers: Enabling the Trust that Society Needs to Thrive. O'Reilly, Sebastopol (2012)
4. Yan, J.: Security design in online games. In: Proceedings of 19th Annual Computer Security Applications Conference, ACSAC 2003, pp. 286–295 (2003)
5. Yan, J., Randell, B.: A systematic classification of cheating in online games. In: Proceedings of 4th ACM SIGCOMM Workshop on Network and System Support for Games (NetGames 2005), pp. 1–9 (2005)
6. Four crooked referees (in Chinese). https://baike.baidu.com/item/%E5%9B%9B%E5%A4%A7%E9%BB%91%E5%93%A8

How Does Match-Fixing Inform Computer Game Security? (Transcript of Discussion)

Jeff Yan(✉)

Linköping University, Linköping, Sweden
Jeff.Yan@liu.se

Fabio Massacci: Sorry, but how can you tell that a person is cheating to lose? Cheating to win is fine, but cheating to lose, also in the normal sport, cannot be measured, because you can play badly for whatever reason.

Reply: Yeah, exactly, that's why, as we argue, it's difficult to design a good countermeasure against match-fixing. And that's also why I believe we have a good proposal to deal with the problem.

Fabio Massacci: This is always outside the protocol. Cheating to win, it's fine, because you can measure it. But cheating to lose, just a bad player.

Reply: It is a tough problem, and that's why we need some new thoughts to figure out different ways of dealing with it. That's something we'll talk about later. Soon.

Frank Stajano: Frank. You had a contradiction between bullet point two and bullet point three. If some stakeholders cheat to lose, and then in the next page you say, all stakeholders desire fair play enforcement, well, no, some stakeholders don't desire fair play enforcement, because they want to cheat.

Reply: Yeah, it's a good point, thanks a lot. I did spot that contradiction. I need to revise that slide. But actually the point I wanted and want to make is that fairness enforcement is still the goal for security design in the games, even with the consideration of match-fixing. Bad guys would like to rig the game one way or another.

Frank Stajano: You mean honest players want honesty enforced, dishonest players don't, right? Is that what you mean?

Reply: I think as a security engineer, our focus is the same as before. We still want to enforce fairness in games. That's the point I want to make.

So far, this is just a simple revisiting (of security notions for games). I think it is more interesting to look into countermeasures of the problem. If you look into match-fixing, as Fabio commented, this is a tough problem. But there is a possible solution. For example, if you track, profile, analyse each player, and each team per play very carefully, then you might have a chance. Of course there are pros and cons with this method. The fact is that following this line of thinking, coarse tools and algorithms exist already. But they are ineffective in dealing with match-fixing. If we want to further develop this line of defence, technically game developers are best positioned to improve those tools and algorithms. But my argument is that they have little incentive to do it. In my observation, similarly,

V. Matyáš et al. (Eds.): Security Protocols 2018, LNCS 11286, pp. 171–178, 2018.
https://doi.org/10.1007/978-3-030-03251-7_20

game developers would not be very interested in cheat mitigation unless their business model gets jeopardised.

Frank Stajano: I think my comment maybe is related to Fabio's in some way. There are types of cheating which can be unequivocally detected. And there are types of cheating where you can suspect the cheating, but you can never prove it from the viewpoint of an external observer. And some people who design games say, well, I would forbid people from doing the other ones, but the ones that I cannot check, I would not make a rule about it because it's pointless.

Let's take a case of the voting for the best talk and the most controversial talk, that I distributed papers for. I said, before lunch, you should not vote for your own talk. But I have no way of policing for that, if I preserve anonymity, and therefore I'm not going to make it a rule, because it would be pointless, I could not punish the miscreants because I would never know. So what is your viewpoint with respect to what the game designer should do? Should you try and police things that you cannot observe, or not?

Reply: No, the game designer shouldn't, because that's not a cost-effective way of doing things. I have a better way of dealing with match-fixing, which I will propose soon.

Before I talk about the solution I like, I'd like to argue that game developers are better-off with investing in other elements of a game, not in match-fixing or cheating detection. For example, they would be better-off with improving game play, which used to be the only priority for game developers. And they would be more interested in developing dedicated eSport features for pro competitions, because you really want to attract the best players into your game. And the game developers would be more interested in offering enhanced spectator support, because this way you grow your game community and increase this game's stickness. So, all these would make a lot more economic sense to the game developers than working on cheat detection.

Now we assume game developers put in place a beefed-up cheat or match-fixing detection system. Ironically, they won't be a stakeholder that benefit the most. The one that benefit the most will not be the game developers, but gambling sites. Little gain for the game developers to spend a lot of money and effort on offering a very sophisticated technology. So, this is a misaligned incentive, isn't it?

Ian Goldberg: Do gambling sites really take a hit when match-fixing happens?

Reply: They are probably not taking a hit, but they ought to care about match-fixing. If people manipulate the game results to do money-laundering, for example.

Ian Goldberg: Unless, well, they could be in on it.

Reply: Yeah, that's a possibility, too.

Ian Goldberg: Obviously, that aside, if they are, if unbeknownst to them, the match is fixed, I guess that, because they will mis-predict the odds that they're giving, they will take a financial hit, is that the argument?

Reply: No, they will not necessarily lose money, but the gamblers lose money, because the odds are manipulated. The gambling sites are likely to receive a lot of complaints from the gamblers. There's not much the gambling sites can do with it. That's why they might be interested in the solution I'll offer.

Ian Goldberg: So, I'm not familiar with e-sports so much, or gambling sites, especially e-sports. Is it the case that gambling sites work like the house in poker, or work like the house in blackjack?

Reply: Just like the house of lottery. It is legitimate in the UK, say if you go to High Street in Cambridge, you can see a few shops, where you can do betting.

Ian Goldberg: So, in poker, the house always will take a cut, no matter what happens in the game, the house gets paid.

Ross Anderson: That's called a totalisator. And it's one of the betting models. There's other betting models, where bookies will guess the odds, and then adjust them as the bets come in. In the latter case, the bookies can take a hit from match-fixing.

Ian Goldberg: So what case are you talking about here? the former model?

Reply: I think I cover all those cases. I do not have to differentiate between those threats. The solution I will propose can address them all.

Ian Goldberg: Okay.

Reply: Okay, let's look into "The way forward".

Because of our analysis of incentives, I believe a third-party solution for match-fixing detection looks like the best. It makes it easier to align incentives. For example, we can have an independent service that only monitors and analyses the betting patterns and the fluctuations of game odds. This is just like intrusion detection or anomaly detection, and we will spot anomaly in the patterns. But the problem with this solution is false positives and false negatives, just like in any other intrusion detection systems. Baddies could evolve their strategy to stay below the detection bar.

Therefore, I have another solution which is also third-party type of thing. I think we can build a crowd-sourcing platform for match-fixing detection. First of all, it's incentive-compatible. The gamblers who bet on eSport, all have a stake in the betting result. Therefore, they would be willing to participate in monitoring each game they bet a lot of money on. And also, it's likely for the gambling sites to support this platform, because this is aligned with their interest as well. Eventually, probably an exit route is to sell such a service to some gambling sites.

Another argument for this crowd-sourcing platform is we can accumulate a lot of useful data such as game-play, evidence and suspicions, and our brains still perform a lot better than AI. Many things still cannot be tractable, using AI technologies.

Another good thing with my proposal, is I think this works for both eSports and traditional sports. That's some additional benefit.

So far, I've tried to answer my second question. Now, the third question: As match-fixing goes digital, will it reduce or raise the cost of money laundering? John Chuang from UC Berkeley deserves credit for this question. It was raised in our discussions. We have agreed that answering this question either way will have policy implications. We tend to agree that match-fixing will reduce a bad guy's cost for money laundering, partly because now there are a lot of esports games played everyday. I haven't figured out yet how we could collect data and finish off an empirical study to show the result either way. How to do an empirical study? How to get data? Do you have some suggestions?

Fabio Massacci: So if you have lots of people giving the possibility of match-fixing, probably the cost will reduce, but the problem is then what Frank said before. For collusion, you may have ability to show, okay, there was something that was not possible, also for poker, when people who were supposed to share information that is not possible to do it. But for under performance, I really don't see how we could tell the guy just has a cold, and played badly, versus he agreed to underperform. The problem is under performance. You have no way to distinguish normal under performance from cheating under performance. And therefore this creates a sort of a noise in the data, which is very difficult for me to give any difference.

Reply: If we have only a single observation, indeed nobody can draw a conclusion whether some underperforming is witnessed or not. We can do nothing about them. But the argument is, this kind of thing is just like a drug. When you get a lot of money out of this match-fixing, you get addicted. You definitely do it again, if you stay undetected. So the argument is, when you do this again and again, you may be caught. That's the only thing that we aim to achieve. We don't claim we detect any single case of match-fixing, which is impossible.

Ian Goldberg: Two things, so one, are you trying to catch the players underperforming, or are you trying to catch the bettors who are in on the fix?

Reply: We are trying to catch the players who under perform to screw up the game odds.

Ian Goldberg: So you watch it, so the crowd-sourcing you were talking about.

Reply: Yeah, observing game-play.

Ian Goldberg: Are watching the player, saying that was really...

Reply: That was weird.

Ian Goldberg: He threw that.

Reply: Yes.

Ian Goldberg: Okay, so my other question is, so you're asking about the cost of money-laundering here. So can you explain what the actual procedure is by which a match-fixing can launder money?

Reply: Okay.

Ian Goldberg: So someone comes in with bad money, and does what with it?

Reply: For example, you do the first match-fix, and you lose a lot of money to somebody. Then the next time, that somebody will lose this to somebody else. So if these two things cannot be linked together, then the money becomes clean.

Okay, now I wrap up my talk. I have asked three questions. The first one is about security notions: will match-fixing change security notions for computer games? Second, match-fixing (digital or not), what's the optimal countermeasure? Third, as match-fixing goes digital, will it reduce or raise the cost of money laundering? My last question: any other interesting questions to ask in this line of research?

That's it. Thanks.

Ilia Shumailov: Sorry, can you explain, do people launder money that way?

Reply: Oh, indeed. There are huge sums laundered by match-fixing.

Ilia Shumailov: So is there any regulatory pressure on them? I mean, do they have to do any sort of money-checking before they accept it?

Reply: No. Whenever you hand in money to the Jocky Club in Hong Kong to buy these horse-racing tickets, you just do it, and nobody will check the money. I don't think they will care.

Patrick McCorry: I just want to understand the solution. So you're saying that the crowd will decide if it's match-fixing or not. So you're crowd-sourcing the answer to that.

Reply: Not exactly, the people who contribute to crowd-sourcing will provide only initial feeds, like suspicious signals. But those things alone cannot lead to a match-fixing accusation. They only contribute raw clues. Afterwards, some efforts, serious efforts, are needed to aggregate those signals, and do the analysis and inference.

Alexander Hicks: So you're saying the crowd component could help, so I guess clues that there might be match-fixing. What kind of clues are those?

Reply: Let me think about a concrete example. Okay, let's talk about soccer. I mean football, in English term. That's probably the most seriously hit by money laundering. For example, a particular footballer underperformed in some critical events. And then you observe the gambling markets. And there are some abnormalities with the odds. Then we can lock on him.

Alexander Hicks: Yeah, but surely you can observe, it's not really the crowd that observes that, I mean a lot of that data might be internal, where you can observe it without requiring the crowds.

Reply: It is important for us to collect those video-tapes, those game-play, etc. Those data may be available there, but it is difficult for artificial intelligence to make good use of them. So my argument is, why don't we encourage gamblers to observe suspicious things and then mark them down, treating each suspicious behaviour as a signal. Then we put these stuff online, and other people can build on them, and etc. Eventually one day we can pin down some fixers.

Ilia Shumailov: So surely the problem with money-laundering can be solved much easier. Surely you can just impose regulations on those betting services, to do the money-checking before it gets into the system. And this way you will not get any dirty money in the system. And then what you can do is say, if the betting service itself accepted the dirty money, you just impose fees on it, that way incentivising the actual betting service to check the money before they take it.

Reply: In one sense you raise a very good point. But on the other hand I have counterarguments. If it is so easy to do this money-checking, then money-laundering shouldn't be a problem in the first place. But now it is still a big problem.

Ilia Shumailov: We haven't presented our paper yet.

Fabio Massacci: I think your question may be the solution. So instead of monitoring the players only, maybe you should monitor the players and the betting site, or something. It's the correlation of both that may give you an idea of, okay, the player's going to play well, and there are certain site where the odds are in his favour, he does badly.

Reply: That's exactly my argument, too.

Fabio Massacci: Monitor not only the players, but the players, and ...

Reply: And the odds anomaly. Yes, the correlations.

Fabio Massacci: Different betting sites and so on, to see if there is an event.

Reply: Yes, we need that correlation to make any sensible inference.

Frank Stajano: How do I know that there isn't a criminal gang in Saudi Arabia that is betting millions on a particular match, and doing something? They don't appear in the New York Times listing. They may be crooks that use this particular match to do their things. And they're not advertising on the high street. How can I monitor all the possible crooked gambling houses?

Reply: No way. Because they are simply off the radar. So, nothing we can do with them. I don't think I can offer any solution to that problem.

Virgil Gligor: By definition, the stakes are not high.

Fabio Massacci: But I think you have a problem. Frank's problem of the people hidden in Saudi Arabia betting on it is not a problem, because if you want to do for money-laundering, it needs to be an official place. Because you need to good, honest money of the normal bettors, being mixed with bad money. So therefore it has to be something on the New York Listing, or I mean, not that, like an esport. Because you need the good money to be mixed with the bad money. So it has to be something public and sort of official. If it's something in Saudi Arabia, nobody knows about it, you don't get any money-laundering out of it.

Reply: Mark Lomas is an expert in anti-money-laundering.

Peter Roenne: So by the crowd-sourcing solution, you mention that they have high-stakes. So if you play to someone, and you see them lose, you're probably likely to say, maybe there was something going on. Do you have any mechanism ...

Reply: I didn't get the last bit of the question.

Peter Roenne: So if you have a high stake in the game, if you really want to playing on this game, and you're part of this crowd-sourcing, you could use the mechanism to try and raise a flag, and say, "something is going on, this is not fair game." Because you are going to lose, you are seeing that you are losing.

Reply: But it's still a single input, a signal from a single participant, it cannot decide a final result.

Peter Roenne: It's an incentive not to play correctly.

Just thinking whether you could put some mechanism onto these crowd-sourcers to make them play fair.

Reply: I hadn't thought about that. Thanks for your suggestion, I will think about that further.

Mark Lomas: I think it might be useful to distinguish between two different types of fixing. If you try to fix a football match, you have to do something active in the match which might be observed. So if a player chooses to miss a goal, everyone sees them do that. They might not be able to prove they're dishonest. But thinking about a different game. Imagine we're playing online poker, and I want to cheat. I might cheat by playing completely honestly, but I leak my hidden cards to another player. So anyone observing me doing that, none of my behaviour is at all suspicious. Some other player may benefit from it, but it doesn't get seen. And that's why it's worth distinguishing between football and poker, because the mechanism for cheating, or, more importantly, the mechanism for detecting cheating must be different.

Bruce Christianson: But won't their behaviour be suspicious? Because they'll play differently from how they would do if they didn't know your cards?

Mark Lomas: It would, but it won't be vastly suspicious, because what they will be doing, if they're clever about it, is they only bet when it's consistent with their cards, but they realise the odds are slightly better. So they seem to be a bit luckier than the other players.

Bruce Christianson: Yeah, so that's suspicious, but only if someone watches all the games, and not just the ones where they cheat.

Reply: I agree with your point in general. But in this particular case, poker is not an esport game. Spectators do not bet on poker. That's different. For the e-sport gaming, you see each team's play frame by frame. Nearly everything is observable, and there's no hidden things. In poker, there are hole cards, which are hidden from players but known to spectators. That's why spectators cannot bet on poker.

Mark Lomas: Yes, but the distinction here is that poker players are both the player and the gambler, whereas a football player is illegal to be the gambler.

Reply: Oh, I see that point. Thanks. Last question.

Alexander Hicks: So another thing, another suppression one would make would be, because now you're looking at players making bad decisions, which might be reported by people watching, which I agree with. The other question is very subjective kind of bias. Those things considered, and the match-fixing, and you mentioned football earlier, so there were a lot of reports with like the 2010 world cup, there groups saying matches were fixed. And the people getting paid there weren't the players, but it was the referees. And somebody even in Italy in the past have been sanctioned based on players paying off referees. And so that's usually kind of the point of failure. But at the same time, if you're kind of looking at trying to observe referees in the states, in a game like football, you kind of end up with every premier match being accused of match-fixing. So how do you kind of deal with that?

Reply: I think that's one of the reasons I am in favour of crowd-sourcing, rather than artificial intelligence. Because it gives us the flexibility. Those gamblers are supposed to be familiar with a particular type of game they are betting on. We can let them to define what should be on the radar, and what count as suspicion and what do not.

Alexander Hicks: Yeah, I mean that the point was refereeing, now we understand that big mistakes happen in every game. And both sides usually agree that the referee was horrible. So if you're asking people to record that the match was fixed because of the referee. So I guess, you can say if a really good player does something bad, that happens quite rarely. But something like referee mistakes happen multiple times per game, every game, every weekend.

Reply: That is a problem which I haven't thought about yet. I will think about that, thanks a lot.

From Secure Messaging to Secure Collaboration

Martin Kleppmann(✉), Stephan A. Kollmann, Diana A. Vasile, and Alastair R. Beresford

Department of Computer Science and Technology, University of Cambridge, Cambridge, UK
{mk428,sak70,dac53,arb33}@cl.cam.ac.uk

Abstract. We examine the security of collaboration systems, where several users access and contribute to some shared resource, document, or database. To protect such systems against malicious servers, we can build upon existing secure messaging protocols that provide end-to-end security. However, if we want to ensure the consistency of the shared data in the presence of malicious users, we require features that are not available in existing messaging protocols. We investigate the protocol failures that may arise when a new collaborator is added to a group, and discuss approaches for enforcing the integrity of the shared data.

Keywords: Group communication · Collaborative editing Secure messaging

1 Introduction

Secure messaging apps with end-to-end encryption, such as Signal, WhatsApp, iMessage and Telegram, have broken into the mainstream: for example, WhatsApp alone has 1.3 billion monthly active users [16]. The success of these apps demonstrates that it is feasible for protocols with strong security properties to be deployed at internet-wide scale, and that their benefits can be enjoyed by users who are not technical experts.

However, secure messaging alone is not sufficient for protecting all forms of sensitive data exchange. Some communication takes the form of collaborating on some shared resource, such as a document, or database. For example, journalists collaborate on sensitive investigations by interviewing sources, analysing documents, and sharing their notes and drafts with colleagues [11,12]; lawyers collaborate on contracts and other sensitive documents while communicating with their clients under legal privilege [10]; and medical records are maintained by several specialists involved in treating a patient. Most currently deployed systems for these forms of collaboration rely on a server that is trusted to maintain the confidentiality and integrity of the data.

In this paper we discuss how existing protocols for secure messaging can be leveraged to bring end-to-end security to scenarios in which several users collaborate on a database or a set of shared documents. We give a brief overview

V. Matyáš et al. (Eds.): Security Protocols 2018, LNCS 11286, pp. 179–185, 2018.
https://doi.org/10.1007/978-3-030-03251-7_21

of existing algorithms and technologies, report on lessons learnt from our initial implementation of secure collaboration software, and highlight some open problems that we hope will stimulate further work in the information security community.

2 Threat Model and Security Objectives

We assume that the collaboration software has any number of *users*, each of whom may have one or more *devices* (which may be desktop or laptop computers, or mobile devices such as tablets and smartphones). Users and their devices may form groups of *collaborators*, and the collaborators in each group have shared access to a particular document or dataset. Each collaborating device maintains a copy (replica) of the shared data on its local storage.

Devices may frequently be *offline* and unable to communicate, for example because they might be mobile devices with poor cellular data coverage. We require that devices should be able to modify their local copy of the data even while offline, and send their changes to other devices when they are next online.

The system may also include some number of *servers*, which store messages for any recipient devices that are offline, and forward them to those devices when they are next online. Devices may communicate with each other directly (e.g. via a LAN, Bluetooth, or peer-to-peer over the Internet), or indirectly via servers. Furthermore we assume the existence of a public key infrastructure (PKI) through which users and devices can authenticate each other.

We consider the following types of adversary:

Network Attacker. This adversary has full control over any network via which devices communicate, including the ability to observe and modify all traffic.
Malicious Server. This adversary controls any messages sent via or stored on a server, including the ability to observe and modify any messages.
Malicious User. This adversary is able to create any number of devices that may participate in group collaboration, and which may deviate arbitrarily from the protocol specification.

In the face of these adversaries we seek the following security properties:

Confidentiality. The data shared between a group of collaborators cannot be obtained by an adversary who is not a member of that group.
Integrity. The data shared between a group of collaborators cannot be modified by an adversary who is not a member of that group.
Closeness. A user or device can become a group member only by explicitly being added by a group administrator.
Convergence. When any honest group members communicate, their local copies of the shared data converge towards a consistent state (even if some other group members are malicious).

We propose encoding the shared data and any modifications as messages, and using a secure group messaging protocol to exchange them among collaborators. Existing secure group messaging protocols maintain the confidentiality and integrity properties in the presence of all types of adversary [4,15]. Closeness is sometimes weaker in existing protocols: for example, WhatsApp does not guarantee closeness in the presence of a malicious server [13]. However, group key agreement protocols that ensure closeness have been studied previously [7], so we do not consider this property further in this paper.

Thus, when building a secure collaboration protocol on top of a secure messaging protocol, the primary security goal is to ensure *convergence* in the presence of the aforementioned adversaries.

3 Convergence of Shared State

Since we allow the data on a device's local storage to be modified while the device is offline, independent modifications on different devices can cause their copies of the shared data to become inconsistent with each other. Fortunately, this problem has been studied extensively in the distributed systems literature. We propose using *Conflict-free Replicated Data Types* or *CRDTs* [8,14], a family of algorithms that provide abstractions and protocols for automatically resolving conflicts due to concurrent modifications.

CRDTs provide a consistency property called *strong eventual consistency*, which guarantees that whenever any two devices have seen the same set of updates (even if the updates were delivered in a different order), the data on those devices is in the same state [6,14]. This property implies that the state of a device is determined entirely by the set of updates it has seen.

Thus, we can achieve the convergence property for collaborative data by encoding every update as a message and sending it to other devices via a secure group messaging protocol. On each device, we use a CRDT to interpret the set of messages delivered to that device, and derive its local copy of the shared data from those messages. Now, the problem of achieving convergence is reduced to ensuring that all honest group members receive the same set of messages.

In the context of secure messaging protocols, ensuring that group members receive the same set of messages is known as *transcript consistency* [4,15]. (Sometimes transcript consistency is taken to mean that all group members must receive the same sequence of messages in the same order; for our purposes, it is sufficient to require the weaker property that collaborators must receive the same set of messages, regardless of order.) Not all messaging protocols provide this property; for example, Signal does not ensure transcript consistency in the presence of a malicious user [13]. However, the property can be implemented as a separate layer on top of an existing messaging protocol.

A simple approach based on a hash function is illustrated in Fig. 1: whenever a device sends a message to the group (e.g. message m_4), it includes a hash of the last message it sent (m_2), and the hashes of any other messages it received in the intervening period (m_3). A recipient accepts an incoming message only after it has received all prior messages that it depends on, which are referenced by their hashes. Assuming preimage resistance of the hash function, whenever two devices observe the same message, then they must have also received the same set of prior messages (namely those that are transitively reachable through their hash references).

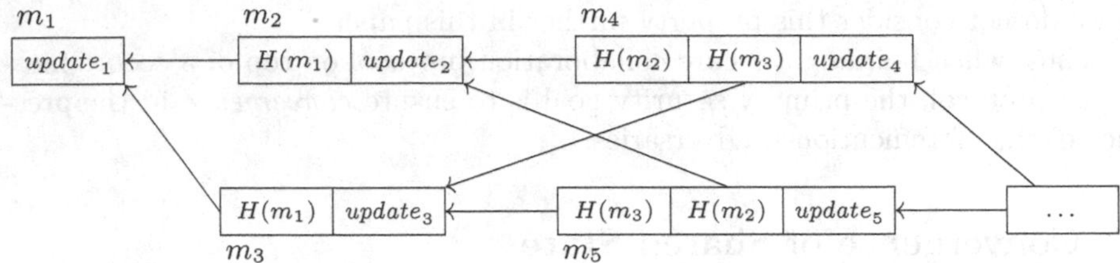

Fig. 1. Chaining messages by referencing hashes of previous messages.

The construction in Fig. 1 is similar to the internal structure of a Git repository [3], in which each commit references the hash of one or more parent commits.

4 Adding New Collaborators

The approach in Sect. 3 ensures convergence in a static group of collaborators, where all members are added when a group is created. In this setting, every message in the history of the group is delivered to every member device. However, if the membership is dynamic – that is, if group members can be added or removed – additional challenges arise.

With most group messaging protocols, when a new member is added, that member is able to receive any messages that were sent after they were added, but no prior messages. However, in the context of collaboration on some shared data, receiving later messages is not sufficient: the new member also requires a copy of the shared data to which any subsequent updates can be applied.

The simplest solution is to give the new member the full update history: that is, the administrator who invites the new member also sends the new member a copy of all past messages sent in the group. If a hash-chaining construction like in Fig. 1 is used, the new member can check the integrity of this message history by computing the hashes of the messages and comparing them to the referenced hashes.

However, sending the full update history has two downsides. Firstly, it may be much larger than a copy of the current state, and thus inefficient to store and transmit. Secondly, the full update history includes every past version of the data, including any content that has been deleted and is no longer part of the current state. For privacy reasons, the existing collaborators may not want to expose the full details of former versions of the data to the new collaborator.

5 Checking the Integrity of Snapshots

If it is not acceptable to send the full update history to a new collaborator, a snapshot of the current state of the shared data must be sent instead. However, a naive snapshot protocol would lose the convergence property in the presence of a malicious user: namely, the user who sends the snapshot may send data that does not match the true current state, and thus cause the new collaborator's state to diverge from the rest of the group. For example, the malicious user could claim that another user wrote something that, in fact, they never wrote.

We are exploring protocols that allow the new collaborator to verify that a snapshot is consistent with the prior editing history of the shared data, without revealing the full update history to the new collaborator. Approaches include:

1. The snapshot can be sent to all group members, not just the new collaborator. Existing group members can then check the integrity of the snapshot, and vote on whether they believe the snapshot to be correct or not. A Byzantine consensus protocol [2,5] can make this voting process resilient to malicious users, provided that a quorum (typically, more than 2/3) of voting members is honest. However, this approach requires members to be online in order to vote. If members use mobile devices that are frequently offline, as proposed in Sect. 2, a voting protocol may introduce prohibitive delays before the snapshot integrity is confirmed.
2. As an alternative, the new collaborator could initially trust the first snapshot it receives, and then run a consistency-checking protocol in the background. This protocol would not prevent the new collaborator from seeing an inconsistent snapshot, but it could ensure that any inconsistency is eventually detected, provided that the new collaborator eventually communicates with an honest group member. This approach is analogous to Certificate Transparency [9], which does not prevent certificate authorities from misissuing certificates, but which deters such behaviour by making it detectable and irrefutable.
3. There may be cryptographic constructions that allow the creator of the snapshot to prove to the new collaborator that the snapshot is consistent with the full message history, without revealing the message history. For example, we are currently exploring the use of redactable signatures and one-way accumulators [1] for this purpose.

In general, we may differentiate *fail-safe* and *fail-secure* approaches to snapshot integrity checking. A fail-secure (or fail-closed) approach in this context means that the new collaborator must wait until the integrity of the shared data has been fully verified, e.g. using some voting protocol or cryptographic proof, before they are allowed to see it. On the other hand, a fail-safe (or fail-open) approach would allow the new collaborator to immediately see the snapshot—even if it might be incorrect—and resolve any inconsistencies after the fact.

6 Conclusions

End-to-end encryption is now in regular use by over 1 billion people for secure messaging. Yet, end-to-end encryption is not currently used by collaborative applications where multiple people modify some shared resource, such as a document or database. In this paper we have outlined a method of building collaborative apps on top of secure messaging protocols, providing not only confidentiality and integrity in the face of network attackers and malicious servers, but also the properties of closeness and convergence. Handling the insider threat of a malicious collaborating user is more challenging, and we highlighted snapshot integrity as a particular issue which requires further work to fully address.

References

1. Benaloh, J., de Mare, M.: One-way accumulators: a decentralized alternative to digital signatures. In: Helleseth, T. (ed.) EUROCRYPT 1993. LNCS, vol. 765, pp. 274–285. Springer, Heidelberg (1994). https://doi.org/10.1007/3-540-48285-7_24
2. Castro, M., Liskov, B.H.: Practical Byzantine fault tolerance. In: 3rd USENIX Symposium on Operating Systems Design and Implementation (OSDI), February 1999
3. Chacon, S., Straub, B.: Pro Git, 2nd edn. Apress, New York (2014). https://git-scm.com/book/en/v2
4. Cohn-Gordon, K., Cremers, C., Garratt, L., Millican, J., Milner, K.: On ends-to-ends encryption: asynchronous group messaging with strong security guarantees. Technical report, 2017/666, IACR Cryptology ePrint, July 2017. https://eprint.iacr.org/2017/666
5. Correia, M., Veronese, G.S., Neves, N.F., Verissimo, P.: Byzantine consensus in asynchronous message-passing systems: a survey. Int. J. Crit. Comput.-Based Syst. **2**(2), 141–161 (2011). https://doi.org/10.1504/IJCCBS.2011.041257
6. Gomes, V.B.F., Kleppmann, M., Mulligan, D.P., Beresford, A.R.: Verifying strong eventual consistency in distributed systems. In: Proceedings of the ACM on Programming Languages (PACMPL), vol. 1, no. (OOPSLA), October 2017. https://doi.org/10.1145/3133933
7. Kim, Y., Perrig, A., Tsudik, G.: Communication-efficient group key agreement. In: Dupuy, M., Paradinas, P. (eds.) SEC 2001. IIFIP, vol. 65, pp. 229–244. Springer, Boston, MA (2002). https://doi.org/10.1007/0-306-46998-7_16
8. Kleppmann, M., Beresford, A.R.: A conflict-free replicated JSON datatype. IEEE Trans. Parallel Distrib. Syst. **28**(10), 2733–2746 (2017). https://doi.org/10.1109/TPDS.2017.2697382
9. Laurie, B., Langley, A., Kasper, E.: RFC 6962: certificate transparency. IETF, June 2013. https://tools.ietf.org/html/rfc6962
10. Lerner, A., Zeng, E., Roesner, F.: Confidante: usable encrypted email: a case study with lawyers and journalists. In: 2nd IEEE European Symposium on Security and Privacy, pp. 385–400, April 2017. https://doi.org/10.1109/EuroSP.2017.41
11. McGregor, S.E., Charters, P., Holliday, T., Roesner, F.: Investigating the computer security practices and needs of journalists. In: 24th USENIX Security Symposium, August 2015

12. McGregor, S.E., Watkins, E.A., Al-Ameen, M.N., Caine, K., Roesner, F.: When the weakest link is strong: secure collaboration in the case of the panama papers. In: 26th USENIX Security Symposium, August 2017
13. Rösler, P., Mainka, C., Schwenk, J.: More is less: on the end-to-end security of group chats in signal, WhatsApp, and Threema. Technical report, 2017/713, IACR Cryptology ePrint, January 2018. https://eprint.iacr.org/2017/713
14. Shapiro, M., Preguiça, N., Baquero, C., Zawirski, M.: Conflict-free replicated data types. In: Défago, X., Petit, F., Villain, V. (eds.) SSS 2011. LNCS, vol. 6976, pp. 386–400. Springer, Heidelberg (2011). https://doi.org/10.1007/978-3-642-24550-3_29
15. Unger, N., et al.: SoK: secure messaging. In: IEEE Symposium on Security and Privacy, pp. 232–249, May 2015. https://doi.org/10.1109/SP.2015.22
16. WhatsApp Inc.: Connecting one billion users every day, July 2017. https://blog.whatsapp.com/10000631/Connecting-One-Billion-Users-Every-Day

From Secure Messaging to Secure Collaboration (Transcript of Discussion)

Martin Kleppmann(✉)

Department of Computer Science and Technology, University of Cambridge, Cambridge, UK
mk428@cl.cam.ac.uk

Frank Stajano: Among the people who come up with these conflict resolution algorithms, is there agreement about what to do in a situation where the edits look fundamentally incompatible to a normal person? For example, while we are offline, I delete a paragraph, whereas you add a word in the middle of that paragraph.

Reply: That's a good question. There are a few different consistency models that people use, but on the whole, they are fairly primitive in terms of what conflict resolution they do. In your example, where one user deletes an entire paragraph, another user changes something in the middle of that paragraph—I actually tried this with Google Docs. The merged result is a document in which that paragraph is missing, but that one changed word from the middle of the paragraph is still there. So you've essentially got a 'stranded' word in the middle of the document.

Frank Stajano: Are real human beings happy with this way of resolving?

Reply: Well, millions of people seem to be using Google Docs successfully, so I'm just going to assert that it seems to be good enough in practice. It would be nice to have a user interface that warns you, saying: "Hey, there were some edits made here to the same place in the document. You might want to check this is a valid, merged result." All the algorithms do is to ensure that everyone ends up in the same state, and that state doesn't lose any data, if possible.

Ilia Shumailov: I think the general flow of action is, because they keep the history of changes, you can always just go back to another change and re-merge the text yourself. At least that's what I do every time I have a conflict.

Reply: Yes indeed. They keep the editing history, and you can look backward in the editing history as well. However, from the point of view of our discussion today, take conflict resolution as a solved problem. I'm just going to assert that these algorithms work, under the assumption that the same set of messages are delivered to everybody in the group.

We have proved that for several of these protocols, if several nodes have seen the same set of operations, but maybe in a different order, then they converge towards the same state. What we need to ensure now in the protocol is that all of the participants see the same set of operations, and that's where security protocols come in.

V. Matyáš et al. (Eds.): Security Protocols 2018, LNCS 11286, pp. 186–191, 2018.
https://doi.org/10.1007/978-3-030-03251-7_22

(Presentation continues, describing the threat model and security objectives from Section 2 of the paper.)

Ian Goldberg: When you define confidentiality rigorously, it's not enough to say that non-collaborators cannot access the data, because you could have a non-collaborator colluding with a collaborator. So you have to rule out colluding collaborators, and then it gets really complicated really fast. It's not only a closed group, you have to deal with what happens when people leave the group, or what happens if you have two colluding people in the group and one of them leaves the group. How do you stop that person?

Reply: If there's existing literature on defining these things, I'd love to hear more about that.

Ian Goldberg: It's very complicated. And just in the context of group messaging, this is active research right now and my group works on that exact thing. And you have problems involving adding and removing group members.

In the secure messaging realm, what you're talking about is sometimes called *transcript consistency*, and then there are a couple of different kinds of transcript consistency. There is *global transcript consistency*, which is a guarantee that everyone in the group sees exactly the same messages in the same order. That's very hard to do, and the UI for that is ridiculous because you may actually receive messages out of order, but then some BFT-like protocol runs and it says, "oh, that message really should have gone there". And so what is the UI going to do? You see messages and then this one jumps up four messages? It's kind of crazy.

Reply: Yeah, what we want here is a weaker kind of transcript consistency, which doesn't enforce ordering, just enforces that the set of messages is the same.

Ian Goldberg: Right. You probably do still want *causal transcript consistency*, which means a reply to any message will necessarily appear after that message.

Reply: Yes, but that's much cheaper to achieve, I think.

Ian Goldberg: Exactly, it's much easier.

Frank Stajano: I have somewhat similar comments with respect to integrity, where the fact that non-collaborators cannot modify the content is necessary but insufficient. For example, if David and I have a shared document containing the expense reports for our company, and both of us are collaborators and authorised, but neither of us should be able to go back and change some expenses that we've already approved. There may be many other integrity properties of the document besides the fact that people who are not collaborators should not be able to modify.

Reply: Yes, absolutely. Underneath the shared document is a message log containing all of the changes that ever happened. And you can have stronger integrity properties on that log, so you would not be able to tamper with the message log, for example.

(Presentation continues with Sections 3 and 4 of the paper, and posing the problem of checking the integrity of snapshots.)

Daniel Weitzner: It's an interesting problem. I wonder if you have a bit of a concurrency-versus-privacy problem? If the first two users are still actively editing and at some point – as I think Ilia suggested – they want to go back in history, then what about the user who was invited later? Does the user who joined later get to see the history after whatever snapshot you did? Do you end up with two different versions of the document based on when you joined? If you've flattened out all the state then you've lost a lot of information for the first two users.

Reply: Yes, potentially. In particular, if there's some editing happening concurrently to the state snapshot being taken—

Daniel Weitzner: Or just afterwards. It doesn't even need to—

Reply: Yeah, "concurrently" in the distributed sense, that means, they're not aware of each other. Then yes, it could absolutely happen that this other edit can't be applied to that state, because it's assuming some kind of metadata that has been flattened out. That's absolutely a potential problem, yeah.

Frank Stajano: You say it's a problem that two thirds of the participants have to be honest, and online. I'm not sure about online, but is it not going to be the case that, in order to accept the newly invited guy, the previous guys have to agree to let him in? And therefore, at the time they say "okay, I think the new guy is alright", they could also say "this is the snapshot" (or hash of snapshot or something like that) that could contribute to the new guy having a view that they concur on.

Reply: I guess it depends what kind of permission you want to require for new people to be added. At least with Google Docs, and I think with most of the group messaging protocols, any one of the existing participants can just unilaterally invite a new person. So they don't require any kind of agreement from the group—

Frank Stajano: If this is the protocol, how can you even start worrying about privacy if any guy around can invite any of their pals? Then of course privacy goes out the window, right?

Reply: Well no, it's already the case that any one user, if they want to, can just send a copy of the document to their mates, completely outside of the protocol. There's no way of constraining what these individual people can do with their decrypted copy of the data.

Frank Stajano: Then why are you worried that they might see a past edit, if any of these guys can send it anyway, by your own assertion?

Reply: Well, the intention is that if the existing users don't want to share the past state, they have a way of sharing only the current state. Of course, if they wanted to leak the past state they could do that, but we are trying to avoid inadvertently leaking that past state when inviting a new user.

Ilia Shumailov: I think the goal is to save yourself from the server, not from the collaborators.

Frank Stajano: He's eliminated the server, hasn't he?

Ilia Shumailov: Yeah, but how do you keep it consistent?

Frank Stajano: Right, yes.

Reply: Keep what consistent?

Ilia Shumailov: The version of the document, all operations.

Reply: These algorithms will work perfectly fine without a server because they're tolerant of messages arriving out of order. You can run this on top of peer-to-peer protocol without any problems really.

Ilia Shumailov: Yeah this is just an optimisation not to share all of the operations for all of the documents with every new peer. Another interesting question would then be: what happens when the person who was offline joins in with a completely separate state of operations? Does that imply that, in order to impose new rules as a malicious user, you start DoSing all of the legitimate users? And then all of the non-legitimate users can form a current consensus with the online users, and distribute their own version of the document.

Reply: I guess that could happen, yes. I hadn't really considered users DoSing each other, but it's conceivable.

Alexander Hicks: This question is related to what you were discussing with Frank a few minutes ago. If you only want to share the latest state, I'm going to take the example of Google Docs here—it's a bit contrived, but can't you just create a new document, copy and paste what you want, and you've shared the latest state successfully? And you can even have access to your past edits by going back to your other doc if you want, without any risks. Obviously, it's maybe not practical to always open a new document, but it seems like it's doable at least.

Reply: Yes, the only problem is that there is no way for the new participant to tell whether the new copy of the document, that copy-and-pasted document, is actually consistent with what happened previously. So the person who does the copying and pasting of the document may well manipulate the document at the same time, and there is nothing stopping them.

Alexander Hicks: True, but then I guess from there on they would be satisfied they have the latest copy. Unless they're assuming that you're also editing the other copy, but then you can't really avoid that anyway.

Reply: But if you want the existing collaborators to still be able to continue editing, all three have now become equal collaborators, so you want to ensure that all three of them are in the same state. If you copy and paste the entire document into a new one, that means that all of the other participants also need to switch over to the new one, and presumably the participants would, in the process, do some comparison and checking whether the document still agrees with what they thought it was before the copy-and-paste.

Alexander Hicks: Sure, but you could probably generate some proof of that without necessarily revealing the past changes.

Reply: Well yes, that's exactly what we're trying to work out. Are there cryptographic techniques that we can use to prove the integrity?

Alexander Hicks: Something like a light client, I guess.

Reply: Like what?

Alexander Hicks: I guess maybe Paddy [Patrick McCorry] can say... for Bitcoin you have light clients, which only verify up to the past few blocks—is that correct? Something like that could probably work.

Reply: Yes, sounds conceivable. I don't know very much about Bitcoin.

Ian Goldberg: At the end of the day, you can always just run a SNARK, right? So you have a circuit that applies a change to a state, yielding another state, and the SNARK just checks that that was done correctly. It will not be cheap to generate, but it will be cheap to check. And then you can just, along with the latest state, carry a proof that this latest state was generated correctly, without revealing any of the inputs.

Reply: Yes, that would be interesting to try.

Patrick McCorry: This is sort of similar to state channels, where everyone agrees on the new state, so it's n out of n – everyone has to sign it. And when the new person joins, everyone has to agree to that as well. Is it the same process here when someone joins the collaboration? Do you require everyone's authorisation?

Reply: No. At the moment, the way we're thinking about this is that any one member of the group can add new members without having to coordinate with the others. That works nicely if these are mobile devices that are offline most of the time, where we really don't want to have to wait for someone else to come online. Even more so if, for example, one of the devices has been dropped in the toilet by somebody, and so it is never going to come back online again. In that case, we can at most wait for some kind of quorum, but we wouldn't want to have to wait for everybody.

Ilia Shumailov: Well, then that definitely completely destroys your technique here. You said that you wanted two out of three legitimate users. Then you just add a lot of users who have copied state from you, and just say "okay, this is the new state". Right?

Reply: Yes certainly, if you allow arbitrary Sybil identities to be created, then any sort of majority voting seems a bit meaningless. Though the nice thing with these redactable signatures is that they don't depend on any majorities: we can verify the signatures with respect to all of the previous users without waiting for any communication with them.

Ilia Shumailov: Oh, so that implies that with each one of them, you actually make a confirmation that this is the document.

Reply: Yes.

Ilia Shumailov: Well, does that not imply that if I add a bunch of copies of myself and claim that this is the new document, it's still going to work? What happens in the case of conflict?

Reply: Editing conflicts within the document are on a separate layer above this. Here, at this layer, we just need to ensure that everyone sees the same set of messages.

Ilia Shumailov: So, if I clone myself a number of times, and then I say, "okay, this is the new document", what happens with the guy who comes in?

Reply: In this snapshot, part of the information are the user IDs of who wrote what. Those user IDs might be a hash of their public key, for example. So if you don't have the private key for the other participants, you wouldn't be able to impersonate edits from the other people. You could still make a brand new document, in which only you have made the edits, and there have been no edits from others. For that document you would still need some kind of checking with the other participants, and they would at that point say: "hey no, this isn't the document that we were working on – this is something completely different".

Requirements for Root of Trust Establishment

Virgil Gligor(✉) and Maverick Woo

CyLab, Carnegie Mellon University, Pittsburgh, USA
gligor@cmu.edu

Abstract. Root-of-Trust (RoT) establishment assures that either a state of an untrusted system contains all and only content chosen by an external verifier *and* the verifier's code begins execution in that state, or the verifier discovers the existence of unaccounted content. RoT establishment is sufficient to assure program booting in *malware-free system states*, and necessary for establishing *secure initial states* for any software system. In particular, it is necessary for software deployed in access control and cryptographic applications despite the presence of an adversary (e.g., persistent malware) that controls that system. In this paper, we define requirements for RoT establishment and their relationships. These requirements differ from those for software-based and cryptographic attestation protocols. We point out these differences and explain why these protocols cannot be expected to satisfy the defined RoT requirements. Then we argue that *jointly* satisfying all these requirements yields a secure solution for establishing malware-free states – a strictly weaker requirement than RoT establishment. However, to establish RoT, it is sufficient to load a family of almost universal hash functions in a malware-fee state and then verify their outputs when applied to state components.

1 Introduction

Suppose a user has a trustworthy program and attempts to boot it in a system state. The *system state* comprises the contents of all processor and I/O registers and primary memories of a chipset and peripheral device controllers at a particular time; e.g., before boot. If any malicious software (*malware*) can execute instructions anywhere in system state, the user wants to discover the presence of malware with high probability. This goal has not been achieved to date. System components that are *not* directly addressable by CPU instructions or by trusted hardware modules enable malware to become *persistent*; i.e., to survive in non-volatile memories of system states despite repeated power cycles, secure-, and trusted-boot operations [1], and to infect the rest of the system state. For example, persistent malware has been found in the firmware of peripheral controllers [2–5], network interface cards [3,6,7], disk controllers [8–11], routers and firewalls [11], as well as that of removable devices [12]. A remote adversary can retain long-term control of a user's system via persistent malware.

V. Matyáš et al. (Eds.): Security Protocols 2018, LNCS 11286, pp. 192–202, 2018.
https://doi.org/10.1007/978-3-030-03251-7_23

Suppose that the user attempts to initialize the system state to content that she chooses; e.g., she includes a small I/O program for loading a trustworthy microhypervisor or microkernel later, initializes the primary memory to chosen values, and reflashes device-controller firmware to malware-free code. Furthermore, her chosen content may also satisfy some security invariants; e.g., the system is disconnected from the Internet, and it has the configuration expected by the microhypervisor. Now the user wants to verify that the system, which may have been infected by malware and hence is untrusted, has been initialized to the content chosen and hence known by the user.

Root of trust (RoT) establishment on an untrusted system assures that a system state comprises *all* and *only* content chosen by, and known to, the user, and the user's code *begins execution* in that state. *All* implies that no content is missing, and *only* implies that no extra content exists. If a system state is initialized to content that satisfies security invariants and RoT establishment succeeds, a user's code begins execution in a *secure initial state*. Then trustworthy OS and application programs booted in a secure initial state can extend this state to include secondary storage. If RoT establishment fails, unaccounted content, such as malware, exists. Hence, RoT establishment is sufficient for (and stronger than) assuring malware freedom and necessary for all access control models and cryptographic protocols, since all need secure initial states.

In this paper, we answer the following questions:

- How can RoT be established without secrets and trusted hardware modules?
- Can past attestation protocols provide a viable solution to RoT? If not, what requirements are not satisfied?
- Can jointly satisfying these requirements lead to a sound RoT establishment protocols? If not, what additional mechanisms are necessary?

Specifically,

- we define requirements for RoT establishment without secrets and trusted hardware modules, and discuss their relationships;
- we show that past attestation protocols have had different goals than RoT establishment, and hence cannot be expected to satisfy the requirements defined herein;
- we argue that jointly satisfying these requirements leads to establishment of malware-free states.
- we argue that loading a simple family of universal hash functions [24] – one per system component – and verifying their outputs when applied to those components yields RoT establishment.

2 Software-Based Attestation - An Overview

To define the requirements for RoT establishment we review the basic steps of software-based attestation [25–29] for a simple untrusted system connected to a *local* trusted verifier.

Suppose that the simple system has a processor and a m-word memory comprising random-access memory, processor, and I/O registers. The verifier asks the system to initialize the m words to chosen content. Then the verifier challenges the system to perform a computation $C_{m,t}(\cdot)$ on a pseudorandom *nonce* in the m words and time t. Suppose that $C_{m,t}(\cdot)$ is space-time (i.e., $m - t$) optimal, $C_{m,t}(nonce)$ is unpredictable by an adversary, and the computation is non-interruptible. If the system returns $C_{m,t}(nonce)$ to the local verifier in time t, then after accounting for the local communication delay, the verifier concludes that the memory state contains all and only the chosen content.

When applied to multiple device controllers, this protocol proceeds from the faster controllers to the slower ones, repeating the attestation of the faster ones, so that they do not end execution early and act as *proxies* for the slow ones [3].

3 Adversary Definition

Our adversary can exercise all known attacks that insert persistent malware into a computer system, including having brief access to that system; e.g., an EFI attack by an "evil maid". Also, it can control malware remotely and extract all software secrets stored in the system, via a network channel. Malware can read and write the verifier's local I/O channel, which is always faster and has less transfer-time variability than the adversary's network channel. However, malware does not have access to the verifier's code nor to the true random number generator.

We assume the adversary *can break* all complexity-based cryptography but *cannot predict* the true random numbers to be received from the verifier. Also, the adversary can optimize $C_{m,t}$'s code in a system at no cost; i.e., it can encode small values of *nonces* and memory content into the immediate address fields of instructions to lower $C_{m,t}$'s space and/or time below m, t, in zero extra time and memory space. Furthermore, the adversary can output the result of a different computation that takes less time than t or space than m, or both. Why is the no-cost code change a prudent assumption in a timed protocol? First, some code changes can take place before a *nonce*'s arrival, which marks the beginning of the timed protocol. Second, to account for (e.g., cache and TLB) jitter caused by random memory access by typical $C_{m,t}(\cdot)$ computations, verifiers' time measurements typically build in some slack time; e.g., 0.2%–2.6% of t [2,26,29–31]. This could enable an adversary to exploit the slack and use unaccounted instructions; viz., [31].

4 Requirements

4.1 Concrete Optimality

Optimality of a $C_{m,t}$ computation means that its lower bounds match the upper bounds non-asymptotically[1] in both memory size, m, and execution time, t. If the

[1] Different constants of asymptotic lower and upper bounds of $C_{m,t}$ cause these bounds to differ for concrete values of m and t.

time bounds differ, the verifier faces a fundamental problem: its measurement becomes either useless or meaningless. If the measurement is checked against the theoretical lower bound, which is often unattainable in practice, then false positives as high as 100% would render attestation useless. If it's checked against a value that exceeds the theoretical lower bound or if it's checked against the upper bound, then it would be impossible to prove that an adversary's code could not produce better timing and render attestation meaningless. In contrast, if the optimal time bounds are non-asymptotic, the only challenge is to reduce the measurement slack in specific systems, which is an engineering, rather than a basic computational complexity, problem.

If the memory bounds differ, the adversary can exercise time-memory trade-offs and the verifier faces a similar measurement dilemma as above. For example, such trade-offs can be exploited in the evaluation of univariate polynomials of degree d in algebraic models of computation, where $t \cdot m^2 \geq d/8$ [32].

Optimality in a concrete computational model. Optimal bounds for any computation always depend on the model of computation used. For example, lower bounds differ with the instruction set architectures (ISA) of a *practical WRAM* model – which is close to a real computer – even for simple computations such as static dictionaries [33,34]. Few optimal bounds exist in these models, even if asymptotic, despite the fact that their variable word length allows the use of the circuit-based complexity hierarchy. Instead, lower bounds for more complex problems have been proved only in the *cell probe* model [40], where references to memory cells (i.e., bits) are counted, but *not* instruction executions. Unfortunately, these lower bounds cannot be used for any $C_{m,t}$ since they can never match upper bounds non-asymptotically, and are unreachable in reality.

Optimality retention in $C_{m,t}$ composition. In abstract WRAM models program optimality is considered without regard of whether extra system code and data in memory could invalidate the program's lower bounds. Input data and optimal programs simply exist in system registers and memory, and *I/O* operations and register initialization (*Init*) are assumed to be done already.

In contrast, a concrete WRAM model must be implemented in real systems, and hence it must include I/O registers and instructions (e.g., for data transfers, interrupt handling, busy/done status) and instructions that initialize special registers and configure processors; e.g., clear/evict cache and TLB content, disable VM. Thus $C_{m,t}$'s code must be composed with I/O and *Init* code, which could invalidate $C_{m,t}$'s lower bounds. Hence, proving its optimality must account for *all* extra code and data in memory when $C_{m,t}$'s code runs, and hence the less extra code and data the better.

Unpredictability of $C_{m,t}(nonce)$. Most optimality results are obtained assuming honest execution of $C_{m,t}$'s code. An execution is *honest* if the $C_{m,t}$ code is fixed (i.e., committed) before it reads any inputs, and returns correct results for all inputs. Unfortunately, the optimality of $C_{m,t}$'s code in honest execution does not necessarily hold in adversarial execution since an adversary can change $C_{m,t}$'s code both before and after receiving the *nonce*, or simply guess $C_{m,t}(nonce)$ without executing any instructions. Before the *nonce*'s arrival, the adversary can modify the code independent of the verifier's *nonce*. After a *nonce*'s arrival, the adversary can check its value, and determine the best possible code modification, at no cost. For example, she can encode a small-value *nonce* into immediate address fields of instructions, and save register space and instruction executions. More insidiously, an adversary could change the entire code to that of another function $C'_{m',t'}(\cdot)$ and $nonce'$, such that $(C'_{m',t'}, nonce') \neq (C_{m,t}, nonce)$, $(m', t') < (m, t)$, and $C'_{m',t'}(nonce') = C_{m,t}(nonce)$.

The adversary's goal is to write the result $C_{m,t}(nonce)$ into the output register after executing fewer instructions, if any, and/or using less memory than the honest optimal code. If adversary succeeds with better than low probability over the pseudo-random choice of *nonce*, then she could execute unaccounted instructions that arbitrarily modify system state before returning the result, which would remain undetected.

To counter all possible adversary behaviors, we require that the adversary succeeds in writing $C_{m,t}(nonce)$ to the output register with low probability over the *nonce*, after executing fewer instructions, if any, and/or using less memory than the honest optimal code. We call this requirement the *unpredictability of* $C_{m,t}(nonce)$. Thus, the correctness and timeliness of $C_{m,t}(nonce)$ must imply unpredictability.

4.2 Protocol Atomicity

The *verifier's protocol* begins with the input of the *nonce* challenge in a system and ends when the verifier receives the system's output; e.g., $C_{m,t}(nonce)$. Protocol atomicity requires integrity of control flow across the instructions of the verifier's protocol with *each* system component; i.e., each device controller and the (multi)processor(s) of the chipset. Asynchronous events, such as future-posted interrupts, hardware breakpoints on instruction execution or operand access [29], and inter-processor communication, can violate control-flow integrity *outside* of $C_{m,t}(\cdot)$'s execution. For instance, a malware instruction can post a *future* interrupt *before* the verifier's protocol begins execution. The interrupt could trigger *after* a correct and timely $C_{m,t}(nonce)$ result is sent to the verifier, and execute code that undetectably corrupts system state [31]. Clearly, optimality of $C_{m,t}(\cdot)$ is insufficient for control-flow integrity. Nevertheless, optimality is necessary: otherwise, a predictable $C_{m,t}(nonce)$ would allow time and space for an *interrupt-enabling* instruction to be executed undetectably.

Verifiable control flow. Instructions that disable asynchronous events must be executed before $C_{m,t}(\cdot)$. Their execution inside $C_{m,t}(\cdot)$ would violate optimality bounds, and after $C_{m,t}(\cdot)$ would be ineffective: asynchronous events could trigger during the execution of the last $C_{m,t}(\cdot)$ instruction. However, verification that an instruction is located before $C_{m,t}(\cdot)$ in memory (e.g., via a digital signature or a MAC) does *not* guarantee its execution. The adversary code could simply skip it before executing $C_{m,t}(\cdot)$. Hence, verification must address the apparent cyclic dependency: on the one hand, the execution of the event-disabling instructions before $C_{m,t}(\cdot)$ requires control-flow integrity, and on the other, control-flow integrity requires the execution of the event-disabling instructions before $C_{m,t}(\cdot)$.

Concurrent all-or-nothing transaction. Protocol atomicity also requires that the verifier's protocol with n device controllers and CPUs of the (multiprocessor) chipset is implemented as a concurrent all-or-nothing transaction. That is, *all* optimal $C_{m_1,t_1}, \ldots, C_{m_n,t_n}$ codes for the n components must execute concurrently and pass verification. This prevents register and memory modification of already attested devices (e.g., reinfection) by yet-to-be attested devices, not only *proxy* attacks [3]. Note that powering off individual devices and powering them one-at-a-time before performing individual attestation is inadequate because some (e.g., chipset) devices cannot be powered-off without system shutdown, and insufficient because malicious firmware can still corrupt an already attested controllers after power-on and before attestation starts.

Concurrent all-or-nothing execution requires that for distinct *fixed* t_i's, the faster C_{m_j,t_j} computations be performed $k_j \geq \lceil max(t_i)/t_j \rceil$ times, where $max(t_i)$ is the optimal time bound of the slowest device controller. As shown in the next section, a protocol does not exist that uses a *fixed* t_i for a given m_i and produces concurrent all-or-nothing execution, and at the same time retains both C_{m_i,t_i}'s optimality m and result unpredictability. Hence, atomicity requires a *scalable* time bound t; i.e., t can be increased independent of the constant memory bound m and yet preserves $C_{m,t}$'s optimality[2].

5 Past Attestation Protocols and RoT Establishment

Past attestation protocols, whether software-based [25,26,29,35,38], cryptographic-based [17,19–21,39], or hybrid [3,41], have *different* security goals than those of RoT requirements defined here: some are weaker and some are stronger. For example, whether these protocols are used for single or multiple devices, they typically aim to verify a weaker property, namely the integrity of software – not system – state. However, they also satisfy a stronger property: in all cryptographic and hybrid attestation protocols the verification can be remote and can be repeated after boot, rather than local and limited to pre-boot time as here.

Given their different goals, it is unsurprising that past protocols do not satisfy some RoT establishment requirements defined here, even for bounded adversaries and secret-key protection in trusted hardware modules. For example, these protocols need not be concerned with system's *register content* (e.g., for general processor and I/O registers), since they cannot contain executable code. Furthermore, they need not satisfy the concurrent all-or-nothing *atomicity* (see Sect. 4.2) of the verifier's protocol since they need not establish any state properties, such as secure initial state in multi-device systems. Finally, since none of these systems aim to satisfy security properties *unconditionally*, they do not require that verifiers are equipped with true random number generators; e.g., pseudo-random numbers are sufficient for *nonce* generation. Beyond these common differences, past protocols exhibit some specific differences.

[2] This is the opposite of *perfect* universal hash functions, which seek a *constant* t independent of the scalable m.

Software-based attestation. Some applications in which software-based attestation is beneficially used do not require control-flow integrity [37], and naturally this requirement need not always be satisfied [31,36]. Here we illustrate a more subtle challenge that arises *if* one uses traditional checksum designs for RoT establishment in a multi-device system, where the concurrent all-or-nothing requirement becomes important. That is, some past designs cannot jointly satisfy concurrent all-or-nothing atomicity and either code optimality or result unpredictability. Software-based attestation models [38] also face this challenge.

Some past $C_{m,t}$ computations are checksums that have a *fixed* bound t for a given m. Let a concurrent all-or-nothing transaction comprise checksums $C_{m_1,t_1}, \ldots, C_{m_n,t_n}$ for n devices. This implies that some $C_{m,t}$ must be executed $k \geq \lceil max(t_i)/t \rceil$ times and its executions $C_{m,t}(nonce_0), \ldots, C_{m,t}(nonce_{k-1})$ must be linked to eliminate idle waiting [3]. Suppose that linking is done by the verifier: optimal $C_{m,t}(nonce_j)$ cannot end execution until it inputs $nonce_{j+1}$ from the verifier. Then $C_{m,t}$ can no longer be optimal, since the variable input-synchronization delays within $C_{m,t}$ invalidate the optimal time bounds t[3]. If synchronization buffers of $nonce_{j+1}$, m also becomes invalid.

Alternatively, suppose that $C_{m,t}$'s executions are linked through nonces: $nonce_{j+1} = C_{m,t}(nonce_j)$. However, $C_{m,t}(nonce_{j+1})$'s unpredictability requires that its input $nonce_{j+1}$ is pseudo-random. This would no longer be guaranteed since $C_{m,t}$ need *not* be a pseudo-random function; e.g., Pioneer's checksum [26] and its descendants (e.g., [29]) are not.

Despite their differences from RoT establishment, software-based attestation designs met their goals [2,26,35], and offered deep insights on how to detect malware on peripheral controllers [3], embedded devices [31,36], mobile phones [30], and specialized processors; e.g., TPMs [29].

Cryptographic attestation. Cryptographic protocols for remote attestation typically require a trusted hardware module, which can be as simple as a ROM module [18], to protect a secret key for computing digital signatures or MACs. If used in applications that require control-flow integrity for the signature or MAC computation, as in RoT establishment, a trusted hardware model in each device must protect *both* the secret key *and* the signature/MAC generation code. Otherwise, these applications would exhibit similar control-flow vulnerabilities as software-based attestation.

More importantly, cryptographic attestation relocates the trust to the third parties who install the cryptographic keys in each device and those who distribute them to verifiers. The trustworthiness of these parties can be uncertain; e.g., a peripheral-controller supplier operating in jurisdictions that can compel the disclosure of secrets could not guarantee the secrecy of the protected cryptographic key. Similarly, the integrity of the distribution channel for the signature-verification certificate established between the device supplier/integrator and

[3] Input synchronization delays for $nonce_{j+1}$ within a $checksum_j$ computation on a network interface card (Netgear GA 620) that takes time t can be as high as $0.4t$ with a standard deviation of about $0.0029t$; see [3], Sects. 5.4.2-5.4.4.

verifier can be compromised, which enables known attacks; e.g., see the Cuckoo attack [13]. Thus, these protocols aim to offer only conditional security.

Nevertheless if the risk added when third parties manage one's system secrets is acceptable *and* protocol atomicity requirements can be met, then cryptographic protocols for remote attestation could be used in RoT establishment.

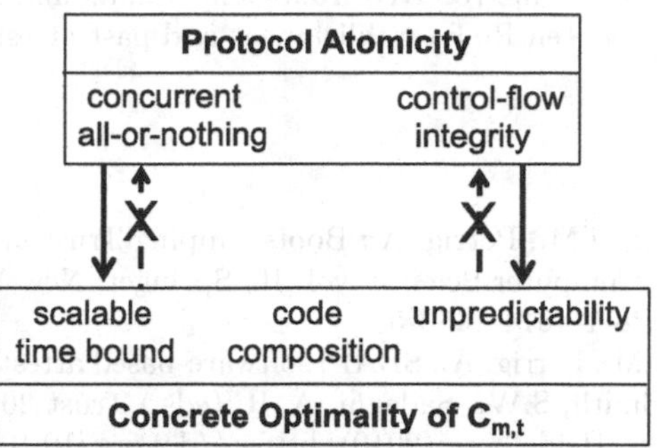

Fig. 1. Requirements for RoT establishment

6 Satisfying RoT Requirements – Overview

Necessity. Figure 1 summarizes the relationships among the requirements for RoT establishment. Atomicity of the verifier's protocol has unavoidable dependencies on both $C_{m,t}(\cdot)$'s scalable time bounds and unpredictability. As illustrated above, identifying dependencies is important because they show which requirements must be jointly satisfied to discharge proof obligations for establishing malware-free states. It is also useful since unnecessary dependencies can introduce cycles that often rule out proofs; e.g., the spurious optimality dependency on atomicity [31].

The concrete optimality requirements must be jointly satisfied independent of protocol atomicity. First, unpredictability must not depend on control-flow integrity: even if an adversary can trace the execution of each instruction of optimal evaluation code, she cannot write the correct result into the output register by executing fewer instructions or using less memory than optimal, except with very small probability over guessing.

Second, unpredictability enables verifiable execution of instructions that disable asynchronous events durably, which achieves control-flow integrity.

Third, a scalable optimal time bound and the implementation of concurrent all-or-nothing transactions based on them will complete the support for establishing malware-free states.

Sufficiency. Note that jointly satisfying the requirements presented above only yields malware-free states – a *strictly weaker* property than RoT establishment. However, it is sufficient to load a family of almost universal hash functions [24] in a malware-fee state and then verify their outputs when applied to state components to establish RoT unconditionally.

Acknowledgment. Comments received from Gene Tsudik and Adrian Perrig helped clarify the differences between RoT establishment and past attestation protocols.

References

1. Parno, B., McCune, J.M., Perrig, A.: Bootstrapping Trust in Modern Computers. Springer Briefs in Computer Science, vol. 10. Springer, New York (2011). https://doi.org/10.1007/978-1-4614-1460-5
2. Li, Y., McCune, J.M., Perrig, A.: SBAP: software-based attestation for peripherals. In: Acquisti, A., Smith, S.W., Sadeghi, A.-R. (eds.) Trust 2010. LNCS, vol. 6101, pp. 16–29. Springer, Heidelberg (2010). https://doi.org/10.1007/978-3-642-13869-0_2
3. Li, Y., McCune, J.M., Perrig, A.: VIPER: verifying the integrity of PERipherals' firmware. In: Proceedings of the 18th ACM Conference on Computer and Communications Security, pp. 3–16. ACM Press (2011)
4. Cui, A., Costello, M., Stolfo, S.: When firmware modifications attack: a case study of embedded exploitation. In: Proceedings of the 2013 Network and Distributed Systems Security Symposium, ISOC (2013)
5. Stewin, P.: Detecting Peripheral-based Attacks on the Host Memory. T-Lab Series in Telecommunication Services. Springer, Heidelberg (2014). https://doi.org/10.1007/978-3-319-13515-1
6. Delugre, G.: Closer to metal: reverse engineering the broadcom NetExtreme's firmware. In: Sogeti ESEC Lab. (2010)
7. Duflot, L., Perez, Y.-A., Morin, B.: What if you can't trust your network card? In: Sommer, R., Balzarotti, D., Maier, G. (eds.) RAID 2011. LNCS, vol. 6961, pp. 378–397. Springer, Heidelberg (2011). https://doi.org/10.1007/978-3-642-23644-0_20
8. Zaddach, J., et al.: Implementation and implications of a stealth hard-drive backdoor. In: Proceedings of the 29th Annual Computer Security Applications Conference (ACSAC). ACM (2013)
9. Mearian, L.: There's no way of knowing if the NSA's spyware is on your hard drive. Computerworld **2** (2015)
10. Raiu, C.: Equation: The Death Star of the Malware Galaxy, February 2015
11. Applebaum, J., Horchert, J., Stocker, C.: Catalog reveals NSA has back doors for numerous devices, vol. 29 (2013)
12. Greenberg, A.: Why the security of USB is fundamentally broken. In: Wired Magazine, Number July (2014)
13. Parno, B.: Bootstrapping trust in a trusted platform. In: Proceedings of the 3rd Conference on Hot Topics in security, pp. 1–6. USENIX Association (2008)
14. Lone-Sang, F., Nicomette, V., Deswarte, Y.: I/O attacks in intel-pc architectures and countermeasures. In: Proceedings of the Symposium for the Security of Information and Communication Technologies SSTIC (2011)

15. Lone-Sang, F., Nicomette, V., Deswarte, Y.: A tool to analyze potential I/O attacks against PCs. In: IEEE Security and Privacy, pp. 60–66 (2014)
16. Kaspersky Lab: The Duqu 2.0 - Technical Details (version 2.1). Technical report (2015)
17. Eldefrawy, K., Perito, D., Tsudik, G.: SMART: Secure and minimal architecture for (establishing a dynamic) root of trust, February 2012
18. Koeberl, P., Schulz, S., Sadeghi, A.-R., Varadharajan, V.: TrustLite: a security architecture for tiny embedded devices. In: Proceedings of the Ninth European Conference on Computer Systems, EuroSys 2014 (2014)
19. Asokan, N., et al.: SEDA: scalable embedded device attestation. In: Proceedings of the 2015 ACM Conference on Computer and Communications Security. ACM (2015)
20. Ibrahim, A., Sadeghi, A.R., Tsudik, G., Zeitouni, S.: DARPA: device attestation resilient to physical attacks. In: Proceedings of the 9th ACM Conference on Security & Privacy in Wireless and Mobile Networks. WiSec 2016, pp. 171–182. ACM (2016)
21. Ibrahim, A., Sadeghi, A.R., Zeitouni, S.: SeED: secure non-interactive attestation for embedded devices. In: Proceedings of the 10th ACM Conference on Security and Privacy in Wireless and Mobile Networks. WiSec 2017, pp. 64–74 (2017)
22. Lipton, R., Ostrovsky, R., Zikas, b.: Provable virus detection: using the uncertainty principle to protect against malware. Cryptology ePrint Archive, Report 2015/728 (2015). http://eprint.iacr.org/2015/728
23. Lipton, R., Ostrovsky, R., Zikas, V.: Provably secure virus detection: using the observer effect against malware. In: 43rd International Colloquium on Automata, Languages, and Programming, ICALP 2016, 11–15 July 2016, Rome, Italy, pp. 32:1–32:14 (2016)
24. Thorup, M.: High speed hashing for integers and strings. CoRR arXiv:1504.06804, September 2015
25. Spinellis, D.: Reflection as a mechanism for software integrity verification. ACM Trans. Inf. Syst. Secur. **3**(1), 51–62 (2000)
26. Seshadri, A., Luk, M., Shi, E., Perrig, A., van Doorn, L., Khosla, P.: Pioneer: verifying code integrity and enforcing untampered code execution on legacy systems. In: Proceedings of the 20th ACM Symposium on Operating Systems Principles, pp. 1–16. ACM (2005)
27. Seshadri, A., Luk, M., Perrig, A., van Doorn, L., Khosla, P.: SCUBA: secure code update by attestation in sensor networks. In: Proceedings of the 5th ACM Workshop on Wireless Security, pp. 85–94. ACM (2006)
28. Seshadri, A., Luk, M., Qu, N., Perrig, A.: SecVisor: a tiny hypervisor to provide lifetime kernel code integrity for commodity OSes. In: Proceedings of 21st ACM Symposium on Operating Systems Principles, pp. 335–350. ACM (2007)
29. Kovah, X., Kallenberg, C., Weathers, C., Herzog, A., Albin, M., Butterworth, J.: New results for timing-based attestation. In: Proceedings of the 2012 IEEE Symposium on Security and Privacy, pp. 239–253. IEEE (2012)
30. Jakobsson, M., Johansson, K.A.: Retroactive detection of malware with applications to mobile platforms. In: Proceedings of the 5th USENIX Workshop on Hot Topics in Security, USENIX (2010)
31. Li, Y., Cheng, Y., Gligor, V., Perrig, A.: Establishing software-only root of trust on embedded systems: facts and fiction. In: Christianson, B., Švenda, P., Matyáš, V., Malcolm, J., Stajano, F., Anderson, J. (eds.) Security Protocols 2015. LNCS, vol. 9379, pp. 50–68. Springer, Cham (2015). https://doi.org/10.1007/978-3-319-26096-9_7

32. Aldaz, M., Heintz, J., Matera, G., Montaa, J., Pardo, L.: Time-space tradeoffs in algebraic complexity theory. J. Complex. **16**(1), 2–49 (2000)
33. Miltersen, P.B.: Lower bounds for static dictionaries on RAMs with bit operations but no multiplication. In: Meyer, F., Monien, B. (eds.) ICALP 1996. LNCS, vol. 1099, pp. 442–453. Springer, Heidelberg (1996). https://doi.org/10.1007/3-540-61440-0_149
34. Andersson, A., Miltersen, P.B., Riis, S., Thorup, M.: Static dictionaries on AC^0 RAMs: query time $\Theta(\sqrt(log\ n/log\ log\ n))$ is necessary and sufficient. In: Proceedings of 37th FOCS, pp. 441–450 (1996)
35. Seshadri, A., Perrig, A., van Doorn, L., Khosla, P.: SWATT: software-based attestation for embedded devices. In: Proceedings of the IEEE Symposium on Security and Privacy, pp. 272–282. IEEE (2004)
36. Castelluccia, C., Francillon, A., Perito, D., Soriente, C.: On the difficulty of software-based attestation of embedded devices. In: Proceedings of the 16th ACM Conference on Computer and Communications Security, pp. 400–409. ACM (2009)
37. Perrig, A., van Doorn, L.: Refutation of "on the difficulty of software-based attestation of embedded devices" (2010)
38. Armknecht, F., Sadeghi, A.R., Schulz, S., Wachsmann, C.: A security framework for the analysis and design of software attestation. In: Proceedings of the 2013 ACM Conference on Computer and Communications Security, pp. 1–12. ACM (2013)
39. Francillon, A., Nguyen, Q., Rasmussen, K.B., Tsudik, G.: A minimalist approach to remote attestation. In: Proceedings of the Conference on Design, Automation & Test in Europe. DATE 2014, 3001 Leuven, Belgium, Belgium, pp. 244:1–244:6. European Design and Automation Association (2014)
40. Yao, A.C.-C.: Should tables be sorted? J. ACM **28**(3), 615–628 (1981)
41. Zhao, J., Gligor, V., Perrig, A., Newsome, J.: ReDABLS: revisiting device attestation with bounded leakage of secrets. In: Christianson, B., Malcolm, J., Stajano, F., Anderson, J., Bonneau, J. (eds.) Security Protocols 2013. LNCS, vol. 8263, pp. 94–114. Springer, Heidelberg (2013). https://doi.org/10.1007/978-3-642-41717-7_12

Requirements for Root of Trust Establishment (Transcript of Discussion)

Virgil Gligor(✉)

CyLab, Carnegie Mellon University, Pittsburgh, USA
gligor@cmu.edu

Frank Stajano: You spoke about establishing a malware-free state. If I give you a bit string, which basically is a dump of all the memory that you're interested in, are you able to detect whether it contains malware? Any possible known or unknown malware? Do you assume you have that capability or not?

Reply: Well, no, it's not easy to figure out whether the memory dump contains malware. Your question is also interesting because a binary program in the memory dump can have different behaviors on different systems[1]; e.g., it can be a perfectly good program on one and malware on another.

Frank Stajano: No, I'm saying a string of bits specifically for your system. If I give you a dump of the state of your system, are you able to tell me whether it had malware or not? Because I don't think it's possible.

Reply: I'm not, and that's not what I'm interested in. What I'm interested in knowing whether my own string of bits, which I know doesn't contain malware, is in my system with high probability.

Frank Stajano: But in one of the previous slides you said that root of trust is established so long as you *knew* what was in the system.

Reply: Yes, since I initialized my system.

Frank Stajano: There's a difference between *knowing* what's on the system and *having the thing you wanted* in the system.

Reply: True. In short, here is what I'm saying: I initialize my system state to certain values, which satisfy whatever security invariants I choose. This defines a *known state*, which is also *secure*, since it satisfies the invariants. Now, root of trust establishment requires that I be able to test that the system contains exactly the values I put in; i.e., all and only content that's known to me, and control is in particular program I initialized.

Frank Stajano: I am making a specific distinction between things that are known to you and things that you put in, because the second one is much stronger.

[1] See S. K. Cha, B. Pak, D. Brumley, R. Lipton, "Platform-Independent Programs," Proc. of ACM CCS, Chicago, Illinois, Oct. 2010.

V. Matyáš et al. (Eds.): Security Protocols 2018, LNCS 11286, pp. 203–208, 2018.
https://doi.org/10.1007/978-3-030-03251-7_24

Reply: Yes. I hope now it's clear what root-of-trust establishment is about[2].

Furthermore, I also want to establish root-of-trust without secrets, trusted-platform modules, or bounds on the adversary power; e.g., without any crypto primitives.

Ian Goldberg: So, you say once you're in the secure state, you've done your root of trust, now you can go boot trustworthy OS code, except how are you going to do that? If crypto doesn't work, you can't have a signature on the OS code, you can't even have a hash on the OS code, how do you know the thing you're about to load is the right OS code?

Reply: I boot my own trusted microhypervisor; e.g., CMU's TrustVisor or XMHF, or any formally verified (trusted) microkernel.

Ian Goldberg: Sure, but you're going to boot into a secure state, that code has to load your trusted kernel, but how does it know that kernel is the right kernel? Normally, you would hash it and check with the hashes, right?

Reply: In this case, I don't need hashes. Suppose that I am in a secure state, which says that my system is not connected to any external device except my phone, which contains my microhypervisor. Now, the question is whether I trust that my phone contains my microhypervisor.

Ian Goldberg: So, you'll just run any code your phone gives you at this point?

Reply: No. I run the system code, which then runs my microhypervisor. In other words, if I have some [trusted] input source that contains my microhypervisor, that is what I load.

Ian Goldberg: Right. And you just trust that it gives you the right microhypervisor, and not malware.

Reply: Yes. If you prefer, I can store my microhypervisor it on a empty storage medium, and then I plug it in. My storage medium can be a USB stick.

Ian Goldberg: Okay. But then, what's the next step? If you don't have crypto and you don't have signatures, and you don't have hashes.

Reply: The next step is different. After I load my trusted microhypervisor in a secure state I can activate whatever type of crypto I want. For example, I can run any complexity-based crypto primitives, which are conditionally secure; i.e., where the adversary has to be polynomially bounded. So, I'm not rejecting use of crypto primitives completely. I'm only avoiding them is establishing security of the initial states of my system.

Ian Goldberg: Okay, so after the root of trust boots, crypto exists again.

Reply: Yes, absolutely. Furthermore, I'm arguing is that root-of-trust establishment this is a necessary step for *all* crypto software. In other words, it doesn't

[2] The above discussion led to the post-proceedings paper clarification that the known state was one chosen and initialized by the user.

matter whether root-of-trust is established for software applications or crypto. Any software, and it doesn't even have to be critical software, that doesn't start in a secure initial state is suspect, and more so in the case of crypto and security software.

Let us remember that the notion of a *secure initial state* has been on the security-requirements books since times immemorial. I do not know of anybody has really bothered to figure out how to establish such states. As a matter of fact, in 1998, we had the paper at this workshop about how to bring a system from an arbitrary state to a state that satisfies a security predicate with a fixed number of commands, and we called that *system administrability.* Clearly, *administrability* is a hyper-property, not a safety or a liveness property, and is simpler than root-of-trust establishment because it does not account for potential malware presence. Even this simple property has not been satisfied in any system that I know of.

Fabio Massacci: I have another question: what happens if the IO kernel of your secure initial state is compromised? Basically your example of the USB stick...

Reply: This IO kernel is a simple *busy-waiting* loop. It's not an operating system I/O kernel, it's not even a microkernel. It is busy waiting on the input device, since all interrupts are turned off.

Fabio Massacci: Okay. So, it just loads whatever you give it...

Reply: Yes, but only on the only channel which the code of secure initial state accepts.

In the paper we argue that neither *software-based attestation* nor cryptographic protocols that compute digital signatures or message authentication codes (MACs) on system states are sufficient for root-of-trust RoT establishment. We summarize the basic steps of software-based attestation for an untrusted system connected to a local trusted verifier, and briefly outline its shortcomings. Then we show why cryptographic protocols that compute digital signatures or MACs fall short also.

Suppose that the system has a processor and memory comprising m words; i.e., r processor and I/O registers and $m - r$ RAM words. The verifier asks the system to initialize the m words to known content, and then challenges it to perform a computation $C_{m,t}(\cdot)$ on a pseudorandom *nonce* in the m words and time t. If $C_{m,t}(\cdot)$ is space-time (i.e., $m - t$) optimal and $C_{m,t}(nonce)$ is unpredictable when computed by an adversary, and if the computation is non-interruptible, then if the system returns $C_{m,t}(nonce)$ in time t, the verifier concludes that the memory state contains all and only known content. When applied to multiple device controllers, this protocol proceeds from the faster controllers to the slower ones, repeating the attestation of the faster ones so that they do not end execution earlier than the slowest one.

Software-based attestation is insufficient for RoT establishment for four reasons. First, it does not provide a computation $C_{m,t}(\cdot)$ that is provably $m - t$

optimal. Its dilemma has been that complexity theory has not offered examples of computations with concrete (non-asymptotic) optimal $m-t$ bounds that retain their optimality in a realistic model of computation; i.e., one that has a modern instruction set architecture (ISA), such as the Word Random Access Machine (WRAM) model. Concrete optimal bounds exist for computations that are limited to few algebraic operations; however, they can be bypassed when using WRAM and real ISAs. In contrast, most bounds obtained in WRAM are asymptotic, and different constants of asymptotic lower and upper bounds cause them to differ for specific m and/or t values; i.e., concrete optimality is lost.

Second, software-based attestation fails to maintain control-flow integrity in the verifiers protocol with an untrusted system. However, without verifiable control-flow integrity (e.g., without proving instruction execution, not merely instruction presence in memory) no proof of RoT establishment is possible. In fact, control-flow integrity had not been a design goal of software attestation.

Third, past software-based attestation protocols have used $C_{m,t}(\cdot)$ computations with a fixed time bound t for a given m. However, with such computations one cannot jointly satisfy the all-or-nothing atomicity of the verifier protocol for multiple devices and retain both $m-t$ optimality and result unpredictability in adversary execution. This rules out RoT establishment.

Note that protocol atomicity also requires that the verifier's protocol with n device controllers and CPUs of the (multiprocessor) chipset is implemented as a *concurrent all-or-nothing* transaction. That is, *all* optimal $C_{m_1,t_1}, \ldots, C_{m_n,t_n}$ programs for the n components must execute concurrently and pass verification. This prevents malicious yet-to-be attested controllers from performing unmediated peer-to-peer I/O transfers to the registers of an already verified I/O controller and then erase its I/O instruction from firmware before its attestation begins.

Fourth, past software-based attestation designs fail to assure that a verifier's time measurements cannot be bypassed by an adversary. For example, to account for cache, TLB, and clock jitter caused primarily by random memory traversals by $C_{m,t}(\cdot)$ computations and large t, typical verifiers' measurements build in some slack time; e.g., typically the slack time is 0.2%–2.6% of t An adversary can easily exploit the slack time to undetectably corrupt $C_{m,t}(\cdot)$'s memory; e.g., see our 2015 paper published at this workshop.

Cryptographic protocols that compute digital signatures or MACs on system states also fail to establish RoT, even for adversaries with bounded computation power. Like software-based attestation, they fail to meet the requirements for verifier's protocol atomicity; viz., the second and third drawbacks above. They have two significant operational security challenges, which are sometimes ignored. They relocate part of the RoT establishment to human protocols for secret key protection and distribution to the verifier, outside the system. For example, they assume that third parties who install the secret keys into device controllers in order to compute signatures (or MACs) on controller state have ability and interest to protect the installed keys. Furthermore, they assume that a secure distribution channel for the signature-verification certificate can be easily established between the device supplier/integrator and verifier; e.g., see Parno's Cuckoo attack. Finally, signature verification protocols cannot establish RoT since they fail to support verifiable control-flow integrity in the presence of asynchronous events and concurrent-all-or-nothing transactions.

Fabio Massacci: So, for the concurrent all-or-nothing computations, do you need to know how many systems you actually have? So, how do you know that? Because in some cases the verifier may actually not know what you have.

Reply: The verifier must know the complete system configuration. There are some daunting engineering problems in finding the complete configuration of a system, but I'm focusing here only on the fundamental requirements.

For unconditional solutions, we can enhance software attestation to satisfy the necessary RoT establishment requirements. The first is the *concrete optimality* of a $C_{m,t}$ computation. This means that its lower bounds of $C_{m,t}$ match the upper bounds non-asymptotically in both memory size, m, and execution time, t. Asymptotic optimality does not work because they would enable an adversary to exploit the gap between lower and upper bounds caused by different constants. As mentioned already, very few concrete optimality results exist and none seem to hold in computational models that are close to real systems; e.g., the Word RAM model with fixed rather than variable word length. However, a fixed word length causes the circuit-based complexity hierarchy to collapse and hence optimality results become harder to prove. Finally, optimality results have to be proves in adversary (or "dishonest") evaluations of $C_{m,t}$ computations where the adversary can adapt evaluation code to inputs, shortcut computations, and even guess evaluation outcomes. Hence, $C_{m,t}$ computations results must be *unpredictable* in adversary evaluations. Meeting this requirement is quite challenging.

Ilia Shumailov: Can you explain again, why do we need concurrency in evaluations? Why we can't we live with something like at attention sequence? Basically you could turn everything off except for one component, you verify it, and then move to the next component, etc.

Reply: That doesn't work. For example, one cannot selectively turn off some devices of the chipset without shutting down the entire system; e.g., devices of the manageability engine.

Ilia Shumailov: Communication channels?

Reply: One can turn off some communication channels, but not the north bridge bus in Intel architectures for example, or the connection to the south bridge. Also, you can turn off some peripheral device controllers. However, there here are other reasons for which turning off device controllers will not work. For example, even if you are able to turn off device controller selectively, there it a time difference between the instance when you bring up a controller for verification and the beginning of the attestation test. This is when malware can act. You don't know whether the test code begins execution before or after malware.

Ilia Shumailov: Unless you put a limit on there as well.

Reply: Yes, but if malware is present on a controller, it controls your device[3].

The bottom line is, establishing any security property unconditionally, is extremely hard, and one needs new theoretical results. That's both our challenge and the complexity theorists'.

[3] The above discussion led to the post-proceedings paper clarification that powering off devices and powering them on one-at-a-time before attestation does not have a desired outcome for all-or-nothing attestation.

User Authentication for the Internet of Things

Frank Stajano[1] and Mark Lomas[2(✉)]

[1] University of Cambridge, Cambridge, UK
[2] Capgemini, London, UK
mark.lomas@capgemini.com

Abstract. The Internet of Things is coming to fruition, but current commercial offerings are dramatically insecure. The problem is not that many individual devices are vulnerable, but that there are billions of such devices and yet no concerted plan to make them secure. Since the IoT is here to stay, and will pervade the fabric of our society in a way that will make it impossible for any individual to opt out without retiring to a cave as a hermit, we must address the problem structurally, rather than with local band-aid fixes. This short position paper presents the basic requirements for a scalable user authentication solution for the Internet of Things. We hope it will stimulate a discussion leading to a coherent user authentication architecture for IoT. Our vision is that even the lowliest and most inexpensive of IoT devices ought to offer such basic security properties, but this will only happen if they are agreed upon and designed in from the start.

1 Introduction

Having been talked about under a variety of names for two or three decades, the Internet of Things is finally coming to fruition. What is still missing, though, is a proper security architecture for it. That currently deployed IoT devices are insecure is testified by the plethora of vulnerabilities that are discovered and exploited daily[1]: clearly "features" are higher priority than "security" in the eyes of the purchasers—and therefore of the manufacturers. But we are talking here of a more structural problem: not "this device is insecure" but "there is no strategic plan and no accepted blueprint to make IoT devices secure". We should also bear in mind that if purchasers do not understand security vulnerabilities, or cannot articulate their understanding, then manufacturers are unlikely to address them.

There is some role for government regulation. Indeed, the currently ongoing "Secure by Design" initiative in the UK[2], and corresponding ones in other countries, aims to establish a certification and labelling scheme that would assure to consumers that a certain IoT product is free from basic vulnerabilities.

[1] The Mirai botnet, which attacks IoT Linux-based IP cameras and home routers, is the one that most people remember, at the time of writing, but it is by no means an isolated incident.

[2] https://www.gov.uk/government/publications/secure-by-design.

V. Matyáš et al. (Eds.): Security Protocols 2018, LNCS 11286, pp. 209–213, 2018.
https://doi.org/10.1007/978-3-030-03251-7_25

In this position paper we do not address IoT security in general: instead we focus specifically on the problem of *user authentication*, addressing which is a pre-requisite of any security architecture insofar as the three crucial security properties of Confidentiality, Integrity and Availability can only be defined in terms of the distinction between authorized and unauthorized users of the system[3]. However, we should not be misled by the word "authorized"; authorized users may misbehave.

2 The Problem

Traditionally, user authentication has been addressed with usernames and passwords. This technology is strongly entrenched and difficult to replace, but it is clearly showing its structural limitations in today's computing context, where even non-computer-experts have to wrestle with dozens of distinct accounts. Although passwords continue to dominate on the web, they would be pathetically inadequate for user authentication to the Internet of Things.

We define an IoT device as:

- an Internet-connected computing device,
- often (but not necessarily) embedded in an everyday object, that
- does not offer a traditional keyboard/screen/mouse UI, and
- connects to the network directly (rather than as a peripheral of a computer).

Examples of such devices include a pet monitoring IP camera, a smartwatch, an IP-controlled central heating system controller, an IP lightbulb, the mythical Internet-connected Refrigerator and, with a tip of the hat to Stuxnet, a remotely controllable[4] uranium enrichment turbine.

Each IoT device can be modelled as an object with methods. Security for IoT is primarily about ensuring that only authorized principals can invoke the methods offered by the object: only I and designated family members, but not a would-be burglar or a stalker, should be able to see through the lens and listen to the microphone of the cat-camera. This clearly requires a definition of "authorized principals", and the ability for the IoT device to distinguish authorized from unauthorized principals. It may also be useful to consider limitations on authorization, especially in the context of delegation: I might permit a neighbour to keep an eye on my cat while I am on holiday but don't want them to watch me while I am at home.

Passwords are inadequate for this job, both because each of us will have many more IoT devices than computers (and therefore the already unworkable

[3] Confidentiality is the property of a system in which certain information may only be read by authorized users. Integrity is the property of a system in which certain information may only be altered by authorized users, and in compliance with designated constraints. Availability is the property of a system to which authorized users have access, with designated guarantees, regardless of attempts by unauthorized users to deny such access.

[4] Don't believe in airgaps.

proposition of a different password per account will never be able to scale) and because IoT devices tend not to have a UI suited to password input.

As first steps towards a solution we seek to define the requirements of a valid IoT user authentication strategy. What are the limitations of existing systems that we would like to address?

3 IoT User Authentication

A valid strategy for IoT user authentication must:

1. scale to thousands of controlled devices (in particular without burdening the user's memory);
2. be suitable for computer-illiterate people (certainly as far as the frequent "login" action is concerned; but ideally also for the comparatively less frequent "account setup" and "device registration" actions);
3. protect, within reason, against impersonation;
4. protect user privacy;
5. ensure that cracking one device does not imply cracking my other devices—and that sharing key material with a device does not assist the manufacturer of that device in cracking my other devices;
6. work even when I lose Internet connectivity.

Desirable additional features include the following.

7. A usable and expressive way of defining who is allowed to use what methods and in what ways (hard and still unsolved research problem).
8. Revocable delegation of a subset of the user's rights.
9. A domain should be able to accept credentials from another, for example when granting my neighbour access to my cat camera.

It is well known that users cannot remember large numbers of secrets. If forced to supply a password for each device they will share the same password with many devices; more sophisticated users may use a password manager to store passwords. However, it is not convenient to use a password manager to authenticate to my fridge or my watch. A physical device holding my credentials and capable of dispensing them wirelessly to the desired verifier when needed, like Pico[5], may be a more useful proposition.

Needham and Schroeder persuaded many of us to adopt authentication protocols and Kerberos popularised that suggestion. Quite correctly they observed that, just because you share resources with other people, that does not mean that you completely trust them. Passwords used to pass across networks in clear. Authentication protocols can protect authentication information against eavesdroppers while in transit.

Although Needham and Schroeder picked on a loose thread they did not continue to unravel the torn jumper. Even when Kerberos is used to protect

[5] SPW 2011, LNCS 7114.

network traffic, an eavesdropper is still able to determine which devices are communicating and when. Or, returning to our main theme, an eavesdropper may be able to recognise that I am controlling my heating system from my office and whether or not my motion-sensitive cat camera is sending data from my sitting room. Either piece of information may be useful to potential burglars. While confidentiality is all about preventing unauthorized access to the data, privacy is also concerned with the metadata.

Mobile devices are often vulnerable to a similar problem. While it may be convenient to unlock my computer using my phone or watch, I would prefer that those devices didn't act as small beacons signalling that I am not at home while typing this paper. How nice things would be if I were able to limit reception of such signals to just the computer I was unlocking—but that's not the way things usually work.

A proximity token like a "modern" wireless car key is not resistant to impersonation: whoever finds it can use it. Some devices compensate for this by requiring a PIN when you first put them on (e.g. the Apple Watch). While biometrics may help with this, some manufacturers compensate for the false accept rate by insisting on a PIN or password at intervals.

The kind of system we envisage as useful is based on the following design principles:

1. Environments (homes, offices, nuclear power plants, etc.) are conveniently divided into domains, similar to Active Directory. Each domain will contain at least one authentication server.
2. We anticipate that many people will not want the complication of a local authentication server at home, so we imagine these might be provided remotely, perhaps as a cloud-based service. However, larger environments may prefer to control their own server so it should also be possible to deploy this locally. We also like to imagine using our devices on a cruise ship which may have plentiful local network capacity but woeful Internet access. We suggest that cruise ships ought to carry authentication servers.
3. To preserve privacy of communicating parties, authentication transactions should not identify participants in clear, although we are willing to permit partial identification as a compromise. For example, it would be very difficult to hide all of the activity in my house while devices there are communicating over the Internet, but it may be sufficient to combine the data from many devices and to transmit spurious data so it is not clear when my cat camera is active (Ron Rivest suggested Chaffing and Winnowing for this purpose).
4. There are facilities for deploying large batches of IoT devices in one go. The symmetric key version is what SecureID does (here is a box of 50 tokens, each with a serial number written on it, and here is a table mapping these serial numbers to the secret keys embedded in the tokens). There is an equivalent but somewhat more secure way of doing it with public key crypto (here is a box of 50 tokens, each with a private key embedded in it that was generated on the device and that no-one else has ever seen, and the serial number is a hash of the public key; here is a table of the public keys and their hashes).

We believe it is relatively easy to identify well-known existing technical security mechanisms that solve each of the above requirements in isolation; that it is somewhat more challenging to combine them so as to solve all the above requirements simultaneously; and that the really serious problem of authentication for IoT is how to do that in a way that remains easy to use for ordinary people.

Acknowledgments. Frank Stajano is grateful to the European Research Council for funding the past five years of his research on user authentication through grant StG 307224 (Pico).

User Authentication for the Internet of Things (Transcript of Discussion)

Mark Lomas(✉)

Capgemini, London, UK
mark.lomas@capgemini.com

This is joint work with Frank, but you can blame me for the presentation.

There's a tradition at these workshops: we were asked to present something to discuss rather than finished work, so I'm going to follow that tradition by essentially explaining something to worry about, but I'm not going to tell you how to fix it.

Before I do that I'm going to go on a slight digression because a number of people have mentioned threat models today, and they've spoken about things like demons attacking your system, or nation states attacking your system. I'm going to just show you an example of an alternative approach which I think is useful to know about. This (Fig. 1), for anyone who may recognise it, is actually an extract from Her Majesty's Government Information Assurance Standard Number 1, which we're unfortunately required to follow as we deliver certain systems to Government departments. I'm not going to go through the whole of their threat model but the thing I want to draw attention to is the distinction between a threat *source* and a threat *actor*. So, when a nation-state tries to attack your system, they're not a threat actor. What they do is they engage a small number of individuals who may want to attack your system and they usually fall into these sort of categories.

The normal users of my system fall here: you may bribe somebody within your organisation to attack something. It may be somebody nearby, a person within range and so on. I'm not going to go through the whole list, but I'm showing you that you look at who actually can attack your system, rather than this sort of omniscient organisation that's got access to everything. So you want to work out who is your actual threat actor.

The other thing is, if you look across to the other axis, we tend to look at confidentiality, integrity and availability, and this lists various ways in which people can misbehave (or just be careless). One of the examples here is that nobody attacks your system at all (!) but one of your users goes and leaves documents lying about. That's something to bear in mind. Just for completeness, there's a number of other threat actors here. As I said, that was a digression but it may turn out to be relevant.

V. Matyáš et al. (Eds.): Security Protocols 2018, LNCS 11286, pp. 214–224, 2018.
https://doi.org/10.1007/978-3-030-03251-7_26

Threat Actor Type	Compromise Methods		
	Confidentiality	Integrity	Availability
Bystander (BY)	**Observes information** *from* Passively observes information in the environment		
	Impersonates a user *of* Impersonates a legitimate user to compromise any Security Property		
	Tampers with equipment *in* Tampers with equipment in any way to compromise any Security Property, including simply stealing equipment or media.		
Handler (HAN)	**Tampers with equipment** *in* Tampers with equipment in any way to compromise any Security Property		
Indirectly Connected (IC)	**Misuses Business or Network connections** *to or from* Compromise any Security Property		
Information Exchange Partner (IEP)	**Misuses Business or Network connections** *to or from* Compromise any Security Property of the FoI		
Person Within Range (PWR)	**Intercepts traffic** *to or from* Intercept communications or emanations from the FoI (including physical media in transit, wired and wireless networks)	**Injects information** *into* Makes unauthorised changes to information transmitted on FoI communication links (including interfering with physical media links, wired and wireless networks)	**Jams** Denies communication links to of from the FoI (including physical media links, wired and wireless networks)
Normal User (NU)	**Accidentally releases information** *from* Performs actions which accidentally result in the inappropriate release of information	**Accidentally disrupts** Performs actions which accidentally result in the compromise of Integrity or Availability	
	Deliberately releases information *from* Performs deliberate actions which result in the inappropriate release of information	**Deliberately disrupts** Performs deliberate actions which result in the compromise of Integrity or Availability	
	Changes the configuration *of* Changes the system to facilitate a compromise of any Security Property		
Physical Intruder (PI)	**Tampers with equipment** *in* Tampers with equipment in any way to compromise any Security Property, including simply stealing equipment or media		
Privileged User (PU)	**Accidentally releases information** *from* Performs actions which accidentally result in the inappropriate release of information	**Accidentally disrupts** Performs actions which accidentally result in the compromise of Integrity or Availability	
	Deliberately releases information *from* Performs deliberate actions which result in the inappropriate release of information	**Deliberately disrupts** Performs deliberate actions which result in the compromise of Integrity or Availability	
	Changes the Configuration *of* Changes the system to facilitate a compromise of any Security Property		
Service Provider (SP)	**Intercepts traffic** *from or to* Intercepts information that passes through the provided service	**Corrupts** Accidentally or deliberately corrupts information that passes through the provided service	**Disrupts** Accidentally or deliberately disrupts either the provided service or information that passes through the provided service
Service Consumer (SC)	**Misuses Business or Network connections** *to or from* Attacks the FoI using their business or network connectivity to a service provided by the FoI to compromise any Security Property of the FoI or the service it provides (e.g. a website).		
	Tampers with equipment *provided by* Tampers with equipment that delivers a service provided by the FoI (e.g. a kiosk) in any way that compromises any Security Property of the FoI itself or the service, including simply stealing equipment or media, installing unauthorised equipment and making unauthorised changes.		
Shared Service Subscriber (SSS)	**Misuses Business or Network connections** *to or from* Attacks the FoI using business or network connectivity provided by a shared service to compromise any Security Property of the FoI. This includes both where the FoI is targeted through the shared service or where the effect on the FoI is from untargeted or "collateral damage" from an attack on the shared service.		
Supplier (SUP)	**Tampers with equipment** *in* Tampers with equipment, either software or hardware, before it is supplied to the business to compromise any Security Property		

Fig. 1. Extract from HMG IA standard number 1.

Going back to the actual main topic: What is an Internet of Things device? This is the definition that Frank and I came up with.

- an internet-connected computing device,
- often (but not necessarily) embedded in an everyday object, that
- does not offer a traditional UI (keyboard, screen, mouse, etc.), and
- connects to the network directly, not as a peripheral.

We're not saying that it's correct, but we're suggesting it as a straw man. Feel free to disagree with it.

The third bullet is actually where some of the problems come up: it doesn't necessarily provide you with a traditional user interface. So when I use my laptop I've got the screen and the keyboard, but if I'm using my camera or a watch, I may have a limited user interface. Some examples here: a camera, or a phone, or a video camera, might be an IoT device.

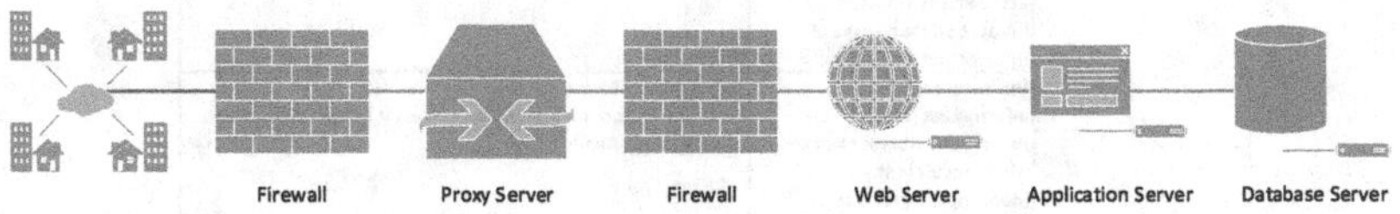

Fig. 2. A common design pattern for providing a service on the web.

This example (Fig. 2) is not an IoT device but, if anyone recognises it, it's a very common design pattern for providing a service. I might have an application server which is front-ended by a web server; it's got a database server that stores the data that it's accessing. The reason I show this here is that if you actually look at the attack surface of it, you can attack it here, where it's exposed to the internet, but if you wanted to attack that database server, you would need to persuade the application server to send it something which exploits a vulnerability in that server. So even if I've got a poorly designed database, which has got vulnerabilities because it wasn't perfect, it's still an uphill struggle for somebody trying to attack it because they have to attack it by getting through the intervening nodes. This is partly why I showed the threat actors, because that's not entirely true, the system administrators within my organisation may have access to all of those components, so in my threat model I have to consider them all. But if I'm looking at somebody who's outside trying to attack it, they'd basically have to attack it there.

Now, the reason I put this up is to make a distinction. If I have an IoT device, I've said upfront it is internet connected so that design pattern in Fig. 2 does not apply, because all of my different components are all actually exposed and they're vulnerable. That worries me.

The other thing that worries me is that these firewalls can be pretty large devices, with a lot of computational power, so I can put in all sorts of cryptographic measures to protect them, whereas I haven't got very much processing power in a watch so I'm unlikely to want to put strong crypto in it.

Or, as the example I give here, I really don't want to carry round a firewall to protect my camera, and it's an expensive proposition to put in into really small devices. You can have a software-defined firewall and put it in a computing device, as I do with my laptop, but I probably don't have that in my camera; or at least I don't know of any cameras that provide that yet as a service.

We're not looking at all of the security properties of IoT but we're interested, for the purposes of this discussion, in login or authentication. I'm not going to look at the totality of things I can do with my devices. So, what do I actually require of an authentication system that supports IoT devices? In the paper we list a series of requirements that we consider mandatory, alongside others that we consider merely desirable.

Well, I want it to be able to scale to thousands of control devices. I may not have thousands of them but they are proliferating and I'd like my system to be able to support a large number of devices, not just one or two.

I want them to be suitable for computer illiterate users, and what I mean by that is if there is an elaborate configuration that you need to apply in order to make your system secure, we geeks may be able to configure systems that way, but the typical user doesn't want to have to go through a complicated process to set up their watch or their camera. They want something that makes it very easy to register the device with some form of authentication service, with minimal intervention by the end user.

Some of these properties I think I won't go through in detail, but I want to guard against impersonation and I want to protect the privacy of the user of my device.

This one I think is an important property: I want to ensure that cracking one device does not imply that you can crack other devices. So, if you can get access to my watch, that shouldn't give you access to my laptop or to my camera. And also, sharing key material with one of my devices shouldn't make it easier for the manufacturer of that device to attack some of my other devices. Because some devices I might consider just convenient, whereas other devices I might have trusted them with something which I regard as quite sensitive, and I don't want a compromise of the less important device to lead to a compromise of a more important device.

These devices may be mobile and so I may end up losing internet connectivity, I don't want the device to stop working just because I happen to be on a train going through a tunnel. I regard those as being the mandatory requirements.

I've put a few desirable requirements but these are the ones where I'm more likely to be willing to compromise. So it would be nice to be able to describe an access control policy but a lot of users won't necessarily want or need that. It would be nice to be able to have delegation of some access rights, in order for instance to allow somebody to use one of my devices temporarily, or use their own device within my domain in order to gain access to some of my information. So a domain should be able to accept credentials from another domain. This is Frank's example: he wants to be able to allow his neighbour to use the cat camera to check up on the cat.

Is everyone happy with those as sensible requirements of an authentication system?

Fabio Massacci: It may be a bit expensive. Since you are talking about devices that would have to be small and cheap, don't you think these requirements are a little bit expensive?

Reply: Oh yes, and that's exactly why I'm giving these examples. So, if you can tell me which requirements I should relax in order to hit a certain target price, that would be an interesting discussion.

Fabio Massacci: We can do this later.

Virgil Gligor: One thing that users are not particularly minded to pay for is privacy. So if you can quantify here the privacy losses then that may be a mandatory requirement, or it may be a desirable one. You don't mean confidentiality, you mean privacy.

Daniel Weitzner: To follow up, I was going ask what you meant by user privacy, in particular considering the question of what the devices are actually going to be able to do.

Reply: I can give you a concrete example, and this is partly why we were thinking about the cat camera. The cat camera, you might think, is not very sensitive: it's just looking at the food bowl in the kitchen or wherever it's been installed. The problem is, you want to access it on the internet. You want to check: "when I'm in the office, is my cat all right?". And what you probably do, when you deploy one of these, is you put a motion sensor in the camera because you don't want to send a complete stream of absolutely everything in the house, because most of it is a static image. So, what you're actually doing is sending motion information outside your environment. It's not that there's something particularly secret within that picture, it's the mere fact that picture suddenly got sent out means "oh, there's some motion in my kitchen". Or conversely, and this is why I'm giving it as the privacy example, if you monitor the information coming from that cat camera, even if it's encrypted, you can work out whether there's somebody at home and whether it's a good time for robbing my house.

Daniel Weitzner: I think the problem is a little worse than that! Because Frank is a nice guy, he may give his neighbour the ability to use the cat camera to check on the neighbour's cat, or even to check on Frank's cat (I don't know what cats you've got); but maybe the camera is in the kitchen and you left on the kitchen table a bunch of subversive political materials that are now in the picture right along with the cat. And that's not what you meant. And what's the device supposed to do about that?

Reply: I'm not suggesting that the device should solve the problem of whether somebody I authorise *should* have been authorised. But I would like it to solve the problem of making sure that only the people I have authorised do actually get to see those pictures.

Daniel Weitzner: I don't think that's privacy.

Virgil Gligor: Confidentiality.

Reply: Okay.

Daniel Weitzner: I just think we should be clear about what you think you actually mean here by "user privacy", that's all.

Reply: I don't feel strongly about the term but I think the reason I put it that way is that you know there's some motion in the kitchen but you don't see me wandering around.

Daniel Weitzner: I understand that. I just think that everything else you have listed is much more precise.

Reply: Yes, and I'm perfectly happy to use confidentiality in there, because I think that's a desirable property too.

Ian Goldberg: I think if you were to just change "protect user privacy" to "protect confidentiality", that would be true but then you'd be missing the big piece of *actually* protecting user privacy. Which I think is also important.

Virgil Gligor: Or "desirable".

Ian Goldberg: Ahem! Not if you ask me, but...

Reply: Yes, I'm perfectly happy with that.

Ian Goldberg: Great! So, from my viewpoint, protecting user privacy means that the user is put in control of how the information (both the data and the metadata) is used, who gets to see it, how it's interpreted, and other kind of meta-information like that. Not just "is the data revealed to this person?". And I think that is a very important requirement.

Reply: Yes.

Graham Rymer: I just wanted to share an interesting side channel which I observed in the university. You can detect the real links that security cameras are connected to because when it gets dark the compression doesn't work so well on the grainy images and you get a bandwidth spike. So actually if I wanted to spy on your house I would probably just kidnap your cat and strap a GoPro camera to it.

Jeff Yan: I didn't quite get the first requirement about scalability. Would you please clarify that a bit?

Reply: I don't want to have just a teeny little authentication system that's just for me. I'd like to have something that generalises so that my device can be one of thousands, not one of three or four. Because, if I were to relax that constraint, I could build a local authentication system that I carry around, maybe just have it in my phone and my devices only talk to it. But I don't think it's useful to use devices in that way.

Jeff Yan: Okay my next question then: is the iPhone an example that satisfies some or all of these requirements? Because actually Apple have designed the devices to meet some of these requirements.

Reply: It meets some, it doesn't meet all of them.

Fabio Massacci: Just a follow up to your answer to Jeff: can devices come and go? Can you have a new device joining anytime, or do you have more or less the same number of devices, with this number rarely changing? And would this be a requirement or not?

Reply: I suspect it depends on time. At the moment these dynamic joining events are probably less frequent but my guess is, as more and more devices become intelligent, you will need to add them frequently.

Ilia Shumailov: What do you mean by "impersonation"? Is it you authenticating to the device or the device authenticating to you? Because one of the things that worries me a lot about IoT devices is the fact that we can produce a lot of them and it's fairly hard to say whether the IoT device you are using at a particular time is actually *your* device, and not somebody else's device. So, to me, IoT security is about *both* the device knowing that I am who I am, *and* me knowing that this device is my device.

Reply: I think that's a good question because what I had as my mental model is *my* set of devices. So I know they're mine, I bought them and I configured them, and I subsequently want to make sure that I authenticate to them. But I think you've added an extra constraint, which is a reasonable one.

So let's try scoring some existing authentication systems against these criteria. If we look at something like Needham-Schroeder (or Kerberos, which is based on Needham-Schroeder), does it scale to thousands of devices? I've put it as an amber tick: it scales in the sense that the authentication protocols themselves scale; but on the other hand if I've got teeny little devices, I've got a major key management problem setting them up. That's why I've put it as an amber rather than a green tick. But I think the other ones are a bit more problematic. How do I *easily* configure my IoT devices to register them with an authentication service? That's quite difficult. Can we guard against impersonation, here? There's a lot of key sharing here, and I don't think it's actually worth going down to this one. Cracking my authentication service, here, reveals information about almost everything in my domain.

Ian Goldberg: What does it mean for a human to run Needham-Schroeder? It's not like I'm going to do DES (or whatever Needham-Schroeder uses) in my head. So are you going to use a device?

Reply: I'm assuming that the device is going to act on my behalf and I want to authenticate it into my domain.

Ian Goldberg: So, I have a watch than I want to authenticate into my domain; but I have to authenticate to the watch? How does the watch know it's me? As opposed to "he takes my watch and...". Or is that not even what you're talking about? You're not even talking about *user* authentication, you're talking about *user's device* authentication. Because you want to authenticate some devices into an existing set of devices.

Reply: Yes, I think so.

Virgil Gligor: I think he's already told us his assumption that this is a watch that he purchased and this is a phone that he purchased. So the associations between these devices and him are implicit in what he is doing, and yes, cracking one of them, or losing one of them, is going to affect the other. So, if you put some of these things together, it turns that he might not necessarily need to authenticate himself through some sort of PIN to his watch or to his phone or whatever. I'm not saying that it's easy to do!

Reply: Yes.

Needham-Schoeder doesn't work when I lose internet connectivity but Kerberos sort of half-heartedly does, because it supports cached credentials. So I can use Kerberos on that device but I'd really mark it as not really supported, because you have to *prepare* for the fact that you're going to be disconnected.

Ilia Shumailov: When you say "suitable for computer illiterate users", do you mean to use or to program? Because in my experience I've found that those two things are very much disjoint.

Frank Stajano: By definition, computer illiterate users will not be able to program. So it's just about use.

Reply: But there's partly an assumption here that, with these personal devices, I need some way of going through a registration process. And, most registration processes I've seen are ones that computer illiterate users wouldn't like to use.

Frank Stajano: It depends if *programming* means writing C code or programming the VCR.

Ilia Shumailov: No, programming means giving a set of instructions for a device to execute.

Frank Stajano: If programming means configuring, then yes, they would have to configure the device. If programming means writing code, they're not expected to write code, otherwise they wouldn't be illiterate.

Reply: Yes, I'm not expecting to solve the problem of teaching users to literally program the device but I do expect them to want to configure it or register it. So, what can we steal from other designs? This first example is here because of the key management problem: it might be all right to type a cryptographic key into my laptop, but it's quite difficult to type a long cryptographic key into a watch. So one of the mechanisms that's been used for doing this, if you've ever used SecurID tokens, when you buy them, they actually come with key material that you put into the authentication service, and the mechanism for registering is actually to use the serial number of the device, which then links the device back to the key. But I'd make a note that, as a method of key distribution, implicitly trusts the manufacturer with key material. The alternative is for certain devices, if you've got sufficient computational power in it, you can say get the device itself to generate public-private key pair and reveal the public key. But then you need to consider what's the user interface for registration and use of that device. So I'll pause at that point and ask: are these reasonable constraints to be looking at?

Virgil Gligor: Yeah, it sounds reasonable to me. I don't mean to harp on privacy but a lot of these devices that you have in mind have built-in side channels. For example, a classic one is your cell phone: voice has priority over data communication. I can tell by pinging your device whether or not you're speaking on the phone or not. So if you keep the privacy requirement in there you open yourself up to all sorts of difficulties in satisfying what people think of privacy. But if you restrict that to confidentiality that's a different world because confidentiality policies are much more restricted than privacy, and somewhat easier to satisfy. So that is why: it's not just a stylistic difference, it's a fundamental difference between the two. Privacy is a lot harder. Built-in privacy flaws exist, whereas built-in confidentiality flaws are more rare.

Fabio Massacci: So the assumption that you have a primary device and all the others authenticate to you, as in some sort of star model. Can the devices talk to each other, like your kitchen talking to the fridge?

Reply: I haven't specified how the solution to this would work. But what we have in mind is some form of authentication service that you register your devices to, in order that it controls the domain. If I'm a large organisation, I might actually run that service. If I'm a typical user at home, trying to cope with the devices I've bought, I might have to use some sort of cloud service, because I don't run an authentication server at home.

Fabio Massacci: Then this makes you still sort of a star-topology, right? There's a sun and then it authenticates all the others and then gives the key to you. The device cannot autonomously set itself up.

Reply: I think yes for the registration process, but I mentioned as one of the constraints that I don't want it to break when I lose network connectivity; so I think that we should be involved in key management and registration, but not in every authentication action.

Virgil Gligor: Consider the devices involved in Pico: you have multiple devices on yourself that form the Pico system. Is that possibly an example of Internet of Things, or not? And how do you differentiate the Internet of Things on the other side, on the side of user wearables?

Reply: I think those devices fall within the definition we had in mind, but the extent to which they actually support that is worth examining.

Ian Goldberg: They're not internet connected. Picosiblings aren't typically internet connected.

Virgil Gligor: Well, eventually they have to be, otherwise it's not useful.

Frank Stajano: I think that, in the things Mark described in a very generic fashion, each Thing in the Internet of Things had its own purpose, for example taking pictures (or doing other things). Whereas Picosiblings are wearable devices whose electronic side is there primarily just to let you unlock the Pico; they don't *also* do another thing. I mean, a Picosibling watch might be a dual-purpose object because it also tells you the time; but if I had, for example, a nose ring Picosibling, it's there for decoration but the only purpose of it having electronics is to establish this Pico authentication aura around me. So it doesn't have any purpose as an IoT Thing, other than being a Picosibling. That is a distinction I would make.

Virgil Gligor: I think it would be good to make the distinction in the paper, because you have networks of wearables that may not fall into that Internet of Things definition that you have.

Frank Stajano: Electronic wearables have to be electronic for a reason. In the case of the Picosiblings they are electronic for the specific purpose of unlocking the Pico. If we are talking about other electronic wearables, we should perhaps first talk about their purpose, and then see to what extent they integrate with the rest of the internet.

Daniel Weitzner: I would like to hear what you think about composability of authentication of the user devices that connect to a lot of other devices. I think users have a particularly hard time understanding that. I think developers have a particularly hard time understanding what models they're living in as things get increasingly connected.

Reply: I have a mental model of devices joining a domain, so creating the "Mark Lomas's devices" domain and then occasionally allowing devices from another domain to authenticate into my domain, and similarly I'd expect you may have your own domain. If you want to allow me to access it, you might want to have some form of cross-domain trust. I'm not saying it *has* to work that way, I'm saying that's the mental model I've got in my head.

Frank Stajano: In response to Fabio: as far as Mark and I have discussed so far, and as he hinted at in his own reply, there's an element of star shape in the initial pairing phase; but, after that, you could conceivably have delegated powers and say: "Dear cooker, now that you're one of mine, I grant you permission to talk to the fridge". Or I don't. In order to be admitted to the house you (as an IoT device) have to talk to me; but, after that, I have rules about what you can do in the house, and you can do them without me being there, if you see what I mean.

Ilia Shumailov: In this distinction of devices and non- devices, the question has to be raised of what constitutes a new device. So for example, in your mobile phone, is the camera a separate device? And the capabilities assigned to different applications within your phone, are they all connected to a device?

Frank Stajano: This is all debatable and could be argued in many ways. I would make a basic distinction based on the network addressability of the Things. If a Thing appears as several network entities then, even if they are in the same box, they're several entities; but if it's one Thing and the camera is a peripheral of the phone, then it's the phone that I'm talking about as a Thing. Mark, do you have anything to add to that?

Reply: Yes. I would agree with that, but I would also add that, if you go back to the computer illiterate user, they're going to have a hard enough time registering something that I don't want to have the additional imposition of asking them to write an access control policy that distinguishes between the microphone, the camera, the fingerprint reader and so on. I just want them to be able to register the phone. That's not to say I would refuse to use a system that provides that, but I think a lot of our users, or the users we have in mind, wouldn't want that complexity.

Ilia Shumailov: Then a clear distinction has to be made between the virtual examples of devices and the physical examples of devices, or maybe you don't want to make the distinction and just say that an ensemble is considered to be a particular separate device as long as it's addressable. But then you raise the question of whether, if you have multiple ensembles which are overlapping between the devices, they are considered to be separate devices or not. And what does it actual mean to be a device.

Virgil Gligor: Well, it seems that Frank answered the question: if I understood his answer, if a device has an internet address, it's part of the Internet of Things. If it doesn't have an internet address, and it's connected in some other way to some other electronics, it may not be a distinct Thing.

Ilia Shumailov: That implies that, if you have some sort of hub to which you can append new devices and you have some sort of library OS running on that hub hypervisor, some of them, through sharing of subsystems, can be considered separate devices, is that right?

Frank Stajano: If you have a printer attached to your laptop, the printer is not an IoT Thing. Your laptop is. If the printer is on the network then the printer is a Thing.

Reply: Yes!

Why Preventing a Cryptocurrency Exchange Heist Isn't Good Enough

Patrick McCorry[1(✉)], Malte Möser[2], and Syed Taha Ali[3]

[1] University College London, London, UK
p.mccorry@ucl.ac.uk
[2] Princeton University, Princeton, USA
mmoeser@cs.princeton.edu
[3] National University of Sciences and Technology, Islamabad, Pakistan
taha.ali@seecs.nust.edu.pk

Abstract. Cryptocurrency exchanges have a history of deploying poor security policies and it is claimed that over a third of exchanges were compromised by 2015. Once compromised, the attacker can copy the exchange's wallet (i.e. a set of cryptographic private keys) and appropriate all its coins. The largest heist so far occurred in February 2014 when Mt. Gox lost 850k bitcoins and unlike the conventional banking system, all theft transactions were irreversibly confirmed by the Bitcoin network. We observe that exchanges have adopted an overwhelmingly preventive approach to security which by itself has not yet proven to be sufficient. For example, two exchanges called NiceHash and YouBit collectively lost around 8.7k bitcoins in December 2017. Instead of preventing theft, we propose a reactive measure (inspired by Bitcoin vaults) which provides a fail-safe mechanism to detect the heist, freeze all withdrawals and allow an exchange to bring a trusted vault key online to recover from the compromise. In the event this trusted recovery key is also compromised, the exchange can deploy a nuclear option of destroying all coins.

Cryptocurrencies have exploded into the mainstream over the last two years and now represent a thriving $700 billion ecosystem. Bitcoin, which was at parity with the US dollar in 2011, briefly traded for $19k per bitcoin in December, 2017, and is now recognised as legal tender in Japan and Germany. A Bitcoin futures contract has been formally launched at CME, the world's largest futures exchange. Amid all this positive press and mainstream recognition, however, cryptocurrencies continue to be dogged by the recurring scandal of hacked exchanges, resulting in billions of dollars in customer losses, and undermining user confidence in cryptocurrencies.

Cryptocurrency exchanges provide several valuable services for users. They serve as a convenient entry point for those wishing to purchase coins using conventional payment mechanisms. Customers can easily use the exchange platform to trade coins from one cryptocurrency to another. Most exchanges also provide user wallets, thus enabling users to participate in transactions while sparing them the hassle of managing cryptographic keys. However, for all this convenience, this

V. Matyáš et al. (Eds.): Security Protocols 2018, LNCS 11286, pp. 225–233, 2018.
https://doi.org/10.1007/978-3-030-03251-7_27

arrangement carries inherent counterparty risk: exchanges have full custody over customer coins and, due to the decentralized nature of cryptocurrencies, in case of theft, customer coins may be irretrievably lost.

As Moore et al. have documented, this risk is real: between 2009–2015 over a third of cryptocurrency exchanges were compromised and nearly half of all exchanges have simply disappeared [8]. The most well-known case is that of Mt. Gox, a Tokyo-based exchange, which at its peak was the world's largest Bitcoin exchange, handling 70% of all Bitcoin transactions, and shut down when $450 million worth of users' coins were stolen. This trend continues to this day. In December 2017, two exchanges were hacked: NiceHash lost 4.7k BTC (i.e. $45m US) [7] but remains operational, whereas YouBit lost 4k BTC (i.e. $39m US) [3], which represents 17% of its assets, and eventually declared bankruptcy.

A number of solutions have been proposed to reduce the risk for exchanges. Prominent proposals include the use of 'cold' wallets to store private keys where attackers cannot access them [26,27,31], hardware security modules to safeguard the hot wallet (i.e. private keys that are always on-line) [2] and the introduction of threshold signatures to distribute transaction authorization across multiple parties [1,11]. However, in spite of these measures exchanges continue to fail. To further evaluate the impact of these failures, we provide a survey on large-scale heists and their cases in Sect. 1.

We argue that one major reason for this continued failure is that most security solutions employ a *proactive*, or preventive, approach. While this approach may be sufficient for conventional financial systems (where a centralized authority can – within certain limits – reverse transactions), it is clearly inadequate for the cryptocurrencies paradigm where damage can be done immediately and irreversibly. Instead, exchanges need to incorporate *reactive* mechanisms into their defense strategies that anticipate failure and allow them to recover *after* a successful attack.

To this end, we propose two reactive mechanisms to complement existing measures: our first solution allows the hot wallet to authorise time-delayed transfers and move coins between wallets within an exchange. This reduces the risk of theft by copying the cold storage's private keys as they may no longer be brought on-line periodically and the associated time-delay provides time for an exchange to detect abnormal transfers between their wallets. Our second proposal is a simple and intuitive failsafe mechanism (inspired by Möser et al.'s proposal of 'vault' transactions [23]) whereby exchanges may effectively detect a heist, freeze all time-delayed transfers, and recover by employing a trusted vault key. If the trusted vault is also compromised, the fail-deadly option can be used to destroy the stolen coins. Both solutions rely on the flexibility and expressiveness afforded by smart contracts and may be deployed on Ethereum without requiring any modification of the underlying platform.

1 Brief Survey of Exchanges Heists

We provide a brief survey on the causes behind large-scale exchange heists which includes the theft of wallets, insider threats and the rise/fall of distributed signing. As we will see, the focus of all security measures deployed by exchanges in response to heists are proactive (and preventive) in nature.

Theft of Wallet (and Address Re-use). Mt. Gox remains the largest heist in the history of cryptocurrencies, with over 850k BTC stolen between 2011–2014. They claimed this heist was possible due to an underlying bug in Bitcoin called transaction malleability, but this was quickly debunked by Decker and Wattenhofer [10]. It was later claimed by WizSec [24] that MtGox's private keys were compromised in September 2011 and the company did not deploy any auditing mechanisms to detect the hack. The stolen set of keys were used to continuously steal new deposits as MtGox re-used Bitcoin addresses regularly and by mid 2013 over 630k BTC were stolen from the exchange. Remarkably, to support this claim, WizSec argues that evidence of the continuous theft can be extracted from transactions on the blockchain.

Reduce Theft Impact with Hot and Cold Wallets. To avoid significant losses as seen with Mt. Gox, many companies incorporate cold and hot wallets. All coins are sent to the exchange's cold wallet and when necessary coins are manually transferred to the hot wallet. If an exchange's server is compromised, then only coins in the hot wallet can be stolen by the thief and thus an exchange can determine the number of coins it is willing to risk. While these hacks are less severe, high-impact heists continued, including 24k BTC stolen from BitFloor in May 2012 [17], 19k BTC stolen from Bitstamp [18] in June 2015 and more recently in December 2017 where 4.7k BTC were stolen from NiceHash and 4k from YouBit. Both BitFloor and YouBit declared bankruptcy as a result of these hacks, whereas BitFloor and Bitstamp remain operational.

Insider Threat. While keeping keys offline makes stealing coins harder, the compromise of cold wallets is not infeasible as witnessed in Feburary 2015, when an exchange called BTER claims to have lost 7,170 BTC from their cold wallet and it is rumoured this heist was due to an insider [14]. Another exchange, Shapeshift has provided a post-mortem [28] on three seperate compromises that led to a heist of 315 BTC. The report mentions the installation of a rootkit and that the thief purchased an SSH key and the username/password of ShapeShift HQ's router from a former employee. Note due to the nature of ShapeShift, most customer funds were not at risk and it was in fact ShapeShift's own coins that were stolen. We highlight this is because ShapeShift only has temporary custody over coins in order to facilitate an exchange.[1]

Compromised Shared Web Hosting. Linode is a web hosting company offering virtual server rentals and several promiment Bitcoin exchanges/wealthy community members used Linode to store their hot wallets. In June 2011, an attacker

[1] ShapeShift is a match-making exchange and sends all customers coins in the corresponding cryptocurrency once the exchange is complete. For example, the customer may send ShapeShift bitcoins and shortly afterwards ShapeShift will send the customer ether.

compromised Linode and targeted the virtual services that stored the hot wallets. Unfortunately this led to the theft of at least 46k bitcoins and the exact amount remains unknown. [12] The victims included Bitcoinia at approximately 43k BTC and Bitcoin.cx at 3k BTC, as well as bitcoin developer Gavin Andresen who also lost 5k BTC. Note after the Meltdown/Spectre disclosure [16,19] in January 2018, companies such as Coinbase highlighted that they still rely on shared web hosting for non-sensitive workloads:

Coinbase runs in Amazon Web Services (AWS) and our general security posture is one of extreme caution. Sensitive workloads, especially where key handling is involved, run on Dedicated Instances (instead of shared hardware). Where we do run on shared hardware, we make it more difficult to accurately target one of our systems by rapidly cycling through instances in AWS.
Philip Martin, Director of Security at Coinbase [21]

Rise and Fall of Multisig. Over the course of 2011 and 2012, Andresen incorporated threshold signatures (i.e. multisig) into Bitcoin [1] which was slowly adopted by the community and we highlight that in Feburary 2018 there is approximately 3.6 m bitcoins (and 11.8 m outputs) that rely on multi-sig.[2] In the aftermath of both hacks of Linode and Bitfloor, Andresen argued that the new multisig feature could reduce the likelihood of heists in exchanges as it requires the attacker to compromise a threshold of machines instead of a single machine. As well, in early 2014, the security company BitGo further declared that the rise of multisig would remove the need for cold wallets (i.e. offline keys) altogether:

"We (BitGo) believe it's time we come together as an industry to end the cold storage ice age and adopt multi-sig."
Will O'Brien, co-founder at BitGo [25]

However, the use of multisig is no silver bullet in itself, and this was proven by another large heist at Bifinex with 119,756 BTC stolen. Bitcoin exchange Bitfinex partnered with BitGo and used them as a third party escrow to audit/approve customer withdrawals. Furthermore it appears that Bitfinex decided not to use cold wallets (and opted for a third-party auditor instead) [6] to take advantage of a statutory exemption in the Commodities and Exchange Act. It was later revealed that BitGo had a special configuration for BitFinex [4] and while a final report on the heist remains unpublished, it appears BitGo simply authorised all transaction requests from BitFinex. This highlights that while the concept of using threshold signatures is attractive, it does not guarantee that the authority to authorise transactions is in fact distributed.

[2] p2sh.info tracks the number of *pay-to-script-hash* outputs which are mostly multi-sig scripts.

Impact of Proactive Security. All security measures deployed so far by cryptocurrency exchanges are proactive in nature with the goal to prevent a heist. The above survey highlights that proactive security measures have evidently reduced the impact of heists, but unfortunately they cannot prevent a heist. Fundamentally, the issue is that once the corresponding private keys are stolen, there is little an exchange can do in order to stop the heist due to the irreversible nature of the blockchain. In the next section, we highlight a potential reactive solution that requires a time-delay on all withdrawals which provides a grace period for an exchange to react and cancel the heist.

2 Reactive Security Measures for Cryptocurrencies

We propose that cryptocurrency exchanges should deploy reactive security measures that allow them to respond in the event of a heist. Our solution has two components which includes time-delayed (and revocable) payments and time-delayed access control of hot/cold wallets.

A revocable and time-delayed payment was first proposed for Bitcoin as a *vault transaction* [23], where a payment is initiated by a key that is held in a *hot wallet*, but can later be revoked (i.e. recovered) within a certain time frame by a key held securely in cold storage [23]. We note that such a mechanism is currently not possible in all cryptocurrencies: while it is trivial to deploy using Ethereum's smart contract language (which we show later in this section), Bitcoin's scripting language requires support for covenants (cf. [23]).

We argue that time-delayed and revocable payments cannot only be used to secure funds, but also to simplify access control mechanisms. For example, an exchange contract may forsee the funds in its hot wallet running low and authorise a time-delayed transfer of funds from cold to hot storage using its hot keys. The cold storage signing keys can stay offline, they are only brought online if the coins need to be transferred immediately or the payment needs to be revoked. In the following, we describe an advanced vault design that combines multiple such mechanisms.

2.1 Time-Delayed Exchange Vaults

We propose Time-Delayed Exchange Vaults, inspired by Möser et al.'s Bitcoin vaults [23], which combine multiple proactive and reactive mechanisms: they allow customers to deposit coins into cold storage, and exchanges to perform time-delayed transfers of coins from cold to hot storage using their online keys and authorise time-delayed customer withdrawals. If an exchange is compromised, the exchange can lock down the vault using an online key (including the compromised key) and effectively freeze all withdrawals. This provides time for the exchange to bring a trusted vault key online and recover from the compromise. We outline the proposed protocol before presenting a proof of concept implementation.

Proposed Protocol. We present how to establish the contract, the three types of keys involved in access control of the coins, the time-delay involved in transferring coins from cold to hot storage and withdrawing coins, and finally the lock down and recovery process.

Contract Set Up and Access Control. There are three sets of keys that must be set when the contract is established in order to facilitate access control:

- *Hot keys:* Always online to authorise customer withdrawals,
- *Cold keys:* Periodically online to transfer coins from cold to hot wallet,
- *Vault key:* Only used to re-issue hot/cold keys and restart withdrawals, or if compromised can destroy all coins in the wallet.

The exchange can store a list of each key type and require a threshold of k out of n keys to sign and authorise moving coins. Two timers $t_{coldtransfer}$ and $t_{withdrawal}$ are required to self-enforce the time-delay, with the former controlling the time required to transfer coins from cold to hot storage and the latter delaying customer withdrawals.

Transferring Coins. There are two types of messages that can be signed by an exchange to authorise moving coins: *cold transfer request* and *withdrawal request*. The former moves coins from cold to hot storage which is instant if signed by a threshold of cold keys or incorporates a time-delay of $t_{coldtransfer}$ if signed by a threshold of hot keys. The latter associates a customer with coins from the hot wallet which can be withdrawn after $t_{withdrawal}$ and must be signed by a threshold of hot keys.

Vault Lock Down. If an exchange has detected a heist, it is responsible for signing a *lock down* message from any key registered in the contract. This message disables all functionality within the contract except for the recovery procedures which can only be accessed using the trusted recovery key. The exchange can set a new list of hot/cold keys and a new recovery key before canceling all withdrawal requests, transferring all coins to cold storage and re-enabling the functionality within the contract. If the trusted recovery key is also compromised, then the exchange can deploy a nuclear option of signing a *destroy* message using the recovery key. This disables all functionality within the contract and removes access to the coins forever. As a result neither the thief or exchange will control the coins.

3 Discussion

Perception of Time Delayed Withdrawals. It is common for users to publicly complain about slow withdrawals of coins/fiat currency. Recent complaints in 2017 include users waiting up to 30 h for withdrawals from Coinbase [9] and the need for Bitfinex to manually verify withdrawals after denial of service attacks between the 4–5th December [5]. While the time delay for withdrawals in our proposed solution is publicly verifiable by the customer, it may be undesirable to further increase the delay for customers receiving their deposits.

Financial Privacy For The Exchange. The benefit of the Bitcoin vault approach is that the underlying nature of Bitcoin's transaction design makes it difficult (but not impossible [22]) to identify the coins held by an exchange as all deposits are distinct sets of coins. In contrast, our smart contract solution provides little privacy as all coins are stored in a single location. This not only leaks information about an exchange's assets and earnings, but also about internal structures and processes as all keys and access rights have to be specified in the contract.

Risks of Smart Contract Wallets. There is a growing list of smart contracts that have resulted in the theft or loss of coins due to subtle bugs in their code. Two prominent examples include TheDAO [13] where a thief exploited a bug to steal over 3.5 m ether and the community was required to co-ordinate a hard-fork to stop the theft, and the Parity wallet [30] bug that allowed a novice user to kill a central smart contract and effectively freeze around 519k ether. We highlight that while there is an accumulating list of methods to formally verify the correctness of a smart contract [15,20,32], it remains to be seen whether an exchange is willing to risk all their assets to a single contract.

Bitcoin Vaults vs Contract Vaults. In vault transactions [23], due to the complexity of Bitcoin's transaction design, each set of stolen coins requires a new signature from the vault key for recovery. Signing multiple (and potentially large) transactions is problematic due to the rise of congested blocks in Bitcoin and significant fees (i.e. $20 or more for a small transaction). Exchanges often have coins spread across a large set of outputs (e.g., Coinbase has more than 1.5 million sets of spendable coins for just 265 BTC [29]), requiring a significant amount of signatures from the vault key. While batching funds is conceivable, the fact that each set of coins needs to store the entire list of access options is a significant drawback of Bitcoin.

Our proposed solution demonstrates that when designing vault transactions for smart contract-enabled cryptocurrencies like Ethereum, the account-based ledger (unlike Bitcoin's complex unspent transaction output ledger) allows a single transaction to lock down and cancel all withdrawals. The expressiveness of smart contracts allows any registered key (and not just the trusted vault key) to perform the lock down which allows an exchange to quickly react in the event of a heist. Finally, more granular access control can be incorporated in the contract to allow the hot keys to transfer coins from cold-storage with a time-delay such that the cold keys no longer need to periodically be brought online and thus mitigate the risk of their theft.

Fail-Deadly Mechanism. A nuclear option to destroy all coins is a strong deterrent against attacks, as the attacker knows beforehand that even if she can compromise keys, all funds will be destroyed before they can be moved outside of the contract. However, it is an open question whether companies would actually make use of such a feature. While it reduces the set of possible attackers (to those that gain indirectly by the exchange having to close), it would ruin the company, could confuse or deter users and might raise regulatory concerns.

Detecting Suspicious Withdrawals. Our solution relies on the ability for an exchange (or a third-party auditor) to detect and cancel a heist while it is in action. As mentioned previously, all transactions are publicly disclosed and in our proposed solution it is clear on the blockchain which coins are transferred from an exchange. This on-chain discovery provides several metrics that can be used in any detection mechanism such as frequency of withdrawals, total coins transferred, etc. However we leave it as future work to investigate detection mechanisms which can be used to detect suspicious withdrawals.

4 Conclusion

In this paper, we show that exchanges have only pursued preventative security measures to protect their signing keys. Both measures include hot/cold keys to reduce the impact of a heist and so-called 'multi-signature' that requires multiple signing keys to authorise a withdrawal. However, as shown time and time again by frequent exchange heists, a single compromise of the signing keys by the hacker will result in the irreversible theft of an exchange's coins. Thus, while preventative security measures are desirable, it is clear that they are not good enough. Instead, we propose exchanges must adopt reactionary security measures which allows them to cancel a heist while it is in action. Our solution is inspired by Möser et al. [23] and it associates a time-delay with all withdrawals. This provides time for an exchange (or a third-party auditor) to flag and cancel withdrawals as supicious. Once withdrawals are cancelled, the exchange can use a trusted (and offline) recovery key to re-issue new (and uncompromised) signing keys for future customer withdrawals.

References

1. Andresen, G.: Pay to script hash. Bitcoin Github (2012)
2. Bacca, N.: How to properly secure cryptocurrencies exchanges. Ledger Company (2016)
3. BBC: Bitcoin exchange Youbit shuts after second hack attack. BBC, December 2017
4. Belshe, M.: Bitfinex breach update. BitGo Blog (2016)
5. Bitfinex: Explanation. Reddit Post, December 2017
6. Brito, J.: What does the CFTC have to do with the Bitfinex hack? Coin Center, August 2016
7. Browne, R.: More than $60 million worth of bitcoin potentially stolen after hack on cryptocurrency site. CNBC (2017)
8. Chavez-Dreyfuss, G.: Cyber threat grows for bitcoin exchanges. Reuters, August 2016
9. Dariusz: Slow withdrawals leave coinbase users annoyed. TheMerkle (2017)
10. Decker, C., Wattenhofer, R.: Bitcoin transaction malleability and MtGox. In: Kutyłowski, M., Vaidya, J. (eds.) ESORICS 2014. LNCS, vol. 8713, pp. 313–326. Springer, Cham (2014). https://doi.org/10.1007/978-3-319-11212-1_18

11. Gennaro, R., Goldfeder, S., Narayanan, A.: Threshold-optimal DSA/ECDSA signatures and an application to bitcoin wallet security. In: Manulis, M., Sadeghi, A.-R., Schneider, S. (eds.) ACNS 2016. LNCS, vol. 9696, pp. 156–174. Springer, Cham (2016). https://doi.org/10.1007/978-3-319-39555-5_9
12. Goodin, D.: Bitcoins worth $228,000 stolen from customers of hacked Webhost. Arstechnica (2012)
13. Hanson, R.: A $50 million hack just showed that the DAO was all too human. Wired, June 2016
14. Higgins, S.: BTER claims $1.75 million in bitcoin stolen in cold wallet hack. Coindesk, February 2015
15. Hildenbrandt, E., et al.: KEVM: a complete semantics of the ethereum virtual machine. Technical report (2017)
16. Kocher, P., et al.: Spectre attacks: exploiting speculative execution. arXiv preprint arXiv:1801.01203 (2018)
17. Lee, T.B.: Hacker steals $250k in Bitcoins from online exchange Bitfloor. Arstechnica, May 2012
18. Lemos, R.: Bitcoin exchange Bitstamp claims hack siphoned up to $5.2 million. Arstechnica (2015)
19. Lipp, M., et al.: Meltdown. arXiv preprint arXiv:1801.01207 (2018)
20. Luu, L., Chu, D.-H., Olickel, H., Saxena, P., Hobor, A.: Making smart contracts smarter. In: Proceedings of the 2016 ACM SIGSAC Conference on Computer and Communications Security, pp. 254–269. ACM (2016)
21. Martin, P.: Coinbase accused of technical incompetence after hoarding millions of UTXOs. Coinbase, January 2018
22. Meiklejohn, S., et al.: A fistful of bitcoins: characterizing payments among men with no names. In: Proceedings of the 2013 Conference on Internet Measurement Conference, pp. 127–140. ACM (2013)
23. Möser, M., Eyal, I., Gün Sirer, E.: Bitcoin covenants. In: Clark, J., Meiklejohn, S., Ryan, P.Y.A., Wallach, D., Brenner, M., Rohloff, K. (eds.) FC 2016. LNCS, vol. 9604, pp. 126–141. Springer, Heidelberg (2016). https://doi.org/10.1007/978-3-662-53357-4_9
24. Nilsson, K.: Breaking open the MtGox case, part 1. Wizsec, July 2017
25. O'Brien, W.: It's time to end the cold storage ice age and adopt multi-sig. BitGo, September 2014
26. Palatinus, M., Rusnak, P.: Multi-account hierarchy for deterministic wallets. Bitcoin Github, April 2014
27. Palatinus, M., Rusnak, P., Voisine, A., Bowe, S.: Mnemonic code for generating deterministic keys. Bitcoin Github, September 2013
28. Perkin, M.: Bitfinex breach update. LedgerLabs (2016)
29. Sedgwick, K.: Coinbase Accused of Technical Incompetence After Hoarding Millions of UTXOs. bitcoin.com, December 2017
30. Shen, L.: Millions of dollars worth of ethereum got locked up. Here's Why. Fortune, November 2017
31. Wuille, P.: Hierarchical deterministic wallets. Bitcoin Github, February 2012
32. Zurich, E.: Formal verification of ethereum smart contracts. Securify, January 2017

Why Preventing a Cryptocurrency Heist Isn't Good Enough (Transcript of Discussion)

Patrick McCorry(✉)

University College London, London, UK

p.mccorry@ucl.ac.uk

Erinn Atwater: So if the attackers compromise one server, why wouldn't they go and compromise all the servers?

Reply: The servers belong to two different companies, Bitfinex and BitGo. But this gets even better, they won't even need to compromise BitGo. This is what I hinted at in the beginning. Bitfinex was a Bitcoin exchange and it partnered with a third-party auditor BitGo. It appears Bitfinex believed the marketing from BitGo and didn't use any cold storage. It also appears they wanted to comply with some regulations which precludes the use of cold storage.

The system was set up as follows: all Bitfinex transactions were associated with three keys and signatures from any two keys would claim the coins. One key was owned by Bitfinex, one key was owned by BitGo, and one was kept as a paper backup (held by Bitfinex). Long story short, of course they got hacked and it was the second largest heist in Bitcoin's history with over 120,000 bitcoins lost. The hack was straightforward, the hacker compromised Bitfinex, stole the first signing key, signed a fraudulent transaction and sent it to BitGo.

At this point, BitGo was expected to reject the transaction, but instead it signed the transaction and gave away all of Bitfinex's coins. BitGo was essentially a signing Oracle, and when this was publicised, BitGo said that they had special configuration for Bitfinex and there was no compromise in BitGo's security.

That is enough about heists for now and instead let's have a quick pop quiz: How do we recover from the 120k bitcoin heist? If you were one of the customers that lost coins during this heist, what option would you select out of the following repayment options? Do you pick proceedings from bankruptcy? Will you accept an IOU from the exchange, where they give you IOU tokens and in one year's time they'll pay you back all your coins. Or do you take an immediate haircut of 80 cents per dollar. So let's do hands up.

Daniel Weitzner: I have a question. Did we pay or have any kind of arrangement with BitGo in advance?

Reply: No, did you mean Bitfinex?

Daniel Weitzner: Bitfinex, yeah. So we didn't work out anything in advance.

Reply: No. Not in terms of recovery options.

V. Matyáš et al. (Eds.): Security Protocols 2018, LNCS 11286, pp. 234–242, 2018.
https://doi.org/10.1007/978-3-030-03251-7_28

Daniel Weitzner: They're just being helpful. And now the question is what kind of help would we ideally like?

Reply: Yeah, exactly. Back to the hands up.

Who would go for bankruptcy? No one, I'd like to mention this was the Mt.Gox option which is still on-going as of March 2018.

Who would accept the IOU? Oh, nobody? This was the Bitfinex option.

Who would do the haircut? Everyone would do the haircut! This was the Coincheck option.

Mark Lomas: How are you actually receiving these 80 cents?

Reply: In dollars.

Mark Lomas: But what I'm getting at is if they try to pay you back in Bitcoin and you already know they have an insecure system, why would you trust them?

Reply: Or with your bank details? I guess they already have your bank details before the heist. That is why I don't use exchanges.

Let's consider the bankruptcy example, because it is a ridiculous situation. Four years ago, Mt.Gox declared bankruptcy and four years later the process still hasn't wrapped up. The ridiculous part is that, because of the exponential rise in the Bitcoin price, MtGox is now in a situation where they can pay all customers back based on the 2014 Bitcoin price ($400) and MtGox can still profit from this situation.

Let's consider the IOU option. Remarkably, Bitfinex actually paid everyone back within the year. So if you want all your money back, IOU is a good option. Finally Coincheck did the haircut option as well which was 80 cents per dollar lost.

Okay, so the big theme of this work is that the community only has two security measures which are cold storage and multi-signature transactions. Both approaches are preventative in nature, where cold storage reduces your risk if there is a heist, and multi-signature increases the difficulty of an attack. My hope for this work is to identify reactive security measures. Is there a way to react and in fact cancel a heist in action? This can be the fail-safe option and it is in fact the motivation behind Bitcoin vaults (and covenants) by Malte Moeser.

Today, if I send Ross coins, then I have no way to dictate how Ross can spend these coins in the future. But with Bitcoin covenants, if I send Ross coins, then I can set some spending conditions such as that, for example, Ross cannot claim these coins for three hours. This helps support the Bitcoin vault idea, where there is effectively a pending transaction, where the transaction is in fact confirmed on the network, and the receiver cannot redeem the coins for three hours. If this pending transaction is in fact part of the heist, then I have three hours to react by bringing a recovery key on-line to cancel the transaction and send myself back the coins.

If we can have good detection mechanisms, then this is nice as we can recover from a heist. But there is a sticking point here as Bitcoin covenants (and thus vaults) is unlikely to be adopted in the future as it requires new consensus rules in Bitcoin.

Mansoor Ahmed: Mansoor. Aren't you also opening yourself up to a double-spending attack? Because you are basically increasing the confirmation times?

Reply: Well, in a sense, the transaction is confirmed on the network and it is in the blockchain. Ross just needs two transactions to claim the coins. One to receive it, the other to spend it after the pending wait period is over. The coins cannot be double-spent as the "pending transaction" is already committed to Ross. The only two options are to either cancel the transaction so the sender (i.e. me) gets the coins back or wait for the expiry to let Ross have the coins.

Mansoor Ahmed: So basically, it increases the latency of the confirmation?

Reply: Yes. In a sense. It's more like a timer that starts ticking after the transaction gets in the blockchain (this is also how payment channels work). The main point is that when you withdraw coins - it is not always likely you will need the coins immediately. You may be happy to wait for four hours until the transaction clears and if this time-delay is publicly verifiable then it might be okay.

Regardless, the point of my discussion so far was that Bitcoin covenants (and thus vaults) is unlikely to be adopted in Bitcoin. But what if we want to deploy this idea today? We propose that it be deployed in a cryptocurrency like Ethereum using smart contracts.

But what is a smart contract? A good mental model for a smart contract is that it is a trusted third party who can only maintain public state. All code is deployed on the network (and it should not be modifiable). All peers on the network deterministically execute the code and as a result all functions are honestly executed. It should also be atomic such that a function either runs or it fails, it is never stuck in an in-between state. Finally, the contract likes to gossip and it cannot keep any secrets. This is one of the reasons I got interested in smart contracts as it motivates the use of cryptography.

How can this be deployed in Ethereum? We can set up a single contract for the exchange which holds all coins on its behalf. Conceptually, the contract can have both cold and hot wallets. When coins are sent to the contract, they are deposited into the cold wallet. Afterwards, when the exchange wants to send coins to the customer, coins can be moved from the cold to hot wallet, and then transferred to the customer. Overall, it is roughly the same idea that exchanges are using today, but in a single contract (as opposed to thousands of unique entries).

This contract can also support two type of keys: the first is a hot key that can do two things. It can send coins from the hot wallet to the customer, but every withdrawal has a time-delay associated with it (i.e. five hours). It can also support transfer of coins from the hot to cold wallet with a larger delay (i.e. 24 h). The second key is a cold key that is only brought on-line if coins need to be moved from cold to hot storage immediately.

Fabio Massacci: Sorry, but if I understood correctly, all the heists took months or years to be discovered, right? So a four hours delay is not going to improve the situation much.?

Reply: Yes, so Mt.Gox took about three years because they had no internal auditing. But in recent cases - a heist is discovered quite quickly.

Fabio Massacci: So, less than four hours?

Reply: It really depends how good the exchange's detection mechanism is (which I don't have access to). But I should also mention that most exchanges have a time-delay anyway (i.e. it might take a few days to get your coins from Coinbase).

Ilia Shumailov: So coming back to Fabio's question, if you imagine somebody deposits 6,000 bitcoins over three years. It's going to be very hard to notice if an exchange is operating on a few millions or a few thousands bitcoins. So I don't quite see how this addresses the actual auditing problem.

Reply: Well, this doesn't do anything for the auditing. The auditing is external to the contract.

Ilia Shumailov: Exactly, so what is this directed at?

Reply: It is directed at the pending transaction grace period. If the contract sets up a pending transaction to withdraw 10k coins, then the auditing mechanism has this time period to detect (and cancel) the hack.

Ross Anderson: I'm a little bit confused about the meaning of audits in this circumstance. I've actually worked for banks and if you've got dual or triple control of transactions, it's very different from auditing which is done by different people in a different department and happens later after bad things are detected. If you're merely doing dual control, if for example it takes your branch manager and branch accountant to release a transaction over a million dollars, then all that can happen is you have two independent people studying the same mandated paperwork. So if your customer is sitting in your office and wants a bank draft for a million pounds so that he can buy a house, then the accountant and manager will do the same thing, they look at the customer, they look at the customer's past, they say 'Nice day Mr. Smith, tell me about the house you're buying.' And they cannot fundamentally do radically different things. I really don't understand what is the extra process that you do within your risk area.

Reply: One thing that helps is also public alerts. For example, a lot of people can watch transactions coming from this exchange. When a heist happens, it can immediately get posted on a public forum, i.e. why is this exchange sending 120k bitcoins?

Ilia Shumailov: If you actually go through those forums you'll find millions of messages like this.

Reply: Yes, there is lots of spam. That is still something that needs to be worked on - in terms of how best the auditing/detection mechanism can work. Ideally, you should be using a third party auditor like BitGo for this type of service, but as mentioned before, this doesn't always work.

Ilia Shumailov: So that implies that you need to know the address belonging to the exchanges.

Reply: Oh, but this is all in one contract. That is one of the limitations of this system, all the coins are in one big pot and everyone can see it. This isn't good for the exchange's financial privacy. It is this pot of money that the third party auditor (or the exchange) looks at to detect fraudulent transactions and it would good to understand the lessons learnt from banks who have been doing this for a long time. After all, banks can and do freeze transactions within 24 h to an extent.

Although so far, exchanges have also been very secretive over their detection mechanism, so it is difficult to work out exactly what they are doing.

Anyway, the next important question that pops up is, what if the hot and cold keys are compromised? The keys can still be used to freeze the contracts, cancel all withdrawals and send all coins to cold storage. The third key is called the recovery key, and it should only be brought online and used in this situation. It is used to re-issue new cold/hot keys and unfreeze the wallet. All three keys together provide the fail-safe approach as it allow the exchange to freeze the contract and recover from the situation, assuming they can detect the heist in progress.

But what if your recover key is also stolen? Then we rely on the fail-deadly option and burn all coins in the contract, so neither the exchange or the thief wins. When I spoke to an exchange about the fail-deadly option, I was told this might not actually be legal. If I am victim to a heist and someone is running away with my coins, I may not be legally allowed to burn them. This needs a further investigation, but is an interesting limitation of the fail-deadly option.

As I mentioned before, there's no financial privacy and you have to trust all your coin to a single smart contract. As we've seen in the past, these contracts keep getting hacked because of weird, quirky bugs in the contract. The party wallet hack for example, they lost 500,000 each which at the time was $150 million dollars. So exchanges may not want this risk.

Graham Rymer: Just an observation. Burning coins is not without precedent. There was a heist in Northern Ireland, in fact.

Reply: Oh, the Northern Bank one?

Graham Rymer: The bank recalled and reprinted their cash to stop the thieves pocketing the coins.

Reply: That was like 10 years ago, wasn't it? I'll put that in the paper, there's actually precedent then of burning coins.

Ian Goldberg: Can you tell us more about this?

Ross Anderson: The IRA scored 50 million pounds from a cash processing centre of one of Northern Ireland's banks. This was after the Northern Ireland peace agreement and the idea was this would provide pensions for all the retiring soldiers. The bank and the government was sufficiently annoyed that they just decided to change the currency so the old bank notes would no longer be spendable. Now in Northern Ireland, as in Scotland, the bank notes are issued by banks rather than by the government. The bank can simply say your bank notes are no longer valid. If you have any, they can be brought to a bank branch with proof of their origin and the bank will re-issue new ones.

Reply: Good explanation. So there is some precedent of removing coins from circulation, I'm going to look further into that.

Erinn Atwater: So that's very similar to the DAO heist where everyone just decided, no, we didn't actually get robbed.

Reply: The DAO was a kickstarter-style contract, and at one point it stored more than $50 million dollars of ether - perhaps around ten percent of Ethereum's market capitalisation at the time. Long story short, the contract was hacked and the thief had 30 days before he could withdraw the coins and the community decided to reverse the hack. This involved 'forking' the network - which means to add/remove consensus rules - which effectively stopped the heist and re-issued everyone their coins. In fact, this is an example of reactive security, but I'd like to understand whether this mechanism can be built directly into the contract itself.

Ilia Shumailov: Just to mention something, don't call this a precedent, one thing when you can burn coins down and recover from it, another is just physically destroying coins.

Reply: I guess. In fact there is actually a proposal under review in the community that locked (or burnt) coins can be released in future hard forks.

Ian Goldberg: So, you're talking about this audit procedure in which you just keep an eye on your coins and see if coins were spent from your account without a corresponding actual withdrawal out of the system. But you made that sound difficult and also that no one actually does it.

Reply: They do, they do internally.

Ian Goldberg: Isn't this as easy as you having you Bitcoin wallet and it just spews out the transaction whenever it sees it on the blockchain?

Reply: Yes, one example is that there is a program that watches the blockchain. I can see the heist in action (i.e. a transaction over 10k bitcoins) and my program automatically signs a transaction to cancel the heist. As I mentioned previously, exchanges are secretive over their detection mechanisms (and I don't know what they are doing) and right now they can't respond to a heist anyway, so they have to rely on their internal mechanisms to prevent key theft.

One issue I foresee with detection mechanisms, if the algorithm is public knowledge, then the hacker could just remain below the threshold and prevent the heist from being detected. I'd also like to see more meaningful time delays, perhaps up to 50 coins can be withdrawn per day (and then we hit the time limit). If over 20% of the coins are spent in a day, then the time limit increases to one or two days, because the contract is sending an abnormal number of coins.

Alexander Hicks: How do I know your contract is secure?

Reply: This is a problem. Would people trust all their coins to a single smart contract? As mentioned before, the DAO hack was audited by the Ethereum core developers (i.e. people who should know what they are doing) and the exploit used was unknown to the community. Although I should mention that Andrew Miller pointed out this style of bug a year before the hack, and his warning was rubbed off as not being a meaningful bug.

Ilia Shumailov: Just to talk about algorithms being public: currently what they are doing at banks (at least what I gathered from communication with a guy who works at one of the companies) is that they hire services from contractors, sort of business-to-business, and ask if they can provide intelligence on whether a transaction is fraudulent or not. Algorithms don't need to be public, but the contractors must provide some explanation of why the transaction is fraudulent. From what I understood, there have to be regulations to prevent racial profiling, etc.

Reply: I see. You can modify the contract in such a way where if auditing were outsourced, then the contractor increases the delay of withdrawal, but not strictly cancel it. For example, the contractor can delay a transaction up to three days. Then both the exchange and contractor can have this communication to determine the reasons why it was flagged as fraudulent. If the exchanges disagrees, the transaction gets approved eventually.

Ilia Shumailov: So, let me ask you a question. Remember back a few slides ago, you mentioned that you don't know how exchanges work inside, they mentioned they have a specific sort of deal with the auditing company.

Reply: BitGo, yes.

Ilia Shumailov: Yeah, so if you're actually working with them and they were issuing you a lot of transactions every day, would you actually keep a very close eye on each one of those transactions? Answer this yourself.

Reply: Well, that was a special configuration. So I'm aware that BitGo actually do have algorithms to detect fraudulent transactions.?

Ilia Shumailov: I'm asking you, if you were to design the system, how would you do it?

Reply: That is one of the outstanding problems in this paper. I would probably do it based on how many coins are moved per day, and then try to get a median based on previous history. But yeah, I don't know what the algorithm is yet.

Ilia Shumailov: But this is the thing, most were probably transferring all their in the peeling chain, or some other way that moves all their coins from one address to the other. This might not raise any sort of suspicion because they keep rotating huge sums of money all the time.

Reply: Yeah, I don't know how many transactions they do actually. I think most of their transactions are internal to their website between users and they just update a database record locally. The ones that hit the blockchain are in the minority.

Ilia Shumailov: So they are never actually doing the transfer?

Reply: There are few types of transactions. There are transactions between customers on the platform, and there are transactions where they take coins out of the platform which also makes it to the blockchain. The latter are all public knowledge and these are the transactions in the minority. That is the only time they would have to talk to a company like BitGo.

Mansoor Ahmed: Seeing that mining is more centralised, would it make more sense to have these fail-safe algorithms between the miners and exchanges, rather than having it encoded into a smart contract?

Reply: Miners should be neutral. Their only role is to include transactions in the blockchain and publish it. We shouldn't have to rely on them to make sure a fail-safe option is enforced. As long as they enforce the consensus rules on the network, then the exchange and some company can do this without the miner's support.

That is the basic idea, a miner's role can be summarised as: "here is a transaction, it's in a block, and I published it." They shouldn't care what the transaction is about.

Mansoor Ahmed: Sure, but they already do a self-selection based on how much transaction fees they are getting. They basically choose which transactions are included. Why don't they include a common sense way of filtering transactions which are fraudulent and notifying exchanges, and then include it if confirmed.

Reply: This sort of goes against the ideology. Miners do have that power, but it's a power we don't really want them to have as they can start censoring transactions. That is what the community wants to try and avoid. I'm not saying they don't have that power, they do have that power. But it would be really good if you could do this without the miner's support. In a sense, you don't have to rely on them to include transactions. That is the real motivation here, the miner's don't need to be included at all.

Alexander Hicks: What do you do if you've got a contract which - let's assume is secure - what do you do if you have a change you need to make because of regulation or how because of how big the time delay is? How do you deal with this with a contract that is permanently in place? Or if you find a bug and you need to transfer the coins to a new contract?

Reply: That is the recovery key's role. If you are transferring coins from one contract to the other, then we might hit the time delay. But if the time delay is one day, then you wait one day for your coins to transfer across. That is not a big deal for an exchange.

Alexander Hicks: But who is authorising that coins are transferred d and why would you trust them not to just transfer those coins randomly?

Reply: Only the exchange can authorise the transfer. The exchange simply transfers coins from contract A to contract B, and we have to wait the 24 h. Once the delay is over, the coins are transferred. So you don't need to make any modification to the contract for that.

Alexander Hicks: Why would you trust that?

Reply: The exchange is authorising it.

Making Bitcoin Legal

Ross Anderson[(✉)], Ilia Shumailov, and Mansoor Ahmed

Cambridge University Computer Laboratory, Cambridge, UK
Ross.Anderson@cl.cam.ac.uk

Abstract. What would happen if the existing laws were actually enforced on the rich and powerful? Social reformers often clamour for new rules but ignore the huge changes that might happen if our existing rules were applied equally to all. And in the brave new world of ICOs and thousand percent cryptocurrency inflation, the rich and powerful are the bitcoin exchanges. What would happen if FinCEN regulations and the laws against money laundering were applied to them, and extended by sensible case law? We argue that this could mitigate most of the worst excesses of cryptocurrency world, and turn a dangerous system into a much safer one. The curious thing about this change is that it would not involve changing the protocol. It would not even necessarily involve changing the law. It might be enough to take some information that's already public, publishing it again in a more easily understood format.

When you come to a fork in the road, take it – *Yogi Berra*

1 Introduction

Bitcoin set out to provide a working online currency outside the control of governments, and has developed from a cypherpunk toy through a way to buy drugs online to a means of getting flight capital out of countries with exchange controls – to an investment product quoted on major exchanges. It has been criticised for wasting a lot of electricity, for being a classic investment bubble, for providing no consumer protection to its users, and for facilitating crimes – from old crimes such as drug dealing, to new ones such as ransomware.

The purpose of this paper is twofold. First, we discuss how the law might actually regulate bitcoin and other cryptocurrencies so as to provide the benefits, ranging from low-cost international money transfers and decentralised resilient operation to competitive innovation, while mitigating the harms – specifically the use of cryptocurrencies in extortion, money laundering and other crimes, and the difficulty that crime victims experience in getting redress. We show that where the relevant case law is used as a basis, it becomes much easier to track stolen bitcoins than previously thought.

Second, we use this discussion to illustrate that the characteristics of a payment protocol can depend much more sensitively than one might expect on the

V. Matyáš et al. (Eds.): Security Protocols 2018, LNCS 11286, pp. 243–253, 2018.
https://doi.org/10.1007/978-3-030-03251-7_29

surrounding context. This may be of scientific interest to the protocols community, and also of practical interest to regulators. Payment systems suffer from strong network effects and it may be harder than it seems to sustain a government-backed 'GoodCoin' in competition with established systems such as Bitcoin and Ethereum. It is therefore important to explore the practical options for taming the systems that already exist.

On the policy front, we have repeatedly seen a pattern whereby the promoter of an online platform claims that old laws will not apply. The Internet was supposed to interpret censorship and route around it; yet child sex abuse images are banned almost everywhere. Napster set out to free all music from the surly bonds of copyright; it was closed down. Uber was going to create a single taxi firm that worked worldwide from a convenient app, regardless of local legacy monopolies; yet when legacy taxi drivers complained about their new competitors working sixteen hours a day, and passenger safety issues piled up, Uber was banned in one city after another. Yet such innovations often make a real difference once a new legal equilibrium is achieved. The music-company mafias have yielded to Spotify and YouTube, which make most music available to anyone who'll listen to occasional ads; competition from Uber has cut Cambridge taxi fares by over 20%; and the Internet has made many more good things available to all.

The key is making online challengers obey the law – and the laws may not need to change much, or even at all. Fixing new problems using existing laws is usually preferable, given the difficulty of getting primary legislation passed.

So where does this leave Bitcoin?

In this paper we assume the reader is familiar with the mechanics of Bitcoin and of blockchains in general. A later paper will present more detail for readers interested in law or policy.

2 Ideal Regulation

The obvious first step towards regulation was to bring bitcoin exchanges within the financial system by applying anti-money-laundering (AML) regulations to them. Thus anyone wishing to exchange bitcoin for cash, or for ether or any other means of payment, has to satisfy know-your-customer (KYC) rules just as if they were opening a bank account, typically by showing government-issue photo ID plus two utility bills as proof of address. This started in 2013, when the Financial Crimes Enforcement Network (FinCEN) directed bitcoin exchanges to register as money service businesses [4]. Most countries have now followed suit, partitioning the world of exchanges into compliant and rogue components.

The second step would be for both enforcement agencies and exchanges to effectively track tainted coins. If my bitcoin wallet is stolen I can now go to the police and report it. The stolen assets are completely traceable through the blockchain and whenever anybody tries to bank them at an exchange, they can be seized. How might the courts actually do that?

2.1 Clayton's Case

Until now, there were two algorithms used for taint tracking in the blockchain – poison and haircut [13]. These taint multisource transactions, of which one input is tainted, either completely, or in proportion. Thus a transaction whose inputs are three stolen bitcoin and then seven good bitcoin has an output on 'poison' of ten stolen bitcoin, and on 'haircut' of ten bitcoin each of which is marked as 30% stolen.

However, this ignores the precedent of Clayton's case, where a court in 1816 had to tackle the problem of mixing good and bad funds through an account after a bank went bust and the outcome depended on which deposits to an account were to be matched with which later withdrawals. The Master of the Rolls set a simple rule of first-in-first-out (FIFO): withdrawals from an account are deemed to be drawn against the deposits first made to it [3].

In order to test this rule, we coded FIFO and haircut taint tracking, and ran them from the genesis block to 2016, starting from 132 well-publicised bitcoin crimes. FIFO turns out to be very much more contained. The 2012 theft of 46,653 bitcoin from Linode tainted 2,694,051 addresses, or almost 5% of the total, using the haircut algorithm, while with FIFO, it's 371,544 or just over 0.67%. The effect is even more pronounced with a shorter propagation period; for example, the 2014 Flexcoin hack (where 'the world's first bitcoin bank' closed after all their coins were stolen) tainted only 18,208 accounts by 2016 using FIFO, but 1,429,794 using haircut. Overall, most bitcoin accounts[1] have zero taint using FIFO, while less than 24% escape taint if we use a haircut approach.

This is a very striking result. Many people assumed that bitcoin tracking was usually impractical, because the taint spreads widely as coins circulate. However once we apply the law and use FIFO, tracking turns out to be much more practical. And FIFO tracking is reversible; you can track forwards from a coin that's been reported stolen, or backwards from a coin you've just been offered. This isn't possible with haircut tainting, as it loses information.

We also looked at bitcoin laundries or mixes. These are based on the idea that if you put one black coin in a bag with nine white ones and shake hard enough, you'll get ten white ones out. But depending on the algorithm in use, FIFO tainting will decide that one of the outputs is black (and no owner of a white coin will want to risk that outcome), or that all coins are a sandwich of black and white components (which is also an undesirable outcome). In any case, mixes have never had the scale, throughput or latency to cope with the proceeds of serious crime; the bitcoin stolen from Mt Gox were traced to BTC-e which was raided and its operator arrested [9].

There is an interesting piece of research to be done here on protocols, documenting the precise effects of FIFO tainting on the various mixing and money-laundering strategies proposed to date, or documented in the wild [12,14,15]. People who have been doing research on financial anonymity without paying attention to Clayton's case have simply been using the wrong metric.

[1] Slightly over 72% of all bitcoin accounts with a nonzero balance are taint-free.

Efficient coin tracing may damage the fungibility of bitcoin. A commodity is called fungible if one unit can replace another; examples are gold coins, and ears of corn. Technology has in the past reduced fungibility. If ten sheep wandered in Roman times from Marcus's field into Pliny's, then the court would let Marcus take any ten of Pliny's sheep; but today, all sheep have electronic tags, so Marcus can get the right sheep back. So too with bitcoin.

2.2 Nemo Dat Quod Non Habet

'Nobody can give what isn't theirs' is a fundamental principle of law in England, with variants in many other jurisdictions. You cannot get effective title to stolen goods simply by buying them; indeed, you can be prosecuted for receiving them. If Alice steals Bob's horse and sells it to Charlie, Charlie doesn't own it; whenever Bob seems him riding it, he can demand it back.

There are a few exceptions. For centuries, if stolen goods were sold at a 'market overt' – a designated public market – between sunrise and sunset, then the buyer would get good title. (So if Charlie had bought Bob's horse in Cambridge market, all Bob could now do would be to sue her for the value, or perhaps have her transported to the colonies.) This rule was abolished in the UK in 1995, following abuse by antique thieves, but it survives in specific forms in some markets to which the idea had spread in the meantime. The relevant case for our purposes is money.

Where goods started to function as money – as with gold – regulation developed to accommodate it. Banks started in some countries as goldsmiths who would give receipts for gold, and on demand would give an appropriate amount of gold back, though not necessarily the same bars. So a gold thief might lodge his loot at a goldsmith, and take the receipt back a week later to get clean bars instead[2].

Fast forward through a lot of history, and you can now get good title to stolen money in two main cases.

1. You got the money in good faith for value. For example, you bought a microwave oven at a high street store and got a £10 note in your change. That note is now yours even if it was stolen in a bank robbery last year.
2. You got the money from a regulated institution, such as from an ATM. Then even if it was stolen in a robbery last year, that's now the bank's problem, not yours.

It is not surprising that the cryptocurrency industry would very much like to have bitcoins declared to be money, as this would enable everyday users to stop worrying about the possibility that some of their bitcoin were stolen. And this is a real fear; the major reported robberies alone account for about 6–9% of all

[2] Monetary law over the centuries has had the same ambivalent attitude about whether money consists of the physical goods that used to embody it, such as coins or notes, or the value they embody – just as bitcoin promoters claim that cryptocurrencies are money or goods depending on which will best help them escape regulation.

bitcoin in circulation [11]. If we add the proceeds of crime more generally we will get a much larger figure but will encounter many complexities of definition, jurisdiction and so on. The proceeds of drug crimes, in particular, are exposed to quite draconian seizure laws in a number of countries.

However nothing in life is free, and being a regulated financial institution has significant costs of its own: capital adequacy requirements, criminal-records background checks for staff, and (most important for our purposes) 'know your customer' (KYC) rules feeding into anti-money-laundering (AML) surveillance systems. Large transactions are reported, as are patterns of smaller ones, and banks demand your passport and a couple of utility bills when you open an account.

Since 2013, the US Treasury Department's Financial Crimes Enforcement Network (FinCEN) has directed bitcoin exchanges to register and follow these rules; other countries have been following suit. Since 2017, several non-compliant exchanges have been prosecuted [7]. The latest development is that the EU proposes to amend the 4th Anti-Money Laundering Directive so as to extend regulation, including a KYC duty, to firms that operate hosted wallet services. That may eventually bring most bitcoin users under the umbrella. The question then will be how the regulators will discharge the responsibility they have now assumed. Might they do something to reassure ordinary investors that they won't lose money as a result of buying stolen bitcoin? Of course they could demand that registered exchanges make good any customers to whom they sell bitcoin that later turn out to be stolen, but is there anything else?

2.3 Registering or Even Insuring Title

One way of insuring title would be for the state to register ownership, as it does in many countries with real estate, motor vehicles and patents. But there are subtleties here about whether or not the register is constitutive of ownership, as with patents, or not, as with cars; and whether it provides a guarantee, as with property.

But given the scale of bitcoin thefts and robberies, and the anonymity preferences of bitcoin users, state guarantees are unlikely to be an attractive option for many stakeholders. A government-controlled blockchain would give neither the platform for innovation that cryptocurrencies do, nor the price, performance and market responsiveness of ordinary bank accounts.

2.4 Might the Courts Do the Job?

So far, no government has declared bitcoin to be money, although Japan and Italy have tiptoed around the edges of this. However, courts may find that bitcoin can be treated as money for some purposes. A relevant precedent established that carbon credits are property, and they possess many of the same characteristics as bitcoins [6].

Monetary status might be thought ideal for investors who hold cryptocurrencies in the hope of capital gains. At present, the investor can only check that her asset has not yet been reported as crime proceeds – but most crime reports don't come with public lists of affected addresses. If bitcoin were money, and she got her bitcoin directly from a regulated exchange, she would have good title.

If someone hacks your Bitcoin wallet, or uses ransomware to extort bitcoin from you, or holds you up at gunpoint and forces you to transfer your savings to them – a crime that's become extremely fashionable of late [16] – then the stolen bitcoin can be traced. Now that coin tracing is practical, the victim can trace the stolen bitcoin through the blockchain, and sue the current holder – or any regulated exchange through which it passed.

So honest customers would like the exchanges' addresses to be public, so that anyone tracing stolen funds could see that a coin went through a regulated exchange before they bought it. The exchanges will resist, not wanting to make it easier for theft victims to sue them. Bitcoin enthusiasts might well side with the exchanges, on the principle that bitcoin public keys are pseudonyms. But it's increasingly the investors who're floating the boat.

3 Changing the Rules of the Game

This pressure point may give an opportunity to change the rules of the game. Fox notes "Information about the tainted provenance of individual cyber-coins may be discoverable by specialised forensic techniques. But there is as yet no standard practice of applying them to routine payments" [5,6]. We have shown that coin provenance can be tracked very much more easily than people assumed. The economic pressure point sits on a technical fissure, between the technical community's insistence that the only concept of ownership of bitcoin is control of the private key for the wallet in which it's stored [1] versus the lawyers' insistence that the registration of a bitcoin on the blockchain is not 'constitutive of ownership' as is the case with registered property rights such as patents.

Cryptocurrency promoters and investors will continue to lobby for a law making bitcoin fungible, arguing that governments make money from selling bitcoin confiscated as the proceeds of crime [8] – even if in the past they have ineptly sold bitcoin at way below market value [2]. They will also point out that when the government of Korea tried to crack down on cryptocurrencies, it suffered a public backlash [10].

But even if bitcoin becomes money, the law and the blockchain will still diverge when you buy a bitcoin knowing it to be stolen – or being on notice that it might be, or being negligent that it might be.

For bitcoin to work as some of its promoters wish, governments would have to go further than declaring it to be money. They would have to declare the blockchain to be constitutive of ownership. This would be an extreme measure, and seems unlikely, given that even registers of motor vehicles don't have such a status. The register simply records where speeding fines and unpaid tolls should be sent; it does not establish ownership. If we want to make ownership of bitcoin more certain, we need a different approach.

4 Taintchain: A Public Trail of Breadcrumbs

As Fox noted, tainted provenance can be discovered using forensics, yet applying these to routine payments is not standard practice.

Our critical new assumption is this. Suppose there exists free and open-source software that makes an up-to-date taint analysis publicly available. This will follow the blockchain forward from all reported crimes, and also from crimes whose existence can be reliably deduced from the internal evidence of the blockchain, and will mark every bitcoin in existence with a taint. Either the coin is clean, or some part of it was stolen. In that case, the taint will document the chain of evidence back to the crime and quantify it under certain assumptions (which we discuss later). We call this public trace the *Taintchain*, and propose to make our FIFO tracing software public so that anyone can build one.

There may well be multiple versions. For example, if a Chinese national uses bitcoin to extract money from China in contravention of its exchange control laws, that will not be a crime in the UK which has no exchange controls. Similarly, if a software company in Estonia pays a developer in Ukraine in bitcoin so she can evade both exchange controls and tax, the authorities in Tallinn may well not be interested. Different legislatures take different views of right and wrong; different taintchains are the inevitable result. The machinery of international law – MLATs, dual-criminality checks for extradition warrants, evidence rules – may eventually find its expression in protocols and in chain analysis code.

Let us ignore issues of jurisdiction for the time being, and consider two possible ways forward. First, what might happen under optimal but light-touch regulation? And second, might private law get us there instead – in other words, if the victims of bitcoin crime were to sue to get their assets back, then might decisions in the courts get us to roughly the same place?

4.1 Protocol Research Problems

Suppose the government simply declares that people who purchase bitcoin in good faith from regulated exchanges following established AML and KYC rules will get good title, and that the exchanges must refund theft victims.

Thus when someone pays in a bitcoin amount, of which (say) 8.4% has been reported stolen, the exchange will seize that portion of the deposited amount and apply due process to return either the actual coins or their value to the rightful owners.

There are many technical protocol aspects to explore. Can we support protocols that will let an exchange customer check whether a bitcoin payment will be accepted, or whether some of it will be confiscated as crime proceeds? If an identified customer says 'Hi, what will you give me for UTXO x?' and the exchange replies, 'Sorry, 22% of that was stolen in a robbery last Tuesday, so we'll only give you 78%' does the customer then have to turn over the crime proceeds? We'd presume so. (The exchange has her passport and utility bills on file, after all.)

If someone invented a protocol to check value in zero knowledge, they might be prosecuted for obstruction of justice. Even if not, the exchanges would be as leery of that as the credit card companies are at present of small transactions which might be used by thieves to check whether a card's been reported stolen yet. In fact, the difficulty of doing pre-purchase coin checking is a strong argument for a public taintchain.

Then there are issues familiar to the protocol community, of revocation and freshness. Suppose Alice checks a UTXO against the taintchain, sees that it's OK, and then transfers it to an exchange in good faith in order to cash it for dollars. Meanwhile the victim of a bitcoin robbery reports some of it stolen, and by the time Alice's transaction is mined into the blockchain, it's tainted. Or perhaps the miners refuse to touch it as they don't want tainted mining fees. How do you sort out the mess? What combination of technical measures, social norms and legal rules might put us in a sweet spot? Presumably the exchanges will have to pick up some of the tab, as banks do at present, but what rules might work and what protocols might support them?

This is actually an old problem. Under the common-law statute of limitations, I can sue for negligence for up to seven years, and there is no limit in England for return of stolen goods. Under the old system for cheque clearing, I might be able to claw back funds for a few days to weeks. Under the EU Payment Services Directive, payments become irrevocable after 48 h, and customer complaints must be made within 13 months. The disparity of rules indicates a role for the lawgiver in clarifying grace periods for cryptocurrencies. Clearly law enforcement will lobby for a long period while the exchanges will lobby for a short one.

Further rules need to be explored. Where we can identify clearly conspiratorial behaviour, such as a mix, the whole of the output may be strongly considered tainted, at least in the case of bitcoin being money – where the requirement for good title is to transact 'in good faith'. Curiously, making cryptocurrencies into money would make anonymity harder, at least insofar as it's provided by detectable technical mechanisms. Cryptocurrencies such as Monero and Zcash might forever be incapable of being treated as money, because of their built-in laundromats. There, a default assumption of bad faith seems prudent.

4.2 So What Might Governments Do?

Up till now, cryptocurrency promoters have campaigned for monetary status (often under the slogan of 'fungibility') while governments have largely dragged their heels, no doubt fearing that control would be completely lost, and that the tracing and recovery of crime proceeds would become even harder. We hope we've shown that it's not that simple.

One possible way forward would be the creation of a 'nemo dat exception' for regulated bitcoin exchanges, with a suitable notice period, and more detailed provisions for the extent to which crime victims might be made good beyond that. We propose that exchanges should also maintain a reserve proportional to their trading activities, as banks do, so that they can continue to make victims good even when there are spikes of claims.

An alternative approach might be private-sector title insurance; once we have a good public taintchain, a bitcoin exchange or a bank might simply guarantee title to any bitcoin it sells, and publish its wallet addresses so that the tracking can stop and start there.

A useful starting point for negotiation between governments and exchange operators, or just for incremental policy development, might be the EU's second Payment Services Directive, which encapsulates Europe's experience to date in dealing with consumer-facing payment systems. Just as Uber was brought to heel by mayors saying 'We don't care if you claim to be a platform, whatever that is; you're a taxi company, and you'll get a license or we'll run you out of town', so a sound opening gambit would be to start enforcing the law as it stands.

For any of this to be feasible, a public taintchain may be the key. En route, there are many interesting protocol problems to tackle.

5 Conclusions

The bitcoin protocol is fascinating. It has created what appears to be a global trusted computer out of a mixture of cryptography and incentives, despite the facts that many of the actors are shady and many of the circulating cryptocoins have been stolen at least once.

Out of this swamp, the value of bitcoins has soared to peaks that few would have predicted two years ago. The demand is now largely for investment rather than transactions; so now may be the time to clean up bitcoin. How can we start?

Tracking stolen coins, so that crime victims can sue to get their property back, is the key. Up to now, people have been using haircut tainting to track stolen bitcoin. We've shown that's wrong, as a matter of both law and engineering. The law says you should use FIFO, and when you do so, the engineering works way better. It's much more precise, and is also reversible: in addition to tracing forward from a stolen bitcoin to see where it went, you can trace backwards from any UTXO and get its entire genealogy. In short, FIFO tracking is a powerful new analytic tool.

The way is now clear for financial regulators to apply the existing law on stolen property and on payment services to bitcoin exchanges.

The thought experiment in this paper illustrates a deeper fact. A protocol's security properties can depend in very subtle ways on context. There is some precedent for this; for example, the bug in shared-secret Needham-Schroeder became apparent once people started to consider insider threats.

The contextual change needed for bitcoin is really just a matter of clarity. The taint information is right there in the blockchain, and in the public theft reports; but combining the two so as to work out the taint on even one single UTXO has involved a key conceptual insight (FIFO) and some engineering effort. The output it a public taintchain that makes stolen coins visible to all. Then a test case, or regulation, might create a soft fork between good coins and bad. And as investment demand trumps transaction demand, good coins might drive out bad ones; and miners might also avoid bad ones as they won't want tainted transaction fees.

Honest users of bitcoin would then buy them from regulated exchanges, and pay them in again directly. Bitcoin would still support peer-to-peer payments, and would not in any engineering sense be 'centralised' or otherwise changed[3]. But most users would start to use bitcoin rather like they use other electronic money, which passes from the bank to the customer to the merchant and back to the bank.

In short, we might be able to turn a rather dangerous system into a much safer one – simply by taking some information that is already public (the blockchain) and publishing it in a more accessible format (the taintchain). Is that not remarkable?

Acknowledgments. We acknowledge helpful discussions with David Fox, Shehar Bano, Tyler Moore, Nicolas Christin, Rainer Böhme, Johann Bezuidenhoudt, Lawrence Esswood, Joe Bonneau and various attendees at Financial Cryptography 2018 where we presented some of the ideas here at a rump session talk.

References

1. Bonneau, J., Clark, J., Narayanan, A., Kroll, J., Felten, E.: Sok: research perspectives and challenges for Bitcoin and cryptocurrencies. In: IEEE S&P 2015 (2015)
2. Cheng, E.: US government misses out on $600 million payday by selling dirty Bitcoins too early. CNBC, 3 October 2017
3. Devaynes v Noble. 35 ER 767, 781 (1816)
4. Financial Crimes Enforcement Network: Application of FinCEN's Regulations to Persons Administering, Exchanging, or Using Virtual Currencies (2013)
5. Fox, D.: Property Rights in Money. Oxford University Press, Oxford (2008)
6. Fox, D.: Cyber-Currencies in Private Law. University of Edinburgh, Edinburgh (2016)
7. Hardy, P.: Failure to register with FINCEN sustains guilty please by virtual currency exchangers. Money Laundering Watch, 24 April 2017
8. Higgins, S.: US Marshals Service to Auction Off $54 Million in Bitcoin. Coindesk, 11 January 2018
9. Hudak, S.: FinCEN Fines BTC-e Virtual Currency Exchange $110 Million for Facilitating Ransomware, Dark Net Drug Sales (2017)
10. Kim, C., Yang, H.: Uproar over crackdown on cryptocurrencies divides South Korea. Reuters, 12 January 2018
11. Lee, T.: A brief history of Bitcoin hacks and frauds. Ars Technica, 12 May 2017
12. Meiklejohn, S., et al.: A fistful of Bitcoins: characterising payments among men with no names. In: IMC 2013 (2013)

[3] The maintenance of the taintchain could and should be open, which in itself gives rise to interesting questions of governance, which will lead to protocol design questions too.

13. Möser, M., Böhme, R., Breuker, D.: Towards Risk Scoring of Bitcoin Transactions. Financial Cryptography (2014)
14. Möser, M., Böhme, R., Breuker, D.: An inquiry into money laundering tools in the Bitcoin ecosystem. In: IEEE, eCrime (2013)
15. Narayanan, A., Bonneau, J., Felten, E., Miller, A., Goldfeder, S.: Bitcoin and Cryptocurrency Technologies. Princeton University, Princeton (2016)
16. Popper, N.: Bitcoin Thieves Threaten Real Violence for Virtual Currencies. New York Times, 18 February 2018

Making Bitcoin Legal (Transcript of Discussion)

Ross Anderson(✉)

Cambridge, UK
Ross.Anderson@cl.cam.ac.uk

Ian Goldberg: So if I'm understanding: if you have a transaction, it has multiple inputs and possibly multiple outputs?

Reply: Correct.

Ian Goldberg: So, what is first? Like the order of the inputs and the order of the outputs in the transactions are irrelevant?

Reply: No, they are not irrelevant. They are absolutely relevant. You read through the transaction from the first byte to the last byte, and you apply the FIFO rule like a robot.

Ian Goldberg: Okay. You are imposing a semantics on the order of the transaction?

Reply: Yes, I take the bitcoin as being the definitive record for these purposes, although not for other purposes, as we'll discuss later. It doesn't actually matter what rule you take provided it's a deterministic rule that applies to everybody, and the canonical one is the canonical ones we take by definition. Frank?

Frank Stajano: A couple of slides back you said: the person has three stolen bitcoins and seven newly minted-

Reply: -and *then* seven newly minted bitcoin-

Frank Stajano: Right? Then you said with the haircut, this would count as 30% stolen, and that's the problem. What was the problem exactly? That sounds exactly right.

Reply: That is the definition of haircut tainting. I'm now presenting FIFO tainting, which is different from haircut tainting. In FIFO tainting, if you've got three stolen, followed by seven good, then the first three bitcoin you spend, the first 300 million satoshis are all completely stolen, 100% stolen, and then the next seven bitcoin are 100% good. The taint doesn't diffuse. Every single satoshi is treated as an indivisible quantum.

Frank Stajano: So with the haircut, all of your bitcoins would have been 30% stolen-

Reply: Correct. And I'll explain, but first of all, let's look at the gross output here, and the gross output is that if you look at, for example, the Linode heist in

V. Matyáš et al. (Eds.): Security Protocols 2018, LNCS 11286, pp. 254–265, 2018.
https://doi.org/10.1007/978-3-030-03251-7_30

2012 with haircut taint you end up tainting over two and a half million addresses, whereas with FIFO you taint only 300-odd thousand, so that's over four years you've still got an order of magnitude increase in precision, using FIFO tainting. And over a two year period, flexcoin from 2013 – where almost 1,000 are stolen – you taint one and a half million by 2016 but FIFO goes gives you only the 18K, so that's almost two orders of magnitude increase in precision. Okay? Here at least is an interesting tool.

Now, what other properties does it have, and I think one of the key properties is that FIFO tainting is lossless. Haircut is lossy, very lossy, and when you start implementing the details of what happens with transaction fees – remember whenever you mine a block you might have a couple of thousand transactions, each of which has got a transaction fee, which is what's leftover, as a bid to the miners to include it. If you're doing haircut tainting, you're going to have to do a haircut across these and average the taint across all the transaction fees.

Once you start looking at details like this it becomes obvious that FIFO's the way to do it, because only with FIFO can you actually go backwards. You see, with haircut and poison all you can do is go from a stolen coin forward to the present. So whenever you've got a new coin theft being reported, you've got to stop and do an overnight batch processing run to update your taint index. Whereas if you're using FIFO tracking, you can look at any individual UTXO and you can go back and see its entire ancestry.

Fabio Massacci: So what happens if the outgoing and incoming number of coins are not divisible by one another? You will have X percentage tainted coin?

Reply: Well, typically what happens is that the outgoing amount of bitcoin is less than the incoming amount of bitcoin, and the difference is the transaction fee. That's defined in the software. Anything that's left over goes to the miners, and that's how you bid for the miners' time and attention.

Fabio Massacci: It's called the mining fee, sorry?

Reply: Bitcoin are conserved, because any bitcoin that's not accounted for in the output-

Fabio Massacci: If you have three in and four out and the two numbers are not divisible –

Reply: That's got nothing to do with anything. The number of satoshis in, and the number of satoshis out, they're exactly the same by definition.

Fabio Massacci: No, I'm talking of the tainted part.

Reply: The number of tainted satoshis going in and the number of tainted satoshis going out are exactly equal under FIFO via construction.

Fabio Massacci: Then, will you taint also the miner's fee or?

Reply: We taint the miner's fee if and only if the satoshis that go into the miner's fee were tainted on input.

Fabio Massacci: Okay.

Reply: This is really important. In fact, dealing with the mining fee is the fiddly bit of the cord. That's what has been keeping Ilia up evenings and weekends, getting it to work. Once you have cracked that we believe you have cracked the problem. That's the operationally and conceptually difficult part of it. Once you've got it running, you can run.

So the interesting thing for this workshop is what are all the effects of FIFO. Because basically we say that people who have been thinking about taint tracking have been using the wrong algorithms: they've been wrong in law, and the algorithms that they use are lossy, and difficult to deal with for that reason. And as a result, when people try and do tracking of stolen bitcoins, they bring in all sorts of AI and ML, and that's very fashionable, and people tend to believe anything that says "AI/ML" is good, but of course, when you actually go and buy due diligence reports on some target transactions, you find very, very variable results. We found, for example, going to one of the due diligence companies, that we asked for a report on the publicly known address of sheepmarketplace, and they said, "Hey, that's fine."

So what's going on in the companies who sell due diligence is as far as we can see snake oil, and we will have a later paper this year where we will have a systematic analysis of this. So what can be done about this?

Peter Roenne: Have you looked into what happens in other countries? What is the state of the law there?

Reply: We've spoken to one or two people, and we'll be continuing. Former Commonwealth countries appear to follow the FIFO rule, and I'm going to Paris on Thursday to speak to a bunch of lawyers over there.

Peter Roenne: Just to follow, under which law do you ...

Reply: We'll discuss this at length in a later paper this summer. The purpose of this talk is to talk about the protocols aspect.

David Llewellyn-Jones: Do you keep track if they get stolen twice?

Reply: Yes. That is an interesting issue, because ... This slide comes to it. Basically the answer is that the FBI should then give back the coins to the person from whom it was stolen first, because the person from whom it was stolen second never owned it, and has no property rights whatsoever in it, and they're jolly lucky if they don't get sent to jail for receiving stolen goods.

So yes, that is something we've thought about. Now, the big principle here according to the laws is a Roman principal, 'nemo dat quod non habet': nobody gives what they don't own. If Bob steals Alice's horse, and sells it to Charlie, then whenever she sees him riding it she can demand it back. It's as simple as that. Now, there are one or two exceptions to the nemo dt rule, and they're, until 1995 there was an exception in England called the markets overt, thanks to King Edward the First of Blessed Memory. That said that if you sold stolen goods in a public market between dawn and dusk, then the buyer got good title.

In this case, if Bob has sold Alice's horse in Cambridge market, then Charlie would own the horse, and Alice could then get Bob hanged or sent to Virginia, or whatever.

But that rule was abolished in 1995 after abuse by bent antique dealers. The situation in Britain now is that there's no statute of limitations for theft, and so long as bitcoin are just a commodity – which is the current position – a stolen bitcoin stays stolen forever. You can't have it unstolen, except possibly in one or two weird edge cases where a court gives an order. For example, if the owner of it died, and his will went through probate, there is an argument that the heirs now own the bitcoin, but that, again, is something that people would argue, and it's not something that scales to general relevance.

Sp what's happening in practise is that the bitcoin folks are relying on the difficulty of tracing, and they said that their policy goal is fungibility, that is that no bitcoin should be differentiable legally from any other.

Frank Stajano: Ross, when you said, "A stolen coin can never be unstolen" you mean even if the FBI gives it back to Alice?

Reply: If the FBI gives it back to Alice then that's correct, then it has been returned to its rightful owner, but you can't cause a stolen property to lose its stolen status by any other means than giving it back to its rightful owner, or by having some kind of court order which says, for example, that the rightful owner wasn't the rightful owner.

Another edge case is what happens if it's confiscated as proceeds of drug crime, and the FBI then auctions it, and there are all sorts of possibilities here for a conflict of laws. If an American Sheriff declares your bitcoin to be drugs proceeds and auctions it, but a British court says that it actually belongs to Fabio, then you get into the whole morass of international legal disputes. Again, this is something we'll discuss in greater detail in a future paper.

Ian Goldberg: Yeah. I'm still stuck a little bit on the semantic issue. Bitcoin wallets today output a transaction worth the input and the outputs, sometimes in an intentionally random order – or in numerical order by just like lexicographic order – so as to hide which is the change output and which is the payment output, for example. And I think many of these either authors or users of bitcoin wallets would be surprised to learn that the random order that the wallet chose suddenly has major effects on whether the coins you hold are stolen or not stolen.

Reply: Exactly so, and I'm going to press on because I'm going to come to this later.

Ian Goldberg: All right, great. Thanks.

Reply: The market overt loophole was closed over 20 years ago, but what if bitcoin becomes money? Well, there are two exceptions. You can get good title to a 10 pound note that was stolen in a robbery last year if you get it in good faith for value, in other words, if you get it in change from John Lewis if you buy a microwave oven for 40 quid and get this 10 pound note in change, the 10 pound note is yours. If you got it from a regulated back, so if you got it from an ATM in the street, then it's yours and the fact that it was stolen last year is now the bank's problem.

So, the bitcoin folks push for bitcoin to become money, and would this help them? Well, in this case it wouldn't, because of the good faith clause. I believe I have that on the next slide: if you've got a bitcoin mix, or laundry, then first of all, if you've got the kind of laundry where you put one black bitcoin in a bag with nine white bitcoins, and you shake them up, and each of the bitcoin owners pulls one out at random, then once you've got FIFO taint, game theory says nobody who owns a white coin will ever do that ever again, and if they do, that's tough, and that's part of the answer to Ian's question. The order in which these things appear in the blockchain is absolutely determinative of stolen status or not, and if you intended otherwise then you're a wicked person for trying to launder money, and serve you right. Okay? Don't do that again. You were silly, right?

Now, what about things like coinjoin and satoshi dice, and so on, where you chop and change lots of transactions? What then happens is that you get the good faith condition killing off there as well, because you've got tangible evidence of the laundry, because when you trace the tainting through, then the output bitcoins look a bit like puff pastry, you know, with some white here and a bit of black, and some white here, and a bit of black, and so on. That's completely obvious.

So you have got the visible evidence of the efforts to obstruct justice – pardon me, to provide financial privacy – are absolutely there in plain sight. The takeaway model here, which is the first big protocol point, is that the people who have been doing research on what they call financial privacy, or transaction anonymity, have been using entirely the wrong threat model. If you believe that FIFO tainting is what the law demands, and if you play with our software and see how it works, then you will fairly quickly see that attempts to provide mixes basically don't work.

And at a macro scale, they also don't work, go read Sarah Meiklejohn's paper. She went and tested a number of laundries, a number of them simply stole her money. Others turned out to be fat wallets with the property that you pay in bitcoin, and it would pay you back .95 bitcoins two days later. It was a very nice business model. But again, this fails the FIFO tainting, because that Mafia-owned wallet will have some white stuff in it, and some black stuff in it, and you may be unlucky and get black stuff out. You're entirely trusting the Mafia on that point, so good luck.

There's a piece of research here: going through all the various bitcoin, laundry techniques and looking how they fare with the FIFO tainting and with other approaches.

Virgil Gligor: I don't quite understand the wrong model question, because basically we know that anonymity and traceability are in conflict from the start, it doesn't have to be in this area. So something's either traceable or it's anonymous, but you can't have both.

Reply: Well, exactly.

Virgil Gligor: Which one is the wrong model?

Reply: Well, exactly. Go and read the papers that people have written about providing privacy overlays for bitcoin, and criticise them. Set that as an exercise for students.

Virgil Gligor: Well I think that we have conflicting requirements, and if they are conflicting requirements, they'll always be conflicting.

Reply: Well, I would suggest that in some sense these are nonsensical requirements!

Virgil Gligor: That's true-

Reply: And some of the more recent forms of cryptocurrency have kind of acknowledged that. So in Z cash for example, if you want to properly launder a coin you give it back to the miners and they re-mine it in this round so that you get out money that's indistinguishable cryptographically from all the other coins mined this round. But if I were the FBI, with my FIFO-tracking software, and I were looking at this, I would simply say that, "Well, a stolen coin was mined at block X into Zcash, so all the coins mined at that round are now contraband," and I would simply contact the regulated exchanges, saying, "Don't touch any of the following coins on Zcash."

Then, if Z cash does persuade all its users to start mining all the stuff in at every round, then the whole thing becomes a money laundering scheme, and I blacklist it. That's the logical outcome of what happens if you've got a really good money laundering scheme, which becomes mandatory on all users, the logic is that you ban that entire coin. You simply tell regulated exchanges not to touch it.

Virgil Gligor: Basically you prefer traceability to anonymity here?

Reply: Well, that's a policy decision.

Virgil Gligor: Right.

Reply: Let's get on to the next protocol point. Suppose bitcoin becomes money, or the bitcoin lobbyists manage to say that a regulated exchange will give good title, then the next thing that happens is that the customers are going to want its addresses to be made public. This is something mentioned in the previous talk.

But the problem is the exchanges aren't going to like this because then theft victims can sue the exchange easily, and remember it's not just thefts now. It's robberies, you know? The crime du jour, now that bitcoin's worth so much money, is somebody comes to your house, sticks a revolver up your nostril, and gets you to transfer all your bitcoin to him. Assuming that he doesn't just shoot you on the way out, you can then get our software and you can trace where the bitcoin have gone, and then what you want to do is to turn these addresses into physical addresses, so that you can go around with legal paperwork, and seize your coins back.

The exchanges aren't going to want to do this. There's all sorts of firms who employ people who make small transactions to and from exchanges, and then they're clustering, so that they can figure out which addresses belong to which exchanges. Right? So what happens here?

Well the fix we believe to this tension is that you just publish a list of all the stolen coins. And that's what we're proposing to do. Because once we put our software, public domain, then anybody can run it on the blockchain and go away for a day, and come back, and then they've got a list of which coins are stolen and which aren't. Once you've got a public list of which coins are stolen, then of course you cannot give value for those stolen coins in good faith.

That's the interesting thing, because all of a sudden you see we're not creating any more public information here. We're just making public something that's already public, but we're making it public in a way that's visible, actionable, and usable. That, we believe, changes everything. That's one of the really interesting points from the point of view of the context of this workshop. How do you change the effect of a protocol by context?

Frank Stajano: Your tainting in the FIFO style needs to start from the first thing that says, a coin was stolen. Which authority says that coin was stolen, the police?

Reply: Well, there's 132 published heists that we worked forward from. There is a separate conversation about the process for reporting a coin stolen. Clearly, any individual can claim, "I was robbed. The UTXO sold was such and such, and here is a taint that I've computed forward from it." They can put up a wanted poster, or whatever. They can go to a court. They can get an order. They can serve the order on every licensed bitcoin exchange in the world. There is work to be done on figuring out what legal mechanisms might be used too.

Frank Stajano: Who's going to check that the wicked person like me isn't first buying something from you for bitcoins, and then reporting the bitcoins stolen?

Reply: Well, this is further work for a later paper. There's already some writing on it, albeit in German, by Rainer Böhme, who's got a bitcoin project in Innsbruck, where they've been thinking about having a public taintchain of publicly reported stuff, and of thefts that have been decided by a judge, and then a private taint chain which is owned by the prosecutor, which are those thefts that have been reported but have not yet gone to court.

But there are issues with this. We think the simplest thing is just that, if your horse is stolen, you put up a notice in the market square saying, "Wanted, horse. Here's a picture." Right?

Frank Stajano: Yeah.

Reply: Otherwise, you would end up with tens of thousands of prosecuting authorities worldwide, each having their own taintchain, and somebody who wanted to check their coins before spending them would have to do some kind of zero knowledge proof with 40,000 different people before they could do it.

Frank Stajano: The wanted poster is the same as that?

Bruce Christianson: What's to stop Frank from putting up a picture of a horse he doesn't own?

Reply: What's to stop DDoS attacks?

Bruce Christianson: Yes.

Reply: Well, my own gut reaction to that is if you want me to put the stuff in the taint chain, I want to see a crime number. I want to see you having gone into a police station with your physical, arrestable, body, having put your passport on the counter, sworn a statement, and that if the statement turns out to be untrue, the police can go and grab your body, and throw it in jail for perjury like Lord Archer, and serve you right. Is that a sufficient block against sybil attacks?

Virgil Gligor: Not clear.

Reply: That is for later discussion.

Frank Stajano: You realise someone going through these things, and checking the veracity, and then going to the police – this guy, should he actually show a passport?

Reply: Okay, I'm going to make progress at this point because here's the regulatory background. Since 2013 the US Department of Treasury's Financial Crimes Enforcement Network has insisted that bitcoin exchanges register as money service businesses, and last year they went around and busted a whole bunch of people who hadn't complied, and now even in places like the Philippines, you have to show your passport and utility bills to buy bitcoins.

This January, the European Union announced that it was planning to regulate wallet hosting service providers too, and given that most bitcoins are held in hosted environments now, this means that you can do stolen coin tracking for the great majority of bitcoin holders, making spending of reported stolen bitcoins in the future very, very difficult. Then the next question that we go through is why not just enforce payment services directly from the regulated exchanges and force people to provide a helpline, and arbitrate queries, and deal with customer complaints, and have financial reserves to make good people whose stuff was stolen and couldn't be caught because it went out to a Russian exchange or whatever ...

So there are regulatory questions here, and this brings us to the discussion questions. First, Patrick was saying, "Do you want miners to act as enforcement?" Then you said no. Patrick I take a different view. I say I do want miners to act as enforcement people, because I want them to start avoiding stolen coins. If I'm a miner, I do not want my mining fees to include tainted input, because the outputs will then also be tainted. So can we provide a system that's big enough and scalable enough that the miners can stop and check each of the input coins to a transaction before they take it from the mempool and start mining it into the blockchain?

That means that you've got to pre-compute, you've got to basically have a lookup table that people can look at. You can't even have an online service. Okay? You don't want 12 different mining pools, each doing 10 queries per second of your taintchain.org or whatever, because that's just going to melt the front end. There's some interesting engineering questions here, but if you can persuade miners to start avoiding stolen coins, then that gives you an interesting enforcement mechanism.

Second, is there no room whatsoever for bitcoin privacy protocols, or can you only use bitcoin privacy protocols, which are covert, which are low-observable, which look like normal transactions? Even if you believe it's ethical to do that, is it even possible to design them? In other words, the target for the anonymity engineer is a very much more difficult target than had been suspected.

Patrick was talking about auditing on withdrawal. Clearly you have to audit on deposit as well.

Daniel Weitzner: So, listening to this, it all sounds quite plausible, and it sounds like the right way to address the legal environment that people are used to, but what really strikes me is that the miners are getting away with murder here, because –

Reply: Yup.

Daniel Weitzner: – we've ... What you've done is, this continues to internalise the cost of the security checking, the integrity checking on the blockchain, but it spreads to the rest of society the cost for dealing with theft. I think it seems to me if you really follow this all through, what you've got is you created just another payment system that isn't necessarily distinguishable that much from other kind of payment systems that we're used to, and doesn't have what I think is the interesting property of a lot of these cryptocurrencies, which is to decentralise by distributing costs.

Reply: Bitcoin isn't decentralised. There's a small number of large mining cartels that run the whole thing and most of them are based in China, so President Xi could just turn around one day and say, "A wicked person mined a contribution to the Dali Lama 20 blocks ago. Undo it now." People would say, "Yes, sir," and they would go back and they would just use brute force to mine the chain forward. And all of a sudden then nobody could rely on simply waiting for six blocks before thinking something was final. So you don't have distribution at present.

Daniel Weitzner: I would agree with that point as well. What I think is just notable here is that you have made much more transparent the cost of actually having a trustworthy system, but it's not obvious to me how those costs are going to be borne.

We were talking last night about the fact that no police force here will deal with financial fraud under what was your number, a million pounds? 10 million? I don't know, whatever the number was, so to me this just illuminates the challenge of making this a real payment system.

Reply: Well, a lot of it will come down to operational details. Now, where you've got a coinbase transaction, that is where the miners got a couple of thousand mining fees plus his 12 and a half, or whatever it is, bitcoin mining reward, how's that going to be dealt with by regulated exchanges? If the miners aren't bloody careful, then every coinbase transaction's going to be tainted, okay?

Daniel Weitzner: Yeah.

Reply: Figure it out, because a quarter of addresses are tainted, so what's the odds that if you've got 2,000 mining fees the entire thing is white as the driven snow? Basically zero. If the regulated exchanges basically put tainted transactions into some kind of warm storage, and then run a number of transactions to undo the tainted bits and return them to the lawful owners, then it will become an absolutely royal pain for the miners to cash in on their transaction fees. So then the incentive is on the miners, right, to run the taint chain.

Daniel Weitzner: Yeah.

Reply: This is all down to the effect of the first court cases that are brought around and about this against exchanges, and what the FinCEN guys do in terms of telling regulated exchanges to hand back stolen bitcoin.

Another thing there, I put down in the list of things to think about, is providing evidence of bitcoin theft. This is something that Frank was raising earlier. How do you prove that your bitcoins were stolen? Now, I don't think that this amenable to a cryptologic solution, because if somebody is sufficiently farsighted to know that next Wednesday a guy's going to come and put a revolver up your nostril, and demand your bitcoins, then you just won't be there, or you will have done a multisig wallet, or something like that.

So I don't think that you can build in technical mechanisms to report theft automatically when it happens. You're going to have to rely on input from the real world, that is from people walking into Parkside nick and making a crime report in person. That's about admin, that's about dealing with how costs scale, that's about legal precedent. But there may be certain technical things that can be done to facilitate that, and that's perhaps an interesting field of protocol research.

And finally, we've been hearing how protocols change with context through a number of talks at this workshop. The thing that struck us about this is that once you realise that bitcoin tracking on the blockchain is relatively easy, and deterministic, and once you've got software that does it, isn't it amazing how bitcoin changes? Because all we're doing is making public information, public.

It's like the arrival of search engines. It's something that actually changes the world.

Patrick McCorry: Just two points I'd like to make. So this idea that things sort of emerged in 2013 with Mike Hearn, and he was really pushing for this. One issue is that if I receive a bitcoin, I have no guarantee it won't be tainted in the future. So I have no incentive to ever receive bitcoin, because if it gets tainted in two hours' time I can't use it any more.

Reply: Yeah, well in that case you just shouldn't ever hold bitcoin. Now, we will be discussing this in a later paper, but this is one of the reasons that you expect bitcoin exchanges to have reserves. So if you go to Coinbase, and you say, "I've got the following UTXO, will you give me so much for it?" and they say, "Yes," and at that time it's mined into the blockchain it's been reported stolen – then is that your tough luck or is that Coinbase's tough luck? That's down to the regulator.

If there was a deal which says that regulated bitcoin exchanges must provide consumer protection, then in a case like that you might expect that Coinbase would take it on the chin – unless they can show that you were collusive. That again, is an entire area of jurisprudence and operational practise that still has to be developed.

Patrick McCorry: Okay, then my second point's to do with the miners. You should have alluded to it as well, where most of the mining pools are in China in the moment. I mean, in 2015, there's a really famous photo of a panel session of eight miners, and they represent like 87% of the hash rate. The problem of the miners having this extra power to order the transactions, is that China can effectively centre any transactions they want. I mean, they could do this for the past eight years and they just haven't done it yet, which is a bit strange.

So one area of research that people are pursuing now is getting transactions in the block chain before miners can validate it, as in we should have commit and reveal. You commit that this transaction's going to happen, and the miners shouldn't get to see what happens there, and then you reveal it and it gets confirmed, and that's sort of line a submarine transaction. Now people are trying to remove this power from miners.

Reply: Well, if I was a miner I'd be dead scared of that, because if somebody commits to something that's forbidden in China, picture of the Dalai Lama or whatever, and then reveals it, and then all of a sudden you can't mine bitcoin anymore, and you've got to get all your mining equipment on to lorries, and take it to Russia, and sell it to somebody. Well hey, that's not an acceptable outcome, is it?

Patrick McCorry: Yeah. Well that's sort of to do with the distributed nature. In the ideal world, the Chinese miners should not be have the influence to stop other miners doing that, so then they either go along with the flow or they get removed from the network.

Reply: No. Hang on, in an ideal world they'll be proper governance mechanisms, because whereas a society we build mechanisms to arbitrate human effort, we build machines with multiple wheels that turn at different speeds. We not only have the policemen out there able to arrest people, you have got the deep statute law providing the backdrop behind that, you've got courts which can alter that by means of precedent when need be, you've got constitutions, you've got mechanisms that change constitutions, which typically take a long time, perhaps a plebiscite. But you don't just throw something into the public domain and say, "This is an immutable, infernal machine that will run forever, and if it runs you over that's your tough luck because we're making lots of money from it." That's not an acceptable way of building systems.

If the result of this work is that bitcoin becomes no longer fungible, and so bitcoin falls out of fashion, well then that's an acceptable outcome, isn't it?

Patrick McCorry: Yeah, well I don't think bitcoin's fungible at all. I mean, obviously it's not fungible because you can taint everything. That's more of a way you exit. If you are in China and you want to have your money outside China, it's a way to exit. I mean, that's the main selling point for all these cryptocurrencies.

Reply: Well, exactly. Bitcoin first took off as a means of trading drugs on Silk Road, and then it become a vehicle for ransomware, and the current bull run started when China tightened its exchange controls. Now, we may not care about that since Britain has no exchange controls, and so exchange control offences aren't offences here. But you know, how many more offences are going to be facilitated in one country or another by cryptocurrencies before they're brought under control?

If you're not prepared to just go nuclear and say that cryptocurrencies are a strict liability offence everywhere like child porn, then how can you use existing laws to bring the thing under control? If that has a side effect of making certain types of cryptocurrency, such as perhaps Monero and perhaps Z Cash into contraband, well so be it. The potential upside from this is that if you can regulate this so that theft becomes unattractive, and becomes capable of being dealt with, then what you get left with is perhaps, Ethereum, a cleaned up Ethereum as a platform for smart contracts.

You remember at Financial Crypto, the keynote that we had there about the chap from JP Morgan, saying that they were, their future bet was an enterprise Ethereum, where they use it as a smart contract platform, and they would not let any unidentified individual be a player in that ecosystem ever.

Patrick McCorry: Yeah.

Reply: Only if you're a regulated bank could you play in that space. Now, is there some way in which you can make smart contract platforms that are available to the public rather than just closed ecosystems? If you're going to do that, then you're going to deal with the regulatory issues. That means if you have to do the kind of stuff that involves tracing stolen coins. You have to do the kind of stuff that you find in the Payment Services Directive too. How do you make crime victims good? How do you find the bad guys, and all the rest of it.

Virgil Gligor: You reinvent the current financial system?

Reply: Yup.

On the Incommensurability of Laws and Technical Mechanisms: Or, What Cryptography Can't Do

Joan Feigenbaum[1(✉)] and Daniel J. Weitzner[2]

[1] Computer Science Department, Yale University, New Haven, CT 06520, USA
joan.feigenbaum@yale.edu

[2] Internet Policy Research Initiative, Massachusetts Institute of Technology, Cambridge, MA 02139, USA
weitzner@mit.edu

Abstract. We examine several technology-policy debates in which technical and legal perspectives are so at odds that they approach incommensurability. Investigating the use of digital rights management systems in the online-copyright debate and the dispute over the impact of end-to-end encryption on lawful surveillance, we offer an analysis of the source of this incommensurability. In these two policy debates, both sides invoke the rule of law to support their position, but in each case they draw selectively from the constituent parts of the rule of law, resulting in seemingly irreconcilable differences. We show that the rule of law is actually composed of rules (susceptible to deterministic evaluation against a set of facts) and principles (expressing important values but not susceptible to purely formal evaluation). The clash between rules and principles exacerbates the difference in perspective between system designers, who favor formal rules, and policy makers, who are more comfortable with situational application of principles. Following our observation that the rules-principles gap makes for incommensurate debate between legal and technical actors, we identify steps that each discipline can take to move toward more coherent policy for the networked, digital environment.

1 Introduction

With the rise of the Internet and other globally deployed technical infrastructures, we have seen frequent clashes between claims of legal and policy experts about how technical systems ought to behave and claims of architects and engineers of technical systems about what type of system behavior is both possible and desirable. At the root of these disputes, one often finds incommensurate views about what it would mean for a system to "work," *i.e.*, to actually "solve" a real-world problem. Generally speaking, a technical system is judged to have succeeded if it provides a *fully specified, correct solution* to a *well defined and well understood problem* and is *implemented and maintained according to sound engineering practice*. By contrast, legal regimes are judged according to very different standards. A proposed law or regulatory framework is judged successful if

V. Matyáš et al. (Eds.): Security Protocols 2018, LNCS 11286, pp. 266–279, 2018.
https://doi.org/10.1007/978-3-030-03251-7_31

its constituent rules are *proper expressions of the society's values* and have the necessary *indicia of legitimacy.*

In this paper, we examine this design incommensurability in the context of the socio-technical debate about encryption and surveillance. Our goal is to arrive at legal and technical design principles that lead to the development of technology that complements applicable laws and promotes society's values. Here, we begin by presenting the criteria by which legal regimes are judged. We then briefly revisit another socio-technical domain in which the incommensurability of law and technology led to stalemate, *i.e.*, digital rights-management (DRM) systems. Finally, we offer two technical and legal design patterns and discuss their potential for moving the debate forward and achieving our long-term goal.

2 Related Work

Many cryptographers, computer-security researchers, law-enforcement officials, and others in both the legal world and the technical world have remarked upon the tension between law and technology in the area of surveillance. Much of the discussion focuses either on the technical aspects or on the legal and human-rights aspects of the issue. We take a cross-disciplinary approach by providing what is, to the best of our knowledge, the first *structural* jurisprudential explanation for this tension. We now briefly review the main positions that have been taken on the question of encryption and surveillance.

At one end of the spectrum is the view that the technical community is simply thwarting the lawful exercise of warrants and court orders authorized by statute and the relevant basic law: the Constitution in the case of the United States. Under this view, the tension is resolved by the fact that both individuals and organizations are obligated, under the All Writs Act [9] in the US and similar laws in other democratic countries, to provide necessary assistance to government agencies in the execution of warrants and, more generally, in "the proper administration of justice." Hennessey and Wittes [8] give good explanations of both the All Writs Act and this general view of the tension between law and technology. A related position is given in detail by Rozenshtein [15], who explicitly rejects "technological unilateralism" of the type endorsed by crypto maximalists. Rozenshtein draws our attention to the technical and political centrality of *surveillance intermediaries* such Google, Facebook, and other large-scale Internet platforms.

Certainly the All Writs Act obligates individuals and organizations to assist the government in the administration of justice; however, because the scope of assistance subject to mandate under the Act is far from settled, it does not fully resolve the tension between lawful surveillance and end-to-end encryption as a legal matter. In the FBI vs. Apple case [9], for example, Apple's claim that complying with the US government's order to develop the software needed to unlock a dead terrorist's iPhone represented an "undue burden," that it put the security of Apple's operating-system software at risk for all Apple users, and that it violated Apple's First Amendment rights against compelled speech inasmuch as the Government sought to require Apple to write new software was vigorously debated and never resolved in court. Beyond the specific requirement proposed by the government in the case, Apple's concern that there may be unacceptable cybersecurity risks created by some proposed exceptional access requirements are well substantiated. Once a technical capability is built into a system, there is always a possibility that it will be misused. History demonstrates that this is not a hypothetical possibility; in the Vodafone Greece scandal [14], for example, a wiretapping capability mandated by United States law was used against Greek government officials. In summary, a general legal obligation to assist the government does not answer the question of what specific assistance is required in a given case, nor does it provide definitive guidance on the broader policy question about what obligations, if any, ought to be imposed on service providers with respect to encryption.

At the other end of the spectrum, there is the view that governments, including democratic ones, routinely violate privacy rights. Because privacy is a fundamental human right, the tech community is therefore morally obligated to build user-friendly strong encryption into as much of the computing and communications infrastructure as possible and *not* to build anything that facilitates governments' decrypting any user's data against that user's will. In response to the Snowden revelations, a large group of distinguished cryptographers and computer-security researchers wrote [2]:

> Indiscriminate collection, storage, and processing of unprecedented amounts of personal information chill free speech and invite many types of abuse, ranging from mission creep to identity theft. These are not hypothetical problems; they have occurred many times in the past. Inserting backdoors, sabotaging standards, and tapping commercial data-center links provide bad actors, foreign and domestic, opportunities to exploit the resulting vulnerabilities.

Schneier [10] adheres to this view, emphasizing that, since the 9–11 attacks, there has simply been far too much mass surveillance and that the only logical response is mass encryption. A more general theory of the morality of encryption is given by Rogaway [16]. Once again, we believe that, while there is a great deal of truth in this view of the situation, it does not satisfactorily resolve the question of how to accomplish *lawful* surveillance in a mass-encryption world. In response to government agencies' fear that perfectly legal surveillance, authorized by judicial warrants and viewed by most of the public as a legitimate tool in the fights against crime and terrorism, could become ineffective if most of what it yields is ciphertext for which decryption keys are unavailable, the proponents of ubiquitous encryption simply say "find other ways to get the data." Some point out that the warrants in question grant only the authority to intercept a communication or to seize a device; they don't guarantee that the sought-after information will be found in the communication stream or on the device – or that it can be decrypted if it is found in encrypted form.

None of this is to say that these commentators are anarchists or that they reject the rule of law. To the contrary they often invoke the rule of law as motivation for their views. They just seem to have lost confidence in the effectiveness of the legal system's ability to provide an adequate level of privacy protection.

Orthogonal to these two legal and policy claims is a set of technical arguments about the risks that mandated exceptional access poses to the global information and communications infrastructure used by billions of people around the planet. A number of proposals for exceptional-access systems create serious security risk. Once those exceptional-access mechanisms are installed for law enforcement, the private communications of all other users also become more vulnerable to attack by malicious criminals and terrorists. Exceptional access for law enforcement means storing the secret keys to communications and data around somewhere, possibly for months or years, to enable police to gain access when they need it. Such a design forces security technologists to backtrack on lessons learned over the years about how to design systems [1].

> Exceptional access would force Internet system developers to reverse forward secrecy design practices that seek to minimize the impact on user privacy when systems are breached. The complexity of today's Internet environment, with millions of apps and globally connected services, means that new law enforcement requirements are likely to introduce unanticipated, hard to detect security flaws.

This is a general summary of a number of more specific critiques of exceptional-access systems provided over the years.

Recognizing that both sides in the polarized debate over this issue have made legitimate points, we seek to bring an alternative framing to the discussion and illuminate possible paths forward. Thus our contribution is orthogonal to the policy and technical positions that have been laid down. We recognize individuals' rights to privacy, companies' legitimate desires to serve their customers, and companies' obligations to assist governments in executing warrants, provided such assistance is legally justified and technically feasible. The extent to which all of these goals are compatible is an open question that is properly the subject of democratic debate, legal research, cryptography and security research, and tech-industry product design.

3 Rules vs. Principles in Legal Regimes and the Contrast with Technical Systems

The tension between technical and legal views of sensitive issues such as encryption and surveillance is illuminated by applying the jurisprudential lens. We are guided in our understanding of the incommensurability between technical systems and legal regimes by the work of Prof. Ronald Dworkin, the leading liberal scholar of western jurisprudence. Dworkin [5] shows that liberal legal systems, manifesting what is generally understood as "the rule of law," are actually composed of *both rules and principles*. Legal "rules" can be understood as logical propositions that are expected to yield answers about what is and is not permitted using formal reasoning capabilities. By contrast, legal "principles" articulate values and policies that must be reflected in a legal system but do not necessarily dictate an unambiguous outcome in any given case.

At first blush, one might think that laws should be commensurate in nature and structure with the logical rules expressed by computer code: formal statements that can be used to evaluate a given set of facts, yielding a determination about whether a given action is legal or not. However, in Dworkin's formulation, "rules" are only one component of "law." Rules are applied in a deductive fashion and yield a clear result. (That terms in a legal rule are sometimes vague and require further interpretation by legal authorities does not diminish their status as logical statements amenable to formal evaluation.) An example of a legal rule is:

If a person dies intestate, then her estate is passed down to her spouse and any surviving children.

However, the rule of law also depends on a set of "principles." A principle is a "standard to be observed in the resolution of a legal dispute because justice demands it." It may also be a "policy that advances some social or economic goal." Dworkin offers two examples of principles:

(1) No one shall be permitted to profit from his or her own fraud.
(2) In a society with such significant reliance on automobiles, the car manufacturer is under a "special obligation with respect to the construction, promotion and sale of his cars."

Although both of these principles strike citizens of modern democracies as plausible and just, they are *not* ordinary legal rules. In particular, courts must apply these principles, but the result of doing so is not always clear. Courts generally do apply (1) in the disposition of a will. In a straightforward application, if an heir is found to have murdered the testator, he or she will not be allowed to inherit from the estate. However, Dworkin identifies many less straightforward applications in which the law *does* allow an individual to profit from fraud, *e.g.*, the law of "adverse position": If an individual occupies property illegally for some period of time without objection from the property owner, then the fraudster may successfully claim ownership of that occupied property.

Principle (2) regarding the obligations of automobile manufacturers is a *policy*, applied in certain cases to prevent a manufacturer from using a sales contract to limit its liability for harm from accidents. This principle was accepted by courts (in the days before more comprehensive automobile regulation) as superseding the ordinary law of contract. In applying this principle, courts showed themselves to be unwilling to apply legal rules in a mechanical fashion that would make them instruments of injustice or bad policy, as measured by principles such as those stated here.

Principles, in Dworkin's understanding, must be applied to certain legal disputes but do not necessarily yield a specific outcome. The scope of either (1) or (2) is neither clearly defined nor susceptible to mechanical application. In short, while principles are an essential part of the legal system, they do not function like rules. As principles are not subject to the same logically decidable evaluation as are rules, they cannot be applied in a manner that will necessarily yield a deterministic result.

Needless to say, the incorporation of principles that cannot be applied mechanically or counted upon to result in obviously "correct" outcomes is not what one expects as a component of technical-system design. Computer-system design certainly does have core principles (*e.g.*, "separation of policy and mechanism"), but the application of those principles in the context of a particular set of system requirements is supposed to result in a sound and complete system specification that can be translated into code. The difficulty of incorporating Dworkin's more complex and less deterministic notion of a "system" into the design and implementation of computer systems is in fact the crux of a number of currently unresolved disputes between computer scientists and lawyers.

3.1 Rules vs. Principles in DRM

Digital rights-management systems were designed to enable digital distribution of copyrighted works while at the same time preventing unauthorized copying of those works. The designs were proposed to address the interests of copyright owners, who believed that the ease of making perfect digital copies of copyrighted works combined with the extremely low cost of (globally) sharing digital copies online would fatally erode the market for legitimate copies of digital works. Hence, rights holders sought to deploy DRM systems that prevented *any* unauthorized copying or distribution. In response, fair-use advocates rejected these systems, because they unduly restricted public access to copyrighted works.

Recall that US copyright law states that copyright owners have certain "exclusive rights," including the rights to reproduce the copyrighted work; to prepare derivative works; to distribute copies through sales, rental, lease, or lending; to perform the copyrighted work publicly; and to display the copyrighted work publicly. On the other hand, the law also stipulates that there are some exceptions to these exclusive rights: circumstances in which members of the public may make "fair use" of a copyrighted work, *i.e.*, reproduce, distribute, display, *etc.*, it without the permission of the copyright owner. Fair use, also known as fair dealing in some copyright laws, protects the public's ability to make limited use of copyrighted material for critical reviews, satire, and educational purposes, among other things. The copyright status of a piece of work is generally clear enough that it can be the subject of a rule, such as "this work may not be copied without permission." By contrast, the operations of fair use are not so easily defined. Copyright owners' rights form the basis of traditional "creative industries," and the "fair-use doctrine" is essential to the flourishing of scholarship, criticism, satire, and many other treasured forms of expression. In Dworkin's formulation, owners' exclusive rights are legal rules, and the fair-use doctrine is a principle.

The controversial nature of DRM technology is directly traceable to the inability of these systems to implement both the *rules* of copyright law together with the *principles* guiding the application of those rules. The primary design goal of DRM technology is to provide consumers easy access to copyrighted content while preventing *any* unauthorized copying. However, the goals of copyright law are broader than this goal inasmuch as the law also includes fair use and fair dealing. DRM systems should both protect owners' exclusive rights (enforce the rules) and permit end users to make fair use (embody the principle). Unfortunately, current DRM technology is not able simultaneously to enforce copy-restriction rules and embody the fair-use principle. In mass-market content-distribution systems targeted at consumer-electronics devices, it is infeasible to give end users the technical ability to make fair use of copyrighted works without also giving them the technical ability to make arbitrary unauthorized use of the same works. Each DRM technology applies its own set of permissions and restrictions that do not, in fact, implement the rules of US or other national copyright law. So none of the technologies satisfies either copyright owners or fair-use advocates. We believe that this impasse perfectly captures the incommensurability of law and technology and that it is analogous to the impasse in encryption and surveillance.

3.2 Rules vs. Principles in End-to-End Encryption and Surveillance

Since the Snowden revelations, the technology and law-enforcement communities have been in a pitched battle. Computer-security architects are pushing end-to-end encryption protocols further and further into the Internet, Web, and mobile communications infrastructure. In response, law-enforcement agencies from all over the world (US, UK, India, and Australia to name a few) have demanded that encrypted-communication systems be built to accommodate their ability to execute legally authorized surveillance. Why do so many people in the technical community feel the need to resist lawful government surveillance by technical means? As this is a socio-technical question, the current answer has both social and technical components. Alongside the question of how legal principles ought to apply to surveillance is the very real systems-security question of whether it is technically possible to build in "exceptional-access" capabilities without incurring unacceptable high security risks for other users [1]. While we are well aware of the importance of these systems-security questions, they are not the main focus of this paper.

From the technical community's perspective, the US government suffered a major loss of credibility as a result of the legally and morally excessive mass surveillance exposed by Snowden. In the words of Schneier [10], "the NSA has turned the Internet into a giant surveillance platform." More notably, wholly establishment figure Brad Smith (then General Counsel, now President of Microsoft) has defined the government as an Advanced Persistent Threat: Smith [12] wrote that the government-surveillance practices revealed by Snowden "threaten to seriously undermine confidence in the security and privacy of online communications. Indeed, government snooping potentially now constitutes an 'advanced persistent threat,' alongside sophisticated malware and cyber attacks." The solution, according to the conventional wisdom in the computer-security community as articulated by Schneier, is to recognize that "we have made surveillance too cheap. We have to make surveillance expensive again." Smith elaborates: "Many of our customers have serious concerns about government surveillance of the Internet. We share their concerns. That's why we are taking steps to ensure governments use legal process rather than technological brute force to access customer data."

Smith's belief that governments should "use legal process ... to access customer data" provides a segue from the social and political aspects of the problem to the technical aspects. The Fourth Amendment of the US Constitution states that citizens have a right to be free from "unreasonable searches and seizures," a key source of the right to privacy. An extensive body of laws and court decisions provides guidance about what constitutes a "reasonable" search or seizure, *i.e.*, about when a government agent can get a warrant to violate a citizen's privacy.

Over time, the general privacy *principle* in the Fourth Amendment has been expressed as a set of more concrete *rules* in the form of electronic-surveillance statutes such as the Electronic Communications Privacy Act (18 USC 2701 et seq). Most other democracies have similar statutes. In Dworkin's terms, the "rule" is expressed in these statutes, establishing what procedures law enforcement has to follow to conduct electronic surveillance, how courts should consider those requests, and how citizens' rights will be protected in the operation of those rules. Today, with the combination of new technologies that enable a substantial expansion of surveillance power and the loss of trust from the Snowden disclosures, the technical community is standing up for privacy principles (as opposed to rules) by aggressively propagating end-to-end encryption. This proliferation of encryption technology is also, of course, just good security practice, but there has been an unmistakable and otherwise unexplainable growth in the use of end-to-end encryption throughout the public communications and information infrastructure since the Snowden revelations.

Just as there are privacy and civil-liberties protection principles at stake in the encryption debate, so too can law enforcement invoke principles beyond just the rules in surveillance statutes. Law-enforcement officials from the US, the UK, Australia, and elsewhere have all challenged the tech industry's decision to implement end-to-end, surveillance-resistant encryption on the grounds that such designs thwart the principle that companies have the obligation to assist in the execution of lawful court orders such as wiretap warrants. This principle does not have the weight of the Fourth Amendment or other fundamental rights, but it *is* established in law. As explained in Sect. 2, the leading example of this challenge from the law-enforcement community is the FBI's claim under the US All Writs Act that Apple should create a modified version of the security features in its iOS operating system to enable the FBI to unlock a phone used in the San Bernardino terrorist attack [8]. While there is a *general* obligation in US law to assist the government in fulfilling lawful court orders (such as search warrants), in this and other cases, US courts have declined to find that technology companies have an arbitrarily broad obligation.

As the debate over encryption and surveillance has played out. both technical and law-enforcement communities have made earnest but incomplete arguments. Law enforcement invokes the "rule of law" but comes closer to advocating for the "rule of rules." In its appeal to the obligation to assist the government in executing court orders, the government side seems to ignore both the historical limits on that *rule* and to give short shrift to the importance of the *principles* associated with limiting the scope of government surveillance. By the same token, frequently heard arguments from the technical community cite the *principle* of privacy protection as a reason to refuse to design systems that might address law-enforcement needs, and thus place the principle of privacy protection above all other rules principles that are properly part of our rule of law framework. In neither case do we attribute bad faith to these two opposing communities. Still we can see that failure to account for the complete role of both rule and principle in the rule-of-law system leads to incommensurate policy positions.

4 Design Patterns that Address the Tension Among Rules and Principles

We have shown that the incommensurability of the technical-design and legal-system perspectives arises from a failure to distinguish between rules and principles. Conflict and confusion between the technical and legal contours of rules and principles have repeatedly muddled both design decisions about technical systems and the effective operation of law in the digital realm. What's more, this confusion has created a nearly existential strain between the technical community and governments around the world. To help disentangle this confusion, we offer two design patterns that will bring greater clarity and engender progress in difficult digital-policy debates. The first is a challenge to the legal community to make rules clearer and to reduce the gray area between principles and rules. The second is a design goal for the technical community, *i.e.*, to design systems with increased transparency and accountability, thus enabling an open dialogue about how legal principles should operate in new contexts.

4.1 Socio-Technical Design Pattern #1: Reduce the Gray Area Between Rules and Principles

When the resolution of a legal question depends on both the evaluation of a rule (something computer systems can do well) and application of a principle (something that is generally undecidable for any logical system), confusion follows. DRM systems are controversial because they are designed to give effect to a set of rules that reflects neither the full range of the law nor the full operation of fair-use principles, producing a result that appears unjust. When surveillance rules appear to accord governments intrusive power beyond what principle says they should have, then some system designers take matters into their own hands.

Clarifying rules and narrowing the cases in which principles have to enter into the evaluation of surveillance authority would bring stability and increased trust to surveillance law. In most countries, electronic-surveillance rules are decades old (with the notable exception of the UK) and fail to account for the substantial intrusive power associated with many new technologies that extend the reach of both government and commercial surveillance. As an example of how the gray area between rules and principles might be reduced, consider the question of how law enforcement is able to gain access to location information in the course of a criminal investigation.

Location privacy is one of the more contentious privacy and civil-liberties issues in the United States. The underlying technology has changed dramatically, and there is significant contention about how rules and principles ought to be understood in determining how law enforcement can access this very sensitive data. To begin with, in the years since cell phones first became popular, mobile communications devices have incorporated hardware and software that reveal the real-time location of most individual users. Courts trying to decide what rules should govern law-enforcement access to location data have generally settled on a 1994 law that was written not to cover location data but rather to protect the privacy of email and web-browsing logs (18 US Code 2703(d)). This rule conditions police access to data on the ability to present a court with "specific, articulable facts" showing that the information sought is relevant to an ongoing criminal investigation. This particular standard is a much higher burden for the police to meet as compared to what they have to demonstrate to get access, for example, to a target's bank-account information. Yet it is lower than the full "probable-cause" standard required by the Fourth Amendment of the US Constitution for wiretaps and other access to "content" such as email.

Conflicting views of how privacy principles ought to shape rules for location access has left the current rule under attack by both law enforcement and civil-liberties advocates for alleged violation of Fourth-Amendment principles. Civil libertarians claim that it under-protects privacy for failing to extend full Fourth-Amendment probable-cause protection to citizens' location information. On the other hand, law enforcement invokes yet another constitutional principle known as the "third-party doctrine." This principle [17] provides that, when an individual voluntarily surrenders personal information to a third party, he or she has waived privacy interest in the information, and therefore no warrant is required. Law-enforcement officials argue that this principle applies, because mobile-phone users have voluntarily transmitted their location information to mobile-network operators and thus waived any privacy interest in it. Civil libertarians argue that location data is highly sensitive and deserves protection from government intrusion notwithstanding the fact that third parties such as mobile network operators or Internet platforms handle that data.

This tangle of rules and conflicting principles has brought the dispute to the United States Supreme Court twice. The first case, United States v. Jones [19], failed to resolve the underlying dispute with certainty, but it indicated that access to historical location data (records of past locations) over a long period of time (28 days) was a privacy intrusion. The Supreme Court is expected to issue another decision in this area shortly.[1] While this debate continues in the legal system, computer-system designers face legitimate questions about whether they should be building tools that help users obscure their location data from law enforcement or rather defer to the legal system to protect privacy. The gray area created by an inconsistent combination of rules and principles could stand to be clarified and simplified with a straightforward set of legal rules that address *all* aspects of location privacy, as opposed to just those aspects addressed in the Carpenter case that the Supreme Court is now considering [4]. (See Footnote 1.) This would increase confidence in the legal system and reduce the perception that the only way to protect privacy is through unilateral action by technologists. Of course, computer security is an important component of privacy and thus a responsibility for all system designers, but we should not have to rely on technical means alone. Privacy protection is a fundamental responsibility of the legal system in democracies.

In addition to location information, there are numerous security and privacy rights at risk that remain unprotected under law. Just to name a few, we need more clear rules governing the privacy and law-enforcement access conditions of personal data collected by new "smart-city" technology, travel patterns revealed by automatic license-plate readers, and data collected and analyzed by in-home listening devices such as the Amazon Echo and Google Home. All of these technologies raise pressing privacy questions. The legality of many such privacy issues is decided in a tangle of principle and rule. To the extent possible, we should narrow these gray areas and work toward explicit privacy rules. This will increase user trust and reduce the burden on technical designers to solve problems that more properly belong in the legal sphere.

4.2 Socio-Technical Design Pattern #2: Bring Transparency and Accountability to the Operation of Principles

The legitimacy of the legal system depends on the ongoing and transparent application of principles alongside the adjudication of specific rules. Technical mechanisms that bring more comprehensive transparency and accountability serve two important functions. First, systems that function with more complete transparency enable fact-based consideration of whether laws are working properly, addressing the democratically desired balance of interests. Second, accountability mechanisms [6] increase public confidence that laws are actually being followed

[1] Note added in July 2018: On June 22, 2018, the Supreme Court ruled [4] that historical location data is subject to full Fourth-Amendment privacy protection, rejecting a lower-court decision [18], which had found that, in some circumstances, the police could access location data even without the traditional Fourth-Amendment proof of probable cause. Although it is an important step forward for privacy protection, the Carpenter decision still leaves open numerous digital-privacy questions, including what standard of privacy protection the United States Constitution provides for real-time location data.

by enabling citizens and their representatives both in government and civil society to monitor the application of law to the operation of systems, pointing out and seeking remedies when violations of rules occur.

Transparency is vital to sound technology development, because so little is known about how new systems work and how they affect society's values. Systems with better transparency properties could help provide policymakers and the public with a sound basis on which to make surveillance policy and with adjustments to privacy, security, and law-enforcement needs based on actual facts about how systems behave in public. A variety of cryptographers including [7] have shown designs of cryptographically sound systems that provide comprehensive statistics on surveillance operations without disclosing details of specific law enforcement investigations. The debate over encryption and surveillance is a classic example of one in which more transparency about actual system operation is needed. Since 2014, when then-FBI Director James Comey called for Internet companies to redesign their systems to assure law-enforcement access to encrypted content, facts about the surveillance environment have been in short supply. As law enforcement claims substantial harms to investigations due the end-to-end encryption on mobile devices, there have been questions about the actual magnitude of this harm. For some time, the FBI claimed it was having trouble quantifying the impact of encryption, then claimed that encryption hampered investigations in more than 7000 mobile devices. But in the end, the actual number appears to have been closer to 1000 [3]. This is just one area in which more technical contribution is necessary to bring increased trust to the online environment. Lack of transparency leads to distrust and efforts to achieve protection through purely technical, rather than legal, means.

Accountability in the operation of surveillance systems is also vital to public trust and good governance. When surveillance systems seem to operate in an opaque fashion, the public in general and the technical community in particular feel that the broader principles of privacy protection and limited government power over citizens' liberty are left legally unprotected. Building accountable surveillance systems requires formal statements of what surveillance has been authorized, reliable logging mechanisms, and appropriate deployment of secure computation techniques and zero-knowledge proofs that provide guarantees of lawful behavior without disclosing sensitive information about ongoing law-enforcement investigations. Several such designs [7,11,13] have now been proposed, but much more work is required to bring full accountability to information usage and surveillance.

While we exhort the policymakers to disambiguate principles and carve out the elements that can be turned into rules whenever possible, there will always be circumstances in which the application of rules to a set of facts is incomplete or undecidable without the broader contribution of legal principles. That is certainly the case in the intersection of powerful new information technologies with fundamental rights such as privacy or free expression. Hence, system designers ought to consider how to bring greater transparency and accountability [20] to the design and operation of their systems, and policymakers ought to put requirements for greater transparency into the law.

5 Conclusion

We have observed that some in the cryptology research community believe that the only effective way to support privacy principles is to deploy end-to-end encryption capabilities as widely as possible. As we have shown, we understand this stance to reflect the belief that the legal system has failed to respond appropriately to the spread of new surveillance technologies and otherwise abused its authority. Legal rules in place are inadequate to protect privacy in the face of powerful new surveillance techniques. Building technical work-arounds to protect users from inadequate legal privacy protection is an understandable stance and may be justifiable in the near term. But surveillance-avoidance technology alone will not create the kind of privacy-respectful society called for by our democratic values. On the technical side, we should broaden efforts to build more transparent, accountable systems. These systems will help provide the public with information necessary to assure that the legal system strikes the right balance between legal rules and applicable principles. The obligation on the law and policy community is to shrink the gray areas where unclear or outmoded rules leave privacy principles unprotected. With the increased sense of trust that a more transparent, accountable environment brings, it should also be possible to re-create a more cooperative relationship between the technical and law-enforcement communities, so that the police have the tools and expertise necessary to protect society, and citizens are confident that the law ensures that privacy will be protected, both as a matter or rule and principle.

Acknowledgements. Feigenbaum was supported in part by US National Science Foundation grants CNS-1407454 and CNS-1409599 and by the William and Flora Hewlett Foundation grant 2016-3834. Weitzner was supported in part by the William and Flora Hewlett Foundation grant 2014-1601.

References

1. Abelson, H., et al.: Keys under doormats: mandating insecurity by requiring government access to all data and communications. J. Cybersecur. **1**, 69–79 (2015). https://doi.org/10.1093/cybsec/tyv009
2. An Open Letter from US Researchers in Cryptography and Information Security, 24 January 2014. masssurveillance.info
3. Barrett, D.: FBI repeatedly overstated encryption threat figures to congress, public. Washington Post, 22 May 2018
4. Carpenter v. United States, No. 16–402, 585 U.S. (2018)
5. Dworkin, R.: Taking Rights Seriously. Harvard University Press, Cambridge (1978)
6. Feigenbaum, J., Hendler, J., Jaggard, A., Weitzner, D.J., Wright, R.: Accountability and deterrence in online life. In: Proceedings of the 3rd International Web Science Conference. ACM, New York, June 2011. Article no. 7. https://doi.org/10.1145/2527031.2527043
7. Frankle, J., Park, S., Shaar, D., Goldwasser, S., Weitzner, D.J.: Practical accountability of secret processes. In: Proceedings of the 27th Security Symposium. USENIX, Berkeley, August 2018

8. Hennessey, S., Wittes, B.: Apple is selling you a phone, not civil liberties. Lawfare, 18 February 2016. https://lawfareblog.com/apple-selling-you-phone-not-civil-liberties
9. In re Search of an Apple iPhone, 2016 WL 618401
10. Jackson, J.: Security expert seeks to make surveillance costly again. Computerworld, 7 November 2013. https://www.computerworld.com/article/2485721/data-security/security-expert-seeks-to-make-surveillance-costly-again.html
11. Kroll, J., Felten, E., Boneh, D.: Secure protocols for accountable warrant execution. Working paper. https://www.jkroll.com/papers/warrant_paper.pdf
12. Meisner, J.: Protecting customer data from government snooping. Microsoft Technet: The Official Microsoft Blog, 4 December 2013. https://blogs.technet.microsoft.com/microsoft_blog/2013/12/04/protecting-customer-data-from-government-snooping/
13. Pato, J., Paradesi, S., Jacobi, I., Shih, F., Wang, S.: Aintno: demonstration of information accountability on the web. In: Proceedings of the 3rd International Conference on Privacy, Security, Risk, and Trust and 3rd International Conference on Social Computing, pp. 1072–1080. IEEE Computer Society, Los Alamitos, October 2011
14. Prevelakis, V., Spinellis, D.: The Athens affair. IEEE Spectr. **44**(7), 26–33 (2007). https://doi.org/10.1109/MSPEC.2007.376605
15. Rozenshtein, A.J.: Surveillance intermediaries. Stan. Law Rev. **70**, 99–189 (2018)
16. Rogaway, P.: The moral character of cryptographic work. Cryptology ePrint Archive, Report 2015/1162 (2015). https://eprint.iacr.org/2015/1162
17. Smith v. Maryland, 442 U.S. 735 (1979)
18. United States v. Carpenter, 819 F.3d 880 (6th Cir. 2016)
19. United States v. Jones, 565 U.S. 400 (2012)
20. Weitzner, D.J., Abelson, H., Berners-Lee, T., Feigenbaum, J., Hendler, J., Sussman, G.: Information accountability. Commun. ACM **51**(6), 82–89 (2008). https://doi.org/10.1145/1349026.1349043

On the Incommensurability of Laws and Technical Mechanisms: Or, What Cryptography Can't Do (Transcript of Discussion)

Daniel J. Weitzner(✉)

Massachusetts Institute of Technology, Cambridge, MA 02139, USA
172641@mail.muni.cz

Frank Stajano: [Picking up on the discussion of why the principle that one may not profit from ones own fraud supersedes a rule that children inherit from their parents.] In the meta-framework, is this because there is here another stronger principle that conflicts with and overrides the rule? Or is there some other reason such as tradition that dictates that the principle supersedes the rule?

Reply: It is some combination of the two. In some cases, there are some well-articulated principles. In the case of adverse possession, it is largely because it becomes hard to administer the opposite. If someone occupies land and builds on it, and if the other owner doesn't complain, and if other legal requirements are met, then it doesn't seem so bad. Maybe then the fraud is not so bad, or fraud is hard to establish. It might have been the result of a mistake; so courts just say: "We're not going to try to go too far to interrogate the reasons behind that change in boundary. We're just going to accept it."

Frank Stajan: I appreciate having a practical example to talk about, but I am absolutely not interested in "adverse possession. I am interested in the meta-framework. Is it the case that there are rules, which are practical things, and there are principles, which are more important and more general and vague, and that principles override rules? Is there a hierarchy between principles and rules?

Reply: Dworkin would certainly say that principles override rules, but not consistently and not necessarily predictably. Let me give you one more example, just to illustrate. There was an early case in the 1940's, before we had much regulation of automobile safety in the United States. Someone bought a car, and in the course of driving it had an accident, which was caused by a defective part. The car was declared to be "totaled, meaning that the accident rendered it worthless. The owner sued for damages, including replacing the car. The car company said: "The sales contract between us clearly established that the company liability was limited to replacing defective parts; so we should not have to pay for the cost of replacing the car, only that part that failed." And the court came and said: "Well, yes, that was the contract, but the reality is that we as a society (the United States in the 40's) are coming to depend more and more on cars, and that creates a special obligation on the part of the auto manufacturers to

V. Matyáš et al. (Eds.): Security Protocols 2018, LNCS 11286, pp. 280–288, 2018.
https://doi.org/10.1007/978-3-030-03251-7_32

exercise more care than might ordinarily be required." So the normal principle, *caveat emptor*, or buyer beware, beyond anything that's not warranted, didn't apply. That was a court exercising discretion, saying: "It's the right policy for society to put more burden on the car manufacturer." The principle overrides the rule.

Mark Lomas: I wanted to suggest that adverse possession is actually a special case of the principle about taking action within a particular period of time. What you don't want to do is to go to a court and say: "Something happened 20 years ago ..." Because if I go and build a fence in your garden, you can evict me. You could tear it down. But the fact is that you let it stand for a long period of time.

Reply: Yes, and this is what I meant by administrability. It's very hard sometimes to wind the clock way way back and figure out who did what to whom. Sometimes courts just say: "Don't expect us to do that." There's a presumption made about the inaction of the other property owner. Absolutely. But that's not stated explicitly in a rule; it's something that courts will bring.

Let me give two examples of how this interaction of rule and principle applies. First is the case of DRM, which I'm going to talk about very quickly. I assume everyone is familiar with digital rights management systems and roughly familiar with the debate. DRM systems were designed for the benefit of copyright owners, who wanted to be able to distribute copyrighted digital works widely and make them easily available to consumers but didn't want to make it possible for anyone to make *unauthorised* digital copies. Because it was very easy to do that; it is much easy to copy a mp4 file than it is to copy a 35 mm reel of film. So DRM systems were designed *solely* to enforce the rule in copyright law. The rule is that, as a copyright owner, you have an exclusive right to control who makes copies of your work, and there's no real debate about the fact that that's a rule. But there is also an intervening principle – the principle of *fair use* or *fair dealing*, depending on what legal system you're operating in. It says that, recognising free-expression principles and the desire to support the free flow of information in society, sometimes we *do* allow individuals to make unauthorised copies or unauthorised uses of copyrighted works. You're all familiar with this. One notable fair-use exception concerns educational purposes and critical-review purposes: If someone writes a review of a book in a newspaper, he doesn't have to get the permission of the book author to quote a paragraph or a sentence or even a little bit more. The problem was that, the way DRM systems were designed, they precluded completely those fair-use exceptions. There's a lot of legal complexity about how the fair-use system works, but the debate about fair use in DRM systems arose because the systems only implemented the rule, not the principle. Today, if you are, for example, a professor of film who wants to show a bunch of clips of movies, you might only be able to find them on Netflix or Amazon Prime, mediated by some DRM system that's installed on your browser. You are not able to take a clip out of that video stream and assemble it together into something you could use for your class. Whereas, if you were teaching literature, you could quite readily copy text from books and assemble it in the same sort of way. So a way of understanding the dispute we have about DRM systems is that they advantage the rule and preclude the principle.

Now I want to spend more time talking about the question of end-to-end encryption and surveillance and just paint a little bit of background. I will start with a caveat. What we're discussing in this paper is not the question of whether exceptional-access systems create security risks. I am very firmly of the belief that there are a whole number of expectational-access designs that would create all kinds of security problems; nothing I'm saying here is designed to contradict the "Keys under doormats" paper[1] But I want to look with you at how the technical community has responded to the question of end-to-end encryption and surveillance. Take two examples. You're probably familiar with IETF RFC 7258 which identifies bulk surveillance and pervasive monitoring as attacks on Internet privacy. This is a statement from the IETF, a technical standards body, which says: "There's a social problem, a legal problem, a problem I am going to suggest to you arises in the realm of principle as well as rule." Even more notably, because you might write off the IETF's statement as a function of latent anti-establishment tendencies, none other than Brad Smith, who was at the time the general counsel of Microsoft and is now the president of Microsoft, right around the same time said, largely in response to the Snowden disclosures, that government surveillance constitutes an "advanced persistent threat." They treated this question about how much surveillance and what kind of surveillance we ought to have in democratic societies as a technical attack on the systems that they were building, and they determined to make a number of technical design decisions that would make surveillance more expensive and less frequent. Microsoft decided to make technical decisions that would affect the operation of this aspect of law enforcement.

Here we also have a rule vs. principle challenge. We do have a bunch of rules in most democratic societies about how surveillance is supposed to work. In the US, we have the Electronic Communications Privacy Act. In the UK, you now have the newly revised Investigative Powers Act, which pulls together a lot of surveillance law. Most legal systems have rules like these. So there are very clear sets of rules about what law enforcement needs to do to get a warrant. What's interesting is that there's also a conflicting set of principles that are at play. On the one hand, when you hear law-enforcement officials, whether here or in the US or in Australia or elsewhere, talk about this issue, what they say is that there's a principle at stake that says that everyone in society, including companies such as Microsoft, has an obligation to assist in the exercise of lawful orders. The FBI's view, for example, is that they can't understand why people in the technical community and, in particular, in tech companies would think that it was appropriate to design systems seemingly to thwart surveillance, to make surveillance harder, when in fact law-enforcement agencies go to court, they get

[1] H. Abelson *et al.*, "Keys Under Doormats: Mandating insecurity by requiring government access to all data and communications," Journal of Cybersecurity 1.1 (2015): 69–79.

a legally authorised warrant, and there are even laws on the books that require a certain amount of technical assistance.

Mansoor Ahmed: Is it really a contradiction in principle, or is it a conflict in the rules that are used to instantiate the principles? Because it's just an empirical difference about the scope that is allowed. And both of them concede that there is a scope; so it's just about the rules that we use to instantiate the principles.

Reply: I'll explain what the conflict is. Some of this is a conflict in the interpretation of the rules about how warrants apply.

Joan Feigenbaum: And a contradiction in the interpretation of the principle. Because you *do* have an obligation. There are always contradictions with principles, but yes there is an obligation, and there are well known court cases in which companies were forced to assist law enforcement. But everybody also concedes that this obligation is limited. It's not the case that every tech company is obligated to do everything that the FBI asks it to do.

Reply: Right. Even the understanding for example, of what is required by way of technical assistance, under rules such as the All Writs Act or the IPA, really come down to questions of principle, of how far you think a company needs to go to offer assistance to law enforcement. And on the other hand, the principle that I think a lot of people in the technical community, both industrial and academic, are standing up for is a principle that says: "Wait a minute. We're supposed to have limits on the scope of surveillance." And those limits really are expressed, at least partly, at the level of principle. Certainly there are some rules that speak to those limits, but the rules are quite broad. And I think the feeling is that the rules on surveillance do not adequately capture the values we have in our principles. So therefore it's the same rules that get applied to get a warrant, the same rules that get applied to get transactional signaling data. But I think the very clear sense is that those rules now have so dramatically expanded the practical scope of surveillance that the principles are no longer being respected.

Ian Goldberg: I think this difference in rule and principle is shown strongly, for example, when the NSA does surveillance. It is very clear that what it cares about is the rule, not the principle. If the rule says it is legal to do, the NSA says not only "we can do it" but "we will do it". And they will even interpret the words in the rule, words like "collect" and "search" and all these other words. You think you know what they mean, but the NSA has a completely different interpretation of the words in these rules that they don't tell you about; under that interpretation, what they do follows the rule, and they care not at all about the principle.

Reply: I think that's a great point. Let me even go further. In fact, if you talk to people in intelligence agencies and law-enforcement agencies, they say that they believe it's their duty to go as far as they think the rule can take them. Now I think that's an extreme reaction in some cases. But it also has some rationale to it in that, if they think their job is to protect society against X, Y, or Z evil, and they don't use all the tools that they think are available to them, they aren't doing their job. They feel that it is their obligation to interpret the rule to go as far as possible. I think that has ended up being extraordinarily short-sighted. I think they have, in many ways, incited this reaction on the part of the technical community – this kind of unilateral defence of principle. But, yes, I think you're exactly right.

Virgil Gligor: Take the NSA example, in which there were two words: "collect" and "select." Those two words are not commutative in the law, but, until about 2007–2011, the NSA used them commutatively. The rule says you have to select first and then collect based on the selection. If you do blanket collection, *i.e.*, collect everything and then select, that's supposed to be outside the scope of the rule. Between 2007 and 2011, the FISA court did not understand that those two words don't commute. It was a technical argument, but the judges didn't understand it. So the NSA supposedly collected the lot, then out of that collection they started selecting. They're supposed to have selectors defined first, then only collect based on the selectors.

Ian Goldberg: So what they ended up doing is redefining "collect." Now, when they copy the data from the Internet into their database, that's not a "collection." They have another word for it ... "ingestion" or "copying" something like that. I forget exactly what the word is. They put the data in their database; then what they term a "collection" is when you type the selector ... So you do the selection, and, when it fetches what you selected from the database, that is the "collection" in their minds. They are doing "selection" for "collection," and they're abiding by the rules, even if they have to change English in order to do it.

Virgil Gligor: That had to be approved by the FISA Court. Otherwise they could not do it.

Reply: It's tempting to say, "Well these are just a set of rules, if we could just figure out what they are." And Joan and I actually have a little bit of a tension about this. I think Joan just wants to know what the rules are, and that's understandable. Some of the questions in this "collect-select" example are issues that you might say you could resolve just by interpretation. If you were just explicit enough and clear enough, you could say "here's an exhaustive set of rules."

My view is that approach in fact misunderstands the reaction of a lot of us in the technical community and a lot of people in the human-rights community, who have said: "No, the problem is not how you're interpreting those particular terms. The problem is that the terms are being interpreted inconsistently with this other set of principles, which have not yet been fully articulated." A lot of my students have also kind of pushed back on this ... It just still sounds like a set of rules. It's rules and interpretations that just kind of keep going. But I think that this is not the way our legal system works. You can see this when you see courts or legislators struggle with this issue. They're not mostly asking technical questions about how a particular statute should be interpreted. What they're really asking is how broad principles like the Fourth Amendment or "necessary and proportionate" should be applied to the interpretation of a set of rues. They are asking how those rules need to be defined to reflect principles.

Mansoor Ahmed: Isn't the difference basically the whole Hart-Dworkin debate, with your differentiation between rules and principles just being the scope of what the judge is allowed to do?

Reply: Yes. Hart being the positivist. This is the ongoing debate of the century between these two great legal theorists. Dworkin stood for the idea that principles are different and that we have to recognise them as logically different constructs from rules. This is to continue to say that the technical community, and in particular the cryptography community, has shown real concern, not just for questions of security and good system design but really for what I think are very obviously principles.

We take from this that there's something incomplete about the views articulated on both sides of this argument. I'm caricaturing a little bit to say that there's a law enforcement/national-security side over here and a technical side over there. But what we see in this debate is that both sides claim the authority of "the rule of law." Law enforcement says: "We're getting properly authorised warrants. Why shouldn't it be the obligation of companies to help us fulfill those warrants?" But I think that, in a lot of ways, what they're talking about is not the rule of law; it's a rule of *rules.* They have rules that work for them reasonably well, but the technology substrata have expanded their authority dramatically without changing one word of the rules – without, arguably, even changing the interpretation of the rules. So law enforcement's criticism of the view in the technical community has been that the technical community doesn't respect the rule of law. I think where the other side of the argument falls somewhat short is with a kind of a unilateral claim to stand for principles. Not all of the principles are necessarily reflected in the tech community's point of view. Because we do have a principle in law that says we should be helping government to fulfill legal orders. The scope of that principle is not easy to figure out, but it also isn't one that should just be ignored. So what do we do?

I do think there are things that we can do, both on the technical side and on the legal side, to bridge this sense of incommensurability that we've described. Number one: There really are things that law can do. Law can reduce the grey area between rules and principles; that is, it can try to make sure that the rules cover as much as possible. That's the Joan principle: Make sure that the rules are updated and that they reflect what our principles really are in this area. That applies also in the case of digital rights management, where what we would want are DRM systems that somehow accommodate the exercise of fair use in a way that they don't currently.

In the same way, on the technical side, I think it's really important that we try to avoid system design that tries to make automatic determinations about how principles apply. Because, by creating technical *faits accomplis*, facts on the ground, by precluding the ability of law enforcement to exercise warrants in a lot of ways, what the technical community is actually doing is changing the question of what the principles of surveillance and privacy and civil liberties and human rights ought to be from a question that gets decided in the context of the rule of law in the legal system and in society at large to a purely technical question. Our claim is that this is something that cryptography should not do, because it's not good at it.

Ian Goldberg: So I'm going to ask you to expand on another English word that you used that I think is often overlooked in this issue. You said "exercise a warrant." When law enforcement exercises a warrant, does the word "exercise" mean they are guaranteed to succeed in getting what they're looking for?

Reply: No. Certainly not.

Ian Goldberg: If they get a traditional wire tap on a phone, and the people they were listening in on are speaking Navajo, they certainly have no...

Reply: 100%. Let me just say what I mean by this second principle. I think that what we would like to see are systems that do a better job of making it clear of what the dispute is. The question you're raising is a question of principle. It's a question of how far anyone in society should go, if at all, to accommodate the exercise of an order. Today, that question is not answered in a rule. Your question *is* answered in that certainly no target of a warrant has an affirmative obligation to help law enforcement succeed in its exercise. But third parties do have a range of obligations; those obligations are not, in most cases, clearly defined, and they represent only one principle of two. The other principle being human rights that have to be brought to bear in the question of who's responsible for what in the exercise of an order. And our claim is that, to try to make that decision by a set of technical facts on the ground is not actually to serve the rule of law.

Ross Anderson: This is an aspect of what I was saying in the earlier talk. In Bitcoin, the designers decided unilaterally that the person controlling the private key controls the money. In other words that the ledger is constitutive of ownership, whereas the law says this isn't the case. The person from whom the Bitcoin was stolen is the person who owns it.

Joan Feigenbaum: Ian, I think that you're exactly right. One logically consistent and appealing response to law enforcement's claim that "well, we have a warrant! You can't deny us this information" is to say, "Oh no, we're allowed to moot the question of whether this warrant is effective by just using end-to-end encryption that works. Yes, you have the right to collect those bits, but you don't have the right to decrypt them. End of story."

That's not satisfactory, even though I agree that it's appealing. It's not satisfactory in the same way that copyright owners' mooting fair use isn't satisfactory. Their attitude is "Look, fair use is not a right; fair use is a defence against a charge of infringement. So, if we just make it technically infeasible for you to get into a situation where we might charge you with infringement, that's it. We've solved the problem." You know, they haven't really solved the problem. They've done a *reductio ad absurdum* of the problem, and they've done a technical fix of the absurd version. In the same way, the crypto community hasn't really solved its problem, because it hasn't really coped with the fact that there are legitimate warrants, and there are legitimate law-enforcement and intelligence-agency operations. Just having one technical solution, regardless of whether you're in that situation or not, isn't really grappling with the principles. There are conflicting principles involved: the privacy principles and the law-enforcement principles.

Reply: Yes. What I think cryptographers and system designers should do is to make these questions and these disputes about principles more visible. A big part of the problem in the case of the NSA has been that it's hard to tell what's going on at all. The FISA court even said, soon after the Snowden disclosures when they were highly embarrassed at what they had allowed: "Well, we don't really understand what they're doing." And that to me is an urgent technical problem that needs answers, and I think it needs answers in the form of understanding how to collect evidence better. It does, I think, echo a lot of what Ross was talking about: Make visible the question about who should be responsible in one case or another. I think that we haven't yet gotten to the state, in modern privacy, where we're able to get a really clear purchase on how our values apply. These Facebook things come and everybody says: "Oh my god, that's a complete disaster." We really have not gotten our legal system and our political process deeply engaged in the question of how our principles ought to apply and result in rules. Because what's clear is that you can't do this solely based on principle. The Bitcoin world is going to have to settle on some of these rules, and the rules are going to have to be scalable throughout a system like that. But the only way we'll get there is with substantially better transparency and more interaction back and fourth, rapidly, with a lot of iteration, between technical evidence and the legal system.

Mansoor Ahmed: Your first point there about reducing variance between rules and principles is a nice, for lack of a better word, principle. But, when it comes down to ground realities, isn't there a big difference in clock speeds of the legal system and technical developments. Isn't this a losing battle?

Reply: I'm a skeptic about "law is always behind technology." I mean, we've had many of these privacy challenges for at least a decade. This kind of large-scale graph analysis has clearly been possible, it's been understood, it's been known. We've had time to figure it out. So I guess I think it's not that the legal system is behind; it's that society hasn't pushed our legal system to reckon with these new technical realities.

Mansoor Ahmed: Is there a tradeoff between the lag between rules and principles and the degree to which you specify your rules? Because, if you overspecify, then you have to keep updating your rules more frequently as technology changes. So you are basically given a trade-off between ambiguity and lack of guidance.

Reply: Well, or you just increment frequently. And there are a lot of existing regulatory mechanisms that are better at moving faster than having to wait four years to get to the ECJ or the United States Supreme Court.

Virgil Gligor: Surprisingly enough, one of the biggest problems that was noticed is that the law, and in particular the FISA court, did not understand the technology. Once they understood the technology, they fixed the problem. So, for example, with respect to "ingestion": If an agency ingests more than it should, the agency must purge the data within 24 h. Auditably. So they fix things once they understand what the technology is, but often they don't understand it.

Reply: And that happened as a result of a whole series of institutional mechanisms that make that court work better, including allowing more people to appear before the court with different interests and pushing the NSA actually to do a better job of being more internally transparent and accountable. So don't try to determine principles unilaterally. It impedes the operation of the rule of law and is bad for society.

Shatter Secrets: Using Secret Sharing to Cross Borders with Encrypted Devices

Erinn Atwater(✉) and Ian Goldberg(✉)

University of Waterloo, Waterloo, ON, Canada
{erinn.atwater,iang}@uwaterloo.ca

Abstract. Modern consumer electronic devices such as smartphones and laptops are laden with intimate personal data such as past conversations, photos and videos, medical information, and passwords for services that contain information on our entire lives. This makes the devices of particular interest to law enforcement officials during even routine searches. A particular threat to users is when crossing international borders, as we have repeatedly seen reports that the data on these devices is subject to search and seizure without warrants or even suspicion of wrongdoing. In some cases, travellers have even been compelled to provide PINs, passwords, encryption keys, and fingerprints to unlock their devices.

In this position paper, we argue for the use of threshold cryptography to distribute encryption keys into shares, which are then securely transmitted to friends residing at the traveller's destination. When a traveller is subjected to scrutiny at the border, they are technically unable to comply with requests to decrypt their devices. Assuming the traveller is permitted to complete their journey, they must then physically interact with some (user-configurable) threshold number of their friends on that side of the border to recover their encryption keys. In our proposal, attackers must compromise both the traveller *and* a threshold number of the traveller's friends in order to learn anything about the secret key; the friends are unable to collude without the traveller present. We also implement Shatter Secrets, an open-source prototype Android app aimed at realizing this goal.

1 Introduction

Crossing international borders in recent times has become fraught with uncertainty over the privacy and security of our electronic devices. Rather than merely the clothing and toiletries in our bags, our smartphones and laptops contain huge troves of intimate information, including photographs, financial and medical information, and correspondence, that often go back many years. In 2017, the United States Customs and Border Protection agency searched approximately 30,000 consumer electronics devices of travellers—more than triple the number of searches performed in 2015—and generated 250 complaints about warrantless searches [4,11]. Even with the capability to use PINs, passwords, and disk

V. Matyáš et al. (Eds.): Security Protocols 2018, LNCS 11286, pp. 289–294, 2018.
https://doi.org/10.1007/978-3-030-03251-7_33

encryption on these devices, travellers have reported being compelled to provide passwords, being asked to use their fingerprint to unlock smartphones, and having their electronics detained for extended periods of time while law enforcement agencies deploy forensic techniques against the devices [7,11]. While some passengers refuse to comply with these requests (resulting in detainment of their device, their person, or being refused entry to the country [6]), certain international borders have even begun requiring large electronic devices be checked into the hold of the plane, removing the opportunity for the owner to refuse imaging and allowing for surreptitious inspection of the device and its contents [3]. Even the more restrictive guidelines on searches provided by the U.S. Department of Homeland Security in January 2018 allow access without a warrant to any data on the device that does not require a network connection [9].

In this position paper, we argue for using threshold cryptography to make it technically impossible to comply with such attempts to compel a traveller to surrender their passwords or encryption keys (the $5 wrench attack[1]). In our proposed system, the traveller does not *know* their encryption keys at the time of crossing the border and being subjected to security scrutiny, and so cannot be compelled to provide it even under threat of detainment or deportation. It is of course important that this fact be made very clear by the software itself, or possibly being well known via the popular media, so that it is incontroversial that the traveller is unable to decrypt the device, and no amount of threatening or arrest will change this fact.

By using strong device encryption in combination with our method of distributing the decryption key, attackers (including border agents and law enforcement) are unable to access the contents of the traveller's device even with coerced cooperation. This defence anticipates the event of being compelled to provide a password, and fails safe by protecting against data disclosure even when the defender's mind has been compromised.

2 Secret Sharing

Cryptographic secret sharing schemes [2,12] take some arbitrary secret data D and divide it into $n \geq 2$ shares, with the intention of those shares then being distributed to n distinct parties. During the sharing process, a threshold t with $1 \leq t < n$ is chosen such that any subset of $t+1$ shares can be used to recompute the secret, but no subset of t shares reveals any information about the secret whatsoever.

Several others have proposed using threshold cryptography schemes for protecting data on users' personal electronic devices [1,10,13]. Our position builds on this work by proposing using these systems for the specific use case of crossing international borders and placing shares in the hands of the user's friends, instead of (just) their other personal devices. In the next section, we describe some of the modifications we make to account for the unique circumstances of the border-crossing scenario.

[1] https://xkcd.com/538/.

3 Position

We propose using the following system to conceal encryption keys when attempting to cross an international border (or any other situation where the user anticipates being subjected to compulsion of their passwords):

0. Begin with a secret S, which could be an encryption key for a primary device or a password to a cloud service. In the latter case, it is up to the user to ensure they cannot be compelled to reset the password (e.g., via email).
1. Generate a symmetric encryption key K.
2. Choose a set of friends of size $n \geq 2$, and a threshold number of those friends t such that $2 \leq t+1 \leq n$.
3. On a secondary device, use (t, n)-Secret Sharing to split S into n shares, and encrypt each share using K.
4. Send an encrypted share to each of your n friends (using a secure channel such as Signal or TLS); friends should import the share into an app that only allows exporting via NFC.
5. Erase S and all of its shares from memory on both devices; retain K.
6. Travel across the border (or other security checkpoint) with both the primary and secondary devices.
7. Upon safe arrival at the destination, visit $t+1$ friends and tap their phones with the secondary device to retrieve their encrypted shares via NFC.
8. Decrypt each share using K, and use them to recover the secret S.
9. Decrypt the primary device or log in to the cloud service using S.

We employ the use of a secondary device as a convenience mechanism for implementation. Performing both encryption and recovery on the same device would require performing step 9 in a "bootstrap" area of the operating system prior to the device's disk being decrypted, which, for example, would require rooting an Android phone to permit such a modification; however, in the event that the standard Android lock screen incorporates our required functionality, the secondary device would be obviated. We specify NFC as the transfer mechanism for secrets because it makes remote communication of the encrypted shares cumbersome; we do not want security agents impersonating the traveller and requesting their friends read out secrets over the phone, and we absolutely do not want them to be able to simply request the secrets be delivered over the network (even with a confirmation popup on the friends' devices, many people are subject to security warning fatigue and will simply agree to such dialogs without authentication).

One concern is that security agents will image the encrypted contents of the primary device (possibly in secret) and the share decryption key K before allowing the traveller on their way. If the traveller then communicates shares over an insecure channel, they will be subject to interception and subsequent decryption of the primary device. By using NFC, we encourage the user to choose friends that are physically located at the travel destination (instead of, for example, choosing friends in their home country and attempting to communicate shares over the phone later). Another concern is that the initial transmission of encrypted shares might be recorded in global passive data collection if a secure channel is not used, which would permit security agents to retroactively recover the shares when an encrypted device is discovered. Transmitting the shares initially over a secure channel with perfect forward secrecy, and requiring physical interaction to recover the shares, mitigates these concerns. To compromise the entire system, such an adversary would have to compromise some subset $t + 1$ of the traveller's friends' devices to recover their encrypted shares in addition to the traveller's devices themselves.

Encrypting individual shares using K prevents $t+1$ friends from collaborating *without* the traveller to recover their secret (which could allow remote access to a cloud service).

Alternative approaches to solving this problem frequently include the traveller mailing the password to themselves, or downloading their data from a website (which possibly only comes online after a certain amount of time, or after friends have confirmed the traveller's arrival). We note that all of these approaches rely on lying to border agents (which we deliberately do *not* advocate for as part of this position paper), or on actions that can be easily impersonated (such as texting a friend), or on actions that the traveler can be compelled to perform (such as video-calling a friend). We note that all of these approaches rely on lying to border agents (which we deliberately do *not* advocate as part of this position paper), or on actions that can be easily impersonated (such as texting a friend), or on actions that the traveller can be compelled to perform (such as video-calling a friend). Another similar project to ours is Sunder,[2] which aims to allow people to use Shamir secret sharing in a usable manner. It does not, however, focus on the border-crossing scenario as our project does.

4 Implementation

We implemented a prototype of our proposal as an Android app called *Shatter Secrets*, shown in Fig. 1. It is free and open source.[3] Users are asked to make an account on our server, which effectively acts only as a relay server for transmitting encrypted secrets over TLS. At registration time, the app generates a public-key encryption keypair and transmits the public key to the server, to be used for end-to-end encryption of encrypted shares being relayed to each designated friend. (Another option is to use Signal[4] disappearing messages to transmit encrypted shares; there is some precedent in Canada [5] and the United States [8] that text messages are considered private even when sitting on the recipient's device.) The user can enter arbitrary secrets, and the app will carry out the process described in Sect. 3. In our suggested configuration, the user installs Shatter Secrets on a secondary device, and uses an encryption key for their primary device as this secret. Friends are selected by entering the usernames they registered in their respective copies of the app. Once a threshold value is chosen

[2] https://freedom.press/news/meet-sunder-new-way-share-secrets/.
[3] https://crysp.uwaterloo.ca/software/shattersecrets.
[4] https://signal.org/.

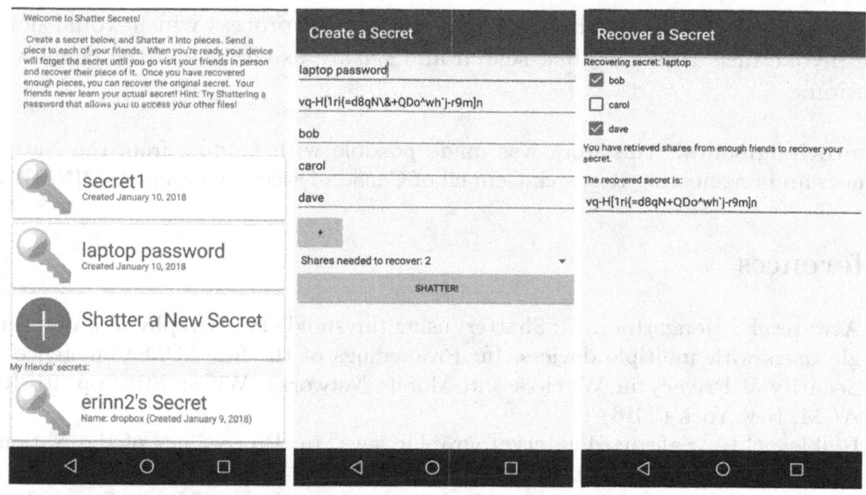

Fig. 1. Shatter Secrets running on Android, showing the list of created secrets and shares received from friends, the configuration screen for sharing a new secret, and a secret being recovered after retrieving shares from two of the three friends.

by the user, the secret is shared using Shamir secret sharing [12] and encrypted shares are sent to the relay server, to be pushed to the selected friends' devices. Encrypted shares are deleted from the server once they have been retrieved, and the user is informed when all of their friends have retrieved their respective shares and it is "safe" to cross the border. After crossing the border, the user must visit $t + 1$ friends in person; each friend confirms they have authenticated the user in person by picking their secret from a list (as shown in Fig. 1b), which will cause the app to then broadcast the encrypted secret via NFC. The friend's device forgets the encrypted share once it has been successfully delivered. When this process has been performed $t + 1$ times, the user's copy of the app decrypts the shares and recovers the plaintext secret for them. If the secret was used for encrypting a primary device, or was a password to a cloud service, the user can then manually type it in on a separate device or app.

5 Conclusion

We argue that international border security agents have no business rifling through the intimate data stored on our personal electronic devices without a warrant or consent. We proposed using threshold cryptography to make it impossible to comply with such attempts on the spot. By distributing encryption keys amongst trusted friends at the traveller's destination prior to travel, the traveller cannot be compelled to provide access to their devices immediately. Instead, some subset of the trusted friends must be approached individually and compelled to provide their share of the key—a process which would hopefully invoke their rights against search and seizure as citizens of the country in question.

Acknowledgments. This work was made possible with funding from the Natural Sciences and Engineering Research Council of Canada Discovery Grant RGPIN-03858.

References

1. Atwater, E., Hengartner, U.: Shatter: using threshold cryptography to protect single users with multiple devices. In: Proceedings of the 9th ACM Conference on Security & Privacy in Wireless and Mobile Networks, WiSec 2016, pp. 91–102. ACM, New York (2016)
2. Blakley, G.R.: Safeguarding cryptographic keys. In: Proceedings of the National Computer Conference, vol. 48, pp. 313–317 (1979)
3. Calder, S.: Security experts astonished by electronics ban on Middle East airlines. The Independent, March 2017
4. CBP Public Affairs: CBP releases statistics on electronic device searches. U.S. customs and border protection, April 2017
5. Connolly, A.: Text messages can be private once received, Supreme Court rules. Global News, December 2017
6. Cope, S., Kalia, A., Schoen, S., Schwartz, A.: Digital privacy at the U.S. border. The Electronic Frontier Foundation, March 2017
7. Fox-Brewster, T.: Feds walk into a building, demand everyone's fingerprints to open phones. Forbes, October 2016
8. Johnson, G.: Justices: people have right to privacy in text messages. Komo News, February 2014
9. Kopan, T.: DHS issues new rules for searching electronic devices at the border. CNN, January 2018
10. Peeters, R.: Security architecture for things that think. Ph.D. thesis, KU Leuven (2012)
11. Savage, C., Nixon, R.: Privacy complaints mount over phone searches at U.S. border since 2011. The New York Times (2017)
12. Shamir, A.: How to share a secret. Commun. ACM **22**(11), 612–613 (1979)
13. Stajano, F.: Pico: no more passwords!. In: Christianson, B., Crispo, B., Malcolm, J., Stajano, F. (eds.) Security Protocols 2011. LNCS, vol. 7114, pp. 49–81. Springer, Heidelberg (2011). https://doi.org/10.1007/978-3-642-25867-1_6

Shatter Secrets: Using Secret Sharing to Cross Borders with Encrypted Devices (Transcript of Discussion)

Erinn Atwater(✉) and Ian Goldberg(✉)

University of Waterloo, Waterloo, ON, Canada
erinn.atwater@uwaterloo.ca

Ilia Shumailov: Just a quick question, so do you know of any instances—every time I cross the border, before I go anywhere, I purge my phone so it's completely empty and you can't use any information from it. Do you know of any instances where people were refused entry to the country or their devices were removed for being completely empty?

Reply: There's been a lot of discussion that I'm aware of around this idea that that is very suspicious, having a blank device. And lawyers kind of think that would be a totally plausible reason for them to deny you entry, especially if you were like a security person like us. It's kind of somewhat obvious that you've done that. But I'm not aware of anyone actually being turned away for that.

Mark Lomas: You mentioned consent. It's probably worth pointing out that there's a change in European law that comes into effect from May, whereas if you suffer a disproportionate disbenefit from consenting, then by law you can no longer consent and the example with the Information Commissioner's Office has given out is if law enforcement asked you to consent to something, that consent is invalid. That may affect border control. Also, what may affect a lot of organisations is if your employer asked you to consent to something, you can no longer consent.

Graham Rymer: Just in response to Ilia, I think if you're super suspicious, you're probably less likely to be detained. For example if you're on a Do Not Detain List because by detaining you're alerting a person that they're under suspicion.

Bruce Christianson: So that's good. They wanted to see who your contacts were.

Reply: So yeah, your rights at the border are very different. And then the United States, as Ian was saying earlier, they like to be very creative with definitions. So the United States has decided to define the term 'border' as being 100 miles thick. And so anywhere there's a US border, within 100 miles of it you're essentially, the ACLU branded it the constitution-free zone. And it looks like this. So if you live in the orange zone, you essentially have no constitutional rights against search and seizure.

Daniel Weitzner: Those are the Hillary Clinton voters. Sorry.

V. Matyáš et al. (Eds.): Security Protocols 2018, LNCS 11286, pp. 295–303, 2018.
https://doi.org/10.1007/978-3-030-03251-7_34

Reply: That's about right, yeah. Because this says 2/3 of Americans live in this constitution-free zone, and she did win the popular vote.

Jean Martina: Technically airports are borders as well. So wherever you have an international airport, you have a 100-mile bubble and that's basically the whole country!

Reply: That's a great point, if you consider airports as international borders, then the orange is where you have no constitutional rights and then this light grey is where you have no constitutional rights. Okay so our position is, you can probably guess, essentially the government has no business rifling through our personal lives. They want to confirm, say that you're not bringing drugs into the country or something like this, sure but they have no business going and looking at photos that you took between your partner 20 years ago that would still be stored on your device, what have you. So our interest is in making it impossible for the government to see these 20-year-old photos. As always, there's a relevant xkcd. With the crypto nerds on the left, of course, trying to end-to-end encrypt everything. Then the reality of the situation, which is they lock you in a small room, only feed you sandwiches or water, or they hit you with a five dollar wrench until you give up the passwords. A lot of people call this 'rubber hose cryptanalysis' in which you break crypto systems by hitting someone with a rubber hose. So our interest as cryptographers, we're normally working on creating this scenario. Today we're interested in protecting against this scenario of the five dollar wrench attack by making it so that even if you decide that you don't want to be hit with a wrench again, and you do want to surrender your password, it's actually technically and physically impossible for you to do so. So that's the piece of technology that we're going to present today.

Daniel Weitzner: So just two quick comments. Borders are horrible because they are neither protected well by domestic law nor does international law touch them because international law won't intrude on the sovereignty of the country whose border it is. It's an inherently difficult legal zone. But secondly, on the positive side, there was just a case that I came across in one of the US Courts of Appeals in which a judge—admittedly in dissent, but this is the dissent panel—actually said that the traditional rationale for allowing border searches without warrants is really about who and what gets brought into the country, so the rationale is "What's in your suitcase? Are you bringing something illegal into the country?" And her argument is that that's not the same as looking at a mobile device that has all kinds of stuff on it. Most of the contents of mobile devices are not items that the government has an interest in excluding, for any legitimate reason. So she's actually applying this view from the US Supreme Court's recent case called Riley which says that there are constitutional rights, 4th amendment rights in your mobile phone and saying that should be extended to the border. So we'll see what happens. It's a dissent but sometimes dissents become majority views.

Virgil Gligor: Interesting story about the borders but there is another law, which says that once you're on the US soil, it doesn't matter where you are from, you are a US person and consequently you have rights of a US person. And lots of people don't know this but unless there is probable cause, they cannot go through all these searches.

Reply: At the border they absolutely can. They don't need probable cause whatsoever.

Ian Goldberg: Once you're outside the 100 miles, you're right. When you're inside the 100 miles though, you're not right.

Reply: In the UK and the US, they can just decide on a whim. It doesn't have to be, "Hey we think you're a drug dealer. I'm going to go through your phone to confirm." They can say, "I'm bored right now. I'm going to go through your phone because I've got nothing better to do."

Virgil Gligor: Interesting. Is this 100-mile border public knowledge?

Daniel Weitzner: It's a change. What it was, it was saying that anyone who the immigration service, who ICE has anything to do with, will be treated as if they're at the border, if they're within 100 miles. So it's not for all law enforcement. It's specifically about how ICE enforcement procedures will be interpreted, which is a very dramatic change.

Virgil Gligor: And this is fairly new?

Daniel Weitzner: Yeah, it's in the last couple weeks. It's very recent.

Virgil Gligor: Oh really?

Daniel Weitzner: Yeah it's a new Trump administration policy.

Ian Goldberg: Well the 100 miles one is like a decade old.

Reply: That picture's from 2013.

Daniel Weitzner: No, but the decision to use that zone for this change in policy is very recent.

Mansoor Ahmed: Does the UK have the same thing? 100-mile zone?

Reply: I don't think so, but I'm not a lawyer.

Bruce Christianson: They used to have a period of time if you're going through a border within the last, I think it was either six or 12 hours. Customs could change their mind and come after you.

Mark Lomas: Can I give a slightly different answer to that? It depends on who it is that wants to search you because HM Revenue and Customs are permitted to declare absolutely everywhere in the UK—a place that they want to search you—they're exempted from the normal rules that apply to law enforcement. So the thing is it depends on what they want you for. If they think that you are smuggling something then we are currently within their jurisdiction.

Reply: So the piece of technology I'm about to present. Our hope is to invoke another right, which is that you can't be thrown in jail for a life sentence or whatever for not divulging a password if you are physically unable to divulge it, they can't throw you in jail for that. There's a case, this will be my last little anecdote before I rush on to the piece of work, but there was a case in the United States of these two Instagram models. It was really dramatic. It was kind of hilarious to watch, but one of these Instagram models, the police suspected there was evidence of some crime on his phone. They said, "You have to unlock your iPhone for us." He said, "I forgot the password so I'm actually unable to give you the password. I don't know it anymore." That went through the courts, and what the judge ended up saying was, "If this were true, that you had forgotten your password, then you would be right. I couldn't charge you for that. However you have failed to convince me that you have actually forgotten it. It's too convenient. You're an Instagram model. You use your phone all the time and you just happen to have forgotten it the moment we locked you up. If you could present some evidence that you had forgotten it, you're right but instead you've got some time tacked on for contempt" on his sentence. So—

Peter Ryan: So you need a zero-knowledge proof of ignorance.

Reply: Okay, so secret sharing. Most of you have heard it. I'm not going to go into the math. There is math involved. Who cares? The idea of secret sharing is you have some secret value. You split it into these pieces called shares. It's not quite as simple as saying, "I have a 1024-bit encryption key. You get 256, you get 256, you get 256." It's not quite like that. If you have not enough shares to put together, you learn no even little piece of the password whatsoever. To recover the secret, you need some number of these shares. You combine them in order to get your secret back. So if you have less than this threshold number, you learn absolutely nothing. So our idea is we're going to take an encryption key for your device. We're going to split it into shares. We're going to send the shares—this is somewhat important, it's subtle—but we're going to send the shares to someone on the other side of the border that you're about to travel across. So not leaving them with your mom at home or even someone suggested leaving them with your lawyer before you leave, which is an interesting idea but what we're hoping is that by sending your shares to friends on the other side of the border, you're then invoking not *your* rights, but *their* rights against search and seizure without probable cause. So when you travel across the border, all border agents get is your encrypted data. They can't decrypt it. They can take an image of it and try to crack it later. But they don't actually get the plaintext at all. Then of course if they try to hit you with a wrench, you can't divulge your password because you don't have a copy of it anymore. It's with your friend, so they've got to go hit your friends with a wrench. Hopefully they're in a place where that's illegal.

Graham Rymer: Just wondering if you considered the threat against availability of the data if, for example, if a threshold number of your friends are unavailable when you reach your destination.

Reply: Yes. So that's a good question. So our software is mainly targeted at people with a threat model where you would rather lose your data than have the government get it, and you would rather be deported than have the government get your data.

Ilia Shumailov: I'm a bit confused with this. So the aim of the person crossing the border is then to withhold the information stored on the phone with the price tag of their physical security.

Reply: Yes. One of the themes of the conference is fail deadly.

Ilia Shumailov: It sounds like it's very hard to imagine a situation in which you actually don't know what's stored on your phone, but at the same time you allow them to damage you and still with damaging, you don't reveal it by physically saying it, for example. That means that some of the information stored within your phone should not be available to you at the time, which implies that it might be much easier to actually have some sort of a key distributed through another medium to the person within the border, and then bring some sort of encryption device stored somewhere with some sort of already encrypted data, such that you actually have no knowledge of what's inside. But that's a very odd threat model, it seems like. Because you're not actually trying to protect your phone. You're actually trying to protect some information of which you don't have any knowledge.

Ian Goldberg: No, you know what's on your phone. You just don't know the password to decrypt the phone.

Ilia Shumailov: But then that implies that through physical damage you can say that this information was on there. They don't really need to know the exact information in many cases. They just want you to actually say that it was there. Like this guy, we're going to meet with him at this location. They don't necessarily need to have a whole chain of messages to say that—

Ian Goldberg: Yeah but they're not going to trust you, like if you say, "Oh yeah, on my phone was a message where it says I was going to meet my girlfriend in the UK." They're not going to trust that.

Reply: Yeah, in the case of the Snowden documents, it took them years to go through it all and figure out what needed to be published, what didn't.

Frank Stajano: So if the main threat is the people at the border being nasty to you because they can do whatever they like in their kingdom. If you have all this set up that first you mail your friends from abroad, some key materials and so on, why don't you just go through the border without any electronics, and once you are there and you've collected a key, you just buy yourself a new Apple store thing, and download the encrypted version on there from your website. Why do you have to travel with the encrypted thing, which is obviously something that is going to put you in trouble.

Reply: So that is security by obscurity. You're relying on them not knowing that you're about to do this because if you have some way of getting your data across the border once you've already passed, they can compel you on the spot in the airport to do whatever that action is. Like if you're downloading your data from your website, they can just say, "Go download it right now from the website."

Ilia Shumailov: But surely this is defeated through just them taking the phone away from you and you lost all the data.

Reply: Denial of service does work. Yeah, it does work against us.

Daniel Weitzner: I'm curious how you think about this in comparison to some kind of deniable encryption scheme or duress password. People have talked about this. It's also sort of unclear legally what happens, what you can be compelled to do. But I'm just interested in how you see it as similar or different or advantageous.

Ian Goldberg: We do not advocate lying to the border agents. So duress passwords are lying to the border agents. They say, "Type in your password." You type in the wrong password which wipes your disk. That's what a duress password is. That is itself a crime. Right? We do not advocate doing something at the border that is illegal. We advocate being actively actually unable to comply with that request.

Daniel Weitzner: I think that's a useful distinction. However, it seems like the same attack as you described for just downloading the data once you cross the border is applicable to this. Which is that if in fact you're really going to be strongarmed at the border, then the border agent will say, "Do you have a way to get this data?" You'd have to answer. You could refuse to answer, but then you could be held under duress. If you don't, you either lie, which is something you say you don't want to do, or you tell the truth. You say, "No, well these five friends of mine can help me get it." So I don't quite understand the advantage of this over the "download it with your key later" scheme.

Ross Anderson: At a previous Protocols Workshop I believe we discussed the steganographic filesystem, where you put one password it gives you the innocuous stuff by decryption and another password gives you less innocuous stuff. If you don't want to take the risk that the second password could be tortured out of you, there's another approach that's actually used by companies who don't want their staff to be subject to duress, which is you just see to it that the sensitive credential, for example, an engineering logon that lets you check out code and alter it, is entirely dysfunctional while the laptop is in China. So your engineer could check your code and work on it in Britain or America or Argentina or India. But not while you're sitting in a hotel room in Peking.

Daniel Weitzner: I don't think this is an easy problem. We've played around with this legal question of, "Is there any way you can construct some sort of deniability scheme such that you are merely not telling the truth as opposed to lying?" Which is a hard distinction. But I still think even, Ross, in your case, if Erinn somehow delegates all of her interesting permissions away, she's going to be asked the same question, right?

Ross Anderson: But if there are three people in China who can recover your file, and if you're compelled to tell the truth, then at the border, you have to give their names and addresses, they're immediately arrested and tortured. And the people's security police get in contact.

Reply: Right. So we're hoping that those people that are there, hopefully, have rights against being tortured.

Daniel Weitzner: So this is for crossing into the border of a nominally democratic rule of law regime.

Reply: Yeah.

Ian Goldberg: And you have to physically go there.

Reply: I'm not going to get to the details, but we've got a few things in the protocol where you do in fact have to do it in person. That's a requirement of the software.

Peter Roenne: Isn't a problem that you cannot prove that you followed the protocol so it would be so much easier just to pretend you followed the protocol, just keep the keys yourself, so you can decrypt yourself so you cannot really prove that you followed the protocol—

Reply: That's lying to the border agent again, which our system is intended for you to not have to lie.

Peter Roenne: The point is they cannot see whether you actually did this or not. You cannot prove that you followed the protocol and they cannot give you the password. So like the standard argument about having deniable encryption is that you will just increase your pain basically because they will just try to torture you, even though you cannot give them anything, but they cannot see that you cannot give them anything.

Reply: So one little piece that we did add in is that there is a giant warning on the main screen saying to the border agent, "This is how the software works. You're going to be unable to compel this person." They can look at the source code of it and see. We also want to get lots of news attention. Release the software and then they can just Google the name of it and see "Hey this is a thing that exists."

Mark Lomas: There's a good principle behind not lying to a border agent. It's the way that law enforcement often catch out criminals, which is they actually find some piece of evidence up front, and they may actually have probable cause to stop you at the border, it's because they've actually found the secret that's in your laptop and they want you to decrypt it in order to correlate the two together. The "don't lie to border guards" protects you against that because if they have some secret which they suspect is in there, and you lie about it, you may then provide evidence of a crime.

Reply: There have been cases, not at borders, where the police will do something like talk to one of your friends and question them about a crime, and then they'll go to you then afterwards and they'll just ask you an innocuous question like, "Have you talked to anyone about this?" And if you say, "No, I haven't really talked to anyone about it at all," and they just spoke to someone about it, then they just arrest you for that. Nothing to do with the crime. They just arrest you for lying about having spoken to someone.

Radim Ostadal: Just a question about this downloading data from the website after crossing the border. What about if you have your own webserver that is offline at the time of crossing the border, and you have just another friend in your home that brings the web server online after the crossing. What's the difference between this scenario and your protocol?

Reply: Yeah, that's an interesting idea. I'll have to think about that more.

Virgil Gligor: You don't lie at the border. You don't use your scheme. You give them your password. Before you do that, you better have a copy of the contents of your phone at home because they may plant evidence on your phone once they have the password. So you actually have to protect yourself because afterwards they cannot prove that bad stuff is yours. So this, by the way, apparently has happened in the OJ Simpson trial when Detective Fuhrman actually planted the glove. And he apparently got caught.

Ian Goldberg: Planting evidence happens all the time.

Virgil Gligor: Yeah so that's why you have to have a copy of your—

Ian Goldberg: That doesn't help you.

Virgil Gligor: Why?

Ian Goldberg: Having a copy wouldn't help you because any testimony you give in your own defence is inadmissible in US law.

Virgil Gligor: Put it on a blockchain.

Ian Goldberg: Anything you say that harms you can be used against you, but nothing you say can be used to benefit you.

Virgil Gligor: Unless you sue them. And then you have a defence, which is what happened in this case. The guy was put on the stand.

Ahmed Mansoor: Honestly, I'd put it on a blockchain.

Ilia Shumailov: Can you actually tell me, because I'm struggling to understand, what's the actual goal of this? Because if the goal is information smuggling into the country—

Reply: Not smuggling. You want to be totally straightforward about the fact that this data exists and you have it.

Ilia Shumailov: Not smuggling, so literally just purge your phone and go like this and give them the password and then no problems arise at all because that phone is empty. Or just don't take the device with you at all

Reply: But you do want to get the information into the country.

Ilia Shumailov: So the goal then is information smuggling into the country.

Reply: Not smuggling, just transfer.

Ilia Shumailov: Illegitimately taking information into the country because this is—it's not legitimate.

Ian Goldberg: No, it's legitimate. You are legitimately—

Ilia Shumailov: So the goal is to actually transfer the information. It's just a lot of different ways by which you can actually transfer information.

Reply: And then there's other concerns like if you are emailing it to yourself later then, this is an adversary that can just monitor the entire internet, and so I didn't get to talk about the protocol which is awesome, we had a great argument, but you have to worry about when you cross the border, the government goes and they look up in their log of the entire internet and all of the traffic, when you sent your shares across the border. So you have to make sure you have perfect forward secrecy and things like that and end-to-end encryption. There's some little nuances in the protocol if you want to have a look at the paper. Or argue over lunch with me about them. In fact I've got a demo of our software also, if anyone wants to see. It's a very straightforward application of secret sharing but yeah. Thank you.

Author Index

Printed in the United States
By Bookmasters